.tive

Thi ... ma,or
the ... ds of
economic and s... in a
comparative context, drawing on material from western societies as
well as those in the wider world. The books are introductory and
explanatory and are designed for all those following thematic courses
in history, cultural European or social studies.

Themes in Comparative History

General Editor: CLIVE EMSLEY

PUBLISHED TITLES

Jane Rendall
 THE ORIGINS OF MODERN FEMINISM: WOMEN IN
 BRITAIN, FRANCE AND THE UNITED STATES,
 1780–1860
R.F. Holland
 EUROPEAN DECOLONIZATION 1918–1980
Dominic Lieven
 THE EUROPEAN ARISTOCRACY 1815–1914
Ken Ward
 MASS COMMUNICATIONS AND THE MODERN WORLD
Pamela Pilbeam
 THE MIDDLE CLASSES IN EUROPE 1789–1914: FRANCE,
 GERMANY, ITALY AND RUSSIA
Ian Inkster
 SCIENCE AND TECHNOLOGY IN HISTORY

FORTHCOMING

David Englander and Tony Mason
 WAR AND POLITICS: THE EXPERIENCE OF THE
 SERVICEMAN IN TWO WORLD WARS
Joe Lee
 PEASANT EUROPE IN THE 18th AND 19th CENTURIES
Rosemary O'Day
 THE FAMILY IN FRANCE, ENGLAND AND THE UNITED
 STATES OF AMERICA, 1600–1850

EUROPEAN DECOLONIZATION 1918–1981: AN INTRODUCTORY SURVEY

R. F. Holland

MACMILLAN

First published 1985 by
THE MACMILLAN PRESS LTD
Houndmills, Basingstoke, Hampshire RG21 2XS
and London
Companies and representatives
throughout the world

ISBN 0–333–31677–0 hardcover
ISBN 0–333–31678–9 paperback

A catalogue record for this book is available
from the British Library.

Reprinted 1992, 1994

Printed in China

Contents

Acknowledgements ix

List of maps x

General Editor's Preface xi

Preface xiii

PART I: 1918–39

1 THE EUROPEAN EMPIRES IN A TRANSFORMING
WORLD 1

Population growth and agrarian crisis in Indo-China 2

The formation of a colonial bourgeoisie 5

Religious revival and national renaissance 8

The colonial world and the Great Depression 11

British strategy and imperial reform: Egypt, India and
the white Dominions 15

Race politics and the colonial order in Africa 26

PART II: 1939–45

2 MOBILIZATION, REJUVENATION AND LIQUI-
DATION: COLONIALISM AND GLOBAL WAR 37

The Japanese revolution in East Asia 38

The consequences of imperial mobilization 47

Colonialism and the Anglo-American alliance 52

The bending of the *Raj* 56

Social change and settler power in Africa 63

PART III: 1945–54

3 EUROPE'S ASIAN STAKE: ADAPTATION, RESTO-
   RATION AND DESTRUCTION   73
   The drive to partitioned independence in India   74
   The emergence of the Indonesian Republic   86
   The war of colonial restoration in Indo-China   93
   Making Malaya safe for decolonization   103

4 BRITAIN, PALESTINE AND THE MIDDLE EAST   113

5 EXPERIMENTATION, CONSOLIDATION AND
   DEADLOCK IN BRITISH AFRICA   129
   Political change in the Gold Coast: a model defined 130
   Racial consolidation in southern Africa   135
   Kenya: the deadlocked state   144

PART IV: 1954–65

6 ORDER AND CHAOS: PATTERNS OF DECOLONI-
   ZATION IN FRENCH AND BELGIAN AFRICA   153
   French West Africa: the management of decolonization 154
   Algeria: the road to Evian   163
   The Belgian Congo: the breakdown of a decolonization 175

7 BRITAIN: THE END OF IMPERIAL STATEHOOD   191
   Suez 1956: the turning point   191
   The changing metropole   200

8 THE CLIMAX OF BRITISH DECOLONIZATION IN
   AFRICA   211
   Ghana: exemplary decolonization and political myth 212
   British Central Africa: the unravelling of Federation 220
   Kenya: the struggle for stabilization   236

9 BRITISH DECOLONIZATION IN THE MEDITER-
   RANEAN   249
   Cyprus: the fatal nexus – strategy, clericalism and
      communalism   250
   Malta: from George Cross Island to Third Worldism 260

PART V: 1965–81

10   THE ASSERTION OF A POST-COLONIAL AGE   269
     East of Suez: the British departure from Aden and the
        Gulf   274
     Southern Rhodesia: the life and death of UDI   279
     Portugal's African empire: revolution from the metro-
        pole   292

     POSTSCRIPT   299

     Notes   303

     Select Bibliography   314

     Index   317

To Hillia

Acknowledgements

THIS book has its roots in an extended seminar programme on modern European decolonization at the Institute of Commonwealth Studies in London University. The author is indebted to the latter institution for providing the facilities to complete this textbook-study. Most of all, however, thanks are due to Peter Lyon and Andrew Porter for bringing their corrective expertise to bear on a much scribbled manuscript. They are responsible for much of the inspiration, but none of the vices, in what follows.

The author and publishers wish to acknowledge the following sources for maps used in the book: Hodder and Stoughton Ltd for the map on p. 16, from Colin Cross, *The Fall of the British Empire 1918–68* (1968); Edward Arnold (Publishers) Ltd for the maps on pp. 28 and 281, from J. D. Fage, *An Atlas of African History* (2nd edition, 1978); Hamlyn Publishing Group Ltd for the maps on pp. 39, 80 and 101, from Richard Natkiel, *Atlas of Twentieth Century History* (1982); Weidenfeld and Nicolson Ltd for the map on p. 121, from Martin Gilbert, *Recent History Atlas 1860–1960* (1960); Chatto and Windus Ltd for the map on p. 194, from Elizabeth Monroe, *Britain's Moment in the Middle East* (1963).

List of Maps

1	The British empire, 1918	16
2	The pattern of alien rule in Africa, 1925	28
3	Japanese expansion, 1941–2	39
4	Indian partition, 1947	80
5	The war in Indo-China, 1946–54	101
6	The partition of Palestine	121
7	The Middle East in 1956	194
8	The pattern of alien rule in Africa, 1965	281

General Editor's Preface

SINCE the Second World War there has been a massive expansion in the study of economic and social history generating, and fuelled by, new journals, new academic series and societies. The expansion of research has given rise to new debates and ferocious controversies. This series proposes to take up some of the current issues in historical debate and explore them in a comparative framework.

Historians, of course, are principally concerned with unique events, and they can be inclined to wrap themselves in the isolating greatcoats of their 'country' and their 'period'. It is at least arguable, however, that a comparison of events, or a comparison of the way in which different societies coped with a similar problem – war, industrialization, population growth and so forth – can reveal new perspectives and new questions. The authors of the volumes in this series have each taken an issue to explore in such a comparative framework. The books are not designed to be path-breaking monographs, though most will contain a degree of new research. The intention is, by exploring problems across national boundaries, to encourage students in tertiary education, in sixth-forms, and hopefully also the more general reader, to think critically about aspects of past developments. No author can maintain strict objectivity; nor can he or she provide definitive answers to all the questions which they explore. If the authors generate discussion and increase perception, then their task is well done.

CLIVE EMSLEY

I do not speak with the same confidence about Venice, Portugal and Spain; I rather think they *are* decadent. But what I wished to guard against was the idea that their decadence could be measured by the decline of their competitive national power. This is a misleading test, and one which people are very apt to apply: e.g. if the British Empire were reduced to these two islands, and the United States quadrupled in population, we might become insignificant as a world power, and yet perhaps not be decadent.

A. J. Balfour to Sir Edmund Gosse,
19 February 1908

Preface

THE undermining and final subsidence of the European colonial empires has been one of the most distinctive themes of the twentieth-century world. Only in recent years, however, over three decades after the climax of Asian decolonization and two decades since the bulk of its African counterparts, has it become possible to develop analytical perspectives on these events of a sufficient subtlety to qualify as 'history'. This is partly because, while most constituents of the old empires had been shunted into the post-colonial age, there were always enough awkward survivals (the Portuguese African dependencies until the mid-1970s and the erstwhile Southern Rhodesia until 1981) to keep alive befuddling myths and rhetoric. Such imperial relics as Hong Kong, Gibraltar and the Falklands apart, however, the slate is now clean enough for dispassionate appraisal to be feasible. Moreover, it is vital that the hitherto simplistic debate on these events be put on a more complex footing. In the 1970s policy-makers in London and Paris could bask in the complacent belief that decolonization (with its assorted bumps and occasional traumas) had been a task well accomplished, and that western Europe could now concentrate its efforts on refurbishing its internal economy. Even leftist commentators, while critical of this position, seemed to share its assumption that the Third World had been effectively marginalized. But by the early 1980s, not least as a consequence of deep recession, this approach had been undermined. The EEC's adequacy as a framework for ordering western Europe's, and particularly Britain's, future had been revealed as, at best, of limited utility; even its survival was in doubt. The old truth that the sustained growth of the advanced world depended on a dynamic relationship with the non-advanced world was proved to be as valid as ever. Reconstructing such a relationship on bases consonant with post-colonial realities, however, cannot be achieved without an accurate and broadly diffused comprehension of the nature of decolonization during the present century. This book is designed to provide an introduction to the latter subject for students and general readers alike.

The end of modern European empire, nonetheless, is a vast subject and this is a relatively slim volume. The methods used to convey the outlines of the story are necessarily oblique, and the selective nature of the account may sometimes be glaring. The Caribbean islands, both French and British, always hovered at the tail-end of the decolonization queue, largely because of the peculiar vulnerability of their often monocrop economies; certainly they are not dealt with here. Politics predominates over economics. The technique employed is that of an assortment of case-studies, pinpointing the instances of decolonization most expressive of particular facets of the process. The focus is chiefly on the demise of British colonialism, on the grounds that this was the largest of the modern empires; treatment of the French, Dutch, Belgian and Portuguese dependency-systems is commensurately more selective. The aim, in short, is relatively modest: to equip the reader with a broad-brush impression of imperial dissolution and to suggest avenues for further reading and reflection.

PART I 1918–39

1. The European Empires in a Transforming World

THE end of the First World War may appear as a somewhat premature point at which to begin an outline history of European decolonization. Indeed, the territorial zenith of modern colonialism was attained only in 1919 with the completion of the Treaty of Versailles, bringing new areas (such as Palestine) within the ambit of European rule.[1] Even more telling is the fact that it was only during the Great War and in its immediate aftermath that westernizing processes began to impinge upon the broad front of non-European societies, and so created the conditions for mass nationalist responses. With this in mind, it might be argued that while the inter-war years were of clear relevance to certain later decolonizations (with one obvious example being the emergence of Gandhian populism in India during the early 1920s), in the main their continuities lay backwards to the age of classical European expansion, not forwards to the era of imperial dissolution. Nonetheless, the sense that processes of decolonization, even in their broadest connotations, only take shape after 1939 is dictated by a falsely based preoccupation with the outward form of political nationalisms among colonial populations. The latter, indeed, were the exception rather than the rule before the Second World War. As we shall see, however, ramshackle political coalitions in the underdeveloped world were only one element – and not the most vital – in determining the end to twentieth-century empires. Decolonization happened because colonialism as a set of nationally orchestrated systems (by the British, French, Dutch, Belgians and Portuguese) ceased to possess the self-sustaining virtue of internal equilibrium, and this spate of disequilibria can best be observed on a time-scale more extended than that provided by the post-1939 decades. Furthermore, it has been argued in the most persuasive account to date of Britain's imperial rundown that this saga is conspicuous for its lack of any progressive, linear shape; it was pockmarked with sharp declensions and prolonged revivals, and the end result was only finally secured by the locking together of various factors about which historians still know relatively little.[2] In the first part of this study, therefore, we shall be concerned to identify those stiffening constraints to which European colonial authorities became subject between 1918 and 1939; constraints which were not necessarily terminal in their implications, but which required fundamental adaptations if relations between metropoles and peripheries were to locate new, up-to-date modes of stability. This general theme will be approached from six disparate directions: agrarian crisis in French Indo-China; the formation of a colonial bourgeoisie; religious revival and national renaissance in Burma and Indonesia; the impact of the Great Depression; British reform strategies in Egypt, India and the self-governing Dominions; and racial politics in 'British' Africa.

I   POPULATION GROWTH AND AGRARIAN CRISIS IN INDO-CHINA

The dominant fact about colonial societies between 1918 and 1939 was that they were expanding. This does not mean that per capita income or gross national product showed increases in their cash values. By these criteria, most colonial economies shrank in the trough of the depression during the early 1930s and over the inter-war period as a whole achieved, in most cases, only very modest progress.[3] Almost everywhere in the colonial world, however, the rate of population growth substantially increased. Thus in the Indian subcontinent between 1901 and 1931 population rose from 294.4 to 352.8 millions; in French Algeria it rose from 2.49 to 4.73 millions.[4] The rate of demographic expansion was accelerating in the decade prior to 1939. The reasons for this trend are obscure. Partly it was because conditions of political stability and improved transportation networks undermined traditional cycles of shortage and periodic famine. Partly, also, it was because after 1918 the application of western medicine in poor societies had a dramatically reductive effect on the death rate, while the birth rate continued at its customary levels. This pattern was testimony, in some respects, to the improving dynamic of the western impact on Asia and Africa. But having effected the conditions for a population explosion, the question arose as to whether the colonial systems could boost food production to a matching degree. It was this agrarian challenge, not political nationalism, which before 1939 constituted the real uncertainty overhanging the long-term viability of European colonialism; and it was the essential failure on this economic front which meant that these imperial systems entered the Second World War in a weakened and vulnerable state.[5] French Indo-China affords a powerful illustration of this situation, not least because of the very distinct linkage which later existed in this area between peasant distress and Communist-led nationalism.

In 1939 the total population of French Indo-China was 23 million. The two great concentrations of population lay in the Tonkin–Annam plains and on the east side of Cochin. But these two regions had different agricultural and social patterns.[6] Tonkin was a land of peasant smallholders with over 90 per cent of farmers owning less than 1.8 hectares. This minute parcelling-out of estates had become as much a function of the political structure as of demographic pressure. The traditional absentee landlords had largely subdivided their lands among the peasantry on a sharecropping basis. The latter had not only to part with a high percentage of their crop (often 50 per cent) but usually had to pay exorbitant interest to moneylenders in order to raise working capital. The net effect was that landlords and creditors were making larger profits, and enjoyed a more stable political hegemony, than if they were to engage upon the hazardous task of modernizing agricultural production. In a society where the hire of human labour cost less than that of a buffalo there was no incentive to introduce novel methods; population growth simply fed into the established channels of local power, and the village bosses suspected that any drive towards higher individual productivity might actually weaken their own mechanisms of control. For the Tonkinese cultivator, the only escape from his increasingly marginal position was to migrate south to less densely populated Cochin, where plantation employment was available. But in migrating the Tonkinese were exploited by ruthless recruiting agents and the French authorities were ineffective in introducing contracts which might have regulated the labour market. It was the resentments and violence attending this flow of surplus Tonkinese which helped to diffuse and accentuate social bitterness throughout Indo-China on the eve of the Second World War. The murder of the French head of the labour recruiting bureau in Hanoi, with a letter pinned to his mutilated body listing his misdeeds, was simply the random expression of anti-colonial reaction rooted in the agrarian dilemma.

In Cochin peasant-owners held somewhat larger farms than their Tonkinese counterparts, but as a group they possessed much less of the total rice area in their region. The pattern of landholding was altogether more varied, with 45 per cent of the rice acreage being in the hands of French, Chinese and Annamite planters whose individual estates usually exceeded fifty acres. Between 1890 and 1937 European holdings in Indo-China had grown from 11,000 hectares to 800,000 hectares, and the preponderance of this expansion was in Cochin. Viewed from a French rubber plantation, the colonial achievement in Indo-China was indeed remarkable.[7] French irrigation development was a model of its kind, boosting land values and rice area, and making Indo-China into the third largest world exporter of rice and rubber. But the Cochin plantation economy was established at considerable social cost: it had limited the escape routes for Tonkinese migrants, clashed with the interests of local smallholders and created a wage-earning rural proletariat.

Confronted with these complexities, French officialdom in Indo-China typified the baffled and defeated character of European rule in Asia during the first four decades of the twentieth-century. The bureaucracy was well aware by the 1930s that the test of colonial government lay in boosting food supply so that rising population could be turned into an asset, not a liability. But the colonial state proved unable to undertake the sort of programmes capable of penetrating the closed agrarian circle. The assumptions of western administration had always been passive, not active; imperial rule worked on the presumption that village structures should be tampered with as little as possible, not that they should be reshaped according to some new formula. Indeed, European power was curiously disengaged from the operations of rural life, so that the bureaucracy had minimal capacity to initiate reform. This was epitomized by the French attempt in Indo-China (and by parallel British exertions in India) to introduce cooperative credit.[8] Since land was required as security for such loans, and since new credit institutions were simply the old village councils in a different guise, the rural elites were able to use this cheap money to fortify their entrenched positions even more. Unable to make administrative contact with the peasant millions, the French authorities fell back happily enough on running well-advertised 'model gardens', refining methods of seed selection and distributing advice on cattle-breeding. All this read well in annual colonial reports, but it could do nothing to shore up the crumbling fabric of the countryside.

The perpetuation of French, British and Dutch rule in Asia had, after 1918, come to hinge on their respective abilities to unscramble the collaborative systems on which they had hitherto rested and create wider coalitions capable of stimulating (and controlling) agricultural change. Whether such strategies *would* ever have proved sustainable, and for how long, cannot be known, because in the event European rulers proved too locked into the existing sets of local alliances to explore the possibilities which lay beyond them. To the extent that colonial authorities sought to tap new sources of support, they looked to the emerging elites of the towns and the few big cities. This made some sense in terms of giving a vicarious sense of renewal to colonial politics. But meanwhile European mastery had lost its footing in rural society at large, and in failing to correct this fundamental weakness the bureaucracies concerned were effectively ensuring the transitory character of their own dominion. It is in this social and psychological sense that colonialism in Asia was dying on its feet even before the Japanese onslaught after 1941 transformed the politics of the region.

II THE FORMATION OF A COLONIAL BOURGEOISIE

The expansion of political activity in modern times has been almost universally related to the activism of a 'new' middle class. Nationalism, one of the great mobilizing forces of the last two centuries, invariably drew its essential character, not from mass proletarian emotions, but from the social and political aspirations of upwardly-mobile individuals. This was the case with the flowering of European nationalisms in the nineteenth century, and it was the case, too, with anti-colonial nationalisms in the non-European world during the twentieth century. It was in the decade after the First World War that the consolidation of indigenous middle classes in certain dependencies raised the basic question: was colonialism an infinitely flexible organism, capable of adaptive responses to social transformation, or was its collaborative fabric so brittle that the existing order (and with it European authority) had to be broken into fragments before a new equilibrium could be established?

In discussing this theme for the pre-1939 period, we are necessarily concerned with Asia rather than Africa. In some African cities western-influenced, literate and salaried *indigenes* formed a distinct grouping (in Lagos, for example) as early as the mid-nineteenth century. Nevertheless, such an African cadre did not generally constitute a broadly dispersed and self-conscious class until the Second World War. In large parts of Asia, however, the more penetrative and bureaucratized nature of European government had led to clusters of 'native clerks' employed in government offices, and opportunities in the lower rungs of the professions, such that newly patterned elites were cohering from 1880 onwards. This was particularly evident in that instance of bureaucratic colonialism *par excellence*, British India, and, not least because of the social and economic changes induced by the 1914–18 conflict, a significant element of the Indian middle classes had by the 1920s entered into an irascible maturity.[9] It was the collective frustration within this social category which propelled the growth of the Indian National Congress and which was the real force behind mass Gandhian protest.

The most powerful and westernized element in these middle-class formations consisted of large-scale capitalists. The inflationary conditions of the First World War had allowed alert operators to accumulate considerable fortunes, and after 1918 these entrepreneurs were engaged in a struggle to consolidate and diversify their activities. Such aspiring oligarchs were well placed to dominate the infant industrial structures in underdeveloped countries, since liquid capital of the requisite size was concentrated in such few hands. The big 'family house' was a characteristic phenomenon in situations of nascent industrialization: the Montazzero clan in Brazil, and the Misr banking fraternity in Egypt, are examples outside the formal British empire.[10] The most outstanding case of a crystallizing capitalist elite within the formal ambit of British colonialism, however, was in India, where a narrow business class had succeeded in using its traditional mercantile activities as a base from which to penetrate the industrial sector.[11] Within this entrepreneurial nexus there was considerable scope for clashes of interest and perspective. Thus J. N. Tata, the great Bombay textile magnate, feared that the flaking apart of British authority under nationalist pressure might have disastrous consequences for labour discipline, whereas G. D. Birla saw no contradiction between his industrial ambitions and becoming the chief paymaster of the Indian National Congress during the 1930s. These passing nuances, however, were less important than the central fact that the emergence of indigenous industrial barons gave weight to the local bourgeoisie which it had previously lacked and, as the economic problems of the inter-war years unfolded, Indian businessmen from all parts of the subcontinent, operating in nearly every sector of the economy, found themselves pitched into united opposition to government policies emanating from Delhi.

Obviously such men as Tata and Birla were not quintessentially representative of the contemporary Indian bourgeoisie. It was only the special conditions of colonialism, putting them on the wrong side of the racial divide, which emphasized their commonality with the mass of social allies which tapered off sharply beneath them. The latter were distinguished from their 'middle' counterparts in the industrialized West not only by their colour and culture, but by their marginality. Thus in Europe the bulk of the bourgeoisie did not live in constant dread of falling back into economic destitution;[12] in India, where the middle orders of society occupied a much smaller role within the polity, such insecurity was the dominant motif of their lives. It was this marginality which bound together the different occupational parts of the bourgeoisie: the minor government officers, the commercial clerks, and the retail and wholesale traders. These cadres, too, had enjoyed an improvement in their living standards during the Great War, and they were profoundly alienated when these gains were clipped back during the immediate post-war recession. It was in this milieu of fear and frustration on the part of marginal urban classes that nationalism located its most vocal constituency.

The typology of these aspirant but vulnerable orders, however, meant that the nationalism to which they frequently inclined was a more complex affair than simple anti-Europeanism. Those Indians, for example, employed within the great departments of state, both at central level and in the provinces and districts, had no desire to see bureaucratic authority diminished and before 1939 few could conceive of a bureaucracy which was not British-controlled. Their concern was to see that the status of the bureaucracy should be protected, and the avenues for Indian promotion within it broadened. These men were, in varying degrees, deeply imbued with

British habits and culture; the more established of them had frequently been to British universities, including Oxford and Cambridge. Thus, while their political instincts drew them to nationalism
after 1918, it was a nationalism which did not embrace a sweeping
rejection of the existing order, and their cultivated urbanity made
them acutely suspicious of other constituencies within the Indian
National Congress which evinced a more pronounced anti-bureau-
cratic, anti-British ethos. Such ambiguities were also prime features
of indigenous response to social change in British Malaya and the
Dutch East Indies, where the nationalist sentiment of the indigenous
peoples was usually related much less (and sometimes not at all) to
any rejection of the legitimacy of European control and more to a
desire to curtail the economic power being amassed by the Chinese
migrants which the growth of modern commercial activities had
attracted to their lands.[13] As we shall see, the Second World War was
to bring nationalism and imperialism into a more direct and unqualified confrontation. But before 1939, while new social groups were
changing the calculus of colonial life, nationalist consciousness
remained shot through with delicate compromises.

III   RELIGIOUS REVIVAL AND NATIONAL RENAISSANCE

So far we have noted two processes, agrarian impoverishment and
urban class formation, which, isolated though they were within the
highly compartmentalized arrangements of colonial society, were
chipping away at European authority in the early decades of the
present century. Both, however, were cut across and textured by a
third phenomenon which requires brief emphasis: that of religious
revivalism. Religious activism was a vehicle for some African responses to modern pressures during these years. The spread of 'Independent Christianity', ideas of the 'Black Messiah' and the spasmodic but
agitational emergence of the 'Watchtower' movement marked a
desire to separate from, and often to reformulate, the European
spiritual legacy.[14] Probably the most commonly retold of these
episodes is that of the Watchtower prophet, John Chilembwe, in
Nyasaland, whose millenarianism developed such political and racial
overtones that, following disturbances of which the detailed events
remain obscure, he was shot by the security forces.[15] While these

strands of African religiosity had only the most tenuous connection with ideas of national statehood, and while they had their principal causes in the spiritual realm, they must nevertheless be seen as one means by which certain Africans in the inter-war years were able to explore ways of acting outside colonial norms. But, again, it was in Asia that the linkage between revivalism, politics and national consciousness can be most clearly seen. In commenting on this we shall look at events in Burma – which until 1937 was part of British India – and the Dutch East Indies.

In Burma the majority Buddhist faith had had to evolve a toughness of will to resist the combined encroachments of Christianity *and* Islam. There was a relationship between this cultural tenacity and continuing resistance to alien authority: anti-European 'outbreaks', legitimated with sacred oaths, recurred in Burma well into the twentieth century.[16] It was from the early 1900s, however, that Burman Buddhists turned to organizational methods of furthering their aims. In 1909 the Burman Mission Press was formed, and this was soon followed by the Young Men's Buddhist Association. Opinion within these two bodies was often socially very conservative and apolitical; in 1916 the Young Men's Buddhist Association began their conference with a rendering of 'God Save The King'. But there was no doubting the assertiveness which came to prevail amongst the priesthood. Not surprisingly, this assertiveness came to adopt an explicitly nationalist form, since the latter presented the most coherent framework within which to develop a response to the burgeoning intrusions of government. Although the religious hierarchy, often closely associated with the British administration, tried to keep priestly dissent within limits, by the 1920s these controls were proving ineffective. Indeed, police management of town disorders had become increasingly problematical, since the crowds were usually led by the saffron-clad clergy whom the authorities were wary of physically manhandling in any way.

The diverse interaction between religious and national revival in Burma can be illustrated by scanning the career of one prominent priest-scholar, U Ottama.[17] In the early 1900s this man spent several years in India and was influenced by Tagore, the philosopher of early Indian nationalism. He then visited Japan and was struck by the racial confidence which had been generated by that country's recent and successful war against Russia. After studying in Tokyo and in the old imperial Japanese capital, Kyoto, he travelled widely throughout the Indo-Chinese peninsula, and finally returned to Burma in 1921. Between then and his death in 1939, U Ottama toured Burma expounding a mixture of religious and national themes, and many priests ascribed their political education to his work. Even such brief biographical details can show how Asian nationalisms were linked in a fertile exchange of ideas and experiences between the great regional centres of politics, learning and faith, and that the period between 1900 and 1939 witnessed a sequence in which European administrative and commercial penetration had begun to fragment local societies and evoke profound anti-western responses.

The shifting sentiments within Burman Buddhism, however, were much less spectacular than the changes occurring within the much more complicated structure of Indonesian Islam.[18] As in Burma, the symbiosis between resistance to European conquest and religious enthusiasm continued after 1900, when there was a suggestive growth in the incidence of riots arising from some alleged 'insult' to the Prophet. An overarching stability was ensured by the fact that the local clergy were securely meshed into the presiding alliance of princely traditionalists and Dutch bureaucrats which distinguished the colonial system of the Netherlands East Indies, but this imposing façade was nonetheless being undermined, firstly by those *ulama* (or preachers) who drew support for their own critique of the Islamic establishment from the distressed peasantry, and secondly by the emergence of a modernist movement amongst younger clergy for whom the idea of a 'purified' nation held growing significance. It was this combination of institutional reform, agrarian discontent and intellectual change which shunted Islam into a prolonged (if rarely explicit) conflict with colonial rule in the Indonesian archipelago.

Dutch official folklore in the Netherlands Indies had long been nervously aware of the legacy of Islamic resistance bequeathed by the nineteenth-century Java wars, and by the significant role played by the Indonesian clergy in the wider Muslim world. The growing obstructiveness which Dutch administrators met after 1910 led them to the conviction that the status quo could only be safeguarded by a rapid westernization of the literate classes and by cordoning off the peasantry from its traditional religious leadership. Thus they tried to break Islam's hold over education, consistently undermined the prestige of the Muslim hierarchy and tried to restrict the flow of pilgrims to Mecca. In some ways the colonial government's strategy was assisted in these tasks by the struggle between orthodoxy, modernism and secularism which split native Indonesian society into hostile factions. The essence of this latter struggle, however, was to seek superior access to the loyalties of the urban and rural masses, and it was this competitive mobilization which, although limited in its operations by official surveillance, served to induct increasing numbers of people into political debate. Furthermore, once the effects of the 1930s depression had panicked the Dutch bureaucracy into an attempt to seal off the peasants and workers from external influences, such that prominent nationalists were imprisoned in remote areas and collective organizations of almost any kind were harassed, the factions of orthodox clergy, the modernist reformers and the secular politicians were bound together in a common determination to break the colonial constraints which hemmed in all three.

At no point did any of the European colonial powers come into untrammelled conflict with the religious institutions and sentiments prevailing in their respective dependencies. Indeed, in the nineteenth century, when the colonizing powers were self-consciously 'Christian nations', they had, in practice, consistently sought to check their own missionary zealots. Nevertheless, during the twentieth century, when Europe had, ironically, shifted far from its own religious certainties and the rhetoric of 'civilizing mission', the indigenous faiths of other continents (above all, Islam) became coloured by a generalized, if restrained, anti-westernism. This is not difficult to explain; it was only after the outbreak of the Great War that the western presence became sufficiently diffuse in the localities of Asia and Africa to challenge existing patterns of authority in all walks of life. It was this cultural and spiritual alienation between 'the west and the rest', engendered by the very intimacy of their economic integration, which, like some miasmic dust, began to clog the machine of European imperial dominance in the twenty years prior to the Second World War.

IV   THE COLONIAL WORLD AND THE GREAT DEPRESSION

Many of the problems attending the European empires which have been outlined so far would have had only minor significance if, after 1918, Asian and African connections with the industrialized world had been a source of sustained and widening prosperity. But this was not the case; instead, the Great Depression of the 1930s proved, along with the two world conflicts, one of the three seminal experiences of the twentieth-century world.[19] One of its basic causes was that industrial and agricultural prices in international markets had moved out of synchronization with each other, the latter falling much more sharply than the former. Thus as purchasing power fell in the primary-producing world, depression spread to the industrial export-ing nations whose marginal surplus could no longer find an outlet. Economic contraction first gained momentum, therefore, in the non-industrialized, often colonized, regions and attained its most virulent forms there; so that however deep pockets of industrial poverty became, it was rural societies which were frequently pressed close to, and in localized cases sometimes beyond, the point of exhaustion. Between 1850 and the mid-1920s the interaction between western capitalism and its dependent satellites in other continents had, on balance, worked to the benefit of each, but for fourteen years after 1925 the market mechanism was a source, not of heightened opport-nities for individuals, but of pinched disciplines and shattered hopes. Anti-colonial nationalisms bred amidst this milieu of material disap-pointment; students rioted in Cairo, Rangoon and Djakarta, not because they felt some political millenium was within striking dis-tance, but because depression had suddenly knocked away the supports which had made colonialism so acceptable to the generation of their parents.[20] The geyser bursts of anti-westernism after 1945, once the constraints of war had been removed, are explicable only as the delayed aftermath of the 1930s experience in which the political understanding between rulers and ruled had been crucially under-mined.

Under the impact of slump, industrialized nations became less sensitive to the needs of their imperial charges. This may seem a strange contention, since it was in the 1930s that welfarist rhetoric on the issue of colonial poverty became widespread. But such liberal colonialism, most notably exemplified (in Britain's case) by the Royal Commission into West Indian social problems following the 1938 riots, was a thin mixture of sentiment and prudence. In fact during the 1930s structural forces were at work which drove a wedge between metropolitan economies and their supplier dependents.[21] Thus the major European powers scrambled to help their own farmers by reducing imports and stimulating home production, regardless of the effects this had in other parts of the world. Even in

Britain, where agriculture had less social, political and strategic 'weight' than in France or Germany, the decade saw a spate of legislation to boost the domestic agricultural sector. Simultaneously, European governments also accorded the preservation of existing levels of industrial employment within their home frontiers a much higher priority in economic policy-making, so that currency manage-ment, for example, was geared to this end rather than to the smooth working of mercantile networks so critical to imperial relations. In short, European states whose economic decisions were being deter-mined by domestic factors could not in the long term keep together empires with an infinite complexity of producer interests. If the reason for this disjuncture was not evident in the village worlds of colonial Asia and Africa, its knock-on effects were concrete enough.

This breakdown in the long-assumed 'complementarity' between metropoles and their dependencies actually encouraged industrial developments in some larger colonial states. In India, for example, the necessity to protect financial stability as agricultural revenues fell meant that the authorities in London and Delhi were driven to shore up the *Raj*'s income by levelling higher duties against manufactured, often British, goods;[22] similar processes were at work in the French and Dutch empires. For the first time large western industrial corporations had a strong incentive to set up local production facilities in these marginal markets.[23] This trend towards nascent industrialization underlay that secular transformation of traditional 'open' (that is, export/import-dominated) colonial economies into increasingly 'closed' commercial systems which after 1945 was to involve the unscrambling of the existing political order; A. G. Hopkins has stressed the importance of the depression years in fuelling these changes in West Africa.[24] Such slump-induced deve-lopments clearly involved tangible benefits for underdeveloped coun-tries, since the resulting employment allowed thousands to escape the deteriorating conditions in the countryside. To the extent that economic diversification was a precondition of future political and social maturation in Asia, Latin America and Africa, these depar-tures can be put on the credit side of the depression experience. But implicit, too, in these processes was the appearance of that urban bias in the political economy of these poorer regions which has per-suasively been portrayed as the cause of much of their distorted late-colonial and post-independence history.[25]

Certainly the cash-crop peasantries of the colonial world were amongst the prime victims of the world recession. One historian has tentatively suggested that in India it was the rending of the rural social fabric which led to a nationalist imperative, since only a fully localized regime could take the sweeping action required to bind the wounds which had been inflicted,[26] while we have already noted how, in Indo-China, colonial governance was too delicate an instrument for agrarian reform of even the most vapid sort. The peasants' plight, however, can best be illustrated by events in British Malaya and the Dutch East Indies, where the imperial economic mechanism had been most effective in enticing 'native' growers (both immigrant and indigenous) into producing for export.[27] After 1918 this southeast Asian peasantry had been locked in a struggle with European plantations for dominance within the commodity sector. The plantation interests in Malaya had tried to block the expansion of the native smallholders' output by introducing restriction schemes in the 1920s, masquerading as pure price-support measures, but peasant production could not be made to 'sit still' quite so easily and actually expanded after 1925 when rubber prices staged a brief recovery. But between 1929 and 1932 the London rubber market collapsed; this time the blow to incentives was so traumatic that many peasants simply reverted to subsistence production. As a consequence, food output rose; the Indonesian archipelago was never more self-sufficient than during the early 1930s. The effect of this retreat from the accumulation of a monetary surplus by leading peasant classes can only be guessed at, but it clearly involved a massive scaling down of individuals' material expectations. Political nationalism barely existed in the British Malaya of the 1930s, and had a vicarious existence in rural Indonesia, but the operations of depression had a fracturing effect on the relationship between colonial authorities and peasant masses that was to prove historically critical.

But if peasants suffered more from commodity price declines than did their European planter competitors, by 1939 the ability of white expatriates to shape local economies in their own image had also been undermined. It was true that European settlers in East Africa, and plantation entrepreneurs in south-east Asia, were able to extract favours from the colonial state to ensure their continued profitability, so that, for example, the refurbished International Rubber Restriction Scheme after 1934 attempted to impose the burdens of contraction primarily on native growers.[28] But such official support could not offset the fact that the high overheads of European-style production made it peculiarly vulnerable to sustained deflation. This was the case in Kenya, where the colonial government's attempt to shift some of its attention to the encouragement of African cash-crop activity after the mid-1930s signified a loss of confidence in the long-term role of white farming as the 'motor' of local economic growth.[29] In southeast Asia, too, the recovery of rubber prices in the latter half of the decade brought indigenous smallholders flooding back into the market, proving the resilience of native capitalism. Indeed, in the latter stages of the depression European plantation interests in Malaya became sufficiently impressed with the fragility of their own position to seek accommodations with Chinese capital. Thus European firms sought loans from Chinese lenders – the Chinese Overseas Banking Corporation was formed in Malaya during 1932 – invited Chinese businessmen on to their boards and employed more Chinese technicians, cheaper and often more reliable than European staff, on the estates.[30] Similarly, in India the old British managing-agencies sometimes struck up alliances with Indian capitalists as the key to their corporate survival, and did so with a shrewd knowledge of the political implications.[31] In south and east Asia, therefore, the depression had effected a change in the balance of economic power between European and indigenous capitalism which afforded the latter a new position in colonial affairs. If it was the making of the 'world market' which had been the central determinant of nineteenth-century colonization, it was changes in the nature of this market which during the 1930s pointed towards shifting political realities.

V BRITISH STRATEGY AND IMPERIAL REFORM: EGYPT, INDIA AND THE WHITE DOMINIONS

Of all the European empires, it was the British which before 1939 was confronted most directly by political nationalisms in its various dependencies and quasi-dependencies. The Dutch in the East Indies, and the French in Indo-China, for example, were able to contain the pressures beginning to work against their rule by essentially police methods; but in Egypt and India the British were forced to experiment with more sophisticated methods of forging new conjunctions between local aspirations and imperial interests. The British self-governing Dominions – Canada, South Africa, Australia, New

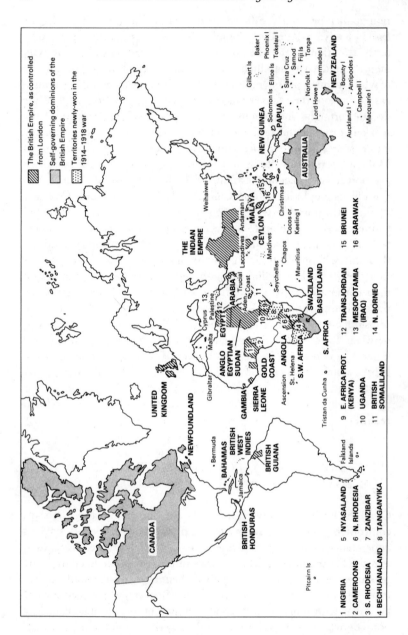

MAP 1   The British empire, 1918

Zealand and, after 1922, the Irish Free State – represented a somewhat different case. Their internal government had been freed from UK control even before 1914, but their involvement in the Great War had shown that this could mean little if in external matters the British parent continued to possess a clear constitutional superiority. The manner in which the hiatus between metropolitan necessities and Dominion nationalism was bridged between 1918 and 1939 represented a model of change which contemporary British statesmen felt to have potential relevance for the empire as a whole. We shall look at each of these three different, but related, experiences in turn.

In the summer of 1919 a spate of riots, looting and assaults on Europeans spread across Upper Egypt.[32] The key to these outbreaks lay in the temporary fusing of peasant discontents and the grievances of landed notables which had been effected by the 'war imperialism' of 1914–18, and which the coming of peace had permitted to surface. What, then, had war imperialism meant for the different classes of Egyptian society? The peasantry had been the chief losers from the inflation, food requisitioning and higher taxes which had character- ized the Middle East in this period.[33] Meanwhile the professional elites of Cairo, and the magnates of the countryside, found that the British had taken a much closer hold on Egyptian government once the Protectorate had been formally set up in 1914, largely to assist the war effort. The traditional leaderships within indigenous society therefore felt that they were becoming hemmed in by British supervision mediated through its local ally, the Court faction, and they sought to stem these encroachments on their privileges by manipulating popular disturbances.

Faced with such burgeoning troubles close to the vital Suez Canal, the British Government had two alternatives. The first of these was to commit more troops to impose order and then to intervene much more powerfully in Egyptian politics, guiding the Protectorate to- wards some variant of the Indian model: a close-knit, British- dominated bureaucracy closely scrutinized by the London authorities and capable of isolating 'troublemakers' – be they peasants or notables. The other option was to uncouple the magnates' grievances from those of the rural masses by announcing the end of the Protectorate, and to seek some new ruling coalition which would guarantee *essential* British interests without requiring constant, and expensive, intervention. Not least because of the demands on UK military resources in Ireland, India and elsewhere in the Middle East, it was the latter possibility which, after considerable debate, was taken up following the Milner Mission to Egypt in 1919. When Lord Allenby, the British High Commissioner in Cairo, finally negotiated an Anglo-Egyptian settlement in 1922, the Protectorate was dismantled while British rights of occupation were recognized, her advisory roles in administration and finance confirmed and her control over Egyptian foreign policy entrenched.

The nub of the British political strategy was clear enough: 'Why worry about the rind', Milner had summed it up 'if we can obtain the fruit?'[34] The Egyptian fruit which seemed a necessary complement to the contemporary British diet was the secure operation of the Suez Canal passage, Egypt's anchorage within a British-orchestrated regional alliance and the efficient servicing of Egyptian foreign debts under negotiated terms. All these appetites were provided for in Allenby's settlement, while the party of nationalist notables, the Wafd, had been appeased by the British retreat from any close surveillance of domestic government. In effect, the British Government had accepted the risks involved in a new equilibrium between imperial strategy and nationalist politics in its key Middle Eastern satellite. It did so on the assumption, which proved largely correct, that in an age of popular protest the Wafd would have as much need of the British as the British had of them, and that both these groups had a vested interest in constraining Egyptian life within the margins of the 1922 agreement. This tacit understanding between London policy-makers and Egypt's landed elites proved robust enough to survive three decades of depression and war; suggestively, it was only the weakening of British influence after 1948 which led to the Wafd's own demise at the hands of the 1952 Army-led coup.

The Egyptian unrest in the immediate post-war period had Indian parallels: 1919 was the year not only of turmoil along the Upper Nile, but also of the Amritsar massacre in Allahabad when British troops opened fire on Indian demonstrators, killing 122 people and wounding many others. In India, too, it had been the pressures of war imperialism – with its conscriptions, taxes and other regimentation – which had upset the old compromises between British rulers and established interests.[35] The years immediately after 1918 might have witnessed a settling down of Indian affairs had it not been for three factors. The first of these was the pervasive effects of the international slump between 1920 and 1923. The second was the Khilafat protest movement amongst the Muslims of northern India sparked off by the British role in destroying the authority of the Constantinople Caliphate; although the significance of Khilafatism ultimately lay in its contribution to the pitching of Muslims against Hindus within Indian society, at the time it seemed much more likely to push Islam into confrontation with the *Raj*.[36] The third factor at work was the mobilizing and integrating role played by Mahatma Gandhi in Congress nationalism, such that his self-styled 'sainthood' provided a framework within which divergent communal, urban and agrarian interests could be reconciled into common political purposes.[37] For these reasons, amongst others, it was in India that the British had to face up to the challenge of a massive (if erratic) nationalism straddling much wider social groups than did the Egyptian Wafd, and hence not susceptible to the rather simple, if sturdy, deal that had been struck in Cairo.

The problem facing the British Government in India was, indeed, much more complicated than its Egyptian counterpart. Fundamentally this contrast arose from the roles which the two countries had been accorded within the UK's world strategy. Egypt's significance lay in the sphere of communications, as a thoroughfare to eastern empire; only a limited degree of intervention was required to secure this objective. India had in the course of the nineteenth century become something much larger: an imperial base through which British power could be disseminated throughout much of Asia. This required broadening the tax base of the *Raj* to minimize the call on the imperial exchequer in London, and recruiting India's martial races into a localized army. But if large segments of India's population were to be progressively engaged in these strategic processes, the consensual nature of the *Raj* had itself to be continuously developed.[38] In the second half of the nineteenth century such a working consensus had been built up by old-fashioned collaboration, with the viceregal machine establishing rapport with key social groups dispersed through the subcontinent; but by the twentieth century the necessary alliances had become so broad and complex that they could be identified and nurtured only through the penetrative, but not always predictable, medium of electoral politics. Thus after 1900 the British rulers had to vacate their stately arbours and trudge through the shifting sands of Indian politics.

The first major instalment of modern constitutional reform in India came with the Morley–Minto Councils' initiative in 1908; the objective was to structure representative politics within a patchwork of local settings. The mobilization of Indian manpower and materials between 1914 and 1918, however, required mass cooperation, and thereby created a popular 'opinion', which went beyond such narrow conciliar realms. In 1918, therefore, the Montagu–Chelmsford reforms extended an element of Indian self-government to the provincial level, while reserving certain crucial areas of policy – such as finance – to the local British administrations headed by the Governor.[39] With mounting instabilities within the east Asian region, it was more than ever vital for the British *Raj* to dig deeper into Indian society for the fiscal and political support which would sustain its base role. But by tracing out these grooves within the towns and villages of India, the imperial government was providing access not only for its own agencies but also for those of its opponents. In this sense imperial necessities and Gandhian populism were inseparable twins, each seeking to penetrate the same fissures in Indian life, and by the 1920s the essence of the struggle was to see which of these forces could tap deepest into the recesses of the subcontinent.

The logic of this contest in political archaeology finally led the British Government to attempt a *coup de grâce*: the 1935 Government of India Act.[40] This monumental piece of legislation was one of the most complicated parliamentary enactments in British history. The Act embodied two main principles: an all-India Federation and provincial self-government through elected legislatures. The proposed Federation was to be composed of three main elements: the eleven responsibly governed provinces of British India, a small number of territories which were to continue to be under the centralized control of Delhi, and the princely states which had hitherto enjoyed the protection of British 'paramountcy'. In legislating for a measure of provincial self-government, some important territorial amendments were also made: Sind was separated from Bombay and the North-West Frontier Province advanced to full provincial status. Provincial legislatures were to be elected on a broadened franchise totalling, in all, some 35 million people; crucially, the mechanism of separate electorates for communal groups, which the British had fostered ever since Morley–Minto days, was to be grafted into the newly extended system. Both at the federal level, where the Viceroy remained responsible to the Secretary of State in London and not to his Indianized Council, and at the provincial level, where the Governors retained control in certain areas of policy and had the discretion to suspend the constitution, a battery of imperial checks was built into the arrangements such that the nationalist Congress rejected the whole experiment as a fraud. In fact the federal provisions of the Act were never operated since the princely states held back from accession, fearing that they would soon come under the whip of a Congress-dominated regime; only the provincial portions were activated when the national elections were held in April 1937 – a date which can be regarded as the birth of democratic politics in India.

Critics of the 1935 Act, both at the time and since, have concentrated their critique on its embodiment of separate communal entities and its creation of additional Muslim-majority provinces such as Sind and the North-West Frontier Province. In this way, it is alleged, the framers of the Act were quite blatantly (and to a degree rare even in the imperial canon) devising methods through which Indian politics could be comprehensively communalized and made more pliable to manipulation from Delhi (and London). The official British response to this criticism was that it was only by constructing communal safeguards that the great minorities of Indian society, both of religion and caste, could be persuaded to accept a measure of democratic innovation; and if this defence is not often articulated by latter-day historians, it is by no means dead.[41] The inner spirit of the 1935 reform, however, is probably to be found in the conviction of the British bureaucratic establishment that they, rather than the diverse elites who ran Congress, were best placed to survive the inauguration of mass politics in India. This belief had been a prominent part of the imperial apologia for many decades; it was decided in 1935 to extrapolate it into a policy. In short, the British strategy was to explore the workings of popular Indian politics until they located that point at which the claims of Congress nationalists to represent the 'teeming millions' could be exposed as a sham; this new equilibrium, in which imperial interests would be secure in the best of all possible (if not ideal) worlds, could subsequently be locked firmly into place. Of course, there was a price for this prospective apotheosis: it meant that the bureaucracy would have to withdraw into its bunker-secretariat in Delhi, leaving provincial government to the political caucuses. But then, under modern administrative and fiscal conditions, it was the centre, not the provinces, which had at its disposal the vital levers which could precipitate events in prescribed directions.

Even before the princes' intransigence blocked the federal aspects of the Act, it was the latter's provincial enactments which mattered most to the British, since it was these which promised to fragment Congress into its potentially divergent parts. It had been obvious from the start that the 'national' leaders of Congress, such as Gandhi, Jawaharlal Nehru and Vallabhai Patel, would attempt a boycott of the legislation, but the British judged (correctly) that the provincial politicians of that party were too hungry for the local powers which it held out to them for such a 'strike' to hold. The scale of the Congress victories which emerged from the April 1937 election results was, however, a blow to the imperial strategists. The Muslim League led by Mohammed Ali Jinnah, which the British had increasingly come to see as an invaluable counter-weight to Congress, did not even win a majority of the reserved seats for Muslims. But it had always been likely that first blood would go to Congress nationalism; it was the working-out of the system over a period of years which was likely to reverse this trend decisively. Indeed, good evidence of this eventuality was provided by the electoral aftermath, when the provincial Congress governments failed to syphon off sufficient patronage to satisfy their Muslim supporters and handed a key opportunity for Muslim League strategists to depict Congress as a Hindu monopoly. Gandhi and his associates in the Congress high command were thus as determined after, as before, the 1937 elections to block the 1935 Act, and it was their good fortune that the outbreak of the Second World War allowed them to do so. The Viceroy, Lord Linlithgow, had declared India's co-belligerency with Britain against Germany without any consultation with Indian opinion. The Congress central leadership sitting in Delhi saw this as a fortuitous opportunity to bring the operation of the 1935 Act to a grinding halt. They prevailed upon their colleagues heading the provincial Congress ministries to resign office until the nation's consent to the declaration of war had been sought (which, under the circumstances, it was not likely to be). This forced the Government of India to activate Section 93 of the 1935 statute, which allowed for the reimposition of direct rule by provincial governors. The Gandhians had therefore thwarted those provincial devolvements of power by the British which had threatened to undercut their position. But they had been forced, nevertheless, into disarray by the British constitutional offensive and the imperial government had gained some political 'space' in which it was subsequently able to bend Indian resources to a war effort which put even that of 1914–18 into the shade. In the battle between imperialism and nationalism in India during the inter-war years, it might be concluded that the former had won on points.

From the vantage point of London, Indian problems, whilst *sui generis*, could never be entirely separated from developments in the sphere of the self-governing Dominions. Dominion Status had been held out in 1917 as the ultimate destination of the Indian polity, and in 1929 the then Viceroy in Delhi, Lord Irwin, revived the suggestion with a shorter, though still undefined, time-scale implicitly in mind. It is therefore of significance that the debate over Indian policy took place against the backdrop of the successful hammering-out of a solution to the frictions within Anglo-Dominion relations. By the end of the 1930s the Dominion model was therefore seen as a precursor for future Egyptian and Indian development.[42] The British encounter with Dominion nationalism before 1939 therefore equipped Whitehall with a tradition of how to manage political change overseas which had reverberations across the whole front of colonial policy, although the effects of these were initially obscured by the imperatives imposed by the ensuing conflict of 1939–45.

In the early 1920s, however, the prospects of stabilizing the white 'Commonwealth' – the term, coined for this descriptive purpose in 1915, was just passing into common use – appeared relatively dim. Almost all the Dominions had set out to scale down their commitments to the imperial alliance. These attempts differed greatly in scale and determination from one Dominion to another, but in all cases they were coloured by an anti-imperial sentiment which the Great War had helped to mesh into their respective national cultures. Thus in Canada a consensus began to form that the nation's future lay in a regional understanding with the United States; in South Africa the defeat of the pro-British General Smuts (Prime Minister since 1919) by the Nationalist Party led by J. B. M. Hertzog in the elections of 1924 implied that the forces of Anglophobia now had control of Union affairs; in Australia the emphasis of economic development came to lie increasingly in the manufacturing sector and so lodged a question mark against the stability of commercial relations with the UK; while the addition of the Irish Free State to the Dominion 'club' after the Anglo-Irish Treaty of 1921 burdened the nascent Commonwealth with a problem which was more likely to break than to make that new-minted institution. Only New Zealand seemed securely strapped into a pro-British loyalism which manifested itself in every walk of its national life. The complexity of contemporary economic problems, not least the dynamic of Dominion industrialization, and the UK's participation in international disarmament seemed likely to deprive the Commonwealth of any lasting rationale. But by 1939 separatist tendencies in the Dominions had, in the main, been deflected, if not destroyed, and all these countries (with the exception of the Irish Free State) entered the war on the side of Great Britain.

During the 1920s, and climaxing in the 1931 Statute of Westminster, the nub of Anglo-Dominion exchanges lay in the constitutional sphere. Irish Free State, South African and Canadian leaders insisted on some definitive proof of constitutional 'independence' from London control to appease their radical, and sometimes anti-British, supporters; the British, for their part, were determined to conserve sufficient elements of legal unity such that the empire continued to be perceived as an operational (and, when necessary, fighting) entity by potential great-power enemies. But the distance between these two desiderata turned out not to be as great as had earlier been feared. None of the Dominion Prime Ministers during the 1920s ultimately wished to dabble in separatist extremes which might alienate them from the centre-ground within their electorates; while the British recognized that their own necessities could be met, not by outdated mechanisms of constitutional control, but rather by the cultivation of unifying symbols – symbols which under war conditions could touch off the sudden burst of loyalty to the motherland which had characterized events in August 1914. The 'deal' which was therefore etched out at the 1926 Imperial Conference, and subsequently enshrined in the 1931 Statute, was one in which the Dominions were accorded full parliamentary autonomy, freed from the antique impositions of Westminster supremacy, while the common monarchy, a monarchy, in other words, which did not function under separate title in the six Dominions, but was one and indivisible, was reaffirmed as the key constitutional emblem of imperial unity. The significance of the latter stipulation was that it preserved the force of the metropolitan adage, 'When the King is at war, the Empire is at war', so that no Dominion could remain neutral in an 'imperial' conflict without having to bring into sudden question its whole constitutional structure. This settlement of old legal frictions left many ambiguities unresolved; certainly, in the case of the Irish Free State, any hope that this stabilization would stick was destroyed by the election of Eamon de Valera and the Fianna Fail party in February 1932, since the latter were committed to republican ideals.[43] Nevertheless, from the perspective of fostering a cooperative Commonwealth, it was more important that the new constitutional understanding should erase tensions in Britain's relationship with South Africa and Canada, whose economies held real strategic import for any British war effort in future, than with the Irish Free State, which Britishers had never accepted as a conventional Dominion anyway, and these prior objectives were largely met. Indeed, in Whitehall particular pride was felt at the way in which Hertzog, the Boer arch-nationalist and anti-British rebel of 1914, had been enticed into concrete (if sometimes concealed) agreements with the UK Government on military and diplomatic matters after 1924. The lesson was clear: provided that British policy-makers could ruthlessly identify what was, and what was not, essential in their empire relationships, a wide scope for accommodation could be opened up for exploration. In particular, the British had learned that if they got the political nuances right, the area of precise constitutional status was one where sweeping concessions could buy goodwill at little real cost.

However skilfully a constitutional 'settlement' in the white Commonwealth had been arranged between 1926 and 1931, it remains likely that all the major Dominions would have continued to diversify their economic and political activities outside the imperial context if external conditions had allowed them to do so. It was not British craftsmanship which stunted these latter movements which had appeared so vigorous during the 1920s, but the commercial and diplomatic constraints which set in after 1931. In this sense the concern with status which threatened Commonwealth stability was not 'solved' by the 1926 Conference and the 1931 Statute; rather, it evaporated before the heat of the world crisis of the 1930s. That crisis underlined the fact that, however real the social and economic development of the Dominions had been in the early decades of the twentieth century, they remained dependent on the UK market as their only sure source of export-income in a highly protectionist world, and even more dependent on UK military protection when other powers were in the grip of military authoritarianism. All this would have been very different if, after 1918, the United States had engaged more openly in world affairs, and offered itself as a sympathetic patron for the economic and political interests of smaller Anglo-

Saxon powers; the Canadians (above all), the South Africans and the Australians would all have beaten a path to Washington's door under these circumstances, whatever the resentment caused in London. But the US remained wrapped in a pervasive isolationism, putting tariff barriers up against all comers and refusing to accept security obligations even in its Pacific backyard. As long as the Americans rejected the mantle of world leadership which their economic weight made possible, the Dominions had little choice but to take refuge under the one umbrella (that of the British Commonwealth) which, however plugged with holes, provided some protection against the storms of the period. In 1939, as in 1914, the Dominions entered a war at Britain's behest, in a somewhat more sceptical and surly spirit, but for the same reason: they could not afford to cut themselves adrift from the one benefactor likely to accord their interests any serious consideration.[44]

In responding to pressures emanating from the white Dominions, Egypt and India, therefore, British Governments between 1918 and 1939 embarked on a search for new means of stabilizing imperial relations. The equations involved in the individual sums were all different, but the mathematical style was essentially the same: the deepening and broadening of the collaborative channels down which the medley of interest groups might travel. In fact whatever successes were achieved along these lines were only very partially due to political management of this kind. External crises, which limited everybody's room for manoeuvre in the period, and the particular dynamic of economic development in still dependent areas, whereby the risks of ending up with *no* patron amongst the industrialized powers rose rather than fell over time, were at least as important in imposing limits on imperial fragmentation. The 1939–45 conflict was to turn this world upside down, and to alter the balances between imperialism and nationalism. But the continuity of a pre-war tradition of how British strategy might set the terms of change in overseas territories was profoundly to influence the subsequent course of decolonization.

VI   RACE POLITICS AND THE COLONIAL ORDER IN AFRICA

One of the difficulties in making general analytical statements about

European decolonization is that the Asian and African experiences were so contrasting. The respective time-scales in the two regions with respect to political change bore little relation to each other. Thus in Africa there were no mass-based indigenous nationalist parties on the Asian model before 1939. This is not surprising, since it was only after the First World War that colonial rule came to reverberate powerfully upon almost all aspects of African society. This might be taken as acceptable grounds for passing over any discussion of African issues until the 1940s, when the continuities with later decolonization became plainer. But the gradual cracking-up of European colonialism in Africa after 1945 will not be adequately understood unless it is preceded by a brief description of how the status quo was exhibiting signs of metal fatigue before the outbreak of the Second World War. This treatment will again be limited to British-ruled territories, because it was in these instances that economic change was most rapid and 'pre-political' pressures amongst the *indigenes* most visible to the historian's naked eye.

Any survey of inter-war Africa should sensibly begin with events in the Union of South Africa: it was in this self-governing Dominion that a complex concentration of economic activities was emerging, based largely on extractive mineral enterprises, and which had already made the country into a 'regional metropole'.[45] But whereas in Asia these economic transformations worked to disrupt the white man's mastery, in South Africa the Europeans hammered out a strategy to reinforce their local dominance. Indeed, they were so successful at doing so that at some point, probably in the inter-war years, the South African situation ceased to be essentially 'colonial' at all and to that extent falls outside the scope of the present study. But South African developments cannot be screened out of any analysis of decolonization. It is vital, for example, to stress how a wedge came to be driven between British administrative styles in their African dependencies and that prevailing in the Union. Had this differentiation, observable as early as the 1920s, not taken place, the subsequent course of decolonization would have been infinitely more contorted. Furthermore, it was the long shadow thrown by South African segregationism which critically stimulated political consciousness in other African societies where the apparatus of the colonial state was less likely to asphyxiate collective responses.

What, then, were the roots of twentieth-century segregationism in South Africa? The answer to this lies in the intersection of industrial

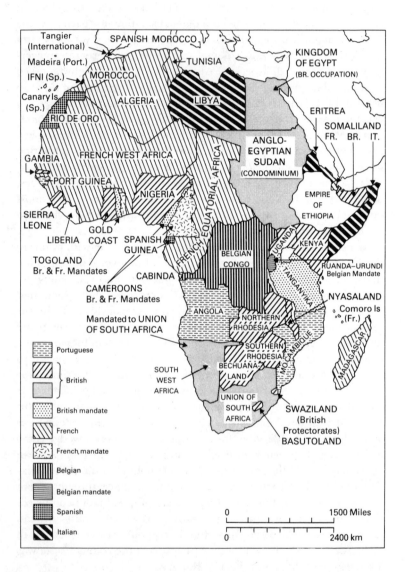

MAP 2   The pattern of alien rule in Africa, 1925

growth and racial politics in a region of white-settler consolidation. Before 1914 South African industrial activity consisted largely of the great concentrations of gold and diamond mining around such centres as the Witwatersrand and Kimberley; after 1914, while extractive enterprise remained at the heart of the economy, the manufacture of secondary goods also became important. Both General Louis Botha and Jan Smuts (Prime Ministers respectively 1910–19 and 1919–24) visualized industrialization as a solution to the Union's twin racial fault-lines between English- and Dutch-speaking whites, and between whites and blacks. Their strategy, however, was at least partially vitiated by the related consequences of rapid economic growth: the formation of a class of 'poor whites' and the flood of Africans into the industrial centres. Thus by the early 1920s one-quarter of South African whites could be categorized as 'poor'. This trend was predetermined by the downward pressure on wage rates in the special conditions of the Union; in the extractive sector the thinning of gold-bearing seams under deep-level conditions meant that the margins of profit were progressively eroded, while the massive reservoir of African labour constantly undermined the going rate for semi-skilled jobs in mines and factories. These black workers were partly pushed into urban employment by the appropriation of their rural lands under the 1913 Land Act, and partly pulled by the dynamic labour requirements of South African industrialism. The peculiar structure of the Union's development therefore pitted whites and blacks against each other at the lower end of the wage-scale, and this conflict naturally extended from jobs and pay to all other aspects of city-living, such as housing and transport.

What effects did this social pattern have on Union politics? It was by knitting together a coalition of poor, usually English-speaking, whites and the traditional Afrikaner farm vote that the Nationalist leader, J. B. M. Hertzog, was able to defeat Smuts at the 1924 General Election. Modern segregationism thus arose from the Hertzogite dilemma between 1924 and 1939: how to make continued industrialization, integral as it was to the South African state, compatible with poor white anxieties?[46] Hertzog's answer was to permit the flow of Africans into industrial conurbations to continue, but only on terms which fitted with European supremacy. Beginning with the Class Areas Act of 1924, which defined and limited African municipal rights, and culminating in the Native Representation Act of 1936, which destroyed the dangerous precedent of a parliamentary franchise open to qualified non-whites, Hertzog sought through a carefully modulated segregationism to ease the rival pressures at work on his regime.

The emergence of South African segregationism had profound effects on African societies to the north, not least because the migrant labour-chains which fed the Union's industries extended outwards to Northern and Southern Rhodesia, Nyasaland and the Portuguese possessions of Angola and Mozambique.[47] Many thousands of Africans whose legal domicile lay outside the Union therefore came to inhabit two worlds: their home locations where their lives were *relatively* free of political intrusions, and their migrant destinations where racial subordination was the dominant motif. Here lay the chief dilemma which confronted the modern colonial African: the search for cash employment held out hopes of material betterment, but carried with it the political-cum-racial structures which crushed personal liberties. The Africans of Nyasaland were caught in this classic ambivalence and were frequently propelled by their personal experiences into political awareness. Many of the leaders of black protest organizations in South Africa before 1939, for example, were Nyasas, and even a goatherd boy in that Protectorate, for example, might have heard of his compatriot, Clement Kadalie, leader of the main African trade union in the Union during the 1920s.[48] It was in these subterranean ways that politics, as Europeans understood the term, entered African life before the Second World War; it was, not least, a defensive response to the segregationist dynamic implicit in South Africa's regional hegemony.

Fear of South African expansion was an emotion which, in some senses, forged common interests between African subjects and British rulers in neighbouring territories. African masses feared Hertzog-style oppression; British authorities feared that the growth of South African influence would chip away at their own prestige throughout the continent. Here is at least one major explanation of that curious suspicion of economic development which often characterized British administrative attitudes in Africa before, and sometimes beyond, 1939; such development was bound to stimulate South African involvements beyond the boundaries of the Union. Meanwhile, in metropolitan circles a liberal critique of the 'native' policies emanating from Pretoria was gaining currency in many quarters, even some not usually noted for radical sentiments. Thus one of the underlying aims of British policy in this period was to ensure that the Union's influence north of the Limpopo River boundary was effectively neutered. In this aspiration British officialdom was enormously assisted by the decision of the Southern Rhodesian whites at the 1922 referendum to reject the proffered incorporation into South Africa, choosing instead to remain a British Crown Colony gifted with 'Responsible' self-government and, thereby, in a much stronger position than their European counterparts in Kenya (this also meant that in Whitehall Southern Rhodesian business was overseen by the Dominions Office rather than the Colonial Office). The referendum result was largely determined by the agriculturalists' instinct that their interests would not receive much attention amidst the scrimmagings of the Pretoria bureaucracy; they were much better off being ruled from Salisbury.[49] But if British administrations elsewhere in the continent were to have no truck with South African conceptions of government, they had to have some guiding set of principles of their own; this need was met by what in the 1920s and 1930s became widely known as indirect rule and imperial trusteeship.[50]

Indirect rule was, in its purest forms, a product of British West African conditions, where a white settler presence did not exist to any significant extent.[51] The concept was evolved during Lord Lugard's Nigerian governorship (1912–18) and classically adumbrated in his book *The Dual Mandate in British Tropical Africa*, published in 1922. Lugard's theme was that the task of colonial administrators was to identify legitimate traditional authorities, invest the more cooperative elements among them with prestige and sanctions derived from the imperial power, and within this stable framework to coax and coach African societies into 'civilization'. In fact the origins of indirect rule lay in the sparse resources of men, money and military equipment which had been available to Lugard in Nigeria, or to other colonizing proconsuls elsewhere in Africa: there had been little choice but to rely on existing institutional arrangements to maintain stability. Lugard's 1922 tract was thus a rationalization after the event, reinforced by his own personal dislike of westernized Africans. Nevertheless, that rationalization was a serious intellectual and practical attempt to meet the widely perceived dilemma of contemporary Africa: the need to minimize the disintegrative effects of western penetration, without stifling social and economic advance. Indirect rule was therefore fundamentally concerned with constructing indigenous agencies through which colonial transformation could be effected with the maximum sensitivity to local mores. In practice, however, indirect rule proved a blunt and ineffective instrument. Many of its imperial exponents, cherishing an image of 'old Africa' entrusted to their care, turned this ideology to crudely preservationist purposes, using it to beat down the 'progressive youth' and 'trousered native' (those stereotypes of African social change) whose half-formed aspirations jarred with the existing order. Some indirect rule chiefs did indeed have traditional standing in their communities, but many were appointed on the most flimsy evidence of ancient pre-eminence.[52] However legitimated or not by family status, these chiefly cadres usually shared one common characteristic: they sought to exploit the power which their special relationship with the British authorities gave them. Hence the Native Authority structures which emerged, equipped with localized Courts and Treasury, often became a façade behind which the ordinary peasantry suffered bitter impositions. It cannot really be argued very cogently that indirect rule *per se* held back African development between the wars: world market conditions saw to this without the necessary adjunct of bureaucratic methods. Nor was it anachronistic in 1939 to the extent that it became so during the Second World War, when the prestige of tribal authority was crucially diminished. But, nevertheless, British observers of colonial administration in Africa became profoundly conscious as the 1930s progressed that indirect rule, far from functioning as an acceptable mode of change, had been distorted in ways that impinged painfully on the lives of the mass of Africans and led them to fear the operations of colonial government.

If indirect rule was rooted in its West African origins, the concept of 'trusteeship' was essentially developed in the setting of British East Africa.[53] Its most striking manifestation was the 1923 statement on 'native paramountcy' in Kenya made by the Colonial Secretary, the Duke of Devonshire. Since this was a territory where the growing body of white colonists had been militating for settler control even prior to 1914, the Devonshire Declaration seemed to reaffirm London's commitment to beating down these European pressures. In fact the situation was more convoluted. The Kenyan administration in the early 1920s was equally concerned with the line of friction being established between African traders and an ambitious Indian merchant class.[54] Thus Devonshire was using 'native paramountcy' as a bludgeon to force back Indian demands, which was why the white settler response was relatively restrained. Subsequently the skirmish in Kenya between the activism of local whites and the officials who resisted any disruptive change persisted, with the latter striking a balance between allowing European settlers to extract favourable treatment from the Kenyan state while blocking the path towards more radical innovations (such as closer union between Tanganyika, Uganda and Kenya) which, by pooling settler resources, might have put them in a position to make a break for the open ground of self-rule on the Southern Rhodesian, not to say the South African, model. Predictably many, and perhaps most, British officials in the East African territories positively favoured closer union, with the prospect it held out of a new white-dominated 'dominion' in a strategic part of the continent. It was from within Whitehall that opposition to such initiatives was strongest, and in the end decisive. Nevertheless, the essential quality of British rule in Kenya during the 1920s and 1930s lay in an attempt to establish a working equilibrium between the three main racial blocks and 'trusteeship' provided the ideological parameters within which such a *modus vivendi* could be evolved. In retrospect, it is possible to see the trusteeship principle as a mechanism which allowed the British-run bureaucracy to foil settler aggressions in the decades when Africans were least able to provide their own political protection. But in 1939 the chances of this 'line' being held were becoming problematical.

The subterranean concerns of the official British mind on African issues are reflected in the fact that during the mid-1930s fears of 'race war' became common. Significantly, it was not assumed that such a scenario would be generated by autonomous African protest; racial confrontation was envisaged as the likely side-effect of international and regional conflicts breaking into the circle of colonial stability. The mid-30s saw the two main inter-war occurrences of this type which threatened to interact explosively with each other: the Italian invasion of Ethiopia, which excited the possibility that a black army might actually defeat European forces, and the perfervid propaganda of white supremacism which began to issue from the South African Government.[55] The swiftness of Mussolini's acquisition of Ethiopia helped to reduce these anxieties, although Hailie Selassie's eviction from his kingdom undoubtedly did, in the longer term, give an enormous boost to the intellectual evolution of black nationalism in Africa.[56] By the end of the decade, however, the more alert members of British colonial administrations recognized that, while organized political opposition did not yet exist, the racial consensus on which colonialism rested had been partially breached.

PART II   1939-45

2. Mobilization, Rejuvenation and Liquidation: Colonialism and Global War

THE Second World War poses some difficult interpretive problems when viewed from the perspective of later European decolonizations. The standard textbook theme on this matter is that the impact of total war on the UK's strategic and, above all, economic capacities was such as to make the loss of empire inevitable, even if the African dénouement was subsequently delayed. In this bald state, however, the argument is facile. The facts were rather to the contrary: the successful orchestration of massive colonial war efforts indicated that Britain still had the leverage to operate an aggressive imperial states-system, if it chose to accept the costs of doing so. In this sense, as John Gallagher has so vividly portrayed, the Second World War was a time of imperial revival, when the traditional collaborative coalitions at the periphery were shocked into a new and powerful, if short-lived, equilibrium.[1] On the other hand, quite clearly the 1939–45 conflict did trigger changes at a variety of levels – diplomatic, strategic and economic – which transformed the contexts of European empire and shifted the odds against, not in favour of, their long-term (and sometimes even their short-term) survival. But there is no contradiction in these superficially contrasting facets: it was the very scope and scale of the colonial war machines which held within them elements likely to react against any return to the pre-war patterns of rule. We shall try to elucidate these processes by looking at five aspects of wartime experience: the effects of Japan's conquests in east Asia after

December 1941; the consequences which sprang from the mobiliza-
tion of colonial societies for Allied purposes; the implications of the
Anglo-American alliance for colonial empires; the course of affairs in
India; and social change and settler power in Africa.

I   THE JAPANESE REVOLUTION IN EAST ASIA

The Japanese presence in Asian diplomacy had constituted a challenge to western domination since the 1890s.[2] Japan's subsequent
commercial expansion, culminating in its massive export-led growth
after 1931, held out the possibility that the British, French and Dutch
empires could be progressively penetrated by Japanese economic
mastery. Indeed, in retrospect it is easy to see that such a strategy of
informal influence eating its way through the forms of European
colonialism would have suited Japanese ambitions best of all; as it
was, Japan gambled all on a war 'and, in defeating the European
colonialists, merely opened the door wide for the Americans and a
medley of local political operators. It is because the Japanese attack
on Pearl Harbour during December 1941 was such a seminal event on
the way to Asian decolonization that some brief remarks on its
rationale must be made.

The key to Japanese history during the approach to war lay in the
astonishing transformation of its economy during the 1930s.[3] In 1929
that economy had remained locked into a textile phase of industrialization, with its prime export commodity, raw silk, as much an
agricultural as a manufactured article; by 1939, against all earlier
expectations,[4] Japanese industry had developed a capital goods
sector and a technological underpinning equal to most of its chief
western competitors. Population growth, far from preventing this
internal revolution, had hurried it forward by concentrating the
mind of the imperial bureaucracy in Tokyo on diversification of
employment and incomes. This route to social stabilization, however,
required access to markets and raw materials in the surrounding
region (in Manchuria, for example) which, under prevailing conditions, could only be secured by force, thus increasing the power of
the army and the xenophobes. By the end of the decade Japanese
industrialism was driven to seek new economies of scale in an Asian
mastery which brought it into inevitable deadlock with western
powers.

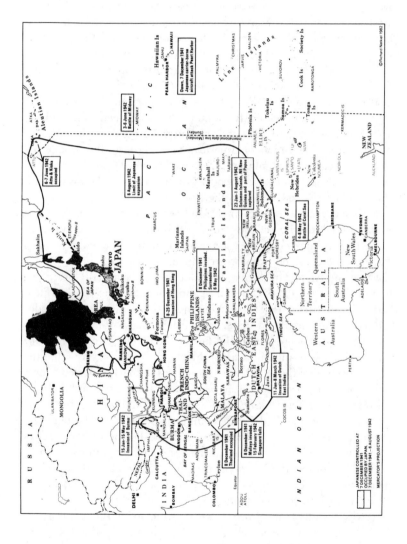

MAP 3   Japanese expansion, 1941–2

The Japanese, however, were curiously convinced right up to mid-1941 that their regional objectives were attainable without a big war. This was because they were confident that ultimately the Americans would join them in a re-partition of east Asia; thus China and the western colonies in the area would be reallocated within Japanese and American 'spheres' and hitched more securely than ever to external metropoles. This Japanese expectation that the United States could be detached from its European partners (above all, Britain) seemed sensible enough in the Pacific context, but it failed to grasp the fundamental Atlanticism of American commerce and diplomacy. Thus the steady Japanese encroachments throughout 1940 on French Indo-China and the Dutch East Indies failed in their general aim of refashioning American policy. But in the process the militarists came to dominate policy-making in Tokyo. An uneasy 'war consensus' finally prevailed in Japan, based on the assumption that one decisive assault upon the Americans would induce them to negotiate a 'new order' settlement. In effect, President Roosevelt was to be forced to choose between the British and the Japanese; in subsequently sticking to the former he made inevitable a prolonged Pacific conflict which transformed the history of Asia.

Once the American Pacific fleet had been substantially destroyed in the attack on Pearl Harbour it did not take long for Japanese authority to extend itself throughout much of east Asia. French Indo-China had already been under effective Japanese domination from August 1940 onwards; with the fall of Singapore in mid-February 1942 the whole of the Malayan archipelago was absorbed within the Japanese empire; the Dutch East Indies was similarly digested. These territories remained under occupation until the atomic onslaught on Hiroshima and Nagasaki in early August 1945. Thus for four years these Asian societies had Japanese influences deeply implanted upon them; the ideology of a 'Greater East Asia Co-Prosperity Sphere' was rooted into the local environment and this bundle of ideas (with its material emphases implied in the title) played a vital historical role in generating an Asian consciousness which, after 1945, could not be forced back into colonial containers.

It was the fall of Singapore, however, which of all the events of this period, has been taken as the vital moment at which western supremacy in the East was broken. The full weight of this point may be somewhat misjudged, reflecting more the shock which the Singapore debacle administered to the British public than to its effects on Asian populations.[5] Nevertheless, the collapse of the British defence of Singapore, the great imperial bastion in the region, indicated the essential hollowness of colonial power in the face of external pressure. To those observers, such as Mao Tse-tung or Ho Chi Minh, who had already grasped a good deal of the theory and practice of revolutionary guerrilla action, here was convincing evidence that determined campaigns using the cover of the jungle could break a colonial system seated in the towns and cities. Meanwhile in Britain there was a pained surprise that the Malay and Chinese populations of Singapore had not risen in loyal defiance of the Japanese, and assisted the British forces in a courageous last-ditch resistance; instead, the civil populations had passively accepted their fate, and the British military preparations proved to be inadequate. From this point onwards the British public had an alternative image of colonialism in Asia, peopled by a whisky-sodden old-guard of administrators and traders incapable of meeting the needs of modern business and government. Certainly it was during the Second World War, and not least under the impact of the Singapore disaster, that colonial rule began to be viewed with dislike and disdain in many quarters of the British home democracy.

In all Japanese-occupied territories, the events which took place in the war years had vital long-term significances. Thus the origins of the Chinese Communist insurgency in Malaya, which broke out in 1948, lay in the 1942–5 period. The chief victims of Japanese rule in Malaya and Singapore had not been Europeans, however bitter the impositions suffered by the white inmates of Changi jail, but the preponderant Chinese population. The Japanese, here as elsewhere, attempted to cow the one Asian race capable of challenging their regional dominance; thousands of Chinese were executed in Singapore to ensure the liquidation of underground leaderships. The experience of this subjugation, however, bound the hitherto disparate Chinese community into a greater degree of solidarity, and the fact that the Communists were the only segment of the Malayan Chinese to effect any outright resistance to Japanese authority invested them, in particular, with great prestige. In fact the Malayan Peoples' Anti-Japanese Army (MPAJA) largely remained in its isolated jungle hide-outs, and only made very rare contact with Japanese forces, but the continuity of their guerrilla existence had political importance. Their survival was helped by the manner in which the Japanese, to reduce the problem of feeding the towns, forced thousands of

Chinese out into the countryside to become rural squatters. This scattered rural migration created pockets from which MPAJA (and, after 1948, anti-British insurgents) could be supplied with food and recruits.[6] Ironically, Lord Louis Mountbatten, as Supreme Allied Commander South-East Asia, reinforced MPAJA's local legitimacy by forging contacts with them in 1944, and establishing a supply-line preparatory to the projected Allied attack on Japanese positions in the archipelago. The suddenness of the Japanese defeat precluded this final drama, and presented MPAJA with a clear opportunity to move into the resulting vacuum before the British had a chance to appear on the scene and take over from the Japanese forces, who had promptly thrown down their arms. In fact MPAJA resisted the temptation to exploit these circumstances, simply paying off a few old scores, in the hope that the returning British would repay them in political kind. It was the sense that their restraint had not been recompensed after 1945 which antagonized much Chinese opinion. Thus in Malaya the war years were crucial in breaking the old balances of colonial politics beyond repair.

Perhaps the dominant fact about Japanese administration in occupied east Asia was that it exercised a looser rein than its British or Dutch predecessors. It was, of course, militarist in nature, and stringently carried out the tasks integral to the war effort, but these terms of reference left much of local society, especially in the countryside, relatively uncontrolled compared to the long-established machines of the old European bureaucracies. Apart from forays by the Japanese secret police, intense but sporadic campaigns of food procurement and some dramatic cases of forced labour (such as the construction of the Burma Road) there was a sense in which the years between 1939 and 1945 were a fresh experience of freedom from external interferences. The organizational vitality of much local Asian politics under Japanese occupation was partly an expression of this situation, although it was, even more, a product of the characteristic style of Japanese supervision.[7] Thus whereas the European colonialists had always sought to break up mass organizations wherever possible, fearing that at some point they were bound to become infected by political or religious assertiveness, the Japanese sought to manipulate opinion through the encouragement of associations and clubs. Above all, the latter tried to diffuse the enthusiasms surrounding the Greater East Asian Co-Prosperity Sphere by allowing Asian youths to participate in mass sport and (under certain controlled conditions) militia training. The classic instance of this was the Pemuda organization in Indonesia, which cultivated the ruthless authoritarian ideals of Japanese militarism. Just how successful this strategy of linking Japanese power with these youthful and malleable cadres might have been is unknowable, since the experiment was cut short by the Anglo-Americans' own brand of technological brutality at Hiroshima. But the organizational initiatives of the period of Japanese occupation galvanized a whole generation into racial consciousness and introduced them to the basic military arts; again, such a massive psychological arousal of these societies created a texture of life radically different from that of the pre-war Asian world.

The relationship which existed between the Japanese authorities and the secular nationalists is particularly worthy of note, since it was the latter who were to rise to prominence, rather than their erstwhile religious allies, after 1945. At first the Japanese had been sensitive to the fact that secularists such as 'Engineer' Sukarno in Indonesia would be more difficult to graft into the Co-Prosperity Sphere than the volatile but pliable revivalism of such religious bodies as the Muhammadija.[8] A competitive dynamic set in during which the secular politicians established 'reading clubs' as a front for their continued activities while the Japanese syphoned off their potential supporters into sporting associations, youth-militias and coordinated religious gatherings; this multiplication of institutions enhanced that splintering of Indonesian political culture which was to be the prime motif of the republican revolution after 1945. But the Japanese were nonetheless careful not to suppress the political nationalists altogether. Sukarno and his associates were given jobs and periodically used as a means whereby the Japanese could communicate with the population through a local agency other than the Islamic authorities. Between 1942 and 1945 Indonesian politicians were continuously being moved out of, and back into, the spotlight; never allowed to become independent actors, they were retained as people who might, one day, have their uses for the occupiers. Indeed, after late 1944 the Japanese did begin to build up Sukarno as a 'man of destiny'. In this way they ensured that, regardless of their own likely defeat in the war against the Americans, the returning Europeans would not be able to piece together the fragments of their old mastery. It was during this last phase of Japanese rule, when local populations were exposed to enormous uncertainties as to the future direction of affairs, that nationalism became a majority sentiment amongst the political classes of many areas, since it afforded a point of anchorage in a confused and frightening world.

Of all the Japanese-occupied parts of wartime Asia, the most anomalous position was that prevailing in Indo-China. This merits particular attention since that area was to figure so largely in later regional transformations.[9] In August 1940 the Vichy authorities in France and the Japanese Government negotiated an agreement whereby the French colonial administration remained *in situ* in Indo-China, while a Japanese occupying force ensured that its constituent territories (above all, Tonkin and Cochin) were meshed into the war economy managed from Tokyo. This humiliating and precarious position not surprisingly split local French residents into Vichyites and Gaullists; such internal divisions did not go unnoticed amongst the Vietnamese cadres whose confidence in their old rulers was instantly affected. Nevertheless, the French Governor-General, Admiral Decoux, sought to shore up his administration by experiments designed to rally local opinion. Educational opportunities were expanded, and the curriculum reformed out of its narrow vocational bias; Vietnamese were admitted to the higher branches of the bureaucracy, a concession they had unavailingly sought throughout the 1930s; and police surveillance of all Vietnamese political life was toned down. Under the impact of war, and with the *possibility* of a decisive Japanese coup never more than days away, Decoux had to broaden and deepen the collaborative link betweeen French authority and the middle orders of Vietnamese society; but in doing so the Governor-General risked the catalysis of social and political forces which were incompatible with any effective restoration of the old colonial regime at the war's end.

Just as important as Decoux's frantic signals to Vietnamese elites, however, was the wartime progress made by the Indo-Chinese Communists, or Viet Minh.[10] The Viet Minh organization had been formed in 1941, and was largely the creation of Ho Chi Minh, who eleven years earlier had set up the Indo-Chinese Communist Party (ICP). The latter body, however, had been almost wholly isolated in Indo-Chinese politics, and was constantly harassed by the French security services. The war, in effect, suddenly opened up new opportunities for Ho Chi Minh just when all had seemed lost. It greatly increased the number of dissident factions which, while not adhering to Communist ideology, nevertheless saw the benefits which could flow from the eviction of the French. It was to attract this new constituency that the ICP leader established the Viet Minh as a popular anti-colonial 'front', but within which Communist control was absolute from the first. Furthermore, the war, by cutting off the local French authorities from metropolitan reinforcement, and by forcing them to concentrate their troops in positions from which the in-coming Japanese garrisons could be kept in some sort of check, meant that the Viet Minh were given a breathing space to establish strongholds in remote areas, particularly in the isolated, upland regions of the south-west. Here were the ideal conditions for the setting-up of Communist guerrilla bases, since the terrain was matched by a population (the tribal Thos) who had long resisted all outside intruders, be they French or Vietnamese. The Viet Minh themselves were hardly welcome guests to the tribal communities, but at least they initially caused less displacement, and therefore less resentment, than the full panoply of colonial administration. By building up a presence in this milieu, therefore, the Viet Minh were able to enjoy a rare period of security in which they could develop logistical procedures, forge a consensus on military strategy and, above all, accumulate weaponry. On this last point it was a matter of vital significance that the most northerly Viet Minh strongholds lay athwart the Chinese border; the warlords of south China supplied the Viet Minh with guns and ammunition during the war on the grounds of a shared enmity with the Japanese. This supply was later cut off, but by August 1945, when the Viet Minh triumphantly marched into Hanoi, the capital of Tonkin, they had large stocks of weapons at their disposal.

But although the war thus helped the Viet Minh construct base-areas, there always remained the possibility that they would be bottled up in these isolated retreats and finally throttled by whoever (French or Japanese) ended up controlling the cities and delta-routes of Indo-China. So why did this scenario not occur and why, instead, did Viet Minh influence spread through Tonkin and, to a lesser extent, Cochin? At the risk of simplification, it can be said that the war brought together two sensations, the combination of which was to prove politically explosive: hunger and nationalism. In an agricultural economy whose excess population always kept it on the verge of food shortage, the wartime disruption of production (with the Japanese appropriation of much of the surplus crop, the frequent conscription of the workforce and the drying-up of rural credit) pushed it over the edge into a famine which killed millions of people. The scale of this dislocation can only be guessed at; the dramatic contortions of post-war Indo-China arose, in no small part, from this collective trauma. Meanwhile the Viet Minh were careful to play down their Communist identity and adumbrate their own central position in a nationalist spectrum; they struck a cautiously ambivalent note on land reform, so as not to alienate landlord classes; they even liquidated, at least officially, their own institutional forms and merged with a new organization, the Dong Minh Hoi, which was allegedly representative of all nationalist factions. By promoting themselves as the spearhead of an anti-Japanese, anti-French front, the Viet Minh leadership were able to tap into profound political emotions at almost every level of Vietnamese society.

Indeed, nowhere were the convolutions of the last stages of the war in Asia more significant for the future than in Indo-China. In March 1945 the Japanese finally moved against the French administration, disarming its forces and interning its political and civil leaders. In this way the Japanese put themselves in a position to arrange a *de facto* Indo-Chinese succession which would confront the Anglo-American allies when they finally fought their way back into the area. An 'independent' government was set up at Hue, with sovereignty over Tonkin and Annam, with Tran Trong Kim as Prime Minister, and Kim, though fearful of taking actions which might offend the western powers on the point of victory, soon found himself besieged by student demonstrators demanding tangible signs of a new autonomy. In northern Indo-China the Japanese had thus unleashed a popular nationalism most likely to embarrass the western 'restorationists'. Meanwhile, in Cochin, with its endemic factionalism, there could be no pretence of transferring power to a single authority, and therefore the Japanese satisfied themselves with arming those groups (including nationalists and religious sects) most likely to oppose a renewal of European authority. This was the position when the Japanese surrender reduced them to mere spectators of Indo-Chinese affairs. In Tonkin the Viet Minh were able to carry out the 'August Revolution', taking Hanoi with barely a short fired. The puppet government at Hue was disbanded. In so far as there could be any certainties under contemporary conditions, it was clear that Ho Chi Minh's new republic represented the only viable point of consensus. The position in Cochin now became dramatically different. Here the neutralization of Japanese authority was the signal for internecine warfare to break out between rival groups, with assassination as the favoured *modus operandi*. The British reoccupation of Saigon in early September 1945 did little to restore stability, and when these (mostly Indian Army) troops were withdrawn following pressure from the Government of India, the British command had to yield responsibility to the French earlier than had been anticipated. By the autumn therefore, a Viet Minh regime was firmly installed in the north, while French reinforcements were beginning to pile up in the south; both these groups were committed to the unification of Vietnam under their own sole hegemony. In this way the stage had been set for the most disastrous of all Asian decolonizations: the Franco-Communist war in Indo-China between late 1946 and 1954.

II THE CONSEQUENCES OF IMPERIAL MOBILIZATION

The key to success in modern warfare has been the ability to effect a rapid increase in industrial and agricultural production, and to keep it at that level long enough to effect a military decision. It might, therefore, be wondered why Great Britain was able even to consider going to war with Germany in 1939, since the latter's economy was, in most important respects, already markedly stronger by comparison. British strategic credibility, however, derived from a very special combination of factors: an advanced industrial base, a position at the centre of the world's commodity trades and island-status (the last fact, usually emphasized as the source of British security, is almost devoid of·explanatory power on its own). It was the UK's ability to act as an imperial economic state, weaving together the varied resources of many societies well out of the Luftwaffe's range, which meant that her potential opposition had always to be taken seriously. Nevertheless, such an imperial *tour de force*, successfully executed in 1914–18, was subject to many uncertainties, and in 1939 there was no guarantee that the necessary formulae for success, in India, for example, still existed. In this sense, the great continental states – the United States, Russia and Germany – could contemplate war mobilization rather more equably, since the materials and manpower to be employed existed very largely within the metropole's own frontiers. For Britain (and France, and Holland) it was, in contrast, necessary to push and pull the administrative levers which connected their societies with such distant and fragile entities as colonial India, Indo-

China and Indonesia. A prolonged war thus exposed imperial relationships at all levels to pressures which were permanently to affect the future course of affairs.

In fact the defeats of metropolitan France and Holland meant that it was only Britain who had to *sustain* the challenge of colonial mobilization. The pattern this took was, in many instances, a matter of improvisation dictated by events. Once the Japanese had overrun the rubber estates of Malaya, British (and American) needs had to be met by shifting production of that commodity to West Africa, significantly extending the frontiers of the cash-crop economy in the latter region. Similarly, food production in East Africa had to be boosted in order to avert the disastrous shortages in that area which had occurred during the First World War; the result was that many more Africans were brought within the money economy than hitherto.[11] It was the network of industrial trade, however, which underwent the most radical transformation as British factories were forced to concentrate on meeting domestic demand for military and civilian goods, and were thereby less able to cater for export markets. Colonial consumers had to seek new sources of supply; sometimes this meant turning to US manufacturers, but often it was domestic industry which expanded to fill the gap. Thus, as we noted earlier, revenue pressures in the 1930s had pressed some colonial governments towards a modest, tariff-nurtured industrialization; wartime foreign exchange and shipping shortages continued this transformation. Again, the most striking example of this process can be found in India. Before 1939 industrialization in India had largely been limited to consumer articles; between 1939 and 1945 the British bureaucracy actually encouraged local entrepreneurs to enter the capital goods sector, such as the manufacture of chemicals, motor cars and light tanks.[12] By 1945 the consolidation of this industrial master class at the heart of the Indian economy gave it the resources and patronage to do what, in the 1930s, had been unthinkable: to face the *Raj* as a co-equal power. India, of course, is a rare example of such dramatic wartime change; mostly, where the internal availability of skills and raw materials were distinctly limited, industrialization meant little more than the growth of such activities as cement- and brick-making, or food-processing. Nevertheless, it can be seen that the Second World War had entailed a massive rejigging of production structures in many parts of the British empire; for this reason alone the political relations which span from these economic facts were bound to be discontinuous with the pre-1939 world.

A nice example of what war mobilization meant in a particular case can be found in the allied Middle East Supply Centre (MESC). The necessity of building up local production in this region was obvious from the start of the war, since the proximity of the Italian Navy made Anglo-American supply especially difficult; not only did British armies in North Africa need a continuous flow of material, but so did the civilian population of Cairo – after all, the prospect of riots in the rear of the desert campaigns was a potential nightmare for British commanders. In 1939, however, the Middle East had only a very limited capacity for modern economic activity; Egypt, at least, had a relatively developed railway system, but in most other respects lacked the assets for self-transformation, while neighbouring states were characterized by a pervasive rural stagnancy. The task of the MESC[13] was to nullify these disadvantages by building roads, distributing seeds, exploiting existing machinery to the full (sometimes pooling equipment drawn from a variety of localities into a single productive centre) and only where absolutely vital importing capital goods. For the duration of the war economic expansion in the Middle East was much less subject than hitherto to the constraints of market values and the absence of local skills, and instead was driven by the Allies' military and political necessity. Naturally, this expansion of modern productive activity was very localized, and the military situation set up blockages of its own, but the MESC provides one illustration of how Anglo-American mobilization reworked the fabric of those underdeveloped societies which found themselves exposed to its full weight.

Such resource mobilization, however, inevitably involved inflationary consequences. The presence of Allied armies, and the boost to local commodity production, increased money circulation just when the availability of consumer goods was being curtailed, pushing up prices to record levels.[14] This inflation was predictably at its peak in the grain markets, where the large landowners and mercantile cliques made fortunes out of hoarding and speculation. Three chief effects of these processes can be isolated. Firstly, wartime inflation advanced the conjunction of urban and countryside elites, adding strength and coherence to local ruling classes. Thus landed magnates equipped with liquid funds from grain profits invested them in urban assets and so extended their own range of contacts and influence; such tightening links between rural and town cadres were a precondition of modern mass nationalism, since previously the European authorities had alone been able to span the contrasting social worlds in colonial territories. Secondly, rising prices diffused grievances amongst those urban 'middle orders' who did not have access to their own food stocks and who were especially vulnerable to grain speculation; those on fixed incomes, which meant (among others) the employees of the colonial bureaucracy, saw their living standards critically eroded during the war years. Thus individuals who, when educational access had expanded during the 1920s and 1930s, rushed to equip themselves with the weapon of literacy and then scrambled their way to a clerical job in some government office, found these slender gains being clipped back by the impact of inflation and shortage in the 1940s; it was among this 'petty bureaucracy' that nationalism was to lodge with such explosive power in the post-war era. Thirdly, rising prices also put light consumer goods out of reach of the mass of colonial peasantries. Of course, the effective purchasing power of peasant incomes had been low before the war, but the flow of western goods had represented a marked improvement in living standards for rich and middle peasants; their sense of deprivation when this flow was greatly diminished gave political nationalism a vital means of access to the rural masses. In all these ways the inflationary effects of war government broke the traditional balances of colonialism and quasi-colonialism; new alignments, grievances and leverages were created within local societies which made it much harder for the old mechanisms of European power to operate.

The British dilemma over wartime inflation (whether in India, Egypt or elsewhere in Africa) illustrates the bind in which colonial rule was now caught. To some extent inflationary pressures could be reduced by freezing the sterling credits which the UK came to owe colonial governments for war expenditure; indeed, there was no way to pay these debts under war conditions anyway – and there were many, not least the Americans, who took the view that they were not UK liabilities at all, but legitimate contributions by colonial populations for their own protection. The British Government, looking to its future relations with indigenous bourgeois classes, was not prepared to go this far down the path of appropriation, but it made sure that the funds used to requite the colonial economic effort remained in paper form and securely stashed away in the Bank of England, and so did not add to the 'ready' cash flows in the areas concerned.[15] But the line against inflation could not be held so easily as this. There was, for example, the problem of the *working* funds which were necessarily pumped directly into local economies through military procurement and increased civil employment in factories, canteens and transport functions. These extra monies alone, relative to the size of the economies involved, were enough to threaten a ripping inflation, the only hope of controlling which lay in stringent price controls. The attempt to impose such controls, and under extreme circumstances to requisition scarce grain supplies, pitched the British authorities against those elites on whose collaboration the colonial polity had always depended. The emergence of black markets in British-ruled Asia and Africa marked not only the determination of local producers to maximize the market opportunities which the war economy had held out to them, but also a line of political cleavage between ruler and ruled which was bound to have long-term consequences. British wartime propaganda, therefore, was packed full of the statistical successes of colonial mobilization; what went unnoticed, except by a very few, was the manner in which, amidst this flurry of official achievement, the delicate structure of local collaborative understandings had been shattered.

One adjunct of this 'collaborative decomposition' lay in a heightened competitiveness between political factions in colonies and quasi-colonies which made the efficacy of imperial intervention more than ever problematical. What, more specifically, this could mean can be deduced from the Egyptian crisis of 1942, when the King, eager to keep open his lines of communication with the growing anti-British sentiment in his country, appointed a new Prime Minister whose credentials anything but pleased the British Ambassador, Sir Miles Lampson.[16] Lampson acted with characteristic decisiveness, surrounding the royal palace with tanks and effecting the rapid appointment of a new premier. However, this action gravely undermined the popular prestige of the monarchy, on which the 1922 Anglo-Egyptian settlement was not least founded, and the events of 1942 can be seen as inaugurating that decline of royalist politics which led to the Army coup of 1952 and so to the anti-British regime of Gamal Abdul Nasser. The British were therefore able during the Second World War to shunt their dependent (and semi-dependent) partners into a massive war effort which helped them to victory in the strategic theatres of a world-wide conflict, but this (perhaps surprising) success created patterns of social and political antagonism inimical to longer term British interests.

III   COLONIALISM AND THE ANGLO-AMERICAN ALLIANCE

Recently historians have devoted considerable attention to the course of Anglo-American relations during the Second World War.[17] Shifting away from the old preoccupation with the 'Great Alliance', these investigations have focused on the divided perspectives within the London–Washington relationship. In fact Allied objectives in Europe between 1941 and 1945 remained a matter for relatively easy consensus, despite differences over tactical priorities; it was in relation to non-European theatres that the British and US Governments were at loggerheads. Thus, for the Americans, the war was a great opportunity to forge access to regions which hitherto the UK had monopolized. Indeed, US interests had been attempting to penetrate the Middle East since the 1920s, with some success; the historic alliance struck between President Roosevelt and the ambitious Saudi monarch, Ibn Saud, on board USS *Murphy* in February 1945 marked the end of Britain's success in choking off the intrusions of great-power competitors into Middle Eastern politics.[18] If the Saudis provided the Americans with a *point d'appui* in Arab affairs, Washington circles looked to General Chiang Kai-shek to provide them with similar facilities in the crucial case of China. Roosevelt wished to elevate China to the status of a great Asiatic power whose voice, characterized, of course, by a distinctively American accent, would be heard on all the chief regional issues; it was with this end in view that Roosevelt insisted that Chiang Kai-shek and his formidable wife should attend the Cairo Conference in November 1943. The US President, in short, tried to direct the future shape of Asian affairs in ways that shifted power and influence from those states long held within the European orbit (India, Indo-China and Indonesia) to a Nationalist China firmly brought under American patronage.[19] Implicit in this, too, was Roosevelt's consistent desire to foster the congruency of aims between American strategy and anti-colonial nationalism, an axis which seemed to hold out limitless possibilities for the moulding of world affairs when peace came. Only Chiang Kai-shek's crushing defeat at the Communists' hands, and the inexorable manner in which anti-colonialism and anti-Americanism overlapped after 1945, showed these Rooseveltian subtleties to be streaked with illusion.

Roosevelt's critical attitude towards European empires, however, only partly arose from the lust for a world role which gripped the Washington bureaucracy after 1939 (and especially after 1941). It was also a response towards mainstream American opinion. A profound aversion to 'British imperialism' had always run deeply (if unevenly) in American society. This was particularly marked between September 1939 and December 1941, because it could be held that US treasure was being poured out through the Lend-Lease Act for the support of a British imperial war. America's entry into the war after Pearl Harbour against Germany as well as Japan did not fully dissipate these sentiments, so that Roosevelt required some solid emblem of the fact that the alliance stood, not for the salvage of old colonial privileges, but for a new world of universal democracy. This was the rationale behind the Atlantic Charter, which the President persuaded a reluctant Churchill to sign at the end of the Argentia Conference in August 1941. In fact, Churchill soon contended that the 'freedom' alluded to in the Charter as the touchstone of Allied desiderata referred to that of the European peoples under Nazi subjugation, not colonial populations at all. 'I have not become His Majesty's Chief Minister' the Prime Minister portentously declared in his Mansion Hall speech of that year 'in order to preside over the liquidation of the British Empire.' Nevertheless, the Atlantic Charter could not be unsaid, and although historians have probably exaggerated the significance of this piece of windbaggery, it did play some part in stimulating nationalist ideas in the non-European world by giving them the touch of Anglo-American acceptability.

It was in order to deflect Rooseveltian criticisms of empire that the British Cabinet and Colonial Office set out to articulate a modern variant of colonialism transparently concerned with development and welfare.[20] In 1940 this approach was inaugurated when a Colonial Development and Welfare Act was passed through Parliament, authorizing the expenditure of £5m annually. This legislative action also reflected the burgeoning consensus, which had begun to emerge in the late 1930s, that the gamut of colonial political problems hinged for their solution on the promotion of economic change. This thinking was rooted in an enormous naïvety as to what the implications of, and the constraints upon, such change were. Nevertheless, it was at least recognized that the route to prosperity in the non-advanced world necessarily lay in a closer coordination of resources within 'natural' regions, since individual colonies were invariably too small to form effective units of development. The establishment of the Caribbean Advisory Commission (with US participation) and the appointment of a Resident Minister in West Africa expressed this awareness of the regional dimension; after the war it was to blossom into full-blown federation-making, the fragrance of which was not to prove universally popular. Whether this wartime attempt to cull together the rhetorics of liberal-welfarism and a continuing colonialism actually made any impression on American opinion must be doubted; anti-British sentiment in much of small-town America was too strong for such verbal froth to carry weight. But in the process the interior atmosphere of the British Colonial Office was itself metamorphosed. Its professional mystique became entwined with the progressive enhancement of colonial change – under, of course, Whitehall supervision. This was not so much a case of intellectual conversion, as of collective career strategy, since it was clear that the Colonial Office had to find new ways of projecting itself at a time when its position in the ministerial pecking order was slipping fast. Thus the Foreign Office, which had always resented the Colonial Office meddling in matters of high diplomacy, was determined to see the latter relegated to the lowly position it had occupied in the early part of the century, and by the time of the Yalta Conference in early February 1945 this demotion had essentially taken place. This switch in the bureaucratic culture of the Colonial Office, and its reduced leverage within Whitehall, both had significance for the direction of post-war policy.

Ironically, during the latter stages of the war the US Government did come to view British and European colonialism rather more sympathetically than had earlier been the case. Given the degree to which the UK and US publics had been locked together in dramatic common emotions, it would have been surprising if the old edges of their relationship had not been rounded off. The greater, if still very selective and ambivalent, sensitivity evinced by American policy-makers towards colonial dilemmas by 1944, however, evolved more directly out of a continuing revolution within Washington officialdom. Thus the US military establishment (especially the navy) became struck by the future benefits of acquiring its own string of sovereign bases in the Pacific, and in consequence developed a much more circumspect attitude to political 'rights' on the part of Asian peoples.[21] More broadly, however, the American foreign policy establishment, while reaching out for the global pre-eminence it had come to covet, became conscious that this glittering prize was extremely fragile. Before 1941 anti-imperialism had come easily to an official America whose responsibility for stability in other continents was minimal; by 1944/5 US prestige and interests had become closely bound up with the wider world, such that in administration circles European empires (for all their faults) began to be seen as a means of keeping the lid on Asian and African volatilities, at least until the post-war order had been decided upon and its construction set in motion. When peace came liberationist perorations still sporadically emitted from American lips on colonial questions, but the tone had become one of wavering anxiety.

It was over the planning of the post-war world, however, which had begun in Allied circles in 1942, that British and American views were in real danger of shearing decisively apart. British policy-makers and interest groups had accepted a subordinate role relative to their American counterparts as a necessity of war. They had acquiesced in the stripping of the UK's gold and monetary reserves, and the surrender of many export markets,[22] as the price that had to be paid if Roosevelt was to carry the measures through Congress which allowed him to put the American economy at the disposal of the war effort. At the same time, however, the British were acutely suspicious of American intentions to 'fit them out' for a permanent inferiority along these lines.[23] In particular, there was intense equivocation on the matter of a liberalized international economy under Anglo-American (but mainly American) aegis. This was clearly in the US interest: six million people, including a great mass of women and blacks, had been added to the American labour force after 1941, and this level of employment could only be sustained if export markets remained buoyant. Commercial multilateralism, as free trade was commonly referred to at the time, was not so evidently desirable from the British vantage point, since it was uncertain that UK industry would be strong enough to face the full blast of open world markets after two decades of depression and war. Many British industrialists were adamant that their firms could not survive unless accorded some degree of protection through those tariffs and imperial preferences which had become so inimical – after fifty years of grand tariff-mongering on their own part – to the Americans. British planning of post-war policies revolved around one straightforward but agonizing question: were the prospects of living with American economic hegemony more painful than living apart from it?

The outcome to this debate had profound implications for colonial systems. As the end of the war approached there was no doubt that most informed British opinion accepted that, on balance and given reasonable transitional terms, an expansionist, American-led future was preferable to the sackcloth and ashes of an imperial (but inevitably unstable) commercial alliance. This was the point at which the concept of a British imperial economy finally dissipated, although the Sterling Area was to have tactical significance for years ahead. Furthermore, although the British reluctantly embraced an American-orchestrated free trading order as the lesser evil, they did so with forebodings that led to a new importance being ascribed to the underdeveloped world in general, and especially to those parts of it where the UK still exercised colonial functions. Thus it was argued that the competitive power of the US economy could only be made bearable for other industrial producers if the world market as a whole was rapidly boosted, and that the most immediate scope for such accretions of consumer demand lay in Africa, Asia and Latin America. It was out of this school of thought, essentially concerned with industrial survival in an age of American hegemony, that the theme of 'colonial development' was articulated. In 1945 the British Government pushed a new and considerably extended Colonial Development and Welfare Act through Parliament, and commenced an era of grants-in-aid for infrastructural improvements in dependent areas.[24] Britain's African colonies, with which most of this early 'aid' history is concerned, had become more relevant to Whitehall's wider economic strategy than they had ever been in the backwater days of indirect rule; it was only in the mid-1950s that these commercial calculations were revised, and then blanket decolonizations were not long in coming.

IV THE BENDING OF THE *RAJ*

The colonial dependencies most dramatically affected by the Second World War were those wrested from western rule by Japanese occupation. India was not to be counted among these, although the Japanese offensive through Burma in 1942/3 posed a very real threat to north-eastern India and played a part in dissipating British prestige. Nevertheless, the impact of war on Indian politics and society was to have an enormous significance within the wider story of Indian decolonization. In September 1939 the 1935 Government of India Act was in limited operation, with Congress ministries governing seven provinces. One option for Congress at this stage was to exploit the pressures of war to tilt the operation of the status quo in their own favour. This the Gandhian leadership chose not to do; they were much too concerned that *any* cooperation in war administration would crystallize understandings between the imperial centre and provincial politicians, and so break their ability to control the nationalist movement. The Congress leadership were not bent on effecting changes in the 1935 legislation, but on destroying it by forcing their colleagues in the provincial ministries to resign. In this they succeeded, since those ministries could hardly be seen cooperating with a war effect against the injunctions of Gandhi and Nehru. Subsequently the Congress instinct was to sit on the sidelines, leaving the British administration to break itself in the complex task of mobilization, and awaiting the opportunity to assert its status as the only truly popular political force in the country. In retrospect, this Congress gamble can be seen to have both succeeded and failed: it succeeded in so far as the war effort effectively exhausted the capacities of British rule, and lost because that war effort nurtured the Muslim League and thus broke the Congress monopoly of nationalism in India.

In many ways the resignation of the Congress ministries was a blessing for the British authorities. By returning to direct rule in the old Congress-dominated provinces, the Government of India was able to bend local resources to the war effort without constantly having to negotiate with other parties. But the Viceroy, Lord Linlithgow, could not simply revert to pure authoritarianism; the *Raj* had to maintain some progressive credentials if the enormous conflicts of loyalty felt by the literate classes were to be pacified. This was the motive for the August Offer authorized by the British Cabinet in 1940, which defined India's post-war goal as that of Dominion Status and proffered the inclusion of party representatives in the Viceroy's wartime Council. There was little chance of Congress responding to this formula. It was designed, instead, to communicate Britain's good intentions regarding Indian constitutional advance to three main constituencies: the mass of Indian political opinion, President Roosevelt and the British Labour Party. In the ensuing months, however, this particularly hollow sort of posturing became inadequate. The UK's increasing dependence on US economic assistance meant that the American public's sensitivity to Indian 'freedom' (however mixed in motive) had to be taken into closer account. The fall of Singapore delivered a dramatic blow to the UK's military stature throughout Asia, and profoundly affected the texture of Indian political life. In March 1942 Churchill was constrained into authorizing a radical attempt to break the constitutional deadlock in India; this took the form of a mission to the country by a leading Cabinet member, Stafford Cripps, with a mandate to use the August 1940 Offer as a basis for further negotiation.

The details of Cripps' visit to Delhi and his labyrinthine dealings with British officials, Indian politicians and American envoys (the latter in the shape of Roosevelt's personal representative in India, Louis Johnson) must be obtained elsewhere. The conclusion of one close study of this affair is that Cripps was 'dished' by an alliance of Churchillian conservatism in London and the Viceroy's determination in Delhi to keep Congress out of the administration.[25] By allowing Cripps to hold out the bait of an Indianized and party-dominated Council, but preventing him from giving any reasonably satisfactory promise that the resulting Cabinet would possess the confidence of the Viceroy, Churchill and Linlithgow ensured that the talks would last long enough to have therapeutic effects in certain quarters, not least the White House, while conveniently breaking down in the end. There is no doubt a good deal of veracity to this account, but it seems equally probable that the Congress negotiators themselves had little real interest in Cripps' ramblings. Gandhi and Nehru were both convinced that Congress absorption into war government could be politically fatal to them; the bait of participation in some quasi-Cabinet was never likely to entice them into putting their head inside this lion's mouth. The 1942 mission was a means by which all the participants could posture to their respective constituencies: Churchill to Roosevelt, Cripps to a Labour Party which held him in no great warmth, and Linlithgow and Nehru towards the middle ranks of Indian society over whose loyalties they were in bitter competition.

However, the break-up of the Cripps negotiations left Congress in an intensely vulnerable position. The events of the 1930s had convinced its leaders that British power was slowly crumbling, and

when war came they had looked forward, at some point in its
duration, to being able to impose terms on the *Raj* rather than vice
versa. But after more than two years of war the British position
relative to that of Congress seemed remarkably secure. Outside
India, the Germans had not been able to strike decisively at the
British mainland, the US had entered the war on the UK's side and,
however spectacular the Japanese success at Singapore had been, it
seemed doubtful that the latter would be able to sustain the logistical
feats required for a credible invasion of India. Inside India, and most
threatening to the nationalists, the British authorities had managed to
construct a war machine which in its scale exceeded that of 1914–18.
This *tour de force* was shattering not least because it clashed so starkly
with Gandhian expectations. Here was another explanation for
Cripps' failure to establish a negotiated solution: the only war
administration which Congress could possibly enter was one in which
the British were already hanging limply on the ropes, a state of affairs
which, at least to the naked eye, was not the case. But if in early 1942
Gandhi, Nehru and their colleagues had never expected talks in Delhi
to get very far, they were surprised and appalled at the brazen
confidence exhibited by the British Cabinet and Linlithgow. Indeed,
Cripps' humiliation at the hands of Churchill directly implied, not
only that Congress was being taken less seriously than ever, but that it
was in real danger of being thrust to one side as an irrelevance. This
was why the Congress high command was soon panicked into
unleashing the massive Quit India rebellion of August 1942: it
signalled to the British, in the only conceivable way under the
circumstances, that their organization remained too large an entity to
be bulldozed flat by the processes of war government. It is possible
that Gandhi actually believed that the rebellion, the most widespread
Indian disturbance since the 1857 Mutiny, would bring the *Raj*
staggering to a complete halt; it is much more likely that this subtle
tactician was seeking to staunch the momentum of the war effort and
thus redress the balance of power between imperialism and nationalism. If so, the judgement of the saintly *Mahatma* can rarely have been
so grossly flawed. The Indian Army held firm in British hands when it
came to crushing the outbreak. The Congress leadership, including
Gandhi, were interned in large numbers. This proved one of the great
turning points on the road to partition: for it was the effective
disappearance of Congress as a negotiating force in Indian politics
during the next two years which allowed the Muslim League to

consolidate its claims as legitimate heir to British power in much of north India.

To emphasize the statistical achievements of the Government of India's mobilization for war (the number of battalions recruited, the volume of tanks and munitions produced) is, however, likely to obscure more profound developments which ran parallel with them. The pressures of war, in fact, were consistently undermining imperial rule in India, especially in the rural areas, but not in ways fully compatible with Congress's own ambitions. In this context events in the Punjab are illustrative.[26] British supremacy in this large and fertile province had for decades been based on an alliance between the imperial administration and the more prosperous agricultural classes. With the spread of 'politics' after 1918, this collaboration was expressed through the provincial hegemony of the Punjab Unionist Party, which succeeded in preventing either Congress or the Muslim League from making inroads amongst Punjabi opinion. The system, however, only worked so long as British rule benefited the dominant agrarian interests. War industrialization after 1939, however, clearly favoured big-city groups, villages were starved of consumer goods and, most significantly, grain prices were controlled. Thus while the Punjab provided enormous quantities of manpower for the Indian Army, it was denied the prize of inflated grain profits. The climax of this disillusionment came in 1943 when the authorities in Delhi, badly shaken by the rippling effects of the Bengal famine, ordered the partial conscription of the Punjabi grain surplus as a 'bank' for the deficit provinces. This decision was, under the circumstances, inevitable; the British could not let Bengal continue to starve without reaping a whirlwind sooner rather than later. But each sack of grain requisitioned for a Bengali stomach meant cash filched from the Punjabi growers, so that the latter increasingly turned away from their old imperial partner and sought a new patron in the Muslim League – a process that climaxed in the 1946 provincial elections. The local administrators had forewarned the Viceroy of the effects of his policies on the Punjab, but from the perspective of Delhi the necessities of war far outweighed the shoring-up of a rotting colonial fabric. This point of breakage between the 'centre' decision-makers concerned exclusively with the winning of a war, and the subtly different priorities of administrators in the localities, lay at the heart of the decolonization process in India at this time.

It was the Muslim League advance in provinces such as the

Punjab, where previously it had not had much success in 'stamped-ing' Muslim opinion, which confirmed its President, Jinnah, as a political figure who could not be excluded from any constitutional settlement in India, and which thereby put partition on the agenda, however much Congress or the British, in their respective ways, might resist such a solution to Indian problems. In fact during the 1930s Jinnah – a London-trained lawyer, secularist and chain-smoker – had distanced himself from those political and religious extremists within the League who called for a separate Muslim state, or 'Pakistan'. But at the 1940 Congress of the Muslim League in Lahore the 'Pakistan Resolution' was passed which committed the party to the goal of a partitioned independence in the subcontinent. Quite why this new consensus within the League had come about – and, more particu-larly, why Jinnah's stance had undergone a radical shift – is not clear.[27] There is no doubt that the alleged communal favouritism exhibited by the Hindu-dominated Congress ministries after the 1937 elections had caused a backlash amongst Muslims generally, and Jinnah grasped how this could be turned to League advantage. The origins of the 'Pakistan Resolution', however, probably lie in the specific dilemma facing Jinnah and the League in the months after September 1939. Thus to have meekly joined in the Congress boycott of the British war effort would have confirmed the League's purely subordinate role in Indian political life. On the other hand, to have simply cooperated with the government in Delhi would have allowed Congress to lambast Jinnah as a stooge of the imperial power, and probably broken him politically once and for all. But beating the Pakistan drum allowed the League to reach out for the prizes which collaboration with the British put within its grasp, and to maintain a nationalist legitimacy – albeit a nationalism which had sheared completely apart from Congress conceptions.

However, the wartime growth of the Muslim League was crucially linked to the support it received from the Viceroy, Lord Linlithgow. Obsessed with the threat posed by Congress to India's mobilization, Linlithgow latched on to Jinnah as a weapon to stun Congress into immobilism. Indeed, it was at this late stage in the history of the *Raj*, and driven by military necessities, that British rule began a calculated exploration of Hindu–Moslem rivalries, and when peace came the machine of communal politics could not just be slammed into reverse. But quite apart from Linlithgow's private war on Congress, the process of communalization was knit into the social and econ-

omic impact which the war had on India. After 1939 imperial
mobilization entailed an enlarged bureaucracy, an intensified industrialization and a boost to agricultural production. All of these varied
factors provided wider avenues of personal advancement for some,
while inflicting the pains of inflation on others. Thus as the scope for
economic gains and losses was expanded, individual and group
anxieties were raised to a new pitch, so that Indians thrashed around
to find methods of protection against the displacements of the period.
Under subcontinental conditions, it was logical that this need for
social armour more often than not took the form of communal
loyalism. It was because Jinnah was able to exploit the British need
for a local ally at a point when social divisions were being burnt into
the Indian fabric that the Muslim League was able to become a mass
party capable of defeating Congress in those provinces which had
Muslim-majority populations – although in certain instances, such as
that of the North-West Frontier Province, even this still remained
problematical in 1945. Overall, the British *Raj* was able to achieve
what Congress in 1939 had thought was beyond its power: the
bending of Indian resources towards a grand strategy in Asia.
Nevertheless, the price of such success was to be the loss of that all-
India creation which had always lain at the heart of the British
imperial apologia in south Asia.

   In October 1943 Linlithgow had been succeeded as Viceroy by
Lord Wavell, and as the Japanese threat to India eased, the essential
problem became that of a 're-entry' into civilian politics. The gradual
return of normality also meant the recrudescence of nationalist
sentiment amongst the middle orders of society which had been
unwilling to involve themselves in outright opposition to the war. The
British Government acted at various points in ways that served only
to assist this revival of nationalist fortunes. The use of Indian Army
troops to reoccupy Cochin China and Indonesia at the end of the
war, while triggering old resentments about the use of Indian
revenues for purely imperial purposes, was probably unavoidable at
the time; Wavell's decision, however, to put on trial those Indian
soldiers who had defected to the Japanese and fought in the Indian
National Army *against* the British, and to hold that trial in the Red
Fort in Delhi (symbolic seat of the old Moghul power), was an error
of immense proportions.[28] The intention was to draw a very visible
line beyond which anti-British sentiment was to be severely discip-
lined; the effect was to catalyse nationalist consciousness after four

years of repression. Wavell's instincts in Indian politics, however, fitted into a mould of liberal, if distinctly old-fashioned, paternalism.[29] Towards the end of the war he had become convinced that British interests lay in pushing through a solution to India's future status while the political situation remained fluid and Congress's leaders were locked in a weak bargaining position. Throughout 1944 and early 1945 the Viceroy therefore pressed the British Cabinet to authorize him to convene a conference of Indian party leaders at which the various factions might be levered into a coalition government; amidst this process the moderates (inside and outside Congress) might force an all-India compromise. Gandhi was released from prison in May 1945 in the hope that this would help open the way to negotiation. In the end, Churchill, who was not a little sad to terminate a period of Indian affairs in which Congress had sustained considerable damage, did agree to Wavell's promptings, and the Viceroy subsequently hosted the Simla Conference of June 1945, during which he sought tirelessly to weave together some patchwork of League–Congress understanding to form the basis of a joint interim administration.[30] But when Jinnah insisted on his right to nominate *all* the Muslim representatives in such a government, the proceedings inevitably broke up. Two weeks after the failure in Simla, Clement Attlee became British Prime Minister in a Labour Government. Clearly some new slant on British policy towards India was imminent. But by this point, too, the great imperial war effort was coming home to roost in the form of disintegrating administration and communal tensions far more intense than anything which had been experienced within the living memory of the *Raj*.

V   SOCIAL CHANGE AND SETTLER POWER IN AFRICA

In terms of the great 'theatres' of Second World War strategy, most of Africa was a backwater between 1939 and 1945. Recently the wider military significance of the North African campaigns has been questioned;[31] certainly their rippling effects on sub-Saharan Africa were relatively minor. In West Africa the only fighting was a short, sharp fracas between the Vichyites and Gaullists for control of the French colonies; and although the Italian forces put up some resistance to the British in Abyssinia, there was no East African front on the scale of 1914–18. Politics and society in Africa were therefore not exposed to the same physical and psychological shocks character-istic of much of Asia during wartime. Hence in 1945 western opinion could be under no illusion that a return to pre-war routines in Asia was at all possible, but in European-ruled Africa such an expectation was deeply rooted, whatever the official rhetoric of welfare and development for indigenous populations.

However, no intelligent observer of African affairs could fail to note the important ways in which the massive conflicts elsewhere were reverberating (albeit indirectly) within the sub-Saharan region. The great expansions of output in the Northern Rhodesian and Katangese Copperbelts to meet Anglo-American demands, boosting their turnover of migrant labour, were extreme examples of how the war intensified the rhythms of the modern economy in African life, but few localities were left outside the penumbra thrown by the interaction of war and money. It was between 1939 and 1945 that cities such as Nairobi, Leopoldville and Salisbury 'took off' from the modest scale they had attained in the 1920s, and which had remained relatively stable through the 1930s; shortages, inflation and war-employment boosted wage-labour opportunities and accelerated the drift from village to town, with growing numbers of young, single males drawn to the ill-equipped townships fringing the cities. As important as urbanization in this structural shift to cash-based norms, however, were the administrators' 'grow more food' cam-paigns in the countryside.[32] During the depression there had been some modest encouragement given to African farmers by the state but these bureaucratic pressures were considerably extended after 1939, such that indigenous producers were permitted to cultivate cash-crops which they had previously been banned from growing. Furthermore, although the colonial authorities tried to stifle infla-tionary profits by stringent marketing regulations, there is good reason to believe that African growers were able to obtain consider-able cash returns from the endemic black markets. During these years the opportunities for Africans in commercial agriculture, urban jobs and administration were considerably expanded, although not suffi-ciently quickly to prevent the townships becoming pockmarked by un- and underemployment; for most people standards of living were raised markedly above those prevailing in the preceding decade (although the drift to the towns often had gravely deleterious effects on many villages, not least by depleting them of manpower at harvest times). Inflationary and demographic trends snipped at the margins of these gains, but the massive boost to economic activity which the war entailed outweighed these factors, at least for the duration. In this way the balance was critically affected between what was popularly labelled the 'old' and the 'new' Africa, and a diffused sense of material expectation became characteristic of millions of rural, as well as urban, Africans. The growth of post-war political consciousness amongst indigenous masses was an outcrop of this war-induced transformation.

This African metamorphosis was too striking for European colonial administrations to ignore its implications altogether until the war ended. If only to ensure the cooperation of Africans in war measures, both British and French administrations had to provide some evidence of sensitivity to changing times. They met this necessity in characteristically different style. Thus the 'Free French' Gaullists, with their love of the grand gesture, and conscious of their own tenuous position, convened a conference at Brazzaville in January–February 1944 at which African representatives were feted with talk of self-government; it was, however, stressed that this self-government would not affect the continuance of French sovereign authority.[33] What this actually meant was not clear, and no attempts were made at definition. The British approach to change in wartime Africa was much less vivid; it began with the commissioning of Lord Hailey, perhaps the most noted colonial expert of his day, to produce a revised version of his *African Survey* (first published in 1938).[34] Hailey's conclusions were shot through with evasive caution. In particular the growing disjunctures within Afrian colonial life led him to be very circumspect about any further undermining of the institution of chieftaincy, since it represented, he argued, one of the few reliable anchorages for colonial society in the modern world. This nervous (if responsible) conservatism on colonial issues was characteristic of much of Whitehall thinking and restrained British officialdom from striking extravagant gestures which, though they would have been useful in propaganda terms, might have generated uncontrollable aspirations amongst African cadres – cadres which, in the case of British Africa, were much more mature than in their French-ruled counterparts.

Within the British Colonial Office, however, there was a younger generation of policy-makers who came to the fore during the Second World War, and who were prepared to move considerably in advance of Hailey's hesitant gradualism. These were middle-ranking officers touched by the interventionist culture of the war bureaucracy; they were, in consequence, all for 'doing things', and the only thing which could, under the likely circumstance of the future, be done with the colonial empire – the goal which could provide a career full of drama, with a peerage and a ribbon at the end of it – was to plan and execute its demise. The representative man of this strand in the Office ethos was Andrew Cohen, who later, as Head of the Africa Division in the Colonial Office, was to be the most powerful advocate of rapid constitutional change. According to his biographer, Cohen became convinced during the war that the business of British colonialism was no longer viable and should be put into the receiver's hands.[35] In fact this brand of hardheaded anti-colonialism within British Government did not harden into a consensus until the later 1950s, but it is important to note that such a species of bureaucratic radicalism was first nurtured under wartime conditions.

The balance of Colonial Office thinking between 1939 and 1945 was naturally less adventurous than that taking shape in Cohen's original mind. At bottom, it boiled down to little more than that the educated, detribalized African had now to be recognized as the archetype of progress in his society, and given a role in government to match his social significance; this was the critical assumption which permeated the wide-ranging memoranda surfacing in the Office from 1943 onwards, with their emphasis on municipal elections and broadened rural African representation in provincial councils. In effect, this was an acceptance of 'African politics' within the colonial setting which marked an end to that 'anti-politics' embedded in indirect rule, but the implications of such a departure remained obscure while officials remained above all preoccupied with the main task of keeping the African war effort on the road.

It is all too easy, indeed, to ascribe an undue importance to wartime 'planning' as it affected Africa. Of all Whitehall's myriad planning exercises at this time, those concentrating on colonial areas were most ephemeral and, within this colonial category, those focusing on Africa had a particularly fake portentousness. Thus, whenever the Colonial Office indulged in earnest talk of African 'progress', it really did so (implicitly if not explicitly) with reference to West Africa, where there was no substantive white-settler presence to complicate calculations. On the contemporary dilemmas of white-settled Africa, however, metropolitan officials largely maintained a discreet but pregnant silence. They were (from their own standpoint) wise to do so, since the impact of war was to make these dilemmas sharper and more brittle than they had been in the 1930s. In east and central Africa, while, as elsewhere, the war economy had boosted African material aspirations, it had also entrenched settler supremacy more deeply than ever.[36] The depletion of British administrators through the military call-up had led to their being replaced by local white farmers, so that the latter as a group obtained a purchase on the administration which they had failed to achieve in the inter-war years. Most importantly, the settlers effectively dominated the network of marketing and agricultural agencies put in place after 1939. If this was true in Kenya, it was even more true of Southern and Northern Rhodesia where the stimulus to extractive and secondary industries fed directly into the existing channels of white-settler power. Both 'on the ground' and in London British officials became conscious that, whereas they had succeeded in maintaining a racial equilibrium in these areas between 1918 and 1939, during the war years the local whites had stolen a march on their metropolitan keepers. There were even those, such as Lord Cranborne, the Colonial Secretary in 1942, who allowed themselves to think aloud that the war might provide a convenient cover under which full authority could be handed over to the European settler communities, thus disentangling the UK from a set of conflicts which had gone beyond the realm of the manipulable.[37] This was not a majority view; it would have alienated much of British as well as American opinion, and handed hegemony in Africa to the regime in Pretoria – a defeat which would horrify right-wing, as well as left-wing, elements in the UK. Instead, the British authorities muddled through, saying as little on East African matters as possible. At the end of hostilities the officials turned their minds privately to the rolling back of those positions of power occupied by settler minorities, and the nurturing of African agriculture as a countervailing force. This was implicit in the discussions which Sir Philip Mitchell, about to return to Kenya as Governor, had in the Colonial Office in late 1944 on the subject of East African reconstruction. Even in Kenya, however, such a reversal of wartime developments was to prove exceedingly difficult; in the two Rhodesias it was to prove impossible.

There was one other wartime fact which overhung British possessions south of the Sahara: the growing economic and political power of the Union of South Africa. During the Second, as in the First, World War the British found that organizing African resources on anything like a continental basis required a close partnership with Pretoria; through this collaboration South African influence seemed set to break the regional limits within which the UK had always striven to keep it. Thus South African industry became a chief source of supply for many African territories, and much, too, of the Middle East; between 1939 and 1945 the gravitational weight in the sub-Sahara came to lie decisively within the Union. The British Government feared, quite correctly, that this was likely to generate tensions between blacks and whites on a novel scale, and make European communities in British colonies more insensitive than ever to invocations based on liberal notions of 'trusteeship'. Above all, they feared that the pro-British Prime Minister in South Africa, Jan Smuts, who had regained that office in 1939, might be swept out of power after the crisis had passed (just as he had been in 1924), leaving the Afrikaner Nationalists in control. In the later 1920s and 1930s the British had proved strong enough in regional terms to force Hertzog into a working accommodation; whether they could hope to perform the same feat with any Nationalist successor under the different conditions of the 1940s seemed problematical. By 1945 suspicion of South Africa's expansionist aims was endemic in Whitehall; post-war perspectives in London were to be crucially influenced by this fact.

But although the war had created external opportunities for South African expansion, it had also intensified the internal dilemmas of that country. Rapid economic growth, by increasing the flow of blacks into the industrial areas, meant that the old Hertzogite compromises were breaking down: for whites the limited urban segregation enshrined in the legislation of the inter-war years seemed now to offer insufficient protection against the mounting African presence in European residential districts, while for blacks the more stringent application of influx controls began to impose restraints and humiliations on a new scale. The wartime dissatisfactions of urban Africans expressed themselves in the growth of trade unions and radical political organizations, while the Afrikaner intelligentsia moved towards more thoroughgoing concepts of segregationism; Smuts' attempt to limit these polarities by setting up the Fagan Commission in 1944 to investigate 'reform' could, at the very best, only buy him, and South Africa, a small breathing-space. By 1945 therefore it was in the Union, the economic fly-wheel of much of the African continent, that the critical struggle for the racial balance of power was taking place. This was not because South African outcomes could, in any direct sense, determine events elsewhere in the continent, but they were bound – given the Union's commercial predominance – to dictate many of the assumptions on which Africa's future turned. Against this background, Colonial Office discussions about local government initiatives in Nigeria or the Gold Coast were small beer indeed.

PART III 1945-54

3. Europe's Asian Stake: Adaptation, Restoration and Destruction

THE pattern of colonial change in Asia in the immediate aftermath of the Second World War was profoundly confusing. The British were engaged in a frantic search for some political deal which would disengage them from India with the least all-round costs, while the French and the Dutch were intent on renewing and revamping sets of local alliances which would allow them to re-enter the Indonesian and Indo-Chinese fastnesses from which they had been summarily evicted by the Japanese. The British found in the end that the price of their departure from the South Asian subcontinent was a partition which created a newly delimited India and the novel state of Pakistan; the French and Dutch found that the restoration of their power in east Asia could be obtained only by force. In fact by the latter months of 1954 Europe's political authority had been broken in all these theatres, although in the case of Indo-China France's bitter post-war opponents, the Viet Minh, did not succeed to the legacy entire; it was the American presence which then became the hallmark of Saigon's politics. Europe's withdrawal from Asia marked a fundamental 'break' in the logic of modern empires. Those empires had only possessed a rationale as broadly based systems of power as long as they retained a stake in Asia. Indeed, a great many parts of the British empire had originally been acquired as mere adjuncts to the possession of India. With the evacuation from their old eastern bastions, the British and French empires swung on to a predominantly African axis. The African connection, however, only drew significance from its economic contribution (which many people conceived to be crucial) to west Europe's post-1945 reconstruction; it did not cater to the broader diplomatic and military power of the European metropoles in the way that Asian dependencies had been able to do. The dismantling of colonial structures in Asia between 1947 and 1954 therefore marked, in a sense, the end of empire-as-power, even if – viewed from some Caribbean island or African village – the metamorphosis was not particularly evident. These Asian events need to be set against a wider backdrop than can be covered in this study: most importantly, it was the course of Communist successes in China, culminating in Mao Tse-tung's entry into Peking in 1949, which coloured developments throughout the region. From the narrower perspective of Europe's retreat from formal dominion in Asia, however, we shall look in more detail at events in India, Indonesia and Indo-China.

I THE DRIVE TO PARTITIONED INDEPENDENCE IN INDIA

Few events of modern times have been so extensively written about as the coming of independence to India in August 1947.[1] The analytical problems faced by historians covering the period from 1945 to 1947 are not to do with *why* the British decided to ease themselves out of direct responsibilities in South Asia: the breakdown of the *Raj*'s administrative control, the demands on the UK's military resources in other parts of the world and the Labour Party's victory in the 1945 British general election all pointed towards an early decolonization. The difficult questions, both at the time and since, concern the shapes which the independence settlement in the end assumed. Is it conceivable, for example, that an Indian transfer of power patterned in some other way might have avoided the constitutional butchery of partition of the area into two successor states, and the mass slaughters which such a traumatic adjustment brought about throughout much of north India, but above all in Calcutta and the Punjab? In approaching this problem, the current section will not attempt a chronological narrative such as those readily available elsewhere; it will simply outline the chief calculations and constraints which dictated the final outcome.

Towards the end of the war leaders of the Indian National Congress did not exhibit a uniform hostility to Muslim separatism *per se*. During 1944 Gandhi and a leading associate, Rajagopalachari, evinced a preparedness to negotiate with Jinnah on a basis which recognized the legitimacy of a 'Pakistan' – albeit not one whose territorial extent Jinnah would have considered acceptable. But the internal divisions within Congress ranks on this issue were too great to permit a compromise, even if the League had itself felt that its interests might be served by a deal at this juncture. The absence of coherence and realism within the Congress body has been used to explain the (alleged) 'missed chance' of a united India proposed by the Cabinet Mission to India of February 1946 which, led by Stafford Cripps, was the new Labour Government's initial approach to a solution. The Mission's plan, while including optional arrangements whereby Muslim-majority provinces could constitute separate political units, nevertheless maintained a Central Authority with responsibility for such matters as defence and finance. While Jinnah agreed to negotiate on these terms, Congress, and especially Nehru, eventually spurned the outline proposals. Little over one year later, however, after Mountbatten had (in February 1947) succeeded Wavell as Viceroy,[2] even Nehru was happy to grasp at a settlement based on untrammelled partition of South Asia into two distinct nations. Viewed in this light, the end-piece of Indian independence was a bitter defeat for Congress nationalists: in groping frantically for supremacy in the subcontinent, they had dislodged and shattered the beautiful vase of all-Indian nationhood. How had this defeat (if such it was) come about?

In fact there were good tactical reasons why Gandhi in 1944 had wished to signal a cautious willingness to 'talk Pakistan'. At that time the immediate enemy was not Jinnah, but the British, whose crushingly successful war effort was still in motion. Somehow a nationalist consensus had to be protected from communal discord so that the pressure was kept on the UK Government to honour its pledges of independence once peace had returned. Why, then, did Congress not subsequently jump at the chance offered by the Cabinet Mission of a residual 'Centre' authority which they could hope, in time, to build up at the expense of what would be only semi-autonomous provinces, only very few of which, even amongst those which had Muslim-majority populations, would be firmly under League control? An answer to this is often found in Nehru's burgeoning dominance; his growing vanity, and lack of that earthy realism evident in some of his colleagues, such as S. U. Patel, drove him to accept all sorts of risks in order to keep open the option of all-Indian power. But it is unlikely that Nehru's personality was the prime factor which blocked an Indian political consensus. Even by the time of the Cabinet Mission, events had moved into a phase whereby the Congress's real enemy was not the British, but the Muslim League; this was reflected in the progressive improvement of race relations (that is, white–brown relations) which paradoxically marked the final stage of the *Raj*.[3] Under these conditions the façade of a nationalist consensus disappeared as Indian politicians manoeuvred for position in the struggle which assuredly would follow independence. None was so naïve – except, perhaps, for some old-fashioned Liberals, whose adumbration of compromise was more a matter of Anglophiliac style than real political thinking – as to believe that any delicate equilibrium between an all-Indian centre and provincial-cum-communal devolvements would hold fast in the post-independence world. Hence the Congress evaluation of the Cabinet Mission plan was not based on glib enthusiasm about the principle of a Centre *à la* Cripps, but on whether the powers attributed to it would be sufficient to crush Jinnah and his quasi-Pakistan before it got into its stride. In this sense the plan fell short of Congress needs on two crucial fronts: control of the army and of taxation. Indeed, for Congress, a weak Centre which did not have clear authority in the military and fiscal fields was worse than no Centre at all, since a *real* Pakistan, left to its meagre and disorganized resources, might quickly break up altogether, and leave Congress to impose its will at last. This is what the British fully believed would happen; it was the fact that Congress came to share this medium-term expectation that made partition acceptable to its cadres. That curious affability which built up between British officials and Congress leaders after Mountbatten's announcement of 3 June, shifting the date of independence forward from its original 'marker' of June 1948 to the following 15 August, largely derived from the belief of these two partners-in-decolonization that sooner rather than later they would both be involved in clearing up the debris from the broken experiment of Pakistan. Thus for Nehru partition was not a 'final' defeat at all, but yet another gambit, albeit one imposed by events, in a game which would not end simply because the green-crescent flag flew over government buildings in Karachi. It was only in the decade after 1947, when the Pakistani state, for all its internal problems, showed its ability to survive as a state, that the definitive character of partition became painfully obvious to its larger southern neighbour.

The tactical problems facing the Muslim League between 1945 and 1947 were greater than those facing Congress. Congress could make mistakes and still expect pickings from whatever settlement was finally arrived at; in contrast, the Muslim League, with its fragile roots in the dispersed and, from a party viewpoint, not fully reliable Muslim population in north India, was always in danger of being hauled away from the independence trough by the combined strength of Congress and the British. Furthermore, even if the concept of Pakistan gained grudging acceptance as the deadlock wore on, there remained the crucial question of what *sort* of Pakistan. Jinnah was determined not to be fobbed off, as Gandhi had tried to do in 1944, with a 'moth-eaten' Pakistan which did not incorporate the bulk of Bengal and the Punjab. This explains the twin features of Jinnah's negotiating style; intransigence matched by a willingness to go on talking *ad nauseam*. Thus his intransigence derived from the fact that his maximalist position on Pakistan's territorial composition was close to being his only position; his matching patience derived from the fact that he had to keep the British 'in play', and prevent them from scuttling from the subcontinent in sheer desperation, thus triggering a scramble for power in which the League would be overwhelmed. These necessarily double-edged tactics expressed themselves, too, in the alternating styles of constitutional flexibility and violent self-assertion which marked League strategy. Thus in a short period of time the League initially accepted the Cabinet Mission 'outline' (to pre-empt any British–Congress alignment) and adopted Direct Action protest leading to catastrophic communal riots in Calcutta (designed to show the British, amongst others, that they could not be pushed beyond a certain point). Jinnah knew that in so coaxing and slapping the British into 'even-handedness' between Congress and the League, he was losing their private goodwill; but he knew, too, that ultimately Pakistan could *only* be attained in the teeth of British resentment. Jinnah's realism on this latter point was evident at the end of the partition drama when he rejected Mountbatten's idea that, on ceasing to be Viceroy, he should become not only the first Governor-General of independent India (which had already been agreed with Nehru) but also the first Governor-General of Pakistan. Later commentators have seen in this blocking of the joint governor-generalship formula a lost opportunity for Indo-Pakistani stabilization. In fact Jinnah was simply recognizing the bitter truth that British hopes for their continued influence in the region lay in Delhi and not in Karachi.

What role, then, did communal violence play in this surge to partition? It is estimated that at least 200,000 people were killed in the political disturbances of 1947. Most of these casualties occurred in the Punjab *after* August 1947, and were thrown up by the grinding wheels of the partition process as millions of Hindus and Muslims moved in opposite directions to reach what was for each the 'safe' side of the frontier. Nevertheless, from the moment of Mountbatten's arrival in India during February 1947 the tempo of communal intimidation had increased. This was logically so; by making it apparent with every word and gesture that the British would depart at the earliest opportunity, Mountbatten was stoking popular anxieties throughout northern India. As the stakes of Indian politics rose, politicians were forced to pull the levers of communal violence in order to show the British, and each other, that they and their respective constituencies could not be ignored in the independence settlement. This is not to say that there was a general orchestration of political killing by the major party bosses, but the organizational logic of League–Congress competition, penetrating so deeply as it did into north Indian life, meant not only that politicians had to be hardened towards sporadic bloodletting on either side, but that they had a vested interest in seeing that not all the blood in question was that of their supporters. Predictably, the mobilization of violence after late 1946 emanated from sufficiently obscure levels within the organizational structures that the great national figures could show their clean hands to the world with some degree of sincerity – some rather more convincingly, however, than others.

But if communal violence was a method of Indian politics, it also operated within certain constraints; the major political factions all had to recognize the danger that, in such a divisive and volatile society as India's, levels of confrontration might be generated which would end by breaking the existing order and the elites (be they Hindu or Moslem) which clustered around it. There was thus a sense in which the communal oligarchies, while bitter rivals over the transfer of power in South Asia, had a neutral, class-based interest in limiting the extent of popular conflict. Furthermore, Mountbatten's arrival as Viceroy in early 1947 coincided with the recognition by both Congress and the League that each had the power to unleash a civil war if pressed to the limit; once this logistical and psychological fact was in place, the prospect of carving up the British succession between them became the best of all possible options. It is not surprising, therefore, that as Mountbatten forced the pace of power transfer, both League and Congress wished to shut off the political pressures which they had previously done much to intensify; that Gandhi went into Bihar and East Bengal to play at being a saint; and that India's politicians came to feed out of Mountbatten's hands, desperate that he should get them off the hook of subcontinental disintegration.

It was in this milieu of fear amongst the political classes that Dominion Status moved to the centre-point of the Indian stage. Dominion Status, indeed, had been bandied about as a possible framework for an Indian solution since the First World War. By 1945, however, it had been left behind in India as it had largely been left behind in the old 'white' Commonwealth where it had originally operated; it smacked too much of a continued constitutional inferiority to Great Britain to form the basis of any acceptable independence constitution. But by mid-1947 the fusty garment of Dominion Status suddenly acquired such new attraction that Congress, the League and the British all converged on it in propulsive unison. Predictably the reason for this has nothing to do with the constitutional merits of Dominion Status, and a lot to do with the flaws suddenly apparent in the alternative hitherto favoured by nationalist opinion: a clean-slate, probably republican, constitution forged by a Constituent Assembly. As political violence built up during the Mountbatten viceroyalty, the prospect emerged that any such Constituent Assembly might not be dominated by Congress and the League at all; social conflict might give rise to new contenders for power whom the British might be tempted to graft into the eventual settlement. Both Congress and the League, of course, had a common interest in crowding out such *arrivistes* (parading, for example, under such banners as a free and independent Bengal). Thus, by coming to a rapid agreement that independence would take place under the *existing* 1935 constitution, and that within this framework the fabric of Dominion Status would be drawn down upon two states only, the precise outlines of which would be determined by votes in the sitting legislatures, the presiding bosses of the communal parties ensured that the legacy of the *Raj* would be divided up between the smallest number of beneficiaries possible under the circumstances.

Finally, we must come to the distinguishing marks of British policy-

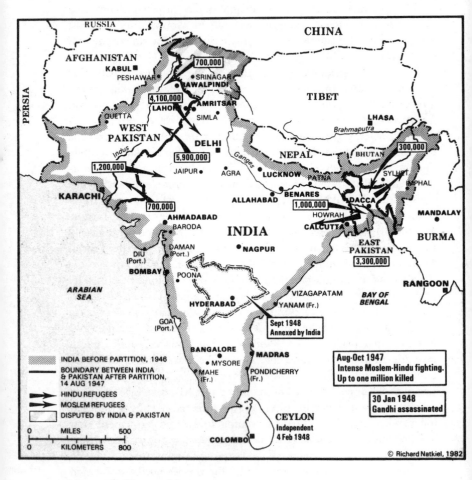

MAP 4   Indian partition, 1947

making in India between 1945 and 1947. In many ways the decisive moment for the metropole was Attlee's dismissal of Wavell and his replacement as Viceroy by Mountbatten in February 1947. Wavell had committed himself to pressing an approach to decolonization upon the UK Cabinet from at least late 1944, but he was attuned to achieving this aim only in the context of a carefully constructed successor-coalition in which no single faction predominated. As the biographer of Allenby's Egyptian career, Wavell sought a 1922-type settlement mirroring most shades of elite opinion in the country. The particular advantage of this strategy was that power might thereby be made transferable on an all-Indian basis without exciting unbearable apprehensions amongst the minorities. Even after the breakdown of the Simla Conference in June 1945, Wavell continued to hope that some such finely-modulated solution might prove possible. But such negotiations would take time and, with communal antagonisms permeating army and police ranks, there was the risk that the whole administrative position might give way to chaos. It was to cater for this possibility, and to jolt the British Cabinet into clear decisions, that Wavell came up with a Breakdown Plan.[4] This envisaged a province-by-province evacuation of British personnel, beginning in the relatively quiescent south and terminating in the turbulent north. Wavell was, through this hypothetical scenario, confronting Attlee's government with a stark choice: either to put more resources (troops, cash and prestige) into India to 'hold the line' while negotiating pressure was stepped up, or to prepare for the inevitable debacle in which the best that might be hoped for was the minimizing of British casualties. It was a choice Attlee refused to face and attempted to evade – as it turned out, successfully – by a rushed dismissal of Wavell and the appointment of Mountbatten.

Far from being prepared to put resources into India as a final push towards a managed decolonization, the Labour Prime Minister was determined to pull resources out as quickly as possible. Attlee (who had served on the Simon Commission in 1929) certainly had a sentimental attachment to the goal of Indian independence, but to this were added much more powerful forces: the need to scale down the number of British battalions serving overseas and to divert UK expenditure into domestic social programmes.[5] But Attlee could not contemplate any approach to independence which risked breakdown procedures of the sort postulated by Wavell; such a humiliating exit from the *Raj* would be a lasting electoral blow to Labour Party fortunes. In short, Wavell's commitment to painstaking coalition-building in India was too complex a conception, and too pitted with uncertainties, for Attlee to stick with it; much more attractive was the option of accepting the inevitability of a narrowly based successor-regime (or, if necessary, regimes) and appointing a new Viceroy with plenipotentiary powers designed to bundle the coteries of League and Congress into some makeshift agreement to divide the prize between them. Once the old-fashioned Wavellite concern with the representative balance of the one or more successor authorities was discarded, decolonization in South Asia became automatically much easier of attainment; Mountbatten's subsequent successes were much more a product of this simple fact than any transcendent personal skills of his own.

By investing Mountbatten with plenipotentiary authority, Attlee put his Viceroy in a uniquely powerful position. This power had little to do with 'ruling' India, since administrative control in the districts was progressively slipping from British hands; rather, it sprang from Mountbatten's capacity at any time to blow the referee's whistle on the scrummaging of the Indian political players around him, to the detriment of whoever happened to be on the bottom at the time. By first announcing on 20 February 1947 that independence would be effected by June 1948, Mountbatten forced Congress and the League into forming an interim government; then by announcing on 3 June 1947 that transfer of power would be implemented by 15 August following, he stampeded the Indian politicians into cooperation during this final phase of the *Raj*. The key to Mountbatten's effectiveness in this situation lay in his ruthless presentation to the Congress and League leaders of the implications which sprang from their own disagreements. No more telling illustration of this viceregal *realpolitik* can be found than the occasion when, meeting with the party representatives on 3 June, Mountbatten began by slapping on the table a memorandum entitled *Administrative Consequences of Partition* and told them to get on with the necessary preparations to avoid chaos.[6] The Mountbatten viceroyalty was a remarkable *tour de force* in which he exploited the conjunction of plenipotentiary credentials from London and the increasing anxiety of the League and Congress that affairs might slip out of their control. Imperial power, in this and other instances of Afro-Asian decolonization, was never more tangible than in arranging its own demise.

There was, however, a price to pay for the conjuration of this terminal form of imperial supremacy. It involved stripping down metropolitan obligations to a bare minimum; above all, it meant abandoning certain social groups who, despite their traditional placements within the status quo of the *Raj*, had become marginal to decolonized relationships within South Asia. Princes, Sikhs and *harijans* (or untouchables) were thus left to negotiate whatever niche they could find for themselves within the burgeoning order that Nehru and Jinnah, in their territorial spheres, saw fit to grant them. The princes, knowing that wealth and prestige afforded them some leverage independent of the British presence, and with some important exceptions such as Hyderabad, concluded accession agreements with their post-independence masters before the deadline of 15 August; if these autocrats were later to lose the great bulk of their political privileges under 'Congress *Raj*', their grip on the one perquisite that really mattered (money) was to remain firm. The untouchables, whose economic and cultural oppression had never been especially alleviated by imperial routines, were also prepared, albeit in a very different spirit, to await whatever a new regime would bring to them. But the Sikhs of the Punjab, true to their warrior traditions, proved to be less malleable material. Mountbatten studiously ignored their demands for special arrangements (in particular, for some form of Sikhistan) in the expectation that they would accommodate themselves to the respective hegemonies of Hindu India and Muslim Pakistan. The Sikhs, after all, while a substantial fragment of the Punjabi population, did not form a majority in any of the major districts of that province. Ignored in Delhi, the Sikh leadership were driven towards a conspicuous involvement in communal violence in an effort to secure consideration of their views. They never received it. Head down, Mountbatten was pushing too furiously towards the 15 August finishing line to pay any heed to distress signals emitted by those whose needs were too awkward to fit the metropolitan schedule.

Here, indeed, is the controversy which will always surround the Mountbatten viceroyalty: did his 'forced march' to independence not only make partition inevitable but also contribute to the communal massacres and mass migration which surrounded this process? In fact the nature of the violence – dispersed incidents across the Punjabi countryside, and butcherings in the Calcutta slums – did not easily lend itself to pacification. The decision not to risk the shaky cohesion of the army and the police by heaping upon them security tasks beyond their ability to carry out was almost certainly the right one.[7] The most balanced judgement is probably that the speed of Mountbatten's decolonization exercise saved, rather than cost, lives by recognizing the partition momentum and foreshortening its course. Nevertheless, some commentators have emphasized that Mountbatten's tactics were flawed in several key respects: the failure to go any way towards soothing Sikh anxieties, and the lack of any real attention by the Viceroy (other than his obsession with becoming joint Governor-General of the successor-dominions, which Jinnah blocked) to the evolution of institutional structures within which Indo-Pakistani cooperation might have been nurtured.[8] There is some force to these criticisms. But any strategy which *had* taken account of aggrieved minorities would not have been what Attlee had in mind when dismissing Wavell in the first place; and it must be doubtful whether institutional tinkering by Mountbatten would have appreciably softened the logic of state-rivalry in the subcontinent, over Kashmir, for example, contained in the bitter compromise of 1947.

A final twist to the story of Indian decolonization remains: any account of it cannot simply terminate in August 1947, precisely because the settlement had taken the half-way house form of Dominion Status. India's later passage to an untrammelled republic, and its absorption into the setting of a reformed 'British Commonwealth', must be noted.[9] It was never likely that the Congress Government in New Delhi, basking in the apogee of the 'freedom struggle', would find Dominion Status psychologically acceptable as a long-term basis for self-government. But psychology apart, Nehru and his colleagues visualized India's future as that of a leading power in the 'New Asia', and the pursuance of this role required that India lay hold of those republican trappings which were the touchstone of prestige in the contemporary 'developing' world. This constitutional imperative, nevertheless, was constrained by the penalties which a total break with the UK seemed to carry in its wake. The most significant of these potential liabilities arose from the fact that Pakistan had publicly announced its intention to remain in the Commonwealth. This held out the prospect that, in all the weighty economic and territorial issues, such as Kashmir and the division of assets, which lay between the two successor-states in South Asia, the British Government would be obliged to support a Commonwealth Pakistan against a non-Commonwealth India. But there were other considerations, too, which went beyond these entrails of partition. In domestic matters (the possibility of a Communist insurgency in Bengal) and in external matters (the remodelling of Indian power in Asian diplomacy) the regime in Delhi recognized that it was still too weak to forfeit British goodwill completely. Post-independence India was therefore caught between the pincers of republican instincts and strategic fragility.

Superficially, the answer to this dilemma was simple enough: India should become a republic, while applying to stay in the Commonwealth. Nehru lodged such an application in London during November 1948. We saw earlier, however, that the conception of Commonwealth after 1918 had come to pivot around the formula of allegiance to the Crown; it was monarchical loyalty, suitably undefined in its full implications, which had constituted the point of consensus between the UK and the 'white' Dominions. The Irish Free State had, admittedly, breached this convention by moving to what was, to all intents and purposes, a semi-republic under the External Relations Act of 1937. But the Irish Free State had always been regarded as an aberrant case (neutral in the Second World War, Eire actually seceded from the Commonwealth in 1949). If the British Government was to accede to Nehru's request, therefore, a coach and horses would be driven through the one institution, the Crown, which seemed to give the Commonwealth a cohesion relatively invulnerable to the political squabbles endemic to any association. Over against this, the authorities in London had to weigh the likelihood that any rebuff to India at such a sensitive stage in her national development would lead Nehru to try another tack altogether: that of leading an anti-British, anti-western crusade in Asia. The British Government was caught in the pincers of a significant imperial tradition and the need to design a fresh, all-purpose Anglo-Indian relationship.

A solution was thrashed out at a special Commonwealth Conference during April 1949, and in the extensive consultations carried out amongst Commonwealth members prior to the meeting. The British solution was that India should become a republic, and yet remain in the Commonwealth by recognizing the reigning monarch as the head of that international 'family'. Even this most vague of obeisances to an alien sovereign was not to Nehru's taste, but he eventually accepted what had emerged as a settlement agreeable to the other Commonwealth governments. Thus if India had been the motor of much of Britain's nineteenth-century expansion overseas, it was

India, too, which forged the framework within which the modern Commonwealth was updated at the end of the 1940s. Refined in this South Asian context, the infusion of a heightened constitutional and political flexibility into the Commonwealth organism was to prove significant in Britain's African decolonizations. It meant that this grouping of states had had a distinctively multi-racial flavour for over a decade before most newly independent African countries were faced with the choice of adherence or rejection; for such leaders of ex-British dependencies as Nyerere of Tanzania and Kaunda of Zambia, therefore, the question of whether to accept Commonwealth participation was not affected by the suspicion of political traps which might otherwise have occurred. We shall not deal further with the evolution of Commonwealth institutions in this study, because it is largely an aspect of post-colonial relations, rather than decolonization proper. But the maturing of that association during the 1950s, blessed with the *imprimatur* of India's presence, formed an important backcloth to events elsewhere in Asia, Africa and the Caribbean.

II THE EMERGENCE OF THE INDONESIAN REPUBLIC

In Indonesia, as in Indo-China, it was British-led forces which first arrived in any strength to secure control from the defeated Japanese occupiers.[10] The fierce nationalist resistance which British and Indian troops encountered around Surabaya in Java during October 1945 was an indication that any reimposition of western political authority – Dutch or otherwise – would prove a prolonged and costly affair. Nevertheless, as the Dutch military commanders regained responsibility with the staggered departure of the British empire forces from late 1945, there were reasons for concluding that the task facing them would be less daunting than that confronting their French counterparts on the Asian mainland. Dutch penetration of Indonesian society had been relatively deep over many decades, and the traditional alliances of metropolitan interests and local classes therefore more susceptible, potentially, to intelligent reconstruction, despite the discontinuities created by Japanese rule. This was particularly likely to prove the case in the outlying parts of the Indonesian archipelago, including Sumatra, where plantation development had been intense and where the nationalist-republicanism centred on Java was viewed by local elites as a threat to their own distinctive interests. If geography always stacked the odds aganst the French in Indo-China after 1945, it seemed rather to assist Dutch hopes of recovering their authority in Indonesia, since in the latter case anti-colonial militias could be progressively pegged back into their Java-nese strongholds as resistance was mopped up in the outer islands. The Dutch, too, were quick to see that the weakness of the republican forces was essentially economic, since Java was especially short of food and also lacked the export-crops which could generate foreign exchange. Thus by securing control of the 'outer' archipelago, and by probing those parts of Java where the republican hold was tenuous, the Dutch could hope to turn the financial screw on the nationalist regime which had established its headquarters in Djokjakarta. This strategy lent itself easily to a federal form; as different regions were 'pacified' by Dutch troops they could be accorded the status of a separate territory within a Dutch-supervised federation, with a locally recruited government as a symbol of legitimacy; and as this satellite-structure was built up, the pressure on Javanese interest groups to cave in and accept a prescribed role within this revamped colonial order would, it was calculated, prove irresistible.[11]

The challenge facing the Dutch in the East Indies was, at least superficially, easier than that to the French in Tonkin and Cochin on one other count: the Indonesian nationalist movement lacked the coherent and confident leadership provided by the Viet Minh, and could not mobilize the peasantry on the same kind of scale. Indeed, Sukarno had only agreed formally to proclaim the Republic in Batavia on 17 August 1945 because he had come under enormous pressure from younger and more radical elements who did not share his constraining anxiety as to Dutch reactions.[12] Even after this breakaway act, the established nationalist politicians were pre-eminently concerned with liquidating rivals who had been thrown up by the machinations of the Japanese, and with doing as little as possible which might rule out a favourable settlement with the Netherlands authorities. Sukarno and his associates at first seemed to be successful in attaining these related ends. The wartime 'peta', or youth, militias were disbanded, and contact was made with Dutch negotiators. The latter soon led to the Linggadjati Treaty of 15 November 1946 which, although only provisional in form, estab-lished a mutual commitment to the formation of a federated Indone-sia in which the Dutch and the republicans would have their mutual needs reconciled. In this desire to come to terms with the old

European colonialists, and so avoid an 'all out' confrontation, Sukarno was no different from Ho Chi Minh. But whereas Ho Chi Minh never saw himself as anything but a co-equal power with the French, Sukarno was an altogether more tentative figure who feared that the nationalist instrument might break in his hands if he tried to wield it too forcefully against his Dutch opponents. It was in this sense that Sukarno was a 'bourgeois' nationalist, only vicariously related to the peasant masses, and who above all represented the interests of Javanese urban classes whose republicanism might easily evaporate at the first news of Dutch armoured vehicles in the outskirts of Djokjakarta.

But although, under the Linggadjati terms, the Dutch and the nationalists agreed on a federal formula for Indonesia's future, the really difficult questions, concerning the distribution of power within such a setting, were left unanswered. Would, for example, the renewed coupling of the Javanese and non-Javanese provinces take place before, or after, full Dutch sovereignty had been withdrawn from the area? Naturally the Dutch were insistent that their sole sovereignty continue throughout the process of federation-making, so that they could determine the character of the new state, while the republicans were eager to see the Dutch *locus standi* reduced as soon as possible so that they could 'mix the cocktail' of independence very much as they wished. The East Indian conflict after 1946 therefore concerned the timing and terms of change, or rather the right to supervise and shape the post-colonial order, not a crude juxtaposition of old colonialism versus new nationalism.

The task of the Dutch Governor-General in the East Indies, Hubertus van Mook, was therefore to construct methods to dictate the course of constitutional reform.[13] His approach was to build a network of compliant states amongst the Indonesian patchwork – known as the Malino states after the conference in July 1946 establishing a formal relationship between them – which straddled the *de facto* borders of the republic, and from which vantage point crushing pressure might be brought to bear against the Javanese heartland. Indeed, had the Dutch been able at this point to impose effective military authority within those parts of the archipelago which they had successfully reoccupied, the republican 'core' would probably not have finally survived – at least not in a shape that nationalists would have considered tolerable. But in fact van Mook was never able to secure stability even within the limits of the Malino sphere. The main reason for this was that, amidst the chaos which had prevailed in the hiatus following Japan's defeat, the traditional civil and religious 'notables' on whom the colonial system had hinged prior to 1942 had been undermined by internecine social warfare; many leading families had been entirely liquidated. This erosion of traditional authority in the localities had created opportunities for new political operators who were either opposed to the Malino regimes or who were happy just to sit on the fence, waiting to see which side finally emerged the stronger; thus the growth of trade unions on the western-owned plantations was an example of this new institutional mobilization. Ultimately the Dutch found that they could not put back together the collaborative pieces of the pre-war order; they were plunged, instead, into uncharted waters in which their accustomed navigational instincts were largely irrelevant. Even worse from a metropolitan viewpoint, as the republicans were increasingly able to establish contact with dissident forces within the Malino states, they succeeded, too, in maintaining a sporadic military presence in areas technically under Dutch control. These facts were potentially disastrous for Dutch prestige, since their Malino allies could hardly be expected to stay loyal in the face of republican pressure. It was, then, to restore Dutch bargaining power, and to shore up the sagging morale of his local allies, that van Mook unleashed what became generally known as the 'first Dutch military action' in late July 1947.

The Dutch offensive was carefully planned and executed. It avoided the seizure of the Javanese capital, Djokjakarta, which would have entailed stiff resistance from nationalist forces and probably shifted power within the republican coalition towards the leftists. Instead, the Dutch economic and military presence was drawn more tightly around the republican-held zone, so that van Mook subsequently held back and awaited the internal fragmentation of the nationalist movement which the heightened pressure was bound to evoke. In this expectation he was not to be disappointed, since in the subsequent talks, climaxing in the Renville Agreement of January 1948, the republicans accepted the new demarcation lines and the inauguration of a United States of Indonesia *before* any commitment by the Dutch concerning a future military withdrawal.[14] At this stage, indeed, the Dutch achievement in the East Indies seemed not inconsiderable. Whereas in India the British had only succeeded in extricating themselves at the cost of partition and the corollary of regional conflict which might later reverberate on their interests in the area, in Indonesia the Dutch seemed to be slotting into place an archipelagic federation reflective of their own needs, from which they could later retreat at a moment, and in a manner, of their own choosing.

The 'first military action' and its immediate aftermath, however, proved to be the high point of Dutch fortunes; afterwards it was downhill all the way. One reason for this was that the Malino politicians began to apprehend that, for all the rhetoric surrounding the offensive, the Dutch had no intention of sustaining a costly military presence in the East Indies, and would in the end do some sort of deal with the republicans at their expense. Under these vicarious circumstances even some of the most enthusiastic supporters of the Dutch presence began to seek covert reconciliations with the nationalists, until the whole Malino structure came to be distinctly vulnerable. This renewed bout of instability led to a crisis within Dutch Government circles, and the replacement of van Mook by the harder-line Louis van Beel. It was van Beel who planned the 'second military action' commenced on 19 December 1948, during which Dutch airborne troops occupied Djokjakarta for twenty-four hours before, under intense criticism from the United Nations, withdrawing once more behind the Renville lines. This was undoubtedly a defeat, but it is important to grasp what the nature of that defeat was. Neither van Beel, nor his metropolitan superiors, had been under the naïve illusion that a fresh offensive at this point would have brought the republic to its knees. Their aim was to reassert a central Dutch role in the bargaining process of decolonization, and nothing could better underline this than an occupation of the Javanese capital for the duration of the negotiations. The failure of the 'second military action' did not make decolonization inevitable, since the logic of independence was already knit into the Indonesian fabric, but it did mean that the Dutch pretension to be the masters of the transition had been broken.

The crucial factor which had fatally lured the Dutch into trying to hasten a settlement through military means was the growing involvement of the Americans in the Indonesian imbroglio. Thus as the US administration began to press for an early end to hostilities, the Dutch had sought to improve their leverage over the republicans on the assumption that the cost in blood and treasure would not have to be maintained for long to earn its reward. The motives of President

Truman in relation to Indonesia at this time are clear: deeply anxious that western Europe should be made strong enough to carry a larger share of responsibility for its defence against the Soviet Union, he was exasperated at the sight of the Netherlands exhausting its scarce resources in a distant and, in great-power terms, almost irrelevant colonial war. Truman's push for a solution in Indonesia was thus but one small reflection of his larger concern with west European reconstruction, a reconstruction in which the Netherlands, the largest of the Benelux countries and situated so strategically on the German border, had a large part to play. Nevertheless, as long as officials in The Hague had been able to point out to their Washington counterparts that the Javanese republicans were Communist-inspired, the US administration could not contemplate the disappearance of the Dutch from the archipelago without some trepidation. But when the republican triumvirate of Sukarno, Mohammed Hatta and Sutan Sjahir had ruthlessly succeeded during September 1948 in putting down a Communist rebellion within their own ranks,[15] Truman perceived the emergence of a republic imbued with that anti-colonial and, above all, anti-Communist nationalism which was its ideal formula in underdeveloped countries. For Sukarno and his fellow leaders, each of whom had taken great risks in switching so much of their military strength away from the Dutch front and against the leftists, such 'acceptability' in American eyes was the key to victory. After the essentially diplomatic debacle which crystallized in the wake of the 'second police action', therefore, the Dutch Government were constrained into putting their whole strategy in the region into reverse. After late 1948 they cooperated with the United Nations Good Offices Committee set up to oversee a return to the Renville 'lines', and agreed to substantive talks, first in Indonesia and then at a Round Table Conference at the Hague. The complicated solution concluded in August 1949 involved the overarching construct of a Netherlands-Indonesian Union, and a United States of Indonesia which allowed for at least some autonomy for the ex-Malino regions from the central government in Djokjakarta. This, however, was largely farce; the Netherlands-Indonesian Union was mere symbolism which nobody expected to last, while the Malino politicians were already scrambling to make whatever terms they could with the Javanese nationalists. Thus behind the constitutional small print it was obvious that Sukarno, Hatta and Sjahir had scooped the regional pool and obtained that essentially unitary and untrammelled republic which had eluded Nehru and the Congress party in India. On the other hand, the Indian Congress had, assisted by the pliability of British policy, maintained a high level of internal party unity through the decolonization experience. In Indonesia, by contrast, the profound tactical choices imposed on the nationalist coalition by Dutch intransigence had served only to heighten the inner cleavages which had always been a characteristic of Indonesian politics. Certainly Indonesia's domestic history in the three decades after independence was to prove more contorted and sporadically marred by mass violence than was the case in India, for all the latter's enormous potential for social conflict. As always, the pattern which individual decolonizations took, while not predetermining the future, certainly shifted the odds for or against the success of the in-coming regime.

There was one especial blot on Indonesia's independence copybook which came to obsess the new republic: the Dutch remained ensconced in Western New Guinea – or West Irian, as Sukarno always referred to it – since that territory had not had its future conclusively dealt with in the final Hague Agreement.[16] At first the Dutch rationalized their continuing presence in New Guinea by claiming that it was intended as a haven for those Eurasians wishing to leave Indonesia, but since the Eurasians showed no proclivity to remove themselves to one of the world's most undeveloped spots, this argument soon fell flat. Subsequently the Dutch contended that the New Guineans could not be handed over to Indonesia until their majority agreement had been secured, and began to construct modest representative institutions, but it was clear that 'politics' was so novel a feature in indigenous life that any 'opinion' on sovereignty would take a very long time to emerge. The real reasons why the Netherlands Government at first refused to hand over the territory to Sukarno after 1950 were probably political and sentimental; it was a way of keeping the Indonesian Republic in its place, and of retaining a residual Dutch presence in the region; once the tempo of the dispute was raised by Sukarno's tirades on a continuation of Dutch colonialism, the authorities in The Hague felt that too much pride was at stake to back down. By the early 1960s, however, Dutch political debate had become so overwhelmingly preoccupied with western European developments that it proved relatively easy for the UN to step in and ease the way for the West Irian's transfer to Indonesia.

This bitter aftertaste to Dutch decolonization in the East Indies almost certainly suited Sukarno rather well, despite the theatrical

outrage of which he was such a master. He needed some external issue
to keep alive the emotions of Indonesian anti-colonialism, since there
was precious little else binding together a new state constructed from
such a patchwork of ethnic, economic and regional interests. In
particular, as the 1950s progressed, Sukarno's failure to move decisively against the local Chinese commercial classes as the Javanese petit
bourgeoisie so keenly desired led him to deflect these resentments by
beating the West Irian drum. Thus Indonesia's apparent drift into
military adventurism during the later 1950s – which continued into
the 1960s, when Sukarno promoted new territorial claims, not least
against Malaysia – simply reflected the regime's need for foreign
policy successes when its economic and social goals had been internally blocked. The poisoned post-colonial relationship between the
Netherlands and Indonesia contrasted sharply with the relatively
smooth bedding-down of Anglo-Indian relations after 1947. But in
the 1950s Britain and India still had a lot to offer each other in the
fields of economics and diplomacy, whereas the Netherlands and
Indonesia had no such interlocking interests with a life beyond
colonialism. Indeed, it was the Netherlands, not the young republic,
for whom the post-colonial age opened up new assets and opportunities: the rich revenue from North Sea gas strikes and the prosperity
generated by the drive towards west European integration. Suggestively, even at the height of the West Irian crisis, the Dutch stock
market had continued its progressive and happy boom; the disjunc-
tion was complete. In retrospect, one might conclude, the Americans,
by elbowing the Dutch out of the Indies in 1949, had done the latter a
considerable favour, forcing them to concentrate on the challenge of
European reform, where the big dividends were to be found. The
French agony in Indo-China, as we shall see, was more prolonged,
not least because the American response to the conflict was so
different.

III THE WAR OF COLONIAL RESTORATION IN
INDO-CHINA

The British empire forces (largely drawn from the Indian Army and
led by General Gracey) which spearheaded the Allied reoccupation
of Indo-China were flown into Saigon on 13 September 1945, only
one week after the first Allied advance guard had arrived in

Indonesia.[17] It is a wry fact that the British, while already thinking in terms of reducing their own exhausting Asian commitments, saw fit to thrust open the Indo-Chinese and Indonesian doors just wide enough for the returning French and Dutch authorities to slip through, only to see them plunge through the trap-flap which lay beyond. Here again was old Albion's clumsy knack of transforming good turns for friends and neighbours into unmitigated disasters. In fact General Gracey's objectives in Indo-China were carefully circumscribed: to secure the disarmament of the Japanese armies south of latitude 16 degrees north (beyond which responsibility lay with the Chinese), to establish order in the key area of Saigon and to assist the French to restore their civil authority. It was generally assumed that, since the Japanese had dismantled the edifice of French rule only as recently as March, and since a large body of interned French officials could be quickly released to assume their previous duties, the reconstruction of the *status quo ante* would prove relatively smooth. This underestimated the political effects which sprang from the establishment of the nationalist republic in Hanoi by the Viet Minh during the previous August, and the Communists' ability to undermine stability in Cochin, not least in Saigon itself. At first reluctant to become involved in overtly political action, General Gracey was forced to move decisively against republican elements in Saigon and to shore up the French position at a time when it might conceivably have collapsed altogether. By early 1946, however, available French forces in Indo-China had risen to 30,000 and by March Gracey had turned over his Indo-Chinese responsibilities completely to Admiral Thierry d'Argenlieu, the newly-appointed French Governor-General. From this point France proceeded to fight a bitter campaign of colonial restoration which ended only after the crushing humiliation of their defeat at Dien Bien Phu in 1954.[18] But before describing this passage of arms, it is necessary to consider the general forces which drove the succession of governments in Paris, even those which had Communist representation, to adopt policies of imperial reconstruction after 1945.

Wartime defeat and occupation by Germany had been a profoundly wounding experience for the French people; May 1940 was the climax of the modern French nightmare of cohabiting the west European mainland with an expanding Germany. For the seven preceding decades French governments, as one of their methods for coping with this situation, had sought to develop an imperial alternative to continental weakness, and national self-respect had become intimately bound up with *France d'outre mer*. Thus the British may have had a bigger empire than the French, but they were, in a sense, markedly less attached to it as a significant political emotion. There was a reflexive inevitability in the way that France moved after the war to recover its old position in Asia, without baulking at the necessary dependence this entailed on British military assistance and which caused such anguish to the Gaullists.

But practical necessities, as well as psychological conditioning, lay behind the French panic regarding colonial restoration after 1945. The economic and social prospects of post-war France were considerably bleaker than those of Britain. UK government and business opinion worried continuously about American hegemony, but at least they had access, however constrained, to the Washington policy machine; French society, in comparison, was in a much weaker position in the race back to normalcy. Indeed, whatever comfort France might have been able to derive from the prostration of Germany at this time, there was the looming danger that she, along with western Europe as a whole, would have to learn to live with whatever crumbs were to fall from the Anglo-American table. Under these conditions, policy-makers in Paris groped for a means to reassert France's status as a great power, and to insist that her voice be heard at a time when the post-war international order was in the making. One of the few methods calculated to achieve this aim was the recovery of that imperial leverage in Asia which the Japanese had brutally destroyed.

In the aftermath of the British–Indian departure from Indo-China, however, the French were restrained in their use of force. Military pacification was essentially limited to Cochin, since this traditional colonial base had first to be secured before any broader Indo-Chinese strategy could be attempted; it was at this early stage that rural *Cochinois* became the victims of terror and counter-terror as the Viet Minh sought to thwart the renewal of French power in the countryside. In Tonkin, by contrast, the French had only a very limited military presence, and were confronted by the secure grip which Ho Chi Minh's republic retained over Hanoi and its environs. The French policy in the north was to avoid any actions likely to make a negotiated settlement more difficult, so that excessive troop concentrations around Tonkinese cities were studiously avoided for fear that the Viet Minh might scuttle back to its mountain retreats as a prelude to a long-drawn-out guerrilla war. In the long series of Franco–Viet Minh talks, which stretched from the Ho Chi Minh –Jean Sainteny agreement of 6 March 1946, through the protracted conferences at Dalat (17 April–11 May) and Fontainbleau (6 July–10 September), the genuine desire of *both* sides to avert an all-out conflict, providing that their minimum political needs could be met, is not to be doubted.

What kind of Indo-Chinese settlement did French negotiators have in mind? Four necessary elements can be isolated. First, the French required to possess a close political control in Cochin. Second, the Laotian and Cambodian monarchies had to be secured in power in their respective countries and the role of such radical, Communist-oriented groups as the Free Khmer kept to a minimum. Third, it was implicit in French thinking that the Viet Minh would be compensated by a leading role in Tonkin, but that this role would have to be shared by other (non-Communist) parties, and Viet Minh activities outside Tonkin would be carefully circumscribed. Fourth, the various territories of the region would be linked in an Indo-Chinese Federation over which the French would exercise a supervisory authority, and through which the government in Paris could dictate the economic and political direction of the area. In short, the French were engaged in a subtle strategy of coalition-building, stimulating conservative forces sympathetic to their regional leadership, and yet finding carefully prescribed room within which potentially dangerous opponents (especially the Communists) could find some soothing compensations. This was colonial restoration of a very real kind; but it was, nonetheless, far from being a blanket reimposition of the pre-war order.

The French belief that they could manipulate the Indo-Chinese world in these ways now appears fantastic. But the calculations involved were, in the circumstances of the mid-1940s, quite logical. Cochin had always been the granary of the region, and Tonkin had not recovered from war famine; control of the food surplus seemed one very potent means of exerting a grip over the Indo-Chinese future. Furthermore, Tonkin had always been too sunk into peasant immobilism for the old French colonial authorities to galvanize it into surplus production; there seemed little reason to believe that the Viet Minh would be any more successful. Ultimately the French judgement boiled down to a shrewd gamble that the cliques which surrounded Ho Chi Minh would opt for the not insubstantial rake-offs available to them in the French scheme of things rather than risk smashing their febrile political organization in a confrontation with a sophisticated European opponent whose capability to bring force to bear within the region was growing all the time. But having pushed and pulled the Viet Minh towards a negotiated settlement, the French reckoned that some decisive action would be required to clinch the argument by confronting the Communist leadership with the hard choice: either to vacate Hanoi and face the acute privations and uncertain outcome of guerilla war, or to close with the French negotiators quickly while their bargaining position remained strong. This was the tactical reasoning which led to the sudden and bloody French bombardment of Haiphong on 23 November 1946, the subsequent landing in strength of French troops and the final occupation of Hanoi in mid-February 1947. These military incursions, however, proved decisive, not in extracting a political capitulation from the Viet Minh, but in making a prolonged war inevitable.

Clearly the French representatives in Indo-China, and the relevant officials in Paris, had misjudged the psychological make-up and logistical capacity of the Viet Minh. In retrospect, the tell-tale signs of the latter's strength were discernible even in 1946: in Cochin extensive tracts of the countryside were under Viet Minh control, in Tonkin the peasantry did respond to the administrative drive for food sufficiency and, throughout the Communist-ruled zone, an insulated economy emerged which succeeded in meeting basic consumer needs *and* the requirements of the militias. This was a remarkable achievement; but it need not be automatically concluded that the Viet Minh had come to embody the legitimate solidarity of the Tonkinese people, let alone of the Indo-Chinese masses as a whole. That the peasantry in the north bent itself to the food effort reflects the scarring effects of famine, not its adulation of Viet Minh commissars. Indeed, Ho Chi Minh at this stage avoided even modest agrarian reforms which might have benefited small peasants, in order that he might engage the loyalties of the landlords and large cultivators. A good part of the Viet Minh success in building up a support structure capable of resisting the hammer-blows aimed at it by the French must be attributed to its ruthless application of intimidatory practices – ranging from political assassination to the arbitrary application of taxes. These observations, however, do not plumb the depths of Ho Chi Minh's achievement in constructing a cohesive movement capable of challenging the French army. Above all, Ho Chi Minh understood that social change, accelerated during the war years, had created popular coalitions – of students, teachers, bureaucrats and soldiers, amongst others – which were deeply frustrated by the traditional patterns of Vietnamese life and were capable of being welded into a movement inherently more likely to outlast the makeshift alliances of French strategy, even if the initial military odds favoured the European power. It was by tapping into the spiralling aspirations of these classes-in-the-making that the Viet Minh had raised itself above the status of being just one more of Indo-China's exotic political factions. But by thus locking themselves into the processes of social conflict in Vietnam, Ho Chi Minh and his associates could not easily cut themselves loose in order to do a deal with the French even if (and this remains hypothetical) they had wished to do so. These complexities went beyond the French calculations of autumn 1946 and the winter of 1947. They occupied Hanoi in the belief that one final push might trigger a scramble towards compromise; in fact it signalled the start of seven years of exhausting warfare.

In the months after the initial French attack on Haiphong the war gradually spread through the peninsula. It was not until early March 1947 that the French army in Tonkin had broken republican resistance in the great urban centres, and by then the Viet Minh had successfully withdrawn their regular forces to the Vietbac zone in the highlands. Meanwhile guerrilla penetration of Cochin had been intensified. It was in the south, therefore, that the rifts within Vietnamese society became most poignant, with individuals and communities having to choose sides. With the *Cochinois* splintering in numerous directions, the French were faced with the task of competing with the Viet Minh for popular support. This was an eventuality they were not prepared for, and about which they had few ideas. The dilemma was clear enough: how to construct an indigenous leadership, capable of operating in the various regions of Indo-China, which was both anti-Communist *and* pro-French. In this insoluble enigma – the enigma of a nationalism sympathetic to French power – lay the origins of what became known as the 'Bao Dai solution'.

Bao Dai, titular emperor of Vietnam, had abdicated at the time of the August 1945 'revolution' which had installed the Viet Minh regime in Hanoi. He had identified himself with Vietnamese independence and yet kept a careful distance from the Communists. He was, therefore, a logical focus for anti-Viet Minh nationalists. But these highly fractionated elements did not have military resources at their disposal. Only cooperation with the French could make Bao Dai into a substantive, as opposed to a purely symbolic, force in the struggle for Vietnamese mastery; yet that cooperation could destroy him politically if it smacked too much of capitulation to the old imperialists. Thus, having given up his sojournings in the south of France for the pickings of Indo-Chinese politics, the emperor's first objective was to carve out a popular base of support by demanding real concessions from the French administration: both theoretical and tangible recognition of Vietnamese independence (the French were much readier with the former than the latter) and a reaffirmation of the constitutional unity of the various Indo-Chinese territories.

Meanwhile, however desperate the French might be for local allies, they had good reasons for holding back from any quick embrace with Bao Dai. For one thing, any agreement with the emperor-nationalist would mean abandoning that Cochin separatism which had always been a significant element in French thinking. Indeed, a series of imponderables surrounded the 'worth' that Bao Dai might hold for the French. Could the emperor, once the French administration had built him up with political and military support, be trusted not to play a double game, renewing his contacts with the Viet Minh? Was Bao Dai a sufficiently credible nationalist to serve the legitimating purpose which the French had in mind? Finally, policy-makers in Paris had to concern themselves with the possibility that their 'old Indo-China hands' in Saigon might jib at a strategy of political concessions which conflicted with their own 'purist' conceptions of French interests. Amidst these uncertainties it is not surprising that the Franco–Bao Dai courtship after mid-1947 was decidedly tentative. In the Along Bay statement of December 1947 the French accepted the principles of Vietnamese independence and territorial unity, but subsequently the negotiations became bogged down; in Paris it was still hoped that a straight military success against the Viet Minh might be achieved, while Bao Dai waited for the French to run out of alternatives. This impasse was broken by the final advance of the Communist armies in China from mid-1948 onwards.[19]

With Mao Tse-tung ensconced in Peking after January 1949, the potential scale of the Indo-Chinese conflict was enlarged. Under these concatenating conditions the French had to accept Bao Dai as the best local ally they could get. But the Communist victory in China held one advantage for them: it made it easier to convince the

Americans that the French military effort was on behalf of 'Western democracy' and not of colonial privilege. From 1949 onwards the Paris authorities strove to portray their objectives in this anti-Communist light. Given the Cold War momentum within the Washington policy machine, they did not have to try too hard, so that in the last four years of the war the United States came to finance an increasing percentage of French military expenditure in the area. The problem lay not in eliciting this flood of dollars through Saigon, but in making sure that the local French agencies retained control over its distribution in the face of progressive meddling by US advisers. The heightened Communist power in the Indo-Chinese region after 1949, however, had one other short-term advantage for France: it forced Vietnamese factions who knew only too well what their fate under a Viet Minh regime would be to collaborate more closely with them. Thus in 1949–50 the French were able at last to construct a pattern of relationships which comprehended Laotian and Cambodian monarchists, a medley of nationalist and sectarian entrepreneurs in Cochin and Annam, and US diplomatic and military expansionists.

Over the ensuing four years, however, the French position in Indo-China progressively caved in. The Viet Minh proved their capacity to carry out 'regular' military offensives in the Red River Delta, and had intensified the mobility of their guerrilla operations. General Nguyen Giap had not only stretched the French supply lines beyond breaking point, but had also, by sudden concentrations of fighting power, inflicted damaging defeats on isolated French garrisons such as that of Cao Bang in October 1950. In an attempt to disrupt the growing logistical effectiveness of the Viet Minh, and to stem their incursions into Laos, the French commander-in-chief, General Navarre, proceeded to reinforce the highland garrison of Dien Bien Phu, close to the Laos border, and it was the overrunning of this force by Giap's troops on 7 May 1954 which effectively secured the end of French empire in Asia.[20]

The failure of the French military effort in Indo-China after 1949 is usually attributed to the obstinate refusal by the authorities in Paris to grant any meaningful concessions to the Bao Dai paper regime which could have made it into a truly popular focus of anti-Communist sentiment throughout much of Vietnam. The French objection to the emperor taking up residence in the Norodom Palace in Saigon, forcing him back to the privations of the Côte d'Azure, is

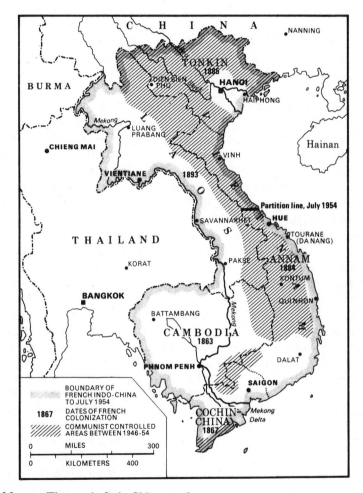

MAP 5   The war in Indo-China, 1946–54

taken to epitomize the petty blindness of French policy which made defeat inevitable. Quite probably, however, these criticisms of French policy-makers are themselves naïve. The French knew Bao Dai was a straw man, and could never be otherwise; they did not waste time and money devolving real power to a political faction incapable of playing a popular role. Above all, after 1950 the relevant officials in Paris knew very well that the transfer of power which mattered was not that from France to the Bao Dai-ists, but that from France to the United States. Quite how far that transfer might go, and what form it might take, crystallized only gradually. Nevertheless, French military strategy in the latter phases of the war (especially under Navarre) was not infused by the illusion that 'victory' against the Viet Minh was any longer possible, at least in the north; rather, it was concerned with the stabilization of existing fronts while certain higher relationships, above all, that between Paris and Washington, were coordinated. Such a Franco-American transition was essentially in place by late 1953; the reinforcement of Dien Bien Phu had the initial tactical purpose of blunting the Viet Minh claims to military predominance at the forthcoming Geneva Conference which was called to discuss, amongst other matters, an Indo-Chinese settlement.

Indeed, the real losers in Indo-China by the time of the Geneva Conference were, in a very real sense, not the French, but the Viet Minh.[21] The latter had fought a long and bitter war for mastery throughout Vietnam, and after 1949 the Communist victory in China had made this goal seem attainable. By 1954, however, not only had both Russia and China become decidedly suspicious of a revitalized Vietnamese nationalism under such regional expansionists as Ho Chi Minh and Nguyen Giap, but they were very eager in the afterglow of the Korean War to de-escalate the tension with Washington. The partitioning of Indo-China, therefore, appealed to the two Communist giants as a means of shutting off any renewal of general war in Asia, ensuring a (restricted) Communist lodgement in the peninsula *and* underwriting Hanoi's dependence on Peking – and thereby on Moscow. Once the great powers, both of East and West, had decided on this slicing of the Indo-Chinese melon, the French and the Viet Minh were effectively relegated to the sidelines. In the event the Geneva Agreement of July 1954 partitioned north and south Vietnam along the seventeenth parallel, and although the small print provided for 'free' elections after eighteen months, nobody really believed these would ever take place. Whatever the rhetorical gyrations in the French National Assembly, it was inevitable that the Prime Minister, Pierre Mendès-France, would obtain the parliamentary sanction he required to end the French entanglement in an Asian war. Neither, in the months after the settlement, could the French authorities have been unduly surprised by the indelicate haste with which the Americans hustled them out of their positions of influence in Saigon, however galling the experience must have been for them. For the Viet Minh, however, the new dispensation could only be viewed with the greatest foreboding. In particular, they had forfeited their old colonial opponent for a new superpower enemy. Of all the great Asian nationalisms the Viet Minh were the most unlucky in that the traditional European rulers had hung on to their old prerogatives long enough for the question of succession to become inextricably enmeshed in the burgeoning rivalry in the 1950s for world power. Giap's military successes had come crucially late to prevent this tragic conjunction of international polarization and Indo-China's future. The human and psychological costs of this fact were, by the 1970s, of incalculable proportions.

IV MAKING MALAYA SAFE FOR DECOLONIZATION

So far in this chapter we have seen how three of the most significant Asian polities came to independence in the decade after 1945. Thus the age of Asian decolonization had, in its vital aspects, been completed even before European rule in Africa moved (after the mid-1950s) into its final crises. There was, however, a degree of chronological overlap in the Asian and African decolonization experiences: Malaya, whose rich natural resources and strategic location made it a significant element in the Asian political system, did not attain full self-government until August 1957, the same year in which the Gold Coast became independent, and one year *after* Sudanese independence. There is, perhaps, a paradox of note here: decolonization in 'big' societies such as India or Nigeria seemed, at times, more manageable than in relatively confined contexts such as Cyprus or Malaya, at least from what might be termed the vice-regal viewpoint. In situations of highly complex and stratified societies, for all the gratings and grindings of competing indigenous groups, the established imperial power had enormous scope for manipulating power transfer; where more simple, almost stark, social structures prevailed the orchestrating capacity of the metropole was fenced in, and sometimes became temporarily incapable of containing the community divisions which an approaching decolonization, by its nature, accentuated. Ironically, pre-war Malaya had been a model of political quiescence and significant economic progress; yet it was here that in the late 1940s and early 1950s the British had to mount a massive operation to defeat a Communist insurrection and make Malaya safe for Westminster-style independence.

The roots of the Communist revolt in Malaya lay in the misunderstandings and frustrations which surrounded the UK Government's constitutional initiatives in the colony after the war.[22] These initiatives had been planned by Colonial Office experts in London during Japan's occupation of south-east Asia, and culminated in October 1945 with the announcement of a new Malayan Union. The Colonial Office, in fact, had derived one advantage from the wartime debacle in Malaya; it had been encouraged to think through its past policy in the area without reference to local groups, be they entrenched British administrators or Malay sultans. The nub of the Malayan Union was that it merged the old separate territorial entities such as the Federated and the Unfederated Malay States into a unitary state, and it amended the old colonial strategy in which the Malays had been accorded a privileged position relative to the other two (migrant) communities, the Chinese and the Indians. Behind these aims, however, lay more general desiderata: to clear the path for self-government on the basis of racial equilibrium, and to accelerate Malayan economic development by giving the Chinese business classes greater scope for their energies.

By mid-1947, however, the UK Government had to accept that the Malayan Union was unworkable and opt instead for a new federal constitution inaugurated in January 1948. How had this come about? The Malayan Union had attracted two principal enemies. The first was the traditional 'Malayan' lobby in Britain, largely composed of British ex-civil servants in the colony who cherished the patchwork of constitutional particularisms prior to 1941 and, above all, the Anglo-Malay 'understanding' which was their pre-eminent characteristic. Affronted by any administrative revision which ran counter to their own predilections, this group had influential friends in Whitehall. The second and most vociferous enemy of the Malayan Union, however, was the Malay community itself. Ironically, there is some evidence that the Malay aristocracy had to be prompted into a defence of its own traditional rights by other Malay groups associated with it.[23] Probably this ambiguity derives from the fact that the sultans knew that their own life-styles were not threatened by the new prescriptions. This *sang-froid* contrasted with the insecurities which oppressed large parts of Malay society after 1945. Thus it was the lower and middle orders of that community which suffered the worst effects of rice shortage after the war and which were vulnerable to the competition of other races, especially the Chinese, for employment. The rash of inter-communal violence indicated the brittle quality of group emotions at a time when contemporary risks, economic and social, all seemed to be on the down side of the ledger. The combination of social vulnerability and, from a Malay perspective, the constitutional onslaught of the colonial authorities led to a novel politicization amongst Malays which took the British by surprise. On 11 May 1946 the United Malays National Organization (UMNO) was inaugurated under the leadership of Dato Onn bin Jafaar, and it rapidly acquired a large membership. Far from paving the way for an easy advance to self-government on a basis of racial equilibrium, the Malayan Union had instead outraged the chief indigenous group and led it to acquire a political arm to defend its prerogatives; Malayan Union, in other words, had accentuated, not assuaged, polarization. Once the British realized this they put the policy into reverse, and in January 1948 the Union was replaced by a federation in which traditional Malay authority would be better placed to survive.

If the British changed their tack after late 1947, so did UMNO. The new party may have indulged in anti-British diatribes to force the withdrawal of the Union constitution, but it rapidly became dependent on the tacit support of the administration, not least in its social and educational programmes central to the construction of mass support. The reason for this relocking of British bureaucracy and Malay leadership lay in the parallel emergence of a dual challenge posed by the (Chinese-dominated) Malayan Communist Party (MCP) and by Indonesian-inspired Malay radicals. Indeed, the worsening imbroglio in Java and Sumatra was the first signal to the British that the road to self-government in Malaya was to be a slower and more hazardous journey than had been envisaged in 1945. Similarly the Indonesian revolution, with its sporadic liquidation of old ruling elites, proved to Onn Dato and his UMNO associates that the British presence was their only defence against a medley of enemies waiting in the wings for their opportunity to take power. Thus the burgeoning government–UMNO alliance was not a stratagem to prolong colonial rule, but a navigational adjustment to make sure that decolonization proceeded in a direction which suited British and dominant Malay interests.

How did the Malayan Communist Party, with its cadres of youthful Chinese, come to be such a significant, if consistently thwarted, force in the colony after the end of the war? First of all, the Communists had won great prestige in the period of Japanese conquest as the only group offering sustained resistance, a fact which gained them a powerful lodgement amongst segments of the Chinese population since that community had suffered most under wartime persecution. In fact the Communist defence front, the Malayan Peoples' Anti-Japanese Army (MPAJA) was rarely involved in actual combat but this went barely noticed amidst the rhetoric of resistance. Subsequently MPAJA would have been overshadowed if the British (and Indian) forces had had to fight their way back into Malaya to 'liberate' its populations, but the sudden surrender of the Japanese created a hiatus in which the occupier's authority had crumbled while the British remained in their Indian and Ceylonese bases. This left MPAJA in control of most of rural Malaya and well placed for a coup. In contrast to the Indo-Chinese and Indonesian revolutionaries, however, the MPAJA leadership, while taking the opportunity to pay off old scores against collaborators and others of whom they disapproved, cooperated in the re-establishment of colonial power, handed in many of their weapons and finally disbanded. After all, the Chinese Communists in Malaya could not rely on majority support in core areas in the same way, for example, that Ho Chi Minh could in Tonkin, and the British were in a better position than the French to crush any opposition to colonial restoration. It was for these reasons, and because the Chinese had reason to believe that the British plans for the future would grant them a more favourable position than before 1942, that the MCP allowed its military wing to be broken up and generally avoided any exploitation of the confusions of 1945–6.

By 1948, however, many segments of Chinese opinion in Malaya had become acutely disaffected. Always more exposed to the rhythms of the cash economy than the Malays, and driven by a more compulsive materialism, it was amongst the Chinese that there were to be found those subgroups hardest hit by post-war inflation and shortages. The Malayan Union was a partial safety valve for these discontents since it held out the possibility that young Chinese would find posts in the civil service and that the state would generally pay more attention to Chinese aspirations. The collapse of the Union, and the looming eminence of UMNO, was like a door slamming in the face of Chinese hopes. The majority of Chinese, nevertheless, remained prepared to work within the status quo. This was particularly true of the big business houses and their clientages, and more generally of all those anti-Communists all too aware that Mao Tse-tung's advance towards Peking made Malaya their only safe domicile, and therefore one not to be lightly put at risk. But many young Chinese who could only see the future through a glass dark with uncertainty were drawn to the MCP as the sole available vehicle for their anxieties. It was, as an American sociologist later showed, precisely this frustrated sense of social mobility which drove individuals to join the guerrilla Communists in the Malayan jungles after 1948.[24] Such a choice was for them an act of protest against conditions which prevented them from exercising their natural bent for competitive self-advancement.

In the three years after 1945 the MCP had a chequered history. The British authorities initially gave it tacit recognition as a legal political party, but once MPAJA was disbanded, and once evidence accumulated that the MCP was actively engaged in penetrating trade unions, the colonial security organs cracked down in the classic manner with temporary incarceration of Communist personnel, the use of informers and harassment of the leftist press. Much of the penetration and counter-penetration of trade unions focused on Singapore, with its dockyard proletariat, an industrial labour force scattered in small workplaces and its large Chinese plurality. Singapore had not been included in the Malayan Union and was subsequently excluded from the Federation, but it remained an important element in the region's political life. Thus if the MCP could win for itself a position of leverage within that great entrepôt, its influence would be all the more powerfully mediated through the adjoining peninsula where the ethnic balances were more evenly drawn. But just when the Chinese position in Malaya was being undermined by the UMNO–British axis, the MCP's industrial strategy in Singapore and on the mainland was also ending in failure. The intimidatory practices of Communist trade union officials had aroused resentment, the Indian labour organizations began to retaliate against MCP attempts to infiltrate the estates where the former had long enjoyed a near monopoly, and the British introduced ordinances to reinforce the position of non-Communist bodies in the industrial field. It was this blocking of the political and industrial routes to power which in early 1948 prompted the MCP leader, Chin Peng, to set afoot preparations for a new strategy which would seek to strike at the British presence through a campaign of rural terror.

On 16 June 1948 three European planters were shot dead at Sungei Siput.[25] It was this event which led the colonial government to declare an Emergency two days later. In fact the local British authorities had failed to act decisively in the face of an earlier accretion of incidents because the prospect of much greater metropolitan supervision was unpalatable for an entrenched and often archaic bureaucracy. Certainly life for the Malayan Civil Service, which had settled easily back into its pre-war life-style, was never to be the same again once the Emergency was under way. But why had the Malayan Communists been tempted to start a military contest which, in retrospect, they had little chance of winning? The answer to this lies in the particular perspectives of 1948. Both in India and in Palestine it had recently been shown that the British were not prepared to sink resources into the retention of key colonial and quasi-colonial possessions. From this it could be deduced that the UK Government was keen to avoid the exhausting involvements which the French had accepted in Indo-China and the Dutch in Indonesia. The Communists in Malaya therefore gambled that the costs of colonialism had only to be nudged upwards for the British to be forced into another scuttle. They failed to identify two interlocking reasons why the British could not leave UMNO to its fate at the hands of an armed MCP in the same way that it had abandoned minorities (or disorganized majorities) in India or Palestine. First, by 1948 the Cold War structure of world politics meant that the one element of colonial society to which the British could *not* bequeath a political inheritance was any Communist (or fellow-travelling) organization; if only to maintain a 'special relationship' with the Americans, the UK Government could not abdicate in the face of Communist competition in one part of south-east Asia while the French valiantly maintained the struggle in another. Second, the MCP strategists underestimated how vital the Malayan economy had become in British calculations since 1945. As pressures on the UK currency reserves had continued, it became necessary that the dollar-earning colonies should boost their exports and lodge the proceeds with the Bank of England; those proceeds were not absorbed, of course, within the UK exchequer, but they did shore up sterling's existing parity. Since Malaya, with its rubber and tin production, had such a consistent surplus in its trade with the United States, British monetary stability partly hinged on Malaya's continued participation in the Sterling Area. This did not mean that Malayan decolonization became undesirable *per se*; but it did mean that infinite care was now required as to whom the beneficiaries of such decolonization might be.

It is hardly surprising that the MCP leadership could not see how these shifting circumstances worked against them militarily. They were convinced that success would come after a brief period in which the local economy was disrupted and 'liberated areas' were established as guerrilla bases. Almost immediately, however, the colonial forces pinned the rebels back into the jungles of Johore and Perak. The Communists were subsequently dependent on the sympathetic help of Chinese squatters who lived on the jungle fringe. These squatters had initially moved to the countryside as a result of wartime persecution by the Japanese, and without this earlier migration the MCP could not long have sustained a rural campaign after 1948. These growers of fruits and vegetables had often been brusquely treated by British administrators as trespassers on Malay lands, and thus sympathized with MCP aims. They provided the Communist fighters with food, and formed the core of the Min Yuen (or Peoples' Movement) which presided over the supply lines connecting town markets and jungle clearings. The tremendous resilience of the guerrilla campaign which, for all its logistical difficulties, continued into the mid-1950s, however, derived from a support base that went far beyond the rural Chinese population. Urban Chinese on the Malayan mainland, especially in Kuala Lumpur, were a crucial source of recruits and finance. The MCP ability to tap into these city classes can be explained by several factors. Mao Tse-tung's final victory in China proper, and his later intervention in the Korean War, sustained the psychological conviction amongst many Malayan Chinese that the MCP had powerful international friends (not least the Soviet Union) who would ultimately ensure success. The reprisals policy of the Min Yuen was a restraint on any who departed publicly from this belief. But perhaps the main reason was that most Chinese were understandably concerned not to back the wrong horse in the

Malayan race, and even those who feared the MCP were often prompted to afford support for the guerrillas just in order to 'hedge' against future eventualities.

How did the British set about cracking this Chinese nut? Between 1948 and 1950 the colonial government was hard pressed to contain guerrilla activity at a low level and construct a military administrative machine capable of a major initiative. Then in June 1950 it unveiled a large-scale resettlement scheme to move the squatter populations away from the jungle edge and re-establish them in new villages. The underlying aim of this was to break the guerrilla–squatter nexus and so cut the rebels off from their supply lines. During the operation one-quarter of the total Chinese population of Malaya was resettled in four hundred new communities, and in these settlements improved social facilities had to be provided to wean Communist supporters away from the MCP. The scale and sophistication of this exercise reflected the enormous effort – which would have been very difficult to contemplate in the first few years after 1945 – which by 1950 the UK was prepared to make in order to arrange its own succession in Malaya. But although the MCP fighters were increasingly short of food, guerrilla activity continued to tie down large numbers of British conscripts, and on 5 October 1951 they gained their most spectacular success when the High Commissioner, Henry Gurney, was killed in an ambush near Fraser's Hill. The result was a massive stepping-up of Emergency operations by the British. In February 1952 civil and military power was combined in the single hands of General Gerald Templar, and over the next two years he proceeded to execute a classic anti-insurgency campaign which effectively broke Communist resistance.[26] The airforce was used to spot and destroy guerrilla food dumps; leaflet 'drops' in the jungle informed the fighters of the amnesty that awaited them if they surrendered; 're-education' procedures were designed to dissolve ideological commitments on the part of those who gave themselves up; those areas, progressively declared 'white' after September 1953, with a 'no incidents' record received highly visible benefits in the form of public works; while in Kuala Lumpur the security services continuously flushed out MCP personnel who were trying to mobilize support for their fighting colleagues. By the time of Templar's retirement in May 1954 the Communists were still sufficiently active for the Emergency to be continued, but they had been pushed far enough into the background for the other arm of British strategy in

Malaya – that concerned with political reform – to be speeded up.

For the first few years of the Emergency, the anti-Communists – be they British, Malay or Chinese – were all too concerned to see their mutual enemy beaten to devote attention to political independence. The most prominent feature of political life in the late 1940s was Dato Onn's attempt to convert UMNO (at least nominally) into a non-racial organization, probably in the belief that this would improve the party's negotiating position and make himself the pivotal figure in Malayan affairs. But the only result was to excite Malay exclusivism within UMNO ranks and force Dato Onn's resignation in August 1951. After this episode it became clear that political progress would take place, not through the evolution of non-racial political institutions, but through a *modus vivendi* between the two great communal parties, UMNO and the Malayan Chinese Association (MCA), the latter having been formed as a Chinese alternative to the MCP. It was the growth of this understanding, lubricated by the improved cash-incomes derived from the Korean War commodity boom, which underpinned the staged introduction of a ministerial system in the Legislative Council, and the extension of Chinese access to jobs in the bureaucracy, without touching off political passions. In early 1952 Oliver Lyttelton, the Conservative Colonial Secretary, stated the British view that Malayan independence would come as and when racial unity was assured, which meant, in effect, when UMNO and the MCA could reach agreement on constitutional forms. The two leaders, Abdul Rahman Tengku and Tan Cheng Lok, engaged in a dialogue throughout 1953 and agreed that they would fight federal elections as a joint Alliance as soon as possible. Such elections could hardly take place while Templar was concentrating all his administrative resources on the anti-insurgency drive, but his replacement by a civil governor, Sir Donald Macgillivray, was a turning point, since the latter saw his own role as an initiator of a new phase in the stabilization of Malaya. In April 1955 a White Paper was published which outlined a programme for an elected majority in the Legislative Council with immediate elections, and once the Alliance had won a huge majority in those contests during July Tengku Abdul Rahman became 'chief minister'. In this way a national and racial coalition had been brought to the point of governmental responsibility just at the juncture when the Communist threat had been beaten off. Thus through a combination of anti-insurgency techniques (representing a heavy financial investment by the UK Government) and deft political management, the British had made Malaya safe for Malay conservatives and Chinese businessmen, and in August 1957 the independent Federation of Malaya was duly proclaimed.

The Malayan Emergency was the most striking evocation of that dimension of decolonization which might be characterized as 'making the ring' of a new politics. Thus the most important task of colonial governments in the final phases of decolonization was political, not economic; it was to ensure that local institutional conflicts could be contained within the broader frameworks set by western interests. The Chinese Communist insurgency which broke out in Malaya in the later 1940s seemed set fair to frustrate this objective in an area whose political direction had great significance for the whole of south-east Asia. One of its most disturbing aspects, viewed from London, was the MCP's apparent success at attracting support from youth, whatever its failures amongst the older, more cautious generation; this hardly boded well for the progressive consolidation of Malayan politics along pro-British lines. The whole purpose of the Emergency was to smash the MCP as a presence in Malayan life, and to draw the boundaries within which aspiring Chinese cadres had to work if they were to retain any hopes of personal advancement. It was this boundary-drawing, both at the institutional level and amongst individuals, which was the real stuff of decolonization as it was implemented 'on the ground'.

4. Britain, Palestine and the Middle East

THE Second World War, as we noted in an earlier chapter, had profoundly affected Middle Eastern affairs. That conflict had deepened and widened local frustrations and resentments in ways which soon meshed with nationalist expectations, and speeded up the displacement of British influence in certain regions by her erstwhile American ally; this latter transition was most complete in the case of the Saudi Kingdom. Even so, there were grounds in 1945 for the belief that the British position throughout most of the Middle East was more defensible than it was, for example, in India, or than the French position was in Indo-China. None of the Middle Eastern countries, including Egypt, sported a credible 'mass' nationalist party such as Gandhi's and Nehru's Congress, and the endemic anti-Communism of these Islamic societies blocked one major way in which this vacuum might be filled under post-war conditions. The British had been busy identifying workable relationships with quasi-autonomous Middle Eastern regimes since at least 1918, and with sensible diplomacy this 'line' could be expected to hold. The intimate and pervasive presence of western economic and political power within the crevices of Middle Eastern society, compared to its more tenuous hold in much of Asia, meant that the possible permutations of Britain's leading role could be almost endlessly refined. Nevertheless, by 1954 this leading role had been fractured in so many places that, of all the western powers active in the Middle East, the British seemed the obvious target on which Middle Eastern nationalists might concentrate their efforts.[1]

At the heart of this Middle Eastern revolution lay events in Palestine, and we must begin by sketching the background to these developments. In 1917 the Balfour Declaration committed the British Government to supporting the Jewish claim to a 'National Home' in

Palestine. At this point the territory had just come under British military control, and the Treaty of Versailles confirmed its status as a British Mandate. But meanwhile Lloyd George's war administration had also embraced obligations – most directly through the famous MacMahon–Hussein correspondence of 1915 – with respect to the sovereign independence of those Arab rulers who had revolted against their long-time rulers (and Germany's current ally), Turkey. Both these sets of commitments were threaded with ambiguity. The Balfour Declaration did not define what was meant by a 'National Home', and what Jewish rights regarding contemporary Palestine flowed from it; equally, it was not at all certain what MacMahon's promises amounted to, and how far they stretched – Palestine, for example, had not been specifically mentioned. This was, from the British angle, a more complicated, tragedy-laden dilemma than simply having given, under wartime pressures, conflicting promises to different factions. British power had cut across two movements (Zionism and Arab irredentism) which were themselves heading for a collision over Palestine's future. The results were bound to be disastrous.

During the 1920s, however, mandatory government in Palestine succeeded in maintaining a rough equilibrium between Jewish and Arab aspirations.[2] Thus Jewish immigration into the territory was allowed to proceed, while the fears of the indigenous Arab community – still easily a majority of the population – concerning their economic and political displacement were assuaged by the British administrative presence. The growth of anti-semitism in Germany after 1930, its intensification after Adolf Hitler's accession to the Chancellorship in 1933 and the spread of similar policies throughout much of central Europe transformed this situation. The considerable increase in Jewish arrivals from Europe into Palestine, and the understandable boost which fascist persecution gave to the Zionist idea, inflamed communal relations in the Mandate during these years. In 1936 an Arab rebellion broke out which, although not very effectual in military terms, prompted the British Government to appoint a Royal Commission under the chairmanship of Lord Peel. In their Report, which was immediately accepted by the metropolitan Government, these commissioners declared in favour of a partition whereby Jews and Arabs were accorded their separate autonomous areas within the framework of Britain's continuing mandatory responsibility. It was the question of partition which afterwards was to dominate Palestine affairs up until the establishment of the state of Israel in 1948.

The conclusion of the Peel Commission constituted a tremendous victory for the 'National Home' movement and particularly for its influential advocate in British political circles, Chaim Weizmann. However unsatisfactory a partition of Palestine's existing boundaries might be, it none the less was the first official recognition by the British that a Jewish state was destined to be formed in the area. But the years after 1936 marked a rapid ebbing of Zionist fortunes. With the approach of war in Europe, it became axiomatic in London that Arab, not Jewish, goodwill would be the most vital to maintain if any conflict were to break out: the importance of oil concessions in Arab territories, and the strategic significance of Egypt, were just two facets of this guiding principle. The climax of the new trend came with the 1939 White Paper on Palestine which now ruled out partition, explicitly refuted the concept of a Jewish state and tightened up immigration procedures. Neither did Zionist prospects improve during the war which soon followed, despite the longstanding sympathy of Winston Churchill for Weizmann's cause. The British military departments remained adamant that Anglo-Arab relations could not be unsettled while Middle Eastern stability was so necessary for the Allied war effort, and it was generally recognized that the Jewish community in Palestine was hardly in a position to withdraw its support in the fight against Germany. In 1945 the Jewish 'National Home' movement seemed, at least superficially, no nearer to its objectives than it had been ten years before.

This dismal outlook for Zionism appeared to improve dramatically, however, with the surprise victory of the Labour Party at the British general election in 1945. That party had, for most of its brief history, been strongly drawn to Zionist ideals, and more recently still to the partition formula. Disappointment on this front, however, was not long in coming. Palestine matters now fell under the aegis of the Foreign Office because of their international ramifications, and the new Foreign Secretary, Ernest Bevin, soon became deeply hostile to Jewish aims in the Mandate. This was, in part, because he quickly proved susceptible to the orthodoxies of a department in which Arabphilism had long been a characteristic. But other factors, too, were at work, and these related to his previous career as one of the pioneer-founders and subsequently General Secretary of the Transport and General Workers Union. Bevin's staunch patriotism was thus of the blunt and volatile kind common to his generation of trade union barons, and he was deeply alienated by the spread of Jewish terrorism (increasingly aimed at British personnel and installations) in post-war Palestine. The fact that Bevin retained as Foreign Secretary the negotiating mentality of a trade union leader was even more important in conditioning his responses on the Palestine issue. He had long before imbibed the golden rule of wage bargaining: never give anything away for nothing. The Arabs had something to give – in Egypt, Iraq and other Middle Eastern territories; it was not at all clear, however, what, if anything, the Zionists had in *their* gift. This calculation was rooted in the belief that international Jewish opinion, to which the ideological Zionists had always to be sensitive, would be guided by the conviction that British friendship was too vital for their world-wide security as a race to risk for the mere bauble of Palestine. In other words, Bevin was confident that he could out-manoeuvre the Zionists within the crucial arena of Jewish politics. This critical gamble proved wildly wrong. As the enormity of the Holocaust experience dawned (not least, ironically, as a result of Britain's exposures of the now liberated 'death-camps' in eastern-central Europe) the Zionist imperative of a Palestinian homeland came to mobilize world Jewry on a novel scale.

Why were the various Zionist groups able to make such rapid headway on the international stage in 1945/6? The deepest causes for this development lie within Jewish psychology in Europe and North America.[3] The Holocaust had been the product of Jewish powerless-ness; only the Zionists, it now appeared to a majority of Jews, had, in their nation-state ideal, a policy to reverse this historic vulnerability. So apposite was this logic under the awful shadow of Auschwitz that the reverberation of a Jewish hegemony in Palestine within Middle Eastern affairs, and, more precisely, the long-term effects that might be felt on the character of Jewish world civilization, were never weighed carefully in the balance. But whatever the Zionist success in mobilizing Jewish opinion in its favour, the British could still nurture the hope that other western governments would cooperate in inter-cepting financial and military resources en route to clandestine Zionist groups, either in Europe or Palestine itself. Here again they were disappointed. The French authorities, predictably resentful at the way in which the UK Government had connived at their eviction from Syria and Lebanon in 1946, tacitly allowed refugee ships to slip out of Marseilles harbour; it was the British refusal to allow these refugees to disembark in Haifa, and their subsequent sufferings afloat, which turned the propaganda war so decisively against the UK. It was not this rather veiled French support, however, which transformed the political and logistical position of Zionism, but the increasingly open sympathy of President Truman in the United States.

One of the basic elements in British optimism regarding the stability of Palestine at the end of the war was the expectation that, if Jewish terrorist groups such as the Irgun went on a large-scale offensive, the US administration would act quickly to cut off the flow of funds and guns to the area. It was, for example, common knowledge that the State Department in Washington was resolutely advising *against* the partition solution on which Jewish hopes in Palestine rested, and it seemed likely that Irgun-style extremism would reinforce the cogency of such advice within US policy-forming circles. Furthermore, it seemed in London that the Truman government was unlikely to risk any wholesale destabilization across the line of Europe's oil supply from the Middle East for the limited benefit of pleasing the Jewish lobby at home. But in fact Truman overrode the State Department and inaugurated a foreign policy line which entailed pillorying the British, not least in the United Nations, for an inhumane attitude to Jewish refugees and, by implication, for blocking that open-ended immigration into Palestine which could alone assuage the needs of displaced Jews.

The factors which led the US Government to move towards an increasingly open support for a partition of Palestine distinctly favourable to the local Jewish population are clear enough in outline, although it is not so easy to see which were the most significant. In the flux that followed the break-up of the Rooseveltian coalition, it is not surprising that Truman should have striven to secure his position in New York politics by staking better claims to the Jewish vote. By early 1947 this meant taking on the colourings of political Zionism. But US policy on Palestine was shaped by other forces than the Jewish lobby alone. Its evolution was also related to that expansionist mood which gripped Washington's bureaucratic and political coteries after 1945/6. The US policy machine became acutely excited at the prospect of a Jewish state as a reliable American ally situated so strategically in the Middle East, and the reluctant State Department was pulled along in its wake. It was this matching up of an Anglo-Saxon *realpolitik* and the strength of the Zionist constituency which critically shifted the terms of governmental debate on Palestine in the United States. Meanwhile the costs of a Palestinian partition seemed quite modest; the Arabs inside and outside the territory showed no capacity for building effective nationalist coalitions able to inflict retaliatory punishment on western interests, and throughout 1945/7 American official opinion was not so solicitous regarding such vital European interests as Middle Eastern oil as it was shortly to become under the impact of the Cold War.

Against this background, Bevin's exhaustive efforts to negotiate Palestinian Jewry into accepting a unitary state with an Arab majority, within which the British could continue some form of mediating role between the two communities, ran continuously into the sand.[4] Essentially, Bevin's aim was to locate the wedge which divided the various Jewish Palestinian factions and to isolate the anti-British extremists. These divisions certainly existed and were intensi-fied during the post-war years, but they no longer turned on rival conceptions of Anglo-Zionist relations. In the altered context of the times all Jewish activists were anti-British, and it was never likely that Bevin would be able to work this monolith loose. By early 1947 the British Foreign Secretary had begun to grasp this fact. The first decisive break in the UK Government's approach came in February of that year when it was announced in London that the Palestine question would be referred to the United Nations. By this ploy Bevin signalled to Truman that if he continued to encourage Palestinian Jews in their hopes for partition, then at some point his adminis-tration would itself have the unpleasant task of supervising the local consequences, since the British would refuse to stay around to do so. Any possibility, however, that this blackmail would prompt the President into whatever covert actions were required to shackle Jewish terrorists in Palestine quickly faded. By mid-1947 a partition of Palestine had become inevitable; the competition between Britain and the US was really to see which of these powers was to be manoeuvred into accepting prime responsibility for its implemen-tation. Thus, with Bevin's dramatic and unexpected anouncement on 26 September 1947 that the Palestine Mandate was to be unilaterally terminated, the British were (as they had recently done in India) unveiling their most powerful weapon: the option of evacuation without any other concern than the minimizing of British loss of life and, as far as was possible under the circumstances, British loss of friends.

The decision of the British Labour Government to evacuate Palestine, however, has to be seen as part of the broader crisis in Britain's international strategies during 1947. At the heart of that crisis lay the relationship with the United States. In 1945 the Americans had extended an emergency loan to the UK, but in return the British (under the subsequent Financial Agreement) committed themselves to making sterling convertible with the dollar in August 1947. Just how willingly the London authorities approached convertibility may be unclear, but its consequences were all too stark: reserves drained out of the Bank of England during September, and controls had to be slapped back on.[5] Although the Truman Administration had not contrived this situation with precise objects in mind, Washington circles hoped that the demoralizing experience would reduce the UK's irritating habit of diverging from American policy in critical matters. Above all, Truman and his key advisors were eager to shake British confidence that they could always be treated as a 'special case' (in the matter of living standards, for example) compared to other Europeans. Here, however, the British Government had for some time been fashioning a retaliatory instrument: if the US authorities tried to undermine their 'special case' status on economic matters, they could start refusing to act like a 'special case' in strategic matters by assuming only those security burdens that were directly relevant to UK interests. This was the significance of the Labour Government's decision in February 1947 to withdraw British troops from Greece, where they had been fighting Communist insurgents;[6] it was a warning shot across the American bows that the British would not hesitate to off-load such costly and complex local involvements on to Washington's shoulders. In playing this game of bluffs and threats, the British policy-makers grossly underestimated the US' preparedness in 1947 to take on these burdens, and in retrospect the American entry into the eastern Mediterranean through the Greek side-door, assuming the anti-Communist role which the British had forsaken, was only a prelude to its more direct penetration through the establishment of Israel. The Anglo-American divisions over the Palestine question after 1945 were thus an integral part of this mutual stalking between two powers who, while increasingly united in their recognition of a Soviet threat, were very far from united as to the modes of power and cooperation within the western-democratic alliance.

Amidst these fluid circumstances it is not surprising that the final phase of the Palestine Mandate gave rise to an extraordinary bitterness on all sides. The United Nations, forced into decisive action following the British abdication-by-referral, voted on 29 November 1947 for a partition of Palestine. This vote served to accelerate the breakdown of communal relations as Arabs and Jews fought for control within their localities. After the UN vote, President Truman continued to hope that the British Government would agree to cede interim authority to some UN-supervised body which could then use the British troops on the ground to impose order – and partition. But the UK Cabinet was too canny to accept a position by which some UN supremo sat in Jerusalem ordering British soldiers to put down Arab resistance. Instead, the Labour Government refused to hand over the mandatory power to any neutral authority. This power was, in the British Government's opinion, non-transferable and would disappear in exact correlation with the progressive evacuation of British troops. Thus the Arabs and Jews fought each other to establish the pattern of demarcation, while the British military commanders concentrated purely and simply on policing the exit routes along which British personnel were moving as quickly as the enormous baggage-train, which there was no intention of leaving behind, would allow.

President Truman had wanted the British presence to continue through the partition process to act as a 'screen' behind which the Israeli state could be set up free from attack by other Arab nations. With the British refusal to play this role, and with the dismantling of the scaffolding of the Mandate, an Arab–Jewish war became inevitable, since the neighbouring Arab states realized that their best hope of reversing the partition fact was at its moment of birth. On 15 May 1948, with the British forces departed, the Arab armies struck: the Egyptians through Gaza in the south, the Iraqis and the Arab Legion of Transjordan (the latter under the command of the Englishman General Glubb) from the east, and the Syrians and Lebanese from the north. During the first month of hostilities the Arab commanders made considerable progress, with Glubb's Legion holding much of Jerusalem and the Egyptians in control of the Negev. In retrospect, it is easy to see that at this point the Arab leaders should have demanded a compromise settlement under UN auspices, which Israel could not then have boycotted. But driven by the belief that the Jewish forces were close to collapse, the Arabs terminated the truce which the UN had succeeded in arranging, only to find that the

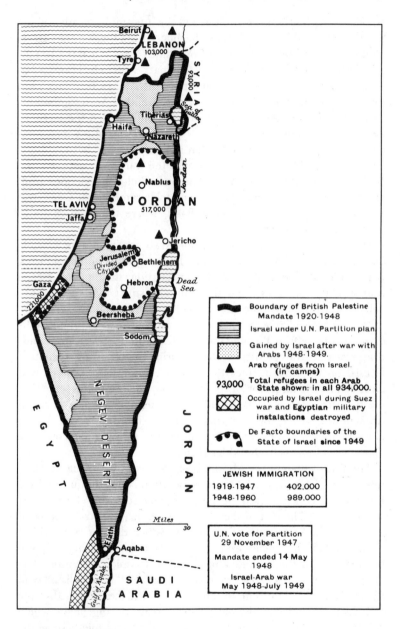

MAP 6 The partition of Palestine

Israeli armies had been re-equipped in the interim: ironically, by the Soviet Union, which at this point harboured the illusion that Israel might orientate itself towards the Communist bloc. When the Israelis counter-attacked, the Arab strategy fell apart, with only Transjordan continuing to offer serious resistance until the end. In February 1949 Egypt signed an armistice with Israel, and the other Arab combatants soon followed suit. As a result, Israel not only gained the territory awarded to it under the original UN partition, but also approximately half of the area which under that dispensation had been reserved for the Arabs. The most visible effect of the war, however, were the 700,000 Arab refugees – the product of wholesale evictions from villages and towns – crowded into ramshackle camps in the Gaza strip and along the rump of the West Bank, where the great majority subsequently remained.

It was this massive humiliation for Arab civilization as a whole during 1948–9 which shaped Middle Eastern affairs in the following years. The British hope that by evacuation they might escape responsibility for events, and their initial instinct that the military debacle at the hands of the Israelis might make Arab politicians more rather than less pliable, proved wildly mistaken. Instead, the Palestinian outcome effected a fundamental alienation between the industrial west and Arab political culture. During the 1950s this alienation focused on the British, since the latter were the most exposed and most vulnerable target for Arab retribution, and it is in this sense that the British presence in the Middle East might be seen as a victim (though not, by far, the most tragic) of the Arab–Jewish war. But to illustrate this we must turn away from Palestine proper and comment upon developments in the wider region.

The British plan in the Middle East after 1945 was to carve out a role as the 'father-figure' of Arab cooperation. With this in mind the UK Foreign Office pressed the major regional states into forming the Arab League. The British thereby hoped to acquire Arab goodwill, and to define Arab nationalism in ways which did not clash with a continued British presence and which allowed Soviet Communism to be portrayed as the chief existing threat to Islamic civilization. The main nodes of such a careful exercise in 'managed' nationalism lay in Egypt, Iraq and Transjordan, and it was with these states that the UK sought to revamp the old pre-war treaty arrangements which had been such a prominent feature of local arrangements since the 1920s. Success attended these efforts in Transjordan during 1946 when King Abdullah extended the UK's right to station troops in his kingdom for a further twenty-five years; but then the Transjordanian state had been a British creation *par excellence*, and was so small as to fear for its continued existence if the British support-system were ever removed. In Iraq matters were more complicated.[7] The ruling monarchy in Iraq was also reliant on its British patron, and yet the royalists could not afford to alienate nationalist opinion which ran wide and deep through Iraqi society. The British evacuation from Palestine only worsened these dilemmas for the Court party in Baghdad; they were anxious to tie up an agreement with the British to prevent the latter's Palestinian scuttle being repeated in adjacent areas, but also scared that any such agreement would now be even more unpopular with Iraqi radical elements since the UK had, in the eyes of most Arabs, treacherously cooperated in the establishment of Israel. The refusal of the 'Parliament' in Baghdad to ratify the 1949 Anglo-Iraqi Portsmouth Treaty, and the fact that the Court reluctantly accepted this road-block, indicated that the old conjunctions between British interests and those of Middle Eastern royalist regimes were shearing apart. If this was true in Iraq by 1949, however, it became even more evident in the most critical test-case of all – that of Egypt.

In retrospect, no doubt, the British should have taken the opportunity to withdraw their military presence from Egypt under the relatively favourable conditions of 1945–6. The UK's war-inflated prestige in the Middle East was then at its peak, and Bevin might have been able to exploit the Anglo-Arab goodwill generated by such an act to consolidate a new style of relationship. In the event, Britain's hasty concoction of the Arab League had a peculiarly sham-like quality since British troops continued to be highly visible in Cairo. The Egyptian political classes, still very much under British supervision, could only sit and watch Lebanese and Syrian 'liberation' from French authority, with a consequent shift of influence towards the intellectual coteries of Beirut and Damascus. For Cairenes, who had basked in the war's apparent confirmation that they occupied the pivotal position within the Middle Eastern world, this was a sudden and painful setback. Indeed, a generation of Egyptian civil servants and businessmen, for whom the war had been a means of rescue from the 1930s depression, and a source of new political and commercial opportunities, quickly apprehended that the British intention was to strap them back into the old immobilism. It is amidst this post-war schism in Anglo-Egyptian understanding that the roots of the 1956 Suez war must be found.[8]

Why, therefore, did the British attempt to maintain their Egyptian foothold, only grudgingly pulling their troops back into the base-area along the Canal marked out in the 1936 Treaty, and consistently evading the Egyptian desire to see that Treaty fundamentally revised? In India at this time the British authorities were thrashing around in search of some convenient mode of departure; in Egypt, where the historic complexities were so much less, they might have been expected to grasp the chance of a clinical severance of an outworn relationship. Nevertheless, it is not hard to see why, under prevailing circumstances, decolonization in South Asia did not give rise to the same qualms as the loosening of the British grip upon Middle Eastern politics. First, Egypt's particular significance derived increasingly from its proximity to the Middle Eastern oilfields. These oil resources had a relevance to the prospects of west European reconstruction which the Indian subcontinental economy entirely lacked. Second, the Soviet Union, still in occupation of northern Persia until mid-1946, posed a more immediate threat to the Middle East than to South Asia. Third, neither the Egyptian monarchy nor the Wafdist party could, from a British vantage point, combine the virtues of 'reliability' and local legitimacy as did the Congress organization in India. In short, whereas the British could rest assured that Nehru could throttle whatever manifestations of anti-British sentiment occurred in India, they could have no such confidence in the tenuous regimes prevailing in Cairo, Baghdad or Damascus. As long as British influence remained firmly entrenched in Egypt, the 'line' could almost certainly be held elsewhere in the region, and so the UK clung to its treaty-presence in that country, hoping to gain time in which the monarchy (or anybody else) could put together a strong and sympathetic government under whose aegis the risks of treaty revision would be kept to a minimum. If these rather optimistic tactics were progressively prejudiced by events in Palestine, they were finally destroyed by the Arab–Jewish war of 1949.

The Arabs' post-partition defeat left them facing the prospect of renewed Israeli expansionism in the not-too-distant future. Their suspicion that the British intended to exploit this weakness to shore up their own position raised Anglophobia, always a strand of contemporary Arab consciousness, into a significant political emotion. Furthermore, Arab politicians, whose popular standing had been shattered by the 1949 conflict, saw that the quickest and most certain way back into mass esteem was by stressing their anti-western commitments, while such anti-westernism was bound to vent itself most forcefully upon Britain, whose imprint upon the Middle East had hitherto been the most profound of all the advanced nations. These processes were not least evident in Egypt, where the military disasters had made King Farouk into a prisoner of the Wafdist factions, and together these elements sought to recoup their losses by vilifying the 1936 Treaty, which they unilaterally denounced in October 1951, and organizing, albeit clandestinely, guerrilla operations against the British base along the Canal. These frantic scamperings after nationalist credibility, however, failed to avert the end of the *ancien régime* with the Neguib–Nasser coup on 23 July 1952. Before then, however, Britain's prestige in the Middle East had entered the beginning of an acute downward spiral when the Mossadeq government in Iran had in 1951 appropriated the Anglo-Iranian Oil Company.

Mossadeq's act of nationalization can only be explained in terms of the long-run political and economic frustrations within Iranian society as that country tried to force its way along the path of modernization after the 1920s.[9] That modernization was recurrently twisted and blocked by the manner in which Iran continued to be buffeted by the mutual rivalries of external powers with an interest in the area, and by the way in which it pitted social groups against each other. Here was a classic example of an underdeveloped nation, possessing a determined leadership and gifted cadres, which nevertheless found that it lacked the institutional and political means to clear away the obstacles to progress, and that the drive to change simply threw up a set of internal divisions which heightened the costs of progress. The frenetic outburst of Iranian nationalism in the early 1950s reflected a need to find some means to break these dual constraints. Thus Mossadeq hoped that, by building a new coalition around the issue of nationalizing the Anglo-Iranian Oil Company, he would obtain the power to shift the terms of Iranian development. This parting of the ways in Iranian politics happened, not entirely by coincidence, just at that point when the British position in the wider Middle East was slipping fast.

Prior to 1949 there is little doubt that such an appropriation of a vital British asset would have evoked a military response by the UK Government. Indeed, in 1946 such preparations had been set in train to reinforce the British position in south Persia. But in 1950 not only was Britain straining its nerves and resources to meet the Korean War emergency, but such a belligerent move in any part of the Middle East would have confirmed the UK's image as the most inveterate anti-nationalist in the western camp. The British were reduced to evacuating their personnel from the vicinity of the great Abadan refinery, and persuading the Americans to intervene on their behalf by employing the argument that Mossadeq had pro-Soviet tendencies.[10] Predictably, however, the US administration was not so easily manipulated, and instead let the Iranian imbroglio develop, waiting for a moment to enforce a settlement which would maximize its own access to decision-making in Tehran. Fortunately for British interests, that moment arrived reasonably quickly, since Mossadeq's movement rapidly ran out of control. Suddenly panicked by the prospect that the Communist Tudeh party might indeed come out on top, the US Central Intelligence Agency engineered Mossadeq's downfall and the installation of a new regime (led by Reza Shah) prepared to take the firm actions required to shape local nationalism in ways that were acceptable to Washington. The settlement which emerged was one in which western oil interests were grouped in a consortium, only 40 per cent of which was credited to the Anglo-Iranian company, and which syphoned-off greatly increased funds to the Iranian authorities. In effect, the Americans had hauled Iranian nationalism off the British back, and used the growing surplus of oil-cash to construct a new framework of western influence in which the UK was ascribed a much reduced role.

Between the two world wars the Middle East had been second only to Asia as a focus of Britain's imperial operations. Over these years, furthermore, the relative significance of these two 'fields of play' narrowed as, on the one hand, the Anglo-Indian economic axis weakened and Japan put the squeeze on UK commerce in China, and on the other hand, the importance of Middle Eastern oil resources became more pronounced. The Second World War accelerated this process, such that in 1945 the apparent inevitability of an early withdrawal from India and Burma was offset by the more heartening fact that Britain's position in the Arab world seemed secure. In this light the reason why the growing unmanageability of Palestine after 1945 caused a greater panic in London than the concurrent shrinking of the *Raj* is discernible. The loss of Palestine to Jewish terrorists had much more disquieting implications for fundamental British interests than the loss of India to the Anglophiliac Nehru; India had become much less significantly knit into these interests, and the Middle East much more so, than in the past. It was the unexpected simultaneity of Indian decolonization and the Palestinian dénouement, indeed, which made 1946–7 an imperial crisis of such intensity. Even then, however, policy-makers in London could still assuage their anxiety with the hope that the emergence of Israel left their leverage in the Middle East still intact. The violent spiral of Arab politics after the 1949 war, however, exploded this final refuge of the mandarin-optimists. By 1954 the British Government had been forced to set off in search of a *modus vivendi* with both local nationalisms of a less malleable variety than their predecessors and American expansionists determined to imprint their own image on Middle Eastern affairs.

Less than a decade after 1945, British imperial power had been relentlessly squeezed out of its Asian and Middle Eastern frameworks. Had either of these remained in existence, the viability of the British empire-state would not have been terminally affected. But with the casings of both broken beyond repair, leaving only the husk of African colonialism still whole, the world system managed from London had collapsed; what was left was a fragmented and (in power-political terms) incoherent set of possessions of doubtful worth. Prime Minister Eden's despairing attempt to topple Nasser after the latter's nationalization of the Suez Canal Company in 1956 was just one measure of the dire wound which recent events in the region had inflicted upon the style and technique of Britain's trans-oceanic *persona*. But before giving an account of the Suez climacteric, we must turn our attention to developments in Africa.

5. Experimentation, Consolidation and Deadlock in British Africa

ONE of the outstanding characteristics of European empires in Africa during the decade after 1945 was how little they were affected by the backwash from the demise of colonialism in Asia. R. Robinson and J. Gallagher pointed out some years ago that Europe's acquisition of African territories in the latter part of the nineteenth century was simply 'scraping the bottom of the barrel' following more important seizures elsewhere;[1] but any expectation that when the barrel of empire began to be emptied of its Asian contents in the late 1940s the African flotsam would be simultaneously ejected proved to be misplaced. In fact the late 1940s and early 1950s were the heyday of African empire, when it seemed to have a coherence and dynamic of its own. This coherence and dynamic was merely the reflection of the passing utility which Africa appeared to have for western Europe in its struggle for post-war economic survival; by the mid-1950s the appearance had faded because one set of metropolitan crises had, as we shall see later, been replaced by another. But these fissiparities were not evident at the time. 'Development and welfare' was the theme of the moment *circa* 1950, and it seemed that within this framework Euro-African relationships were bound to become tighter, not looser, over time.

But if the various regions of sub-Saharan Africa were subject to the same forces emanating from western Europe, and were touched by the same rhetoric, between 1945 and 1955 it looked as if their respective futures were being shaped in radically different ways. This situation needs to be compared with the preceding and succeeding decades, when, for all the contrasts of culture, resources and administrative styles existing over such a vast physical area, those portions of sub-Saharan Africa directly ruled by the European powers were seen as a broadly homogeneous area with convergent, if usually obscurely defined, political destinies. Indeed, one of the most distinctive marks of British administration in Africa before the Second World War had been to limit the divergences in the trajectories of the various states. In the decade after 1945, however, the official mind of European colonialism conceived, not of one future for the African polity, but of several, in each of which the political structures would be subtly (and sometimes not so subtly) different. The main line of division implicit in this thinking was that between those African dependencies with an entrenched white settler presence, and those so-called 'native states' where the European element was largely composed of the thin line of administrators and missionaries; although even in the former case there was scope for graduated projections according to the extent and character of white colonization. It was this emergence after 1945 of two broad avenues of African development, one which involved the progressive dilution of direct European authority and one which involved its consolidation, which is a major explanation for the widespread, if erratic, phenomenon of organized black nationalism after 1955, since by then Africans had become profoundly conscious of the parting of the ways which had opened up before them. In the event these differentiating impulses were at first blunted and then reversed, although not in the exceptional case of South Africa, and not without etching much starker psychological and economic contrasts within African society as a whole than would otherwise have prevailed. We shall trace this experience by looking in particular at the representative cases of the Gold Coast, British Central Africa and Kenya.

Before proceeding further, however, one defect of the case-study method may be noted: it leaves out of account the continental, or cross-regional, dimension of African nationalist growth. The ideal of Pan-Africanism, for example, seemed at the end of the Second World War to have acquired a newly dynamic quality, and to possess considerable potential as a mobilizing force. This was epitomized by the well-attended Pan-African Congress held at Manchester in October 1945, and by the more sober role played by the West African Students' Union (WASU) in London as a homebase for radically inclined young Africans during their stay (usually for educational reasons) in the great imperial capital. Clearly such cross-regional fertilization in the genesis of anti-colonialism after 1945 was a factor of sorts. But it is doubtful whether the panegyrics of Manchester, or the solidarities of WASU, held any substantive short- or medium-term significance. Indeed, subsequently one of the most remarkable characteristics of African nationalisms was their self-containment within narrow territorial worlds; even such relatively mature nationalisms as could be found in the Gold Coast and Nigeria rarely interacted in any significant manner with each other. Thus, when Kwame Nkrumah, who had been a leading figure at the Manchester Congress in 1945, found cause to return to the theme of pan-African unity and continental development in the late 1950s and early 1960s, his adumbrations fell largely on deaf ears. Therefore, in telling the story of African decolonizations in strictly bilateral terms of the metropole's interaction with individual colonial polities, a degree of clarity can be maintained and little of real historical weight left out.

I   POLITICAL CHANGE IN THE GOLD COAST: A MODEL DEFINED

It was seen earlier that wartime British 'planning' regarding the future of colonial government in Africa really had West Africa in mind, uncluttered as the latter was by a white settler presence which elsewhere made all calculations problematical. Even in this regional milieu, however, Whitehall in those years was not contemplating any rapid move towards 'independence', however advanced may have been the views of particular officials. During the war the idea had taken hold (rather conveniently, since it relegated political matters to a subsidiary place on the agenda) that the priority of colonial government should be to foster that economic growth without which any other reforms were bound to founder. This mode of thought was reinforced after 1945 by the vital role of West African commodity production in making the Sterling Area a viable entity, and thus saving the metropolitan pound from an early debacle.[2] Nevertheless, the very economic significance of the larger British West African colonies, and the imperatives set up by the need to stimulate commodity development, meant that Hailey's cautious approach to modernizing indirect rule administration was outdated even by 1945.

During 1946 the governors of the Gold Coast and Nigeria, Sir Alan

Burns and Sir Arthur Richards, introduced new constitutions into their respective territories. The format of these two legislative systems was roughly similiar. Native authorities were no longer to exist in the administrative isolation so characteristic of the pre-war system, since they were to be grafted into a network of Provincial Councils in the Gold Coast and three Regional Houses of Asembly in Nigeria. These latter organs were to elect members indirectly to the central Legislative Councils in Accra and Lagos, where, in conjunction with directly elected members of the municipalities, African representatives would possess a majority of votes over the 'officials'. Overarching all, however, was the Governor's continuing power of veto. The chief objective of these constitutional experiments was to hammer out a colony-wide polity in which the rural conservatives, while pressed into accepting the logic of modernization, would be enabled to dominate the territorial politics which, hitherto, had seemed the natural forum for urban black politicians. This was the strategy behind the Local Government Ordinance of 1947 which, in its overriding concern with nurturing a new African 'politics' susceptible to administrative steerage, was the clearest exposition of post-war Colonial Office thinking.

Such metropolitan concepts of West African change were soon overshadowed, however, by the riots which swept Accra in February 1948.[3] These disturbances had ostensibly arisen from grievances about the inflated price of consumer goods. A local committee had been formed to agitate over the cost of living, and its anti-inflation slogans took on a distinctly anti-European tone. In January 1948 a boycott against the big European agency houses began, and shortly afterwards the Ex-Servicemen's League had announced a prospective protest march in Accra. Permission was given by the colonial authorities for the demonstrators to proceed to the secretariat buildings, but not to the Governor's residence. On 28 February, however, the marchers headed for the old Danish fort of Christiansborg, where the Governor lived, and the security forces opened fire, killing two people and wounding five others. Amid the resulting confusion the police temporarily lost control, and there was sporadic looting and some assaults on Europeans in the city.

At first, predictably, the British officials attributed these events to Communist agitators and several leading African politicians, such as the young Kwame Nkrumah, were promptly arrested. The real import, however, which soon began to be grasped in London, was that petty consumer-capitalism in the large centres of West African population had now emerged as a coherent (if erratic) force which was capable of assuming political forms under pressure. In this context it was obvious that Whitehall's 'planning' exercises between 1945 and 1947 had been a belated adjustment to conditions as they had existed in 1939–40, but had failed to take account of the social flux in train after 1942. The shock which the Accra riots administered to the British lay in its message that urban politicians could now mobilize crowds on economic issues which, given the UK's continuing need to adjust the local economy to Sterling Area requirements, were not likely to be assuaged in the foreseeable future. Thus if the colonial authorities could not be sure of finding economic solutions to these large-scale discontents, it was necessary to find some *political* means of cooling African anxieties.

The intensifying British dilemma in the Gold Coast during 1948, however, arose from constraints in the countryside as well as in the towns. These rural difficulties were epitomized by the swollen-shoot controversy which emerged after 1943. New plantings of cocoa trees had been discouraged by the world cocoa surplus of the 1930s and subsequently by the dislocations of war. This fact alone explained the British concern with the ability of the industry after 1945 to perform its dollar-earning role for the Sterling Area. But the prospects of the cocoa-producers were also darkened by the incidence of swollen-shoot disease. Agricultural experts pointed out that, if cocoa output was to be stabilized and then increased, the infected plants had to be cut out by government teams sent into the growing regions. In the 1930s administrative inertia and political caution would have ensured that such a programme would be introduced only very tentatively. But under post-war conditions government could not contemplate a fall in its revenues and in aggregate production. The result was formidable friction between the growers, who saw their investments of capital and labour being physically destroyed, and the colonial authorities. At first sight this might appear a classic misunderstanding, with native producers resisting advanced techniques of disease control which were actually in their own interest. But the swollen-shoot controversy was another passage in the grower-government relationship which had been deeply troubled ever since the 'hold up' by African producers in 1937. By the later 1940s the cocoa farmers had a shrewd understanding that the government was being impelled to grab an ever-larger slice of agricultural profits. Therefore just as the Accra disturbances took place the British were confronted with difficulties in pursuing their maximizing objectives in the rural economy. But the colonial government could not possibly cope with unrest on the part of rural growers *and* the urban classes. Of these two nascent oppositions, it was the latter which was susceptible to the political gifts which were all that the British had available for distribution in their rucksack. Thus, if before 1948 the idea had been to tame the urban dissidents by bringing rural conservatives into play, after 1948 it was to ensure that the administration had its hands free in the countryside by timely concessions accorded the political cadres in the towns.

One of the first reactions of the Gold Coast goverment to the Accra riots was to set up the Watson Committee to investigate their immediate causes. As a result of its deliberations, the European trade cartel (the Association of West African Merchants) was disbanded. More important, however, was its other key recommendation, the establishment of a new committee to propose a further phase of constitutional reform. The fact that this new body was to be presided over by a distinguished black lawyer, Sir Henley Coussey, indicated the tactical metamorphosis which had taken place within the administration. At this stage, too, there was a change of Governor, and in August 1949 Charles Arden-Clarke was despatched by the Labour Government to the Gold Coast with explicit instructions to 'save' the colony for the British Empire.[4] Arden-Clarke subsequently played the classical role of a decolonizing proconsul, drawing together the threads of constitutional advance, political manipulation and security supervision.

The Coussey Committee delivered its recommendations soon after Arden-Clarke's arrival in the colony. It called for an elected Legislative Assembly of seventy-two members, with a few additional *ex-officio* representatives such as the Colonial and Financial Secretaries. The Executive Council, the Coussey Committee concluded, should consist only of African Ministers collectively responsible to the Governor, but individually responsible for their departments to the Assembly. It was within this new constitutional framework that the British authorities set out to order their relationships with the political classes in the Gold Coast. But constitutional reform was only one aspect of this 'new course'. It was combined with a substantial build-up of the security services, so that if the bureaucracy necessarily accepted a reduction in its direct control over affairs, it compensated for this by extending its information about, and influence upon, the factional struggle taking place amongst local elites.

For while the British were reconstructing the constitution, African politics was itself being reconstructed under the impact of Kwame Nkrumah. Prior to 1948 the only prominent political party had been the Gold Coast Convention Party (GCCP), and even this body was only a loose grouping of the established intelligentsia. The GCCP was well aware, however, that it would have to build up a wider organizational apparatus if it was to contain the popular currents now running strongly through the towns and, by the same token, impress itself upon the British as the most effective local agency with which to bargain in the new era. It was with this in mind that the GCCP leaders invited Kwame Nkrumah back from his studies in the United States to be their Secretary-General. Nkrumah, however, had ambitions which went beyond being the organizational right-hand man of what was essentially a caucus of 'big men' in Accra. He recognized, too, that this caucus, perhaps (ironically) even more than the British themselves, had been left behind by the social changes so evident since 1942. Nkrumah, therefore, soon broke away from the GCCP and set up his own party, the Convention People's Party (CPP). The CPP had, at this stage, one consistent aim: to range the school-educated urban youths, whose numbers had grown well beyond the available employment opportunities, against the GCCP 'fat cats' whose relatively conspicuous wealth made them easy targets. Nkrumah's 'Self-Government Now' slogan, paradoxically, was thus not so much an anti-colonial weapon as a ploy within this inter-African competition. Even at the time of Nkrumah's arrest and imprisonment in February 1948 the CPP had established itself as the only truly popular force amongst the Gold Coast masses; his incarceration served only to heighten Nkrumah's legitimacy as a nationalist hero. It was therefore no surprise that, when the first elections under the Coussey Constitution were held in February 1951, the CPP won a resounding victory. This was the moment of choice for British colonialism in West Africa: could a radical leader such as Nkrumah, whose public image was suffused with the glow of demands for independence, be let out of gaol, installed as Leader of Government Business and then led to cooperate in a British-supervised decolonization?

In fact there was never any doubt that Arden-Clarke would accept the implications of the CPP's success. Already by 1951 the Gold

Coast Governor had been seized by the conviction that Nkrumah himself was the only instrument capable of reconciling progressive African politics and British interests. Perhaps – although this can hardly be known – the local metropolitan officials saw the period of Nkrumah's imprisonment as a useful means of consolidating the mass popularity of a man who, at the same time, was privately attempting to signal his 'pliability' to the imperial power. What is certain is that by the end of the 1940s the British had decided to accept the logic of change in West Africa, newly confident that they could steer it in ways that preserved their own essential stake in the region. This was true of Nigeria as well as of the Gold Coast: the appointment of a new 'liberal' Governor in 1948 in the former territory, Sir John Macpherson, inaugurated a push towards the Africanization of the civil service and a consensus over constitutional reform which left the young radical elements high, dry and isolated. This also brought complications by triggering off a scramble for influence which reinforced the burgeoning Ibo–Yoruba rivalries, as well as divisions between north and south.[5] Nevertheless, British policy-makers in London and 'on the spot' had, in effect, at last identified in the West African setting a 'model' of transition-management capable of forging diverse groups into a workable system of government. This inventive confidence was to mark off British colonial policy in the first half of the 1950s from the anxious caution which had characterized the 1940s.

II RACIAL CONSOLIDATION IN SOUTHERN AFRICA

If events in British West Africa in the decade after 1945 established one pattern of political change, an altogether different pattern was emerging in southern Africa, and given the much greater weight which attached to the latter region within the continental economy, it is arguable that southern African developments were the more significant of the two. They were certainly, as we shall see, more dramatic. Our concern will chiefly be with the bonding of Southern Rhodesia, Northern Rhodesia and Nyasaland into the Central African Federation during 1953. Within five years this Federation had come to encapsulate the British dilemma in 'settler' Africa; and even when the Federation was finally abandoned at the end of 1963, Southern Rhodesia was to prolong the agony for a metropole which had ceased to have any interest in sustaining imperial responsibilities. But before setting the scene for these Central African crises it is necessary to outline the thrust of political change in South Africa, for as always, affairs north of the Limpopo were, in some respects, merely the reflected glow of the racial furnace to the south.

Although Smuts in South Africa, like Churchill in Britain, attained enormous prestige as a war leader, he too found that this did not easily translate into peace-time strength.[6] The bulk of Afrikaner opinion never identified with the war against Germany; an element of this community actively supported fascist doctrines. But even those white South Africans who supported Smuts and the war effort after 1939 soon reverted, when the conflict had ended, to a preoccupation with racial issues, making political loyalties subject to extreme volatility. The wartime expansion of industry had drawn an ever-growing proportion of the African population into urban residence and employment, boosted their incomes and created opportunities for the establishment of black trade unions. African industrial workers were keen to see these gains consolidated and extended when peace came, but found themselves forced on the defensive by post-war shortages, the dislocations endemic to a recivilianized economy and the employers' determination to roll back the wage inflation of the years after 1939. These frustrations welled up in the massive African mineworkers' strike of 1946. The scale, sophistication and prolongation of that strike reflected the emergence of a new radicalism amongst the black working class. The reactive effects on both English- and Dutch-speaking whites were profound. While the war was in progress they had accepted the necessity of a greater African presence in cities and factories without countervailing controls. But with the war ended, whites increasingly favoured exploring policies which could reassert government's ability to limit and direct change.

Smuts misread these shifting moods amongst whites, thinking that it was possible to nudge the latter into an intelligent, tactical liberalism on race questions. This optimism underlay the 'two-man act' of Smuts' post-war administration, with Jan Hofmeyr repeatedly breaking progressive ground in his speeches while the Prime Minister reassured the existing electorate by bringing his impulsive lieutenant to heel. By commissioning and publishing the Fagan Report on South African race relations, Smuts hoped to create an historic opportunity for a new departure. Its recommendations were carefully drawn up to attract moderate African opinion while avoiding a white-conservative backlash. Thus there were proposals for a tentative stabilization of African labour in the towns, for a gradual substitution of influx control by a system of labour bureaux, and for a (possible) voluntarization of the pass laws. After 1945 Afrikaner intellectuals were, in contrast, moving towards a more rigid, rather than more flexible, ideal of race relationships in the Union; they envisaged a broad programme of apartheid geared to the vertical separation of ethnic groups, and this ideology gained incisive expression in the Sauer Report.[7] Meanwhile, however, Nationalist Party strategists avoided taking any position likely to lead moderates, especially English-speakers, to rally around Smuts: the Afrikaner preference for a Republic was played down, the commitment to finance benefits for ex-servicemen was accepted and criticism of the Prime Minister was focused on his involvement in the establishment of the United Nations. In these ways the Nationalists tapped into the mainstream of white anxieties in post-war South Africa, and at the general election of 26 May 1948 they won a narrow parliamentary majority. Dr Daniel Malan succeeded Smuts as premier.

Between 1949 and 1954 the Malan government implemented the first phase of apartheid 'reform'. It is enough here to list some of its key legislative features. The old institutions of the Hertzogian era, such as the Natives Representation Council, were abolished. The Prohibited Mixed Marriages Act of 1949 meant that whites could not have Indian or Coloured spouses, as they had previously been denied black spouses. More significant was the Group Areas Act of 1950, whereby the government equipped itself with powers to demarcate urban zones for the residence of particular ethnic groups; this was a crucial element in Nationalist social engineering, since it allowed commercially successful groups, such as could be found amongst the Indian community in Durban, to be pegged back into defined suburbs. In June 1950 the Suppression of Communism Act entered the statute book, and this shortly allowed the Government not only to harass individual Communists (the party having disbanded itself in anticipation) but also to launch an attack on multi-racial trade unions.

It is perhaps surprising how relatively easily this revolution in South African life was carried through. The main reason for this quiescence, however, is clear enough: the institutions, traditions and solidarities vital for coherent oppositional politics in the Union were not sufficiently developed for the Malan ministry to be stopped in its stride. Nevertheless, there were two manifestations of anti-apartheid mobilization: the War Veterans Torch Commando and the African National Congress-led Defiance Campaign.[8] The Torch Commando was established as a focus for white-liberal protest in April 1951, and quickly acquired a mass membership. However, its essentially middle-class constituency panicked once its organized demonstrations had led to unruly clashes with the police, and the leadership became hopelessly divided when the issue was raised as to whether cooperation should be established with non-white groups in a broad-based campaign against government policy. The Torch episode accurately reflected the realities of white opposition to Malanite policies: however widely spread the liberal emotion on race questions remained, it did not go deep enough to form the basis for effective political action. Significantly, however, the Defiance movement, while African-organized, proved no more successful at pressuring the government. Beginning as a black response to the tercentennial celebrations of Jan Van Reebeck's arrival at the Cape in the seventeenth century, thousands of Africans courted arrest for flouting the pass laws. But the Nationalist regime had skilfully constructed a security apparatus for isolating and dismembering campaigns such as this, and the African National Congress offensive had a minimal effect on the progress of the apartheid-state. Indeed, the legislative momentum now reached a full flood: the Prevention of Illegal Squatting Act had self-evident aims, the Native Laws Amendment Act of 1952 narrowly defined elegibility for urban residence and the 1954 Native Resettlement Act set about evicting blacks from their accustomed homes (in the first instance of this, from western Johannesburg to a new settlement at Meadowlands). By the time of Malan's retirement in November 1954, apartheid-ideology, the brainchild above all of the Justice Minister in these years, J. W. Verwoerd, had been knit into South African life. The fact that this process ran parallel with a more secular development whereby the South African economy accentuated its regional primacy made the implications for Africans in other colonial territories both stark and complex.

While the Smuts era was drawing to a close in South Africa, the sentiment for amalgamation between the white-settler polities of Southern and Northern Rhodesia was gaining strength.[9] We noted earlier that the Southern Rhodesian Europeans had, in 1922, opted in a referendum to reject absorption into South Africa; they had done so largely because the chief economic interest groups had not been confident of making their voice heard in Pretoria. There remained the possibility of uniting in some way with Northern Rhodesia, but in the 1920s and 1930s this, too, was not uniformly attractive: it meant combining with a colony which had a vast African majority and which (unlike Southern Rhodesia) was *directly* administered by the Colonial Office, a fact which made it highly doubtful that any amalgamated entity would be accorded that full Dominion status which was the touchstone of white ambitions in Salisbury. This position changed in several critical respects after 1945. The decisive Afrikanerization of South Africa, and the Union's growing economic hegemony, made absorption into that country both more distasteful for Southern Rhodesian whites and, in the long term, more difficult to fend off. The enormous boost to the Northern Rhodesian copper industry in the war period, however, had greatly added to the cogency of locking together an English-dominated unit in Central Africa. Amalgamation of the two Rhodesias emerged as the least distressing means of achieving what was vital to the status quo: a consolidation of white power to handle the growing material and political aspirations of the Africans. These diverse political motives were superimposed upon the enormous increase in British migration to the two Rhodesias after the end of the war. Such a flow of white manpower seemingly legitimated the vision of a modern European state being carved out of the Central African bush, and imparted an aggression to white ambitions which did not diminish in the years ahead. When Dr Huggins of the United Party defeated his opponents in the Southern Rhodesian elections of September 1948, shortly after the Northern Rhodesian elections had endorsed Roy Welensky and his supporters amongst the elected 'unofficials' in that Crown Colony, it was clear that these committed, if circumspect, amalgamationists would press the British Government to take the initiative in Central African affairs.

In fact, Dr Malan's triumph in South Africa had, of itself, prompted Whitehall to review its regional responsibilities. Concern about South African expansionism had grown during the war years and intensified in its aftermath. Thus, in evaluating British policy which climaxed in the Federation-making of 1953, events must be set in the context of a British strategic tradition, stretching back to the 1870s, concerned with reinforcing structures to thwart Pretoria's authority. This tradition now meshed with the concept of multiracial 'partnership'. For if a Central African framework could be established within which rapid economic growth worked to reconcile settler ambitions *and* African material betterment, then it seemed that the potential dangers arising from the British commitment to this area (fundamentally to do with race war) could be allayed. Not only would the attractive power of South Africa have been blocked, but a model of change would have been set in motion which, unlike its West African counterpart, could be readily transposed on to the East African territories. Thus, whereas 'closer union' in the colonial context was a dirty word in Labour Party circles before the later 1940s, it subsequently took on a distinct appeal. Nevertheless, any such initiative, in order to gain acceptance in Britain, would have to have some visible regard for African interests. It was for such public relations purposes that the Labour Government after 1945, and especially the Colonial Secretary, Arthur Creech-Jones, made it clear that any Rhodesian amalgamation *pur et simple* was unacceptable, since it would have handed over local African majorities to the doubtful care of the European lobbies. Federation, not amalgamation, was the Labour Government's choice, since this would continue to give the colonial bureaucracy in Northern Rhodesia the power to bargain on behalf of Africans. Furthermore, the British were determined to see that Federation be made triangular to include Nyasaland. This desideratum partly arose from a desire to off-load the burden of the Nyasaland debt on to other shoulders than those of the metropole. But since Nyasaland was a classic 'native' state with only a marginal settler presence, its inclusion also had the advantage of equilibriating African and European power (admittedly only partially, and in a demographic rather than political sense) in the federation as a whole. Such an equilibrium was necessary if the experiment was to serve the British purpose of establishing multiracial options for the future.

The perspectives of Rhodesian settlers and British policy-makers were sufficiently close to make negotiations about Central Africa's future possible from early 1949 onwards. But meanwhile, what of African opinion in the territories concerned? There were certain differences here. In Southern Rhodesia blacks exhibited ambiguous sentiments on the federal idea. They were deeply suspicious of the direction in which any new regional combination might move, and yet such a risk still seemed preferable to the other possibility which opened up before them – that of incorporation into the Union. By contrast, the Northern Rhodesian and Nyasaland Africans were uniformly opposed to the proposals. They were well aware that the logic of federation lay in a gradual devolution of power from the metropole to local agencies, and that guarantees of 'protection' of native rights, even if written into constitutional documents, were not likely to be meaningful in the long term. African leaders, such as Harry Nkumbula in Northern Rhodesia and Hastings Banda of Nyasaland, therefore were able at this point to begin constructing political constituencies by beating the anti-federation drum. Ironically, if central African whites had taken up territorial integration not least as a means of throttling any credible African challenge to their hegemony, they only succeeded in generating racial emotions which, under the guise of political nationalism, were within a few years to bring the federation crashing down.

The first of the conferences convened to discuss territorial reform was held in early 1949 at the Victoria Falls Hotel, a venue which was to become renowned in the protracted federation-making and, later, unmaking. This conference was purely local: no Colonial Office representative was present, and Creech-Jones was careful to distance himself from the quasi-amalgamationist resolutions which emerged. In 1950, however, the Labour Government became distinctly warmer towards Huggins and Welensky. There were two reasons for this shift. Early in the year the UK general election had led to the return of the Labour Government with a much reduced majority, but Creech-Jones had lost his seat. His successor at the Colonial Office, James Griffiths, was much less sensitive to the fabian cry of 'African rights' which had been such a feature of Creech-Jones' stylized idealism. But even more important than this change of personnel in London was the deterioration in the international atmosphere, culminating in the outbreak of the Korean War. With the Cold War blowing hot, the British came under great pressure to construct serviceable, if leaky, solutions to the subsidiary problems confronting them in many parts of the world. Thus a conference of four governments (that is, the British Government, the Southern Rhodesian Government, and the colonial administrations of Northern Rhodesia and Nyasaland) was hastily convened in London during March 1951.

The chief antagonists in these proceedings were the Southern Rhodesian delegation on the one hand, pushing for a complete handover of power to a new Central African entity, and on the other the British colonial officials from Northern Rhodesia who, by stressing the precondition of African approval, tried to block a political departure which they deplored. The balance of power in this confrontation lay with the Colonial Office, and in this case with its chief representative, Andrew Cohen. Cohen projected himself as a radical on colonial reform, and had given proof of this with regard to West Africa. Certainly Huggins and Welensky were not his 'natural' allies. But the need to erect barriers against South African apartheid, and to minimize any possible call on British resources when the metropole was bending itself to anti-Soviet rearmament, had become paramount, and in Central Africa this meant doing a deal with the white-settler leaders. In talks outside the formal conference, Cohen, Huggins and Welensky established the outlines of an agreement: the settlers would accept federation instead of amalgamation, while the Colonial Office agreed that the central organs of this federal unit would have significant powers and not be made subservient to 'checks' in the different territories. The details were inevitably, at this stage, provisional. The three colonies would retain their individual constitutions, plus responsibility for 'general' African affairs, taxation and law and order. Nevertheless, there was to be a federal legislature and cabinet to which key responsibilities (defence, economic policy, foreign trade and customs and excise) would be assigned. No one territory would be able to muster an automatic majority in the federal parliament, since Southern Rhodesia was to have seventeen seats, Northern Rhodesia eleven and Nyasaland seven. The real problem was: who, under these ambiguous arrangements, was to have key control over the African populations – the territorial bureaucracies or the federal power? In the Southern Rhodesian case this distinction meant nothing; in the cases of Northern Rhodesia and Nyasaland it meant a great deal. At this point the only attempt to clarify this matter was the plan for an African Affairs Board, which would have an obligation to refer any controversial legislation to the Colonial Secretary. But quite what influence this Board might have where it mattered – in the federal arena – remained unclear.

The British Government published the Conference report in June 1951. This recognized that the African communities were opposed to its main recommendations, but the case for federation was nevertheless made out on the grounds that it would stimulate the economic advancement of the indigenous inhabitants. The British authorities were indeed drawn to federation as an economic solvent for racial tensions, but this was only one motive amongst others; strategic calculations were at least as, and probably more, important. Critics of the plan did not take long to appear. The most cogent (and ultimately proven) of these was that, under Central African conditions, no federation could survive unless it was clear where authority lay in the crucial area of 'native policy'; without any such consensus a breakdown became inevitable. But the British were being driven by too many necessities of their own to listen to such observations. The Colonial Secretary arrived in Northern Rhodesia to go through the farce of 'consulting' African opinion, and he then proceeded to the second Victoria Falls Conference, which began on 18 September. Almost immediately, however, the news came through that Attlee had called a general election in Britain, and the UK ministers reverted to posturings about African rights. Real negotiations would clearly have to be postponed until a new British Government was formed.

The Conservative Party's victory in the October 1951 elections boded well for Welensky and Huggins, and it was not long before they visited London in the hope of extracting further concessions from the new government. In fact the Colonial Secretary, Oliver Lyttelton, would not budge on three crucial aspects: he refused to substitute amalgamation for federation, resisted a unified civil service through which the Southern Rhodesians could achieve regional dominance, and insisted that some elected Africans should be present in the federal legislature. Nevertheless, Lyttelton remained firmly committed to the federation plan even when the Labour Opposition broke with the tradition of bipartisanship on colonial issues and started to attack the policy. It was from this point on that colonialism became the subject of endemic parliamentary squabbles in Westminster.[10] In April 1952 a new conference assembled at Lancaster House and endorsed the constitutional outlines which had already been defined. But the Southern Rhodesian delegation obtained several victories at this stage. African interests were to be supervised largely by specially elected members – where the elections were easily rigged – rather than nominated, while the chairman of the African Affairs Board was to be a federal Cabinet member, a fact which would clearly constrain his independence of action. Although the police and the civil service were to remain under territorial, not federal, control, the Southern Rhodesian Government now felt convinced that they could shape federation in their own image. Even one of the Africans whom Huggins had been careful to include in his negotiating team, Joshua Nkomo, saw fit to speak well, if softly, of the package. A rubber-stamping convention then took place at Carlton House Terrace throughout January 1953; ironically, the only addition at this point was the (in the end fateful) clause that not less than seven or more than nine years thence a review conference would meet to consider the workings of federation. Thus on 14 July 1953 the Rhodesia and Nyasaland Federation Act received the Royal Assent, and the Central African Federation began its short but tempestuous history.

III   KENYA: THE DEADLOCKED STATE

Between 1945 and the early 1950s, as we have seen, strategies for change were established in both western and southern Africa which appeared to have coherent rationales. In the former cases this involved growing administrative and political responsibilities for Africans, in the latter cases, in contrast, an enlargement of white power. In Kenya, the lynchpin state of East Africa, more ambiguous conditions prevailed. During the war the white-settler community had come to possess the institutional leverage they required to block any policies inimical to their privileges; this represented a great advance on the precarious position they had occupied between 1918 and 1939. At the same time, however, the European population in Kenya in the later 1940s still lacked the numbers and the accumulated capital to 'carry' the economic growth of the colony. This recipe – a privileged white minority, clinging to parastatal favours, and whose interest, because of its inherent weakness, lay in freezing, not promoting, economic transformation – was one for stagnation and racial confrontation. When Sir Philip Mitchell returned as Governor in December 1944, he knew that his fundamental task was to reconstruct a pattern of forces in which the British administration occupied a central position from which it could operate to clear the way for African progress without appearing to undermine 'European standards'.

Mitchell knew also, however, that in resuscitating the power of the colonial bureaucracy vis-à-vis the settlers, there could be no return to the pre-war situation in which the latter were kept very much on the outside of the governmental process. Instead, his ideal was to build up a process in which the administration and the unofficial European representatives could work closely together, develop a consensus and gradually find ways of grafting elements of African opinion into this general coalescence. This was the logic behind Mitchell's introduction of the 'member system' in June 1945 under which European settler-politicians undertook quasi-ministerial responsibilities. It was one of the leading white officials, Cavendish-Bentinck, for example, who became responsible for the Department of Agriculture. Mitchell set out not to defeat settler politics, but to nudge the European community into recognizing that intelligent and flexible tactics were required if they were to survive in the face of rising African expectations.[11]

The failure of Mitchell's governorship in Kenya between 1945 and 1952 has often been ascribed to a decision taken very early on following his return: to offer Jomo Kenyatta, the man who before 1939 had led the Kenya African Union (KAU) and who had himself only just come back to Kenya after spending the war years mostly in Sussex, a relatively minor position in a Native Authority rather than a place on the Legislative Council.[12] It is arguable that the radicals of the Kenya African Union – whose underground activities had carried on despite the banning of that organization in 1939 – were progressively pushed and humiliated after 1945 towards subversive action because the opportunity to co-opt Kenyatta at this stage into a mutually acceptable partnership was missed. This view, like much retrospective wisdom, no doubt has a measure of credibility, but is deeply flawed. In fact, the quick legalization of KAU after 1945 would have conflicted with what Mitchell took to be his basic priority, that of drawing European settlers into an acceptance of 'African advancement'. To influence European opinion in this way, Mitchell felt he had to prove his 'soundness' by cracking down on African radicals. Not only, therefore, did Kenyatta arrive home to find only a mere morsel of patronage awaiting him, but the security forces kept constant pressure on the KAU activists in the Nairobi townships. It was under the impact of sustained harassment that some KAU cell-members were driven to contemplate a campaign of rural terrorism as their only means of bringing pressure to bear on the colonial government.[13]

For Mitchell, African progress meant, above all, making agricultural production in the reserves (particularly in the Kikuyu districts of central Kenya) commercially viable. In this way the flow of land-hungry squatters on to the European residential tracts of the White

Highlands could be stopped, and a model for the reform of non-Kikuyu areas delineated. The political necessities of such a strategy were reinforced by the widespread belief that most reserves were facing an ecological crisis brought on by generations of traditional land culture which had dangerously eroded the soil. The years after 1945, therefore, witnessed a determined attempt by the colonial bureaucracy to improve African agricultural practices and so set the scene for a thriving rural capitalism which would leave anti-European radicals isolated in the Nairobi slums. The problem was that such a programme of rural reconstruction in African districts required an injection of resources to underpin model farm experiments and fund loans to small cultivators. But the mass of settler opinion resolutely opposed what they saw as *their* taxes being used in this – allegedly uneconomic – way; despite the fact that much government revenue came from levies on Indian incomes and from import duties levied on goods mainly for African consumption. Thus in the later 1940s colonial service officers were left to carry out rural agricultural programmes with little cash to lubricate the process. In doing so, however, they ran headlong into the forces of African peasant conservatism. African farmers deeply resented being constrained by ordinance into participating in contour-ridging, for example, when the future profits of land reform were all too likely to be cornered by the 'big men' in their midst, principally the chiefs and their kin-groups. Here was the wedge in rural colonial relationships which KAU activists were quick to identify and hammer home. Chiefs who cooperated with the district officers found that their labour force became restive under traditional discipline, while chiefs who had long harboured grievances against local British authority tapped popular support by articulating opposition to reconstruction policies. In short, it was the British drive towards improvement in the countryside which ironically created the tensions which led to the invisible meshing of rural and urban protest.[14]

This fermentation of Kikuyu discontents, also fuelled by the rash of evictions of squatters from European farms, was symbolized by the rash of Mau Mau 'oathing' ceremonies. The taking of ritual oaths, and their association with political issues, was nothing new in Kikuyuland. This was one reason why the security forces were slow to recognize the extent of rural bitterness which had set in by 1950. Later, when an Emergency had been officially declared, however, the Mau Mau oath became notorious for its symbolic elements, such as the holding of earth to the navel, the daubing of animal blood, and the (alleged) performance of sexual acts. Even European observers in Kenya with a reputation for intimate knowledge of Kikuyu society ascribed these reported practices to a disoriented lapse into 'barbarism'.[15] This failure to explore more fully the rational explanations for the outward forms of Mau Mauism reflects the psychological gulf which had come to separate Europeans and Africans in post-war Kenya.

A satisfactory explanation for Mau Mauism must begin by focusing on the complex emotions of individual Kikuyu, particularly those who were or had been normally resident in Nairobi, and who, by the later 1940s, had recognized that their quintessentially modern and material aspirations were not going to be met. The growth of education, townships and cash incomes after the mid-1930s had given rise to a petty consumerism which proceeded to smash itself on the post-war rocks of stagnant employment prospects and inflationary shortages of goods. The only solution to this impasse was to secure control of the colonial state and gear its operations to the sectional needs of predominantly Kikuyu cadres. But there was an acute dilemma implicit in such an anti-colonial revolt: it meant striking out against the source of that modernity which was, in itself, so desirable. Thus the displacement of the white man's rule was, in an important sense, also a displacement of the African mental world as it had been shaped in recent times. The traditional character of the Mau Mau oath was an attempt at collective distancing from western-colonial values, and as a means of psychological reintegration for African individuals, prior to an assault on the established colonial order. In this way unity could be forged and the complexity of motives resolved.

The evidence that initiations into the Mau Mau movement were mounting in early 1950 led the government to ban the organization in August of that year. This merely had the effect of driving the taking of oaths underground, and throughout 1951 Mau Mau became endemic in the Nairobi townships. Nevertheless, even at the time of his retirement in May 1952 Sir Philip Mitchell was convinced that the rumbling but sporadic intimidation that seemed to accompany the new movement was little more than another 'dini' (or temporary outburst of quasi-religious enthusiasms). The senior members of the bureaucracy were less convinced, and in the summer of 1952 began to organize counter-meetings of 'loyalist' Africans and to proffer 'cleansing' ceremonies for those who had been previously compelled to take oaths. This posed an acute problem for the Mau Mau leadership, since the colonial government, equipped with all its institutional panoply, was well placed to win any competition based on the mobilization of 'popular support'; the dissidents simply did not have the requisite levers to win a *political* contest. Their adoption of selective but widespread violence arose from the need to formulate the contest in ways which made the balance of opportunities more even and to regain control of popular protest which had shown disturbing signs of slipping out of its control. The campaign was inaugurated on 17 October 1952 when one of the most prominent Kikuyu 'loyalists', Senior Chief Waruhiu, was assassinated at a meeting. It was this event which shocked settlers and bureaucracy into the recognition that a major anti-colonial offensive was under way in Kenya, and that a huge security effort would be needed to bring it under control. The new Governor, Sir Evelyn Baring,[16] promptly declared an Emergency on 20 October and although the Mau Mau activists were broken as a military proposition by 1956 these special powers were retained until 1960.

The fragile stability of Kenyan society, as we have seen, was thus gravely undermined by the frustrations of school-educated Africans, particularly in the Central Province. Clearly this spiral of blunted expectations has to be set in a wider context before its full weight can be felt: the advances that other Africans were making in the Gold Coast, and the burgeoning segregationism in the south which could all too rapidly be transposed on to the eastern parts of the continent. But perhaps what stands out most prominently in this period is the failure of Kenyan Europeans, despite Mitchell's prompting, to begin evolving any strategy for local survival based on co-opting key African groups into a revamped status quo; the whites' failure, in other words, to experiment with a *new* collaborative system in which their privileges could be put on a firmer base for the future. This peculiar and self-destructive omission may be explained by the simple lack of political sophistication amongst settler communities not noted for throwing up original thinkers. But Kenyan whites remained locked into a negativist, pre-war set of attitudes in which the prime ingredient was a deep suspicion of wily British intentions as represented, above all, by the Governor of the day.[17] No doubt, too, any sensitivity to African demands was blunted by the Europeans' political gains in the war and post-war years, and the optimism as to the settlers' situation which this generated, in the same way as occurred – with rather more foundation – in British Central Africa. This prevented Kenyan whites, as a body, reaching any understanding over colonial reform with Mitchell, and thereby with Whitehall, which might have enhanced their long-term prospects. As it was, the declaration of the Emergency was a reluctant confession by the settlers that African resistence to authority had escalated to the point where UK intervention became necessary. From this moment on settler power was a broken reed, and the initiative lay with the civil and military representatives of the metropole. Paradoxically, the chief contribution of Mau Mau to Kenyan decolonization was not to break British rule, but to reconsolidate the UK's hold over recalcitrant expatriate communities just at the point when metropolitan interests were beginning to question the value of the whole colonial enterprise.

PART IV 1954–65

6.   Order and Chaos: Patterns of Decolonization in French and Belgian Africa

THIS introductory outline of European decolonization has, up to this point, discussed African developments solely with reference to colonies which were either directly ruled by British administrations as Crown Colonies, or were self-governing entities within the British Empire-Commonwealth (the latter cases being those of South Africa and Southern Rhodesia). This by-passing of French, Belgian and Portuguese Africa is glaring given the vast physical extent of the territories involved, and to a somewhat lesser extent, their significant population sizes. The omission, however, is explained by the focus of our study: the dilemmas posed by social and political change were defined earlier and with a much greater degree of sharpness in British Africa. In the Portuguese dependencies, indeed, such a gradual destabilization did not become detectable until after 1960, and did not become acute until after 1970; our brief treatment of this is left until Part V. It was during the 1950s, nevertheless, that French and Belgian colonialism became vulnerable to those forces of change which had long been visited upon their British counterparts. The three significant components of this story which require our attention are events respectively in French West Africa, Algeria and the Belgian Congo. A certain logic attaches to this ordering: in French West Africa political development remained under tight metropolitan control; in Algeria (despite the scale of the war fought between the French and their revolutionary opponents) power was ultimately transferred without subjecting the social fabric to strains it could not bear; while it was the Belgian Congo which came nearest to fulfilling the European nightmare of a decolonization-gone-wrong, not so much because of the number of casualties involved (the bloodshed of the Algerian conflict was far worse) but because the existing institutional frame was profoundly traumatized in the process.

In this context it is worth remarking the irony that the French Republics (the Fourth giving way to the Fifth in the crisis of 1958) presided over one decolonization, or rather set of decolonizations, in West Africa which was a model of carefully constructed consensus, and another, that of Algeria, in North Africa in which the scar-line between the old and the new regimes was amongst the most pronounced in modern transfers of power; it was not until the early 1980s, helped by the election of a Socialist to the French Presidency, that Franco-Algerian relations showed signs of shading into normalcy. The conclusion which emerges from this is that the scope of drawing comparisons between French, British or Belgian styles of decolonization, with the differences being determined by the precepts and tactics of the decolonizing powers themselves, is actually very circumscribed. The enormous range of decolonization experiences was rooted, above all, in the disparity of the local situations. Much of what has been written on French and British approaches to end of empire – with emphases on the former's adherence to 'assimilation', and the latter's concern with the Westminster Model – is at best of tenuous relevance, since this analysis relates to the literary flourishes of officials in Paris and London, not to the real course of events at the periphery. Faced with identical colonial situations, each of the European decolonizers would almost certainly have taken the same decisions and ended up with the same results. But, as we shall see, the situations were rarely alike, and the results ranged from a smooth placidity to profound racial alienation.

I   FRENCH WEST AFRICA:
THE MANAGEMENT OF DECOLONIZATION

So far in this study of European decolonization we have discussed West African developments without touching on the great French possessions in that region. This is largely because, prior to the 1950s, the degree of change occurring in these territories was limited compared to neighbouring colonies. Before the Second World War they had been grouped in a Federation of French West Africa (FFWA), but this had arisen as a fiscal convenience, not as a prelude to greater metropolitan investment.[1] Furthermore, however large the physical extent of such entities as Volta and Dahomey, their populations were relatively sparse; Nigeria alone was bigger in this respect than the whole FFWA put together. Certainly nationalism amongst the *indigenes* had only a very tenuous lodgement before 1950, and even during the ensuing decade was refracted through a prior loyalty to the French metropole. In the end, independence was achieved with remarkable rapidity, applying throughout the FFWA by the end of 1960; but this independence was of a qualitatively different kind from that which had evolved in British West Africa. It is the reasons for this distinction which, above all, need to be elucidated.

As a preliminary, however, it is necessary to dwell briefly on the 1940s, since it would be erroneous to portray these years as ones of complete immobilism in French West African affairs. Between 1944 and 1946 some reforms were implemented in the eight territories which made up the FFWA. The groundwork for these tentative political innovations had been laid at the Brazzaville Conference in January 1944, the chief purpose of which had been to provide a display of Franco-African solidarity for American eyes. But at Brazzaville the French authorities made sure of balancing the effusive language of 'rights' with an affirmation that, given the assimilationist principles of French colonialism whereby metropolitan civil and political status was open to all who met certain educational requirements, independence for colonies was neither a necessary nor desirable destination. Predictably, the restricted franchises and collegial structures which the French knit into their wartime African reforms were hardly likely to affect the status quo one way or the other. Afterwards, during the frantic French constitution-making in the immediate aftermath of the war, there were proposals for the real autonomy of colonial governments within the framework of the new French 'Union'; but when the constitution of the Fourth Republic was finalized in 1946, neither the Federal administration in the FFWA capital of Dakar, nor the constituent parts of that association, were accorded meaningful juridical discretion of any kind. It is often argued that, as a consequence, local politicians had little option but to grab at the bit-part role offered to them under the Union arrangements as deputies in the National

Assembly in Paris. Thus as a political class sprang up to operate the new electoral mechanisms, its leading figures were whisked off to the metropole, where they inevitably allied themselves with one or other of the major French parties. This cut the ground from under the feet of any authentic indigenous nationalism throughout FFWA. Still, it must be considered most unlikely that the African political entrepreneurs concerned saw this as particularly regrettable; the spoils of direct participation in the factional intrigue of the Fourth Republic were much greater than any which could have been extracted from the alternative arenas in Dakar, Abidjan or Cotonou.

African politicians in the FFWA, nevertheless, had a common interest in cooperating to drive up the prices they could impose on metropolitan ministries for their tiny, but useful, bundles of votes. It was with this end in view that an African political congress was held at Bamako during October 1946.[2] But the French Communist Party, with which most FFWA deputies were associated, had so dominated the arrangements for this meeting that African protégés of the Socialist Party, such as Leopold Senghor, absented themselves from it. This merely represented the reality that French party factionalism in the Fourth Republic, for all its own fissiparities, was a more coherent force than the African organizations with which it came into contact: the former was bound to swallow the latter whole. An equilibrium evolved in which African politicians were happy to syphon-off cash from the metropole, and use some of this money to reward their domestic supporters; such funds were small in relation to the norms of political profiteering in Paris, but quite adequate in the narrow political worlds of FFWA to keep clientages happy. However, this stability was upset in 1947 when the Communist Party was elbowed out of the governing coalition of the Republic, since the African deputies connected with it could not afford the ascetic habits of opposition. The political disturbances which broke out subsequently in French West Africa, and particularly in the Ivory Coast, therefore were not so much 'anti-colonial' in nature as protests by assimilated elites at their displacement within the system of metropolitan patronage. Furthermore, the propensity of political parties within the various territories of FFWA to merge on a regional basis, most outstandingly in the *Rassemblement Démocratique Africaine* (RDA), was also given a significant boost, not by any nationalist impulses, but by this modest struggle to maintain access to the corridors of power in Paris. A new equilibrium was finally achieved in

1950 when M. Houphouet-Boigny, the RDA leader from the Ivory Coast, succeeded in eliciting a new patron in the shape of the prominent Radical, François Mitterand, after which the RDA as a whole tramped happily out of the Communist bloc in the Assembly – a most fortuitous move in the light of the future direction of French politics, and one which confirmed Houphouet-Boigny's prestige for decades ahead.[3] It was not least through astute participation in the making and breaking of successive French governments by factional manoeuvring in the confused years of the first half of the 1950s, when the Indo-China war climaxed and the Algerian conflict began, that the FFWA deputies in the Assembly were able to extract a stream of concessions, culminating in the first major constitutional advance in French West Africa, the *loi cadre* of 1956.

It was the *loi-cadre* which marked the opening of a hectic four years which were to see the break-up of the FFWA as a unit and independence granted to the separate territories. But first some salient characteristics of French West African society must be pointed out.[4] Perhaps the most crucial of these was the small size of the school-educated classes. In the Gold Coast and Nigeria these cadres were sufficiently large to constitute a distinct (if fractious) class, with mobile expectations generating an intense anti-colonialism. But in French West Africa, which had been essentially isolated from the mainstream of events during most of the Second World War, educational facilities had not been comparably expanded. There were a few well-known secondary schools (above all, William Ponty High School in Dakar) which catered for the sons of 'big men', but there was not that widening base of schooled males which was emerging in British colonies in the region. The slim shape of FFWA elites thus made it much less costly for the colonial authorities to keep them plied with jobs and patronage, and so made it unnecessary for these cadres to resort to anything resembling mass politics (such as that practised, for example, by the CPP in the Gold Coast) to obtain their wants.

The comparative levels of educational provision between French and British dependencies in West Africa was only one reflection of profounder economic contrasts. None of the FFWA territories embraced a mature producer-class on quite the scale of the Gold Coast cocoa-growers. Thus the opportunities for personal advancement outside the ambit of the civil service were very restricted, so that aspiring individuals could not afford to alienate the local French

administration; in general, the FFWA political classes were occupa-
tionally tied to the colonial bureaucracy to a high degree. To an even
greater extent than in British West Africa, the indigenization of the
civil service, and the consolidation of salary scales, could be modulated to soothe social anxieties when necessary. The 1950 decree, for
example, which assured African functionaries that promotion would
bring with it a European-style income, reinforced the status quo in
these territories at a crucial juncture. In short, the issues which
dominated elite-government relations were found to be resolvable
without recourse to nationalism *à la* Nkrumah. This was just as well
for the local political cliques, since they would have found it virtually
impossible to build popular territory-wide parties of the kind which
existed in British colonies; in the FFWA the discontinuities between
the coastal belts, where western-type activities had made some
impact, and the 'traditional' interior, with its vast tracts of arid
agriculture, were too sharp to allow anything other than a painfully
slow approach to national integration. African political parties in
French-ruled sub-Saharan regions, therefore, did not articulate their
objectives in terms of constitutional independence, since to have done
so would have been an economic and sociological nonsense.

The absence of volatile nationalisms in French West Africa,
however, must also be related to the massive increase in metropolitan
public investment after 1945. Previously it had been axiomatic that
expenditure had to be funded through the local budget. After the
Second World War it was accepted that the metropolitan exchequer
had to play a part in stimulating local development, and in 1947 a
*Fonds d'Investissement et de Développement Economique et Social des Territoires
d'Outre-Mer* (FIDES) was created.[5] The motives for this were analogous to those behind the UK's programmes in this field: in particular,
the concern to boost commodity production in areas where metropolitan buyers would not have to disgorge scarce dollars to obtain their
wants. Between 1943 and 1957 $542.5m were invested through
FIDES in FFWA, a sum which in per capita terms easily exceeded
the level of British expenditure in West Africa. The bulk of this
money was directed towards the coastal units of Senegal, the Ivory
Coast and Dahomey, and proportionately less to the interior territories of Soudan, Upper Volta, Niger and Mauritania. Indeed, a very
high percentage of the funds were concentrated around the few big
commercial centres in the south, equipping Dakar, Conakry, Abidjan
and Porto Nuovo, for example, with modern harbour facilities. Both

between and within these regions, therefore, the effect was to heighten the existing economic polarities in French West Africa. Development was driven by the locomotive of French public investment, and this made any serious clash between African elite interests and French officialdom inconceivable.

It was French public expenditure in West Africa which was, in fact, instrumental in the eclipse of the federal linkage between the constituent parts of the FFWA, such that ultimately power was transferred to a multiplicity of units rather than to a centralized whole. 'Neo-colonial' interpreters of French decolonization regard this eventuality as a deliberate attempt to balkanize the region, on the grounds that French influence would be easier to sustain in the long term if the territorial elements were divided and weak than if the Federation were allowed to mature any further.[6] Metropolitan strategists, however, might equally have opted to *reinforce* Federal institutions through the decolonizing era as their best collaborative bet for the future. Probably the dismemberment of the FFWA is best explained with reference to the purpose of its original establishment, which was to assist the various territories to balance their collective budget. Once FIDES had reduced these fiscal constraints, this rationale had disappeared. Furthermore, the various territorial elites wanted to ensure that French capital was disbursed in ways that fitted with their sectional needs; they did not trust a Federal authority based in Dakar which might prove susceptible to advice that balanced growth required spreading the cash reasonably uniformly across the local economy. Indeed, if there was one means by which the stable relationship of African politicians and French power *could* have been disrupted after 1947, it was by FIDES pumping in money using methods geared to fresh patterns of development rather than to preserving the existing structures of authority and collaboration; but there was never any real risk that such dispassionate economic policies would be allowed to prevail.

Despite all these constraints, the *loi-cadre* of 1956 did represent a fundamental decentralization of power from Paris to French West African colonies. The Territorial Assemblies were to be elected on a universal suffrage and by a single-college system. Their responsibilities were extended to cover public services, previously the sole concern of the French administration. But the chief reform lay in the executive sphere: the territories were to have African-led governments in which ministers had direct charge of portfolios, and were collectively responsible to the Assemblies. This brought their constitutions into line with those prevailing in British West Africa. But why had the French Government taken such an initiative, when, as we have seen, there was no nationalist 'front' in a position to exert any crushing pressure? The Fourth Republic minister responsible, the Socialist Gaston Deferre, explained it in terms of winning African goodwill *before* constitutional demands emerged to polarize metropolitan-colony relationships. This was no doubt true up to a point, since Deferre, seeing developments in British colonies, was well aware that reform could not be put off indefinitely. But the *loi-cadre* probably derived from the more general consideration that at last the Franco-African mechanisms of economic cooperation had attained a strength whereby they could underpin political change. The UK had reached such a point in the Gold Coast at the end of the 1940s; France, with bigger tasks of domestic reconstruction to carry out, did not arrive at this juncture with regard to her African possessions until the mid-1950s. The fact that in 1956 it was convenient for the French Government to win some credit in Africa amidst its growing embarrassments in Algeria may also have been a factor. Probably as significant as this last point, however, was the emergence of Houphouet-Boigny as a local politician whom the Paris authorities felt they could trust and who had attained a pivotal position within the region through his power-base in the Ivory Coast. However fair-weather other indications might have been, it is suggestive that British and French decolonizers never took a major step towards transferring power until they had identified a leader capable of dominating the post-colonial settlement. By 1956 Houphouet-Boigny had become sufficiently integrated into the ways of the Fourth Republic, not least through his friendship with François Mitterand, to be cast for this role; and under General de Gaulle, who assumed power in France during the crisis of July 1958, the Ivory Coast leader became the man whose opinion on African questions was most clearly listened to in the Elysée Palace.

Had the Fourth Republic survived, it is probable that the *loi-cadre* system would have provided the framework for French West African change for at least the next few years: but inevitably Franco-African relations were drawn into the ramifications of the Gaullist takeover. In formulating his 1958 constitution, de Gaulle created a new entity which he termed, with characteristic grandiloquence, the French Community. This was to be a federalized arrangement, but one composed of bilateral dealings between the separate territories and France. The government in Paris was to hold substantial reserve powers, above all regarding defence and foreign policy. In this way French West Africans were presented with a prospect of continued devolution of power, but within the context of a metropole-dominated federation setting real limits to local autonomies. It is difficult to penetrate de Gaulle's thinking in pushing through this change. It is likely that the general was already convinced by the time of his return to power that the restoration of French prestige in the world required decolonization; and the reforms in French West Africa were explorations of a solution which could not yet be applied in Algeria.[7] But perhaps equally relevant at this stage was the coming of Ghana's independence in March 1957, which in the succeeding months had a larger impact on continental politics in Africa than had been generally anticipated. Nkrumah's new-found charisma held out the prospect that English-speaking West Africa would continue to hog the leadership of the region. Thus somehow French West African dependencies had now to be kitted out in constitutional clothing which did not look too fusty in comparison with their British (and ex-British) neighbours.

The French Community provisions of the 1958 constitution as they applied to West African colonies were put to a referendum in the individual territories. In doing so, de Gaulle presented the African governments with a straight choice: they could participate in the new arrangements and ensure the continuance of French economic, political and military aid, or opt immediately for full independence with the consequence that all such flows would be abruptly terminated. This was the crucial test of just how strong were the foundations of French informal hegemony that had been laboriously constructed since 1945. As electoral exercises, these referenda were (unlike their British West African counterparts) not far from pure farce; the existing administrations were usually in a position to rig whatever result they desired. Thus all the territories, with one exception, accepted de Gaulle's offer of Community and cash. The exception was provided by Sekou Touré of Guinea, who used the campaign to denounce the Gaullist plans as a new version of western imperialism. In effect, the Guinean leader was gambling that he could gain enormous prestige from this snubbing of the French patriarch, while negotiating new allies both locally (particularly in the form of Kwame Nkrumah, who was now awash in anti-imperialist rhetoric) and internationally (above all, the Soviet Union). This proved to be a gross miscalculation of what such alternative patrons had to offer in the late 1950s, but such illusions were rife before the Congo crisis in the early 1960s revealed the limits of Soviet interest in African affairs. Sekou Touré's gambit was to prove disastrous for the economy of Guinea, since the French Government rigorously applied its threat to cut off all forms of assistance. But it nevertheless served to highlight the fact that the constitutional realities within the new-mint Community afforded something much less than substantive political (let alone economic) independence.

Guinea's bankrupt fate is ironic in so far as within two years de Gaulle changed his West African stance once again, this time offering untrammelled independence without financial penalty; indeed, France's increasingly powerful position within the Common Market in Europe meant that she was in a position to direct a growing volume of aid to this region. This turnaround in metropolitan policy between 1958 and 1960 is partly attributable to local factors. Guinean independence, for example, made it hard for African leaders in the Ivory Coast and Senegal to fend off criticisms that they were Gaullist stooges. Even Houphouet-Boigny, who liked nothing better than serving as a minister of metropolitan France, ultimately had to recognize that his political credibility at home hinged on ending the ambiguities of the Ivory Coast's position vis-à-vis the old metropole. Furthermore, de Gaulle must have been conscious that, as Nigeria was brought to the point of independence in 1960, it was the ex-British colonies in West Africa who seemed more than ever likely to acquire the political and economic leadership of the region, unless something was done to alter the image of the Francophone territories. However, it is hard to avoid the conclusion that, whatever force may be ascribed to these considerations, by 1960 French decisions south of the Sahara were really a reflection of developments in Algeria, and that de Gaulle was resolving the minor issues of West Africa before facing up to the larger challenge of cutting short the bitter civil war in the North. It is to these Algerian dilemmas that we must shortly turn.

Before doing so, however, mention must be made of the effect which the conclusion of the Treaty of Rome in 1957, and the early phases in the history of the EEC, had on French orientations. One of the crucial attractions for France of the EEC experiment, helping to offset the manifest risks involved, had from the start been the prospect of involving German (and Benelux) capital in the development of the overseas franc zone on terms which continued to favour French trade. In the first six years of the EEC's existence, before any fully fledged Common Agricultural Policy came into operation, it was all the more vital for France to extract benefits from the association in this way. Certainly de Gaulle proved ready to stretch German and Dutch patience to the limit in demanding exclusive preferences for French colonies and ex-colonies within the EEC regime. Thus it was often said at the time that the EEC's formation essentially represented a deal between French agriculture and German industry; here was one way, however, that de Gaulle could show French manufacturers that there was something in it for them as well. But for de Gaulle power-politics was the root of all action, and this consideration was probably paramount. One of the objectives of his strategy, therefore, was to switch the economic leadership in West African development from the Anglophone to the Francophone countries, so that France consistently undermined any separate EEC agreement with Nigeria. Indeed, de Gaulle and his successors were remarkably successful in entrenching a privileged position for the franc zone within the trading arrangements of the EEC which continues to this day – with big spin-offs for French contractors. Therefore, by reinforcing French confidence about the solidity of their economic links with parts of Africa, the Caribbean and the Pacific, the shaping of the EEC after 1957 greatly eased the management of decolonization. But even more significant than this was the growing confidence in Paris by 1960 that France was in a position to determine the course of west European affairs. The euphoria this produced was understandable; after all, no French leadership had been in this position for a century or more. The steeling of French official nerves when faced with the climax of the most severe of all their decolonization challenges, that of the Algerian war, was of enormous importance, since without it events might have taken a radically different course.

II   ALGERIA: THE ROAD TO EVIAN

In July 1954 the French Prime Minister, Pierre Mendès-France, had (as we saw earlier) severed the French entanglements in Indo-China.

In large part, this decision reflected a new determination in Paris to concentrate metropolitan resources on resuscitating French power in Europe. The rapid recovery of Western Germany after 1947 lay behind this shift of priorities; certainly it made the exhaustion of French *matériel* and manpower in the paddy-fields of east Asia appear as a comedy of strategic errors. It was, therefore, an ironic piece of misfortune that, immediately after this withdrawal from Asia, a nationalist rebellion broke out in Algeria on 1 November 1954. The war in North Africa was to last for eight years; in fighting it the French exchequer did not, as in the latter part of the Indo-Chinese conflict, benefit from American subsidies, and among its political ramifications was to be the collapse of the French Fourth Republic. It was not until mid-1962 that Pierre Mendès-France's vision of France freed from colonial burdens and able to devote her national energies to internal renovation came at last within grasp; ironically, by 1962 this grasp was not to be that of Mendès-France's left-radicalism, but of a rampant Gaullist conservatism. How had this come about?

Algeria was always accorded a special place in French colonial thinking because of its proximity to the European mainland.[8] This was also true, logically enough, of France's other North African dependencies in Tunisia and Morocco. But although the issue of decolonization in these latter two instances did contribute to the fractures of metropolitan politics in the early 1950s, and on occasions helped to bring down governments, the reverberations were limited: Tunisia and Morocco both became self-governing states in March 1956.[9] Algeria was different because of the presence of one million white settlers (mostly French, but also including large Italian and Maltese segments) who were known locally as *pieds noirs*. These Europeans had been established in Algeria since the late 1870s, when the wine-making industry had boomed; as such, this settler society was rooted in place even more firmly than comparable British communities in, say, Kenya or Rhodesia. The *pieds noirs* were also distinctive in that they included a significant working-class and petit-bourgeois element which, particularly in the Bab el Oued section of Algiers, lived intermixed, if not intermarried, with the Arab majority. Such groups did not have skills or capital to afford them likely alternatives to their Algerian existence; it was inevitable that they would fight to the last suitcase to retain their privileges if any threat emerged to the status quo.

The basic causes of Algerian-Arab discontents which climaxed in the outbreak of November 1954 will not be outlined here, since they were fundamentally the same as in other colonial situations: a growing population, stagnant agriculture, a flow of migrants to the towns with consequent unemployment, and a wartime cadre of school-educated *indigenes* whose aspirations were suddenly pinched and maimed by post-war realities. In 1945 an attempted nationalist coup centred on the village of Setif was crushed with several thousand fatal casualties (the exact numbers being hotly disputed), many of them the result of an indiscriminate 'pacification' by the French forces.[10] The Setif massacres scarred Franco-Algerian understanding, and probably swung the odds, even at this early stage, against any ordered transition to majority self-government. This was precisely the period, however, when French governments were keen to construct at least the façade of liberal constitutionalism in their colonial possessions; they could hardly do otherwise when the British were serenading themselves out of India with such aplomb. Thus a new Algerian constitution was drawn up in 1947 granting greater civil and religious liberties to Arabs. But this legislation required a two-thirds majority in the National Assembly in Paris, which was never forthcoming. There was probably no significant colonial entity whose internal problems received *less* intelligent and sensitive analysis than French Algeria in the late 1940s and early 1950s.

There were two forces which blocked any rational policy-making on Algerian questions.[11] The first of these was the power of the settler (or *colon*) lobby. Thus, unlike in the British case, these expatriates were directly represented in the French parliamentary system, and did not have to rely on spokesmen whose actual commitment to their cause might break under pressure. But *colon* opportunism was also assisted by the special character of Fourth Republic politics, fragmented as it was into a multiplicity of parties and factions so that no coalition lasted very long before its pieces were rearranged in some new, unstable order. This legislative charade has been described as 'mutual neutralization';[12] no Prime Minister was ever in a position to develop constructive solutions to political problems because of the welter of contradictory commitments made in the course of coalition-making. Under certain circumstances the necessities of national power raised this road-block. Thus in 1954 inter-group rivalries were put into suspended animation while Mendès-France dirtied his hands negotiating peace in Indo-China, but they snapped back into place once the surgery was completed. Such exceptions apart, any parliamentary interest group which wished to torpedo legislation was almost invariably able to do so. This was particularly so in the case of the Algerian lobby which, along with the wine interests, was one of the two largest, best connected factions in the Assembly.

The second force which helped to sandbag-in the Algerian status quo was the quasi-autonomy possessed by French officialdom *in* Algeria. Fundamentally, because of the weak legislative fabric in Paris, French governments abdicated power to the civil service. This actually assisted efficient policy-formation in some areas, as it did with regard to west European integration. But in the colonial sphere the result was a thorough negativism, if only because the Colonial Ministry itself was not much more than a cypher in its dealings with a bureaucracy in Algiers tightly interwoven with *pieds noirs* interests. In short, the operational character of the Fourth Republic meant that decolonization, with its need for firmness and consistency of action, was a peculiarly difficult exercise for French government, and nowhere was this more true than in the case of Algeria.

Curiously, the conclusion of the Indo-China war in 1954 made analogous initiatives in Algeria, especially in the crucial early phases of the rebellion, even less likely than might otherwise have been the case. Pierre Mendès-France had been allowed his moment of glory; the majority in the Assembly were determined to prevent him winning another prize. Mendès-France, indeed, felt bound to soften the resentment towards him by asserting that French rule in Algeria was immutable in ways that had not applied in Indo-China. Even this did not save his government, which was defeated in a parliamentary vote on 5 February 1955. Before the end of his premiership, however, Mendès-France established the two frames of French policy in Algeria which his successors invariably maintained: the massive build-up of a military effort aimed at containing the rebel *Front de Libération Nationale* (FLN), and an approach to political and social reform. More precisely, by December 1954 Mendès-France had despatched an additional 20,000 troops to Algeria, and Jacques Soustelle, a liberally inclined Gaullist, had been appointed Governor-General. The intellectual logic of these tactics seemed cogent enough: the pacification of the rebellion would open up an area of opportunity within which imaginative reform could create more enduring foundations for *Algérie Française*. In fact the policy of pacification consistently aborted the policy of reform. It was the incompatibility, not the interaction, of these aims which, in retrospect, seems to have been inevitable. In part this was so because of the settler-power and bureaucratic subterfuge we have already described. But the contradiction went deeper than this. For the military build-up soon grafted the army into the nexus of *colons* and administrators. When the politicians did at last come round to the view that a French withdrawal from Algeria was essential, the process was contorted by the difficulties of disengaging the army from its Algerian affections.

Indeed, the outstanding feature of the 1954–8 period was the extent to which the French military cadres came to identify with *Algérie Française*.[13] Many officers, particularly at senior levels, went to Algeria with the dry taste of Dien Bien Phu in their mouths. It was widely believed among this group that the Indo-Chinese war had been eminently winnable but for the corrupt and vacillating politicians at home. Some were veterans of the debacle of 1940; many were diverted, too, to the Suez campaign in 1956. In all these instances the lesson had been the same: a successful military solution hinged on exerting whatever pressures were required to keep the ministry in Paris up to the task when the going got rough. For these soldiers, Algeria was the last place where a line between military honour and political cowardice could be drawn. They were therefore determined to crush any hint of reform or negotiation in Algeria. Furthermore, their ability to smother initiatives in this way was boosted by the public adulation accorded, above all, to the mottle-grey-clad paratroopers after 1954. The Fourth Republic politicians did not act to deflate this enthusiastic hysteria because it was seen to be healing the wounds inflicted by the defeat in Asia. In fact this omission was in the end to seal the fate of the regime.

The inherent difficulty facing any French government trying to strike a balance between pacification and reform in Algeria was shown by the events following the advent of Guy Mollet's premiership in January 1956. As a Socialist he held a progressive stance on Algerian affairs, and one of his first acts was to appoint General Georges Catroux, whose colonial record was distinctly liberal, as both Governor-General and Resident-Minister in Algiers. At the same time he announced his intention to make a personal visit to North Africa, a discreet signal that henceforth Algerian policy would be brought more firmly under the wing of the premier. But when Mollet arrived in Algiers on 16 February the *pieds noirs* staged a large-scale demonstration and insisted on the reversal of Catroux's appointment. That night Catroux was dismissed and the post of Resident-Minister was given to Robert Lacoste, an orthodox conservative. It is said that Mollet had gone to Algiers with the image of fat-cat, anti-socialist settlers fixed in his mind; when he found that the *pieds noirs* crowds were made up of ordinary French workers he decided to defend them in the face of adversity. Whatever the veracity of this version, the rest of Mollet's premiership witnessed a tightening-up of the French military effort, culminating in the Special Powers Law of 16 March 1956.

Meanwhile, what of the course and character of the war? FLN tactics from the beginning were essentially hit-and-run. Periodically the incidents were bloodily spectacular, as in the environs of Phillipville on 2 August 1955 when FLN regulars incited the killing of 32 Arabs and 71 settlers, and immediate Army reprisals resulted in the deaths of 1200 alleged 'rebels' – although most of the latter victims were undoubtedly innocent by-standers. But such episodes were not, in their scale, typical. More broadly, FLN objectives were threefold. First, they set out to break the propensity of the Arab community to cooperate with French authority, with pro-French *cadis* (village heads) as a prime target. Consequently the FLN killed more fellow Algerians than Frenchmen during a war which, like most late-colonial conflicts, arose from internal, as much as external, factors. Second, the FLN sought to link up its district military commands, or *wilayas*, into a national network. Third, an attempt was made to maintain a supply route across the Moroccan border. By 1957 the FLN had made variable progress on all three fronts. But by then, too, certain strategic constraints had clarified. Whereas in Indo-China the Viet Minh had been able to carve out secure rural bases from which to launch large-scale offensives, the FLN could not operate in such a 'regular' fashion even in the vicinity of its strongholds in the Aurès mountains. Already by the end of 1955 the French had 400,000 troops in Algeria, most of them draftees engaged on *quadrillage*, or protecting the villages of rural Algeria, while crack para-formations pursued active FLN units. Frustrated at their own inability to obtain prestigious military successes, the FLN leaders at the Soummam Congress in September 1956 decided on a new strategy, for if the Viet Minh had not been able to strike at the heartland of French power around Saigon, their Algerian counterparts were better placed to penetrate the colonial defences in the city of Algiers.

The battle of Algiers, in which the FLN carried out bombing attacks on favourite *pieds noirs* haunts, assassinated 'loyalist' Arabs, and sought to bring the local metropole to a standstill, gained momentum in the end-months of 1956. The dense Moslem population and intricate street lay-out provided the FLN with perfect ground for urban guerrilla activities. These activities were geared to triggering such reprisals and counter-reprisals between Arabs and Europeans as to swamp the traditional accommodations of colonial rule with racial antagonisms; for the FLN knew very well that nationalism without racialism was an empty shell. In this sense, Robert Lacoste's decision in early 1957 to bring the para-units, led by General Jacques Massu, into the city and to give them almost *carte blanche* to break terrorism, marked not only a victory for the *pieds noirs*, who had been demanding better protection, but also for the FLN, who saw it as broadening the interface of Franco-Algerian friction. Massu effectively gave both groups what they wanted. Combining military and police powers, he masterminded a massive operation in which the pursuit of relevant facts through the internment, torture and sometimes murder of suspects was a necessary element. By October 1957 the level of FLN activity in Algiers had been cut to a minimum, and the city subsequently remained calm until early 1961, when it was the turn of the *pieds noirs* to try terror tactics. In the short months of its duration, however, the battle of Algiers encapsulated the dilemmas and brutalities of decolonization more powerfully than any comparable situation of modern times; it was this city trauma, rather than the prolonged rural struggle which dominated the rest of the war, which made Franco-Algerian reconciliation psychologically impossible for almost two decades after independence was finally achieved.

Although some semblance of peace returned to Algiers at the end of 1957, the wider Algerian stalemate seemed more immovable than ever. If the FLN had hoped that French metropolitan opinion would react against Massu's ruthless methods, that some deeply rooted principle of liberal humanism in French society would be evoked as news of police misdemeanours filtered through to the mainland, they were disappointed. There was an organized protest movement which gained momentum at this stage, led largely by the (small) left-inclined press and finding recruits amongst youth, professionals and intelligentsia. But this support was fragmentary at best. Even the Communist Party did not take up the cause of 'civil rights' in Algiers, and it certainly never attacked the actual conduct of the war, because it could not afford to clash with the anti-Arab sentiments of the mass of French workers; this was, after all, a period when economic expansion was bringing many thousands of North African immigrants into mainland French cities. But in fact a subtle transformation was at work throughout French life which, in the end, was to create a milieu in which Algerian decolonization became feasible. After mid-decade the old, pre-war culture of France, with its emphasis on the 'small man' (of which the *pieds noirs* were classic embodiments), and its overriding preoccupation with the defence of established patterns of life, gave way to a new concern with efficient management, new technology and the rationalization of industrial patterns; whereas colonialism had always had an honoured place within the traditional value-system, it had no relevance in an emerging social world whose criteria – geared, not least, to new middle classes very different from the old *haute bourgeoisie*, with its stake in the army and colonial administration – were essentially functional and commercial. By 1957–8 this evolution of attitude was giving rise to a sense (rarely expressed with clarity), not that the war was morally wrong or militarily unwinnable, but that the benefits of victory simply did not merit the huge expenditures involved. Here was the authentic voice of European decolonization. It was a voice which did not blend with, and was considerably more muted than, the shrill entreaties with which the army and settlers in Algiers called for the continued sacrifice of blood and treasure. It was amidst this cacophony of different sounds that in May 1958 the French Republic cracked apart and General de Gaulle, that master of political mood-music, returned to power. Thus in Britain the decolonization sequence never threatened the stability of any government administration, and led to the resignation of just one (middle-ranking) Cabinet Minister; in France the Algerian imbroglio smashed one form of parliamentary democracy and introduced another which, at least in its early stages, fell not far short of a quasi-dictatorship.

The end phase of the Fourth Republic had been inaugurated on 8 February 1958 when the French Air Force strafed a Tunisian village allegedly harbouring FLN activists. Many casualties had resulted and an impassioned debate followed in the United Nations. The British and Americans, concerned to damp down Mediterranean tensions, stepped in with a compromise settlement which the Tunisian and French governments accepted. But the French premier, Félix Gaillard, by bowing to this 'Anglo-Saxon' pressure, effectively sacrificed his own position in the Assembly, and he resigned on 16 April. The usual intrigue of ministry-making followed. But, suggestively, the Algerian lobby now failed to influence the selection of premier, and it was Pierre Pflimlin, who was on record as having recommended talks with the FLN, who formed a government which included in its Cabinet not one recognized champion of *Algérie Française*. This was the moment of truth for the French Army in Algeria: either the Republic would impose on it yet another humiliating colonial defeat, or the Republic had to be forced to be true to *Algérie Française*. Meanwhile the Gaullists waited to seize their chance of regaining power, although whether the general was to do so on the coat-tails of the soldiers, or as an independent mediator *between* Republic and army, depended on the turn of events.

The narrative of events between 13 May 1958, when the *colons* brought on a general strike in Algiers, and 1 June, when de Gaulle was elected Prime Minister in the Assembly, cannot be related here. Gaullist agents carefully guided the settler extremists in Algiers towards open support for the general, so putting their man at the centre of developments. The parliamentary factions shortly found themselves faced with three choices. First, they could refuse to respond to pressures emanating from Algiers and wait for the paratroopers to descend on Paris. The army takeover in Corsica on 24 May showed that this was a probable, not merely possible, outcome of immobilism. Second, the left and centre could attempt to band together in a renewed Popular Front and hope that a public reaction against the military would be fanned into life. Flailing rhetoric along these lines was tried, but the politicians had lost the credibility without which their calls to national unity struck a hollow chord. Third, they could turn to de Gaulle as the only force capable of preserving French democracy against the full impact of military chauvinism. This last choice, in fact was, under the circumstances, the only one which met at least some of the needs of the parliamentary groups. De Gaulle manoeuvred them in this direction with deft hints that, if they did not accept him as premier, then the army most certainly would. On 28 April Pflimlin resigned. After that, the only questions left were technical. De Gaulle had refused ever to set foot in the National Assembly again; the parliamentarians refused to vote his government into existence unless he ritually entered the building. Thus on 1 June de Gaulle, not hesitating to stoop into the gutter for the pearl which lay there, finally went to the Assembly to become the last Prime Minister of the Fourth Republic. But if the army and *colons* had helped to reinstate the general in power, it was, perhaps, they who had most to fear from the ruthless and crystalline concept of metropolitan interests which was the Gaullist hallmark.

What were de Gaulle's intentions regarding Algeria in June 1958? Subsequently disaffected officers and settlers believed that he was determined to effect decolonization from the beginning. What is more likely is that de Gaulle wished to subordinate the Algerian question within the priorities of French government; what this would mean in terms of an Algerian 'solution' was most probably unclear in his mind. But de Gaulle did have two concrete objectives regarding Algeria which he quickly moved to accomplish. The first of these was to reassert the principle of civilian control over the army. Officers of doubtful loyalty were reassigned to posts outside Algeria, and Raoul Salan, a Gaullist who had moved close to the settlers during the May crisis, was replaced as Commander-in-Chief in Algeria by General Challe. Challe's brief was to organize an offensive which, by dashing all possibility of FLN military success, would allow French policy in Algeria to be reviewed without the looming shadow of national humiliation. De Gaulle's second objective was to stimulate economic development in Algeria which, by the mid-1960s, might revolutionize the whole context of Franco-Algerian affairs and make cooperation between Arabs and Frenchmen a necessary part of the regional order, regardless of political frameworks. Thus the Constantine Plan was launched on 3 October 1958, in which pride of place was given to the role of Saharan energy resources in Algerian industrial development.

It was between late 1958 and September 1959, when de Gaulle delivered his famous address on self-determination, that the French leader probably defined his private conclusions on Algeria's future. That address postulated three possibilities: Algerian secession from the French union minus the Sahara, 'assimilation' with France, and qualified self-determination with France retaining rights in the field of economics and diplomacy. The tenor of de Gaulle's statement pointedly marked out the last option as the most desirable. Clearly it did not mean complete independence; but equally clearly it meant the end of the status quo. There is little doubt that de Gaulle was partly influenced in moving down this route by British decolonizations in 1957 in western Africa and south-east Asia. Indeed, the UK was always a Gaullist reference point; the anxiety that the British would score an advantage by shrugging off colonial burdens first was enough to prompt some rapid thinking. But at this time de Gaulle's main concern was in Europe, and with ensuring that the new European Economic Community turned on French leadership. For that to happen French resources, economic and military, had to be switched from North Africa to the European mainland. It was implicit in this approach that the French Army had to be purged of its colonial war mentality, and oriented towards a modernized, continental and nuclear role. Thus by mid-1958 *Algérie Française* had, unknown to itself, collided with the Gaullist vision of France's future; the September statement of self-determination was the revelation of an event which had really already taken place within de Gaulle's supple political intelligence.

De Gaulle's statement was a signal to the army command: they had to choose between him and the *colons*. Hence, when in January 1960 the *colons* barricaded large parts of Algiers, they found that this time the army did not move to support them. It is sometimes argued that, if at this moment de Gaulle had moved swiftly and decisively towards an Algerian settlement, the failed army putsch of April 1961 and, more particularly, its terrorist aftermath, could have been avoided. But such action would not have been in keeping with the silken caution which characterized de Gaulle until any objective was within easy grasping distance. Instead, in March 1960 he visited Algiers and encouraged the army in its anti-FLN offensive, knowing that his own ability to dictate peace terms hinged on its progress. At the same time, by initiating secret talks with individual FLN leaders in the *wilayas* (district commands), he panicked the exiled leadership in Tunis (*Gouvernement provisoire de la République Algérienne*, or GPRA) into believing that any sustained refusal on their part to negotiate might lead to a settlement which ignored them altogether. Finally, in January 1961 he put and won a referendum to the French people which in effect gave him a mandate to construct an entity which was considerably closer to *Algérie Algérienne* than it was to *Algérie Française*. It was the knowledge that de Gaulle might use this mandate to the full in due course that led to the revolt of army elements in Algiers during April 1961. De Gaulle, however, was vindicated in his belief that the growing loyalty to him, especially among the draftees, had cut the ground from under the feet of military dissidents. The putsch collapsed within three days. Subsequently ex-army and *colon* extremists of the *Organisation armée Secrete* (OAS) conducted terrorist operations in Algiers and on the French mainland, including one assassination attempt on de Gaulle which narrowly failed, but the only effect was to blunt the sympathies of metropolitan opinion. After April 1961 de Gaulle was, for the first time, in a position to push towards decolonization in Algeria.

In fact the resumed negotiations with the GPRA which began with the first Evian conference in May 1961 did not reach a final agreement until March 1962. Such prolonged haggling suited de Gaulle; it gave time for his security organs to break the OAS, and to give the various branches of French opinion an interval in which to accept that the Algerian stake was about to disappear. The discussions with the GPRA representatives revolved around three main issues. First, the French argued that the ceasefire in Algeria should begin immediately. Second, they claimed residual rights in the Saharan oil- and gas-fields. Third, the French negotiators sought safeguards for the *pieds noirs* in an independent Algeria, and in particular contended that the latter should be able to retain French citizenship. Predictably, GPRA concessions fell somewhat short of these markers: FLN activities were wound down only gradually, French oil companies had to be satisfied with guaranteed leasing opportunities in Saharan development, while the *pieds noirs*, as long as they clung to French citizenship, were to be eligible for Algerian civil (but not full nationality) rights. The final terms were completed at Evian on 18 March 1962, and a full ceasefire became operational the following day. But if French interests in Algeria were thereby reformulated, those of the *pieds noirs* had ceased to matter, since, outside the realms of the conference chamber, it had become all too plain that they could not stay in North Africa. In the short period before the French Army itself departed, the settlers in their hundreds of thousands, clutching whatever movable goods they could, streamed out through Algiers airport. Most of them returned to France, many remaining in the south, and it is ironic to note that a fair proportion probably ended up as good Gaullists after resettlement. If French participation in the EEC, by diverting metropolitan energies out of its old channels, had helped to evict them from one home, it certainly eased them relatively painlessly into another by virtue of the prosperity which fortuitously marked this period of French history.

Finally, what conclusions can be made regarding the Algerian revolution as a movement?[14] Little is known of its internal history; only the recurrent murders among the leadership echelons, and a few scraps of memoirs, witness to its highly fissile quality. These divisions had ideological and ethnic causes, but their effects were highlighted by the French Army's success in cutting the *wilayas* off from each other, and in erecting a Chinese wall between the exiled leaders abroad and the field units in Algeria. Thus the FLN was prevented from having a dialogue with itself; a consensus on tactics for war and strategies for the post-independence world could never emerge, and the result was an exotic flowering of suspicions and rivalries. Once colonial authority was withdrawn, it was probably inevitable that only the regular army, which had been built up in Tunis and jealously guarded by its commanders from any encounter with French troops precisely to preserve its strength for such a situation, could resolve the tensions surrounding the GPRA by imposing its own will. Here lay the roots of that military authoritarianism which marked post-independence Algeria. Thus, if the French Army had failed to sustain *Algérie Française*, it certainly succeeded in making sure that *Algérie Algérienne* was deformed at birth.

III THE BELGIAN CONGO: THE BREAKDOWN OF A DECOLONIZATION

The importance of the Algerian War in shaping European opinion on colonial issues, particularly during and after 1960, can only be properly understood if it is seen in relation to crises elsewhere in Africa which ran parallel with it, and in this latter category it was the trauma of Belgian decolonization which is of outstanding significance. The Congo – by virtue of its central position in the continent, vast size and mineral wealth – had always been a lynchpin of European rule in Africa. Furthermore, the undisturbed stability of colonial authority in this territory during the mid-1950s meant that the pattern of rapid political change in West Africa did not necessarily have implications for the rest of the land-mass. The suddenness of Belgian decolonization after 1959, and the degree of anarchy which attended the transfer of power, shattered European assumptions as to the 'manageability' of change under contemporary African conditions, and led to the panicky conviction that obligations in this part of the world had to be scaled down as quickly as possible before the costs of decolonization escalated.

Between 1945 and 1959 Belgian rule in the Congo was characterized by a remarkable stability. During these years there was no organization which resembled a broadly based African political party, let alone one with a coherent nationalist programme. The reason for this lies in the character of Belgian colonialism.[15] Because labour shortages prior to 1939 had acutely threatened the basis of the Congolese economy, Belgian administration had developed welfare-oriented policies to smooth Afro-European cooperation. The chief elements of this approach lay in the official encouragement given to the growth of townships and the high quality of medical and other facilities, the latter being applicable to a higher proportion of the rural areas than was the case in other large European colonies. It was the substantial external investment which was drawn to the Congo by its copper and diamond wealth which in part financed this system. One result was that the colonial administrative presence throughout the Congo was more pervasive than in British- or French-ruled regions. This powerful combination of rapid economic growth and administrative penetration meant that the collaborative interface between Europeans and Africans was broad and effective. The dual impact was, if anything, intensified for much of the 1950s when mining capital and Europeans poured into the Congo on a consider-able scale: the European population in the colony, for example, rose from 34,789 to 114,341 between 1946 and 1959.[16] Thus the colonial state in the Congo was a dynamic enterprise which was able to keep ahead of African material aspirations and embrace most social relationships within its administrative procedures. Under these (ulti-mately psychological) conditions, the legitimacy of Belgian authority was not in question.

The dearth of 'politics' in the Congo prior to the mid-1950s was not least the result of the educational system. A larger percentage of Congolese youth were in school in 1955 than was the case, for example, in the Gold Coast, but the instruction given was almost wholly vocational. The balance between primary and secondary sectors was (even by colonial standards) skewed towards the former, and there was no access to university opportunities. In West Africa the scions of chiefly or commercial elites might go to metropolitan or American universities, but in the Congo elite-formations of any kind were too socially ill-defined for such habits to have crystallized. The character of Congolese education was also shaped, like so much else, by the overwhelming Catholic influence. The vast bulk of schools were Catholic missions, and were thus geared firstly to evangeliza-tion, and secondly to the construction of a native clergy. Indeed, higher education in the Congo, in so far as there was any, meant seminary training, and some later nationalist figures only progressed beyond basic education by simulating the desire to be a priest. Thus the one clear route to personal advancement lay through the Church, which was itself the pillar of the colonial status quo. Here was a seamless web out of which black nationalism could emerge only with great difficulty.

Nevertheless, educated cadres (or évolués) in urban employment had emerged as a distinct group in such cities as Leopoldville, Stanleyville and Elisabethville after 1945. This was an inevitable outcrop of the substantial growth of these agglomerations as the economy expanded. Characteristically, the Belgian administration sought to systematize and control this phenomenon by introducing the carte de mérite civil and immatriculation. 'The entire history of this period, for the évolués', Jean Stengers comments, 'is dominated by the history of the certificates.'[17] To enter the magic colonial circle prescribed by these documents, Congolese applicants had to submit their personal histories, habits and homes to inspection by committee. Quite apart from the question of the 'standards' set, this was a forbidding experience which even many eligible candidates under-standably could not face. The Belgian motive was pre-eminently to integrate this social category within prevailing administrative norms. But the effect was also to divide the évolués between the certificated and the non-certificated. The whole system foundered, however, on the failure to establish the tangible benefits attached to immatricula-tion. The authorities had been very cautious in establishing such benefits for fear of triggering a competitive rush to obtain the necessary documentation. But as a consequence the évolués were, as a class, resentful of the Belgian failure to raise the stakes of the game. This resentment did not amount in the mid-1950s to a distinct nationalism, but it did lead to a greater outspokenness on public affairs; the most symbolic evidence of this was the publication during 1956 in a newspaper for the burgeoning black intelligentsia, Conscience Africaine, of a political manifesto which, while gradualist and non-racial in its formulations, was nevertheless explicit about the need for 'total emancipation' in the Congo.

But although between 1956 and 1959 the small African press debated political futures in less veiled and ambiguous terms than hitherto, no mechanisms of political transformation appeared to be at work. Then during December 1959 the capital of the Congo,

Leopoldville, was shaken by riots which actively involved a large percentage of the black population, and which gravely threatened the security of many European residents. It was this event which almost immediately brought the metropolitan government to contemplate independence. Before dealing with this abrupt change of direction in Congolese affairs, it is worth emphasizing the searing repercussions of large-scale riots in colonial situations. We have noted in an earlier section how, in the Gold Coast, big-city disturbances in the late 1940s were able to transmute colonial immobilism into a rapid movement towards reform. The social psychology of colonialism, especially when there was a significant presence of white settlers, was so internally fragile and veined with collective anxieties that breakdowns of order in sensitive locations were liable to traumatize its entire nervous system; like many varieties of political authoritarianism, European colonial rule had a curiously low 'threshold' beyond which the glass casing shattered into fragments. The risks of such an eventuality in the Congo were, perhaps, higher than elsewhere precisely because the Belgians had for so long prided themselves on not being subject to the pressures with which the British and French had had to cope. When the abyss suddenly opened up beneath them, the instinctive Belgian response was to vacate the area as quickly as possible.

What had happened in the few years prior to 1959 which explains the breakdown in Leopoldville? Historians commenting on this have essentially divided their arguments into external and internal factors. They have dealt most fully and factually with the former, since it is outside events whose impact is most easily identifiable, although it is feasible that the latter were the dominant influence. The chief external consideration was that the metropolitan struggle over educational issues was extruded into the Congo. In 1954 Auguste Buisseret, a Liberal, was appointed as Colonial Minister in the Belgian Government. Without having any distinctive ideas as to Congolese political development, Buisseret was determined to reduce the influence of the Catholic Church, and to this end introduced a measure of secular educational provision. The mere fact that such a reform could now be rammed through the Brussels bureaucracy indicated that established colonial interests had lost their footing in the labyrinthine interior of the Belgian state; in this respect Belgian developments ran parallel with similar subterranean swells detectable in Paris and London. Belgian Catholicism, however, was too sturdy an animal to be very easily led by its colonial nose. It organized its supporters at home and, more critically, mobilized a black Congolese constituency as well. The laicists responded by seeking African allies of their own, which was not hard to do under the circumstances. It is ironic that this first major articulation of African 'views' in the Congo was elicited within the framework of a quintessentially Belgian issue. But for many Congolese it was a taste of politics which stuck, and one, too, in which a major colonial institution had been pushed on to the defensive.

The changing terms of the metropolitan debate over the Congo, however, went beyond education. In December 1955 A. A. J. van Bilsen, then Professor of Colonial Legislation at the University Institute for Overseas Territories at Antwerp, published a manuscript entitled *Thirty Year Plan for the Political Emancipation of Belgian Africa*. The arguments employed in this work resembled those surfacing in Paris during the *loi-cadre* enactments. In particular, it was contended that institutional reform and political training had to be pushed forward so that colonial rulers were not overtaken by events. Bilsen envisaged, prophetically as it turned out, that a federal structure would be needed to cushion the impact of Congolese decolonization. He also, as the publication's title stated, considered thirty years to be the appropriate time-scale for the whole operation, although it appears that the author adopted such a cautious estimate in order to lure colonial conservatives into open discussion. Whatever effect Bilsen had on the latter, he certainly influenced black Congolese opinion, and the appearance of the *Conscience Africaine* manifesto in 1956 was a response to, and an extension of, the professor's work. In this way metropolitan liberals and Congolese *évolués* interacted to loosen the conventions of discussion between 1956 and 1959. But this process was obviously caught up in events elsewhere in Africa, and above all elsewhere in French-speaking Africa. The extent to which the Belgian intelligentsia were affected by Algerian events is indeterminate; rather more obvious is the general effect on the *évolués*, first of the *loi-cadre* initiatives, and second, of de Gaulle's speech in Brazzaville, just across the Congo River, in which French Africa south of the Sahara was offered either complete independence or a privileged place within the French Community. The manner in which such a speech, given by such a dominating European personality, exerted its effect amongst the Leopoldville masses is not easily defined, but that its impact was powerful and unsettling is beyond dispute.

If the above 'factors of change' can be designated as external, the most prominent alteration in the Congo's internal condition was the petering out of the economic boom at some point in 1957 as Congolese mineral exports tailed off. The effects were keenly felt. Throughout the 1950s peasant migration to the cities had built up. This flow of labour was a precondition of economic growth, and so administrative controls over the volume of migration had necessarily been curtailed. As long as job expansion in the townships stabilized migrants in their new habitats, the status quo was not threatened. But the onset of recession created pools of unemployment, producing urban tensions and blocking escape from rural life. This was the classic pattern of social decay in modern Africa. It was a pattern which was always greatly complicated when it meshed with mounting concern about the shape of political change. In a sustained boom the prospect of such change is softened because the great majority could clearly expect to share (if unequally) the benefits of national transformation; but recession raised the possibility that any transfers of power might be appropriated by particular groups who would proceed to monopolize whatever marginal growth might be squeezed out of the economy. This approach cannot be taken too far in explaining the Leopoldville riots of January 1959, because in the preceding period substantive 'independence' had not been on the agenda. These riots were aimed at Belgian rulers, not at rival competitors for the post-colonial succession. But the political debate of 1956–9 had led to a heightened visibility of African organizations, which were usually tribal in nature if only because the colonial authorities had favoured the formation of precisely such bodies. In bringing their arguments to bear against the Belgians, Congolese were implicitly and inevitably bringing them to bear against each other. In this sense it may be said that, while the January disturbances represented a coherent anti-colonialism born of economic pressure and political education, they also arose from a collective emotion based on anxiety as to what lay *beyond* colonialism – for this had been the only world that the great majority had known.

The Belgian Government's reaction to these developments was to issue a far-reaching statement on 13 January 1959. 'Belgium intends to organize in the Congo', this read, 'a democracy capable of exercising the prerogatives of sovereignty and of deciding upon its own independence.' This obviously marked a crucial change: 'politics' was going to be invented for mass consumption. But what shape that politics should take, and the precise time-tables to which it had to work, were not clarified. Until the end of 1959 the Belgian authorities continued to think in terms of a carefully staged process in which territorial and municipal elections could be used to identify Congolese negotiators with whom they could work. 'Independence' had been brought into play to hurry forward this aim, but at first the Belgians had no intention of committing themselves to dates until reliable Congolese partners had appeared. But by early 1960 the hope of any such modulated end to empire in the Congo had disappeared, and at the Round Table Conference in Brussels during January the Belgian Government accepted 30 June 1960 as the terminal date.[18] The profound surprise this occasioned elsewhere in Europe and Africa contributed to the wreckage of colonialism's fortunes in that *annus mirabilis* of African political advance. But what had brought Belgian policy-makers to this dramatic revision of policy?

Governmental authority had shown signs of wear and tear in the Congo as 1959 progressed. In large parts of the lower Congo, indeed, it had almost disappeared, and loyalties had recrudesced around local politicians, in this case particularly around the Abako leader, Joseph Kasavubu. Such a hiatus was inevitable, and it did not matter as long as within a reasonable period some leader or political party emerged as sufficiently dominant and 'national' for the Belgians to take into a decolonizing embrace. Together the *ancien régime* and its reversionary partner could damp down the agitations of public mood and see that power was filtered carefully from old vessels into new ones, without leaking too much in the process. But no such consolidating force appeared amongst the Congolese factions. The 13 January statement had unleashed a scramble to form political parties, but far from this splitting of factional atoms exhibiting any tendency to reintegrate at the prospect of gaining real power, they continued to break down into a welter of colliding units. Under these conditions any Belgian attempt to 'play it long' simply meant prolonging the agony of continuing responsibility and slackening control; not surprisingly, the temptation was to scuttle in the expectation that only the immediacy of independence would discipline the politicians in the way required. The British, of course, had taken a somewhat similar approach in early 1947 towards their Indian entanglement, but in that case there were already two powerful local organs, Congress and the Muslim League, to ensure a minimum of political stability; in the Congo the lack of any such entrenched leaderships and institutions with credible claims to nation-wide support meant that the Belgians were in infinitely less charted swamps.

Congolese political fragmentation would itself not have mattered too much if the colonial power was confident of bringing military force to bear when necessary. In other words, as long as any threatened breakdown could be averted by flying in metropolitan forces to back up the Congolese *Force Publique*, then policy-makers in Brussels could still have faced up to the pressures of a graduated approach to decolonization. But the crucial fact was that the Belgian Government had no recourse, in practice, to military correctives as the Congolese situation deteriorated. Throughout 1959 the anti-conscription campaign in Belgium, led by the Socialists but which attracted a broad constituency, made the government all too aware that public opinion would not accept the sacrifice of its blood and treasure for the sake of Congolese considerations. In this context traditional anti-conscriptionism shaded into something rather more novel, metropolitan anti-colonialism. The Belgian state had to be especially responsive to this because, more than its west European counterparts, it contained such deep divisions of its own on linguistic and religious issues. Thus the French state, for all its Fourth Republic confusions, could fight an Algerian war if it chose to; but the Belgian state could not bring resources to bear externally in the same way. It was Belgian public opinion, and the nature of the Belgian polity, which came decisively to limit Congolese options by 1960.

The Brussels Round Table Conference had established a date for independence. It had also authorized a *loi fundamentale* on which independence could be based. But the latter was not a clear document. The Congolese representatives were split as to whether the constitution should be unitary or federal. But nobody was prepared to squabble over this issue to delay the fundamental deal which had been struck: that is, Belgium would continue to guarantee order by ensuring that its nationals stayed at their posts in the civil service and *Force Publique*, while the Congolese politicians sought to establish some consensus amongst themselves regarding the future distribution of power. Thus, whereas in British and French decolonizations in Africa the key indigenous interests (black soldiers, bureaucrats and politicians) were all to be *immediate* beneficiaries of independence, in the Congo a different style of transfer was to take place: Belgian citizens would continue to dominate the chief posts in the army and bureaucracy while the party political cadres arranged a succession to suit themselves. But would the subordinate but equally aspiring Congolese soldiers and civil servants let their political counterparts steal a march on them in this way, boosting their own salaries and monopolizing patronage, leaving only crumbs for those sections of the polity who were to emerge more gradually from direct Belgian supervision? And, anyway, was there a real likelihood that the multiplicity of political parties would throw up some workable form of government in the time required? The splintering effects of the May 1960 elections seemed to heighten these uncertainties. In this way the Congo slithered towards 'freedom'.

Why, observing these instabilities building up around them, did the various elements in the old status quo not sound the alarm? In fact the traditional trinity of local administration, Church and western business interests were no longer bound together; each looked to its best advantage under changing circumstances. The weakest link in this disintegrating chain was the civil service. The only Belgian officials who continued to matter were in Brussels; those 'on the ground' continued to go through their accustomed Congolese motions, but their real attention was on the negotiation of compensated transfer back into the metropolitan bureaucracy. Meanwhile the Catholic Church deftly distanced itself from its traditional partners and sought to remain aloof from political conflict. The clergy's objective was to protect its role in the coming order, and hence it cultivated an air of studied neutrality. Finally, the corporate interests, like the Church, had at all costs to avoid being tarred with the colonial brush. Unlike the Church, however, they relied overwhelmingly on money, not deeply embedded loyalties, to secure their Congolese future, and because it was not clear which local politicians were best able to guarantee that future, business interests financed political parties almost indiscriminately, in the hope of maximizing goodwill – a strategy which naturally served only to institutionalize fragmentation. Well before January 1960, therefore, the colonial state had ceased to exist in the Congo as anything other than a constitutional fiction. This condition of disembodied statelessness, which was implicit in varying degree in all European decolonizations, came to be the dominating characteristic of the Congolese situation, with devastating results.

The independent Congo came into existence on 30 June 1960; within days the country had been swept by large-scale tribal disturbances and renewed external intervention became inevitable. Thus, if decolonization narratives can for the purposes of this study normally be terminated with the formal transfer of power, this cannot be the case in the instance of the Congo. But meanwhile some comment must be made as to why Congolese politics by 1960 had become so uniformly pockmarked by ethnic, rather than alternatively framed, antagonisms. During the colonial period tribal (and subtribal) consciousness had been imposed on the *indigènes* by Belgian administrative device, but such consciousness had also been cultivated by the Africans themselves as a means by which collectivities could adapt to modern pressures. Thus ethnicity, far from decomposing in the urban setting, was refashioned into new uses as individuals sought a group refuge within which to order their lives and promote their interests. The induction of formal politics was quickly hooked into this associational network. 'It is indisputable', one historian writes, 'that the introduction of elections in the cities in 1957 and 1958, without permitting the free organization of political movements to structure the competition, built up a linkage between ethnicity and politics in five crucial urban centres (Leopoldville, Coquilhatville, Luluaborg, Elisabethville and Jadotville) which could not be eradicated by subsequent events.'[19] After early 1959 Congolese *évolués* were positively encouraged to set up new-style political parties, but by this time it was too late for the ethnic temper to be blunted. Furthermore, Congolese leaders could not then afford to spend time building up non-ethnic constituencies, even if they knew that in the long run they would prove more lasting. J. M. Keynes' deprecations on the explanatory validity of the 'long run' in the economic cycle, therefore, can be mirrored in the political circumstances of decolonization; in the short run Congolese politicians needed to garner maximum support in the minimum of time, and that could be done only by dredging the tribal networks into which the masses were already bound. Local Belgian observers did not decry this at the time. Congolese society, after all, had to be stabilized around some set of interlocking relationships, and the temporary use of tribal structures for this purpose had the advantage of continuity with the past. It was, in its way, rational to view the ethnic divisions which burgeoned in the first half of 1960 not only as the predictable accompaniment of all African decolonizations, but also as part of a necessary 'holding action' in which the Congolese were renewing tribal solidarities only as a prelude to building a new, and more enduring, solidarity based on nationhood.

The Congo crisis which lasted from the time of independence until mid-1963, at which point a new equilibrium began to emerge, was initially sparked by the mutiny of the *Force Publique* against its European officers. Disturbances spread throughout much of the Congo between 4 and 9 July, leading to renewed Belgian intervention to protect their nationals. It was the sudden reappearance of Belgian troops in strength which embittered race relations and divided the new government, which was already riven between the forces of Patrice Lumumba, the Prime Minister, and those of Joseph Kasavubu, the President. Subsequently the authority of the Leopoldville regime did not extend to the other main Congolese cities, and sometimes barely within its own immediate environs. So why had the *Force Publique* failed to play the role allotted to it in the decolonization process? The Congolese military cadres had promptly spotted the flaw, from their own point of view, in the deal fixed up at the Round Table Conference: constitutional independence, with most of its pickings reserved for ministerialists and politicians, was to be underpinned by a *Force Publique* in which Europeans continued to occupy the bulk of the middle- and higher-ranking positions. In effect, the army was *not* to be decolonized so that the political factions could enjoy effective protection while they set about rigging the new order. By their revolt, the Congolese soldiery signalled that they were determined to obtain their own leading place in the post-colonial queue, and were prepared to risk complete breakdown to force such access. The politicians were constrained to respond, and the entire European officer corps was immediately replaced by newly promoted Congolese. This was followed by the flight of the mass of Belgian administrators, who had hitherto stayed at their posts but whose confidence had evaporated with the overnight change in the character of the *Force Publique*. 'This unsought revolution', Young comments, 'on top of Africa's most remarkably telescoped decolonization, produced the continent's most Africanized political system.'[20]

Amidst this confusion Moise Tshombe and his allies in the Conakat party had declared South Katanga to be a separate state. This Katangan secession was critically assisted by a medley of European interests: settlers, administrators and, above all, the great mining companies for whom Katangan copper had always been the jewel in the Congolese crown. Thus for African nationalists everywhere and for the international left, Katanga became the symbol of nascent neo-colonialism. This strange alliance of Conakat and Europeans had essentially been brought about by the profound ethnic rivalries which marked this region during the approach to independence. Specifically, Conakat represented a banding together of long-established tribal formations in Katanga who feared that in-coming Baluba 'strangers', with their concentration of strength in the capital of Elisabethville, would move to assert a local dominance. Tshombe's secession was thus in part a response to ethnic anxieties. But ethnicity in Katanga was deeply overlaid by economic issues. This province was easily the richest part of the Congo, and it had traditionally made a large contribution to the national budget. This had always caused murmurings of dissatisfaction by Africans *and* Europeans in the province, but the situation was manageable so long as the Leopoldville authorities kept public finance under control. The trouble was that immediately after independence the politicians gave an enormous hike to ministerial and parliamentary salaries, and were soon forced to duplicate these increases for the administration and the army. The level of public salaries was clearly going to be a permanent drain on fiscal resources, and there was only one source of surpluses which could be squeezed to plug the deficit – Katanga. Thus in the first flush of independence Katangans, who had benefited from economic growth relative to other provinces, were confronted with the prospect of being taxed more heavily than ever to pay for the sinecures of non-Katangans. This was not, viewed from Elisabethville, what independence was meant to be about. The determination with which Conakat forces defended secession in the face of United Nations pressure after 1960 is easily explicable without having to fall back on the simplistic belief, so widespread at the time, that Tshombe was a puppet figure who represented nobody other than western capital out to preserve a little fragment of colonialism.

But how should the European supporters of Katangan secession be characterized? Clearly objectives varied amongst its component parts: mercenaries were after a quick pay-off, while white settlers were striving to defend some Congolese living space of their own. The crux of the matter, however, was the great mining companies, for it was their technical, administrative and financial capacity which kept the Katangan state afloat. Nevertheless, for these interests a separate Katanga was *not* the most desirable solution to their problems, but rather the only one which seemed to offer the possibility of business-as-usual. A unified, stable Congo governed from Leopoldville was always preferred by local western managements, but this was not a realistic option after mid-1960. Also, although in their less lucid moments mining executives no doubt pondered the attractions of a Katangan link-up with its copper-rich neighbours in the Central African Federation, they were too shrewd to believe that western governments would tolerate this sort of white man's surgery in the heart of the continent. In short, the business corporations who supported Tshombe did so, not because they grabbed an opportunity to establish a satellite state, but because it seemed the sole means of cordoning off Congolese disorder from the main centre of the extractive industry. The priorities of western capital were operational, not hegemonic, and after 1961 the companies concerned were, in fact, eager to improve their lines of communication with the Leopoldville factions behind Tshombe's back. Indeed, it was this insurance mentality which was the hallmark of European capitalists' thinking in all African and Asian decolonizations.

What made the Congolese situation so newsworthy was not the extent of the breakdown of law and order (which was very far from complete) but the manner in which it intersected with international developments. It was precisely at this point in the early 1960s that the competition between the western and Soviet blocs seemingly came to focus on the underdeveloped world. In a sense, the very concept of a 'Third World' was shaped by the strategic fashions in Washington and Moscow. Clearly neither of the two superpowers was likely to bring the nuclear confrontation to a climax; the Cuban missile crisis of October–November 1962 only underlined this. Given such a military stalemate, the East–West conflict came to appear essentially political, and its outcome therefore determinable by the 'developing nations' of Afro-Asia and the Americas – a supposition based, too, on a contemporary naïvety as to the cohesion of 'new' states rolling off the decolonization production-line. It was in this milieu that the Central Intelligence Agency could become such a vital part of the US security system, and in which the US Attorney-General, Robert Kennedy, could judicially weigh the pros and cons of assassinating Fidel Castro. Not surprisingly, the US Government was deeply perturbed when Patrice Lumumba was dismissed by the Congolese President, Kasavubu, and the former responded by seeking assistance from the Russians. This served to confirm the rumours that the Lumumbists were the Soviet stalking-horses in the region. Certainly there is no doubt that the Soviets did use the Congo crisis to test their own opportunities in Africa, and assisted the establishment of a rival centre of power in Stanleyville. It was in trying to make his way from Leopoldville to Stanleyville that Lumumba was arrested by rivals within the factional struggle going on in the Congolese capital, tossed to the Katangan separatists and subsequently murdered. At this point it seemed that at the worst the Congo could spark a wider international conflict, and that at the very least the country would be split into mutually hostile blocks, each backed by its ideological mentor.

Under these inauspicious conditions the UN moved to the centre-stage of Congolese affairs, acting, in effect, as surrogate for a dismembered central government. The inspiration for this initiative lay initially with Dag Hammarskjöld, the UN Secretary-General, who was determined that the organization he headed should win for itself some freedom of movement from the American and Russian superpowers by cultivating Afro-Asian support.[21] Katanga, in particular, was the perfect theatre in which this drama could be played out since, by doing battle with a secessionist regime whose nature was seen by the mass of Afro-Asian opinion as quintessentially neo-colonial, the UN could lay claim to radical credentials. Thus, when it became clear that the Congolese army was not capable of responding to the Katangan challenge, the UN despatched forces (mainly from non-western countries, not least India) to Elisabethville. Hammarsk-jöld's aim was not to spark a bloody confrontation, but to impose enough military and political pressure on Tshombe to edge the latter into a negotiated re-entry to the federal arena. Indeed, for all the sound and fury of Elisabethville, with the 'sweeps' of UN forces to weaken the Katangan militia and especially to flush out European technicians, the game was always essentially tactical in nature.[22] It was in order to meet Tshombe for talks that Hammarskjöld was flying to Ndola in Northern Rhodesia during September 1961 when his plane crashed, killing all passengers. By that stage the considerable resilience of the Katangans in the face of external pressure had become clear, and it was not until January 1963, after a continuing escalation by the UN forces in Elisabethville, that Tshombe announced the termination of secession. But by then Tshombe, too, was less interested in sustaining his breakaway state than in regaining a role in Leopoldville.

In fact the gradual reunification of the Congo, in some ways as remarkable as the preceding fractures, had been under way for many months before the Katangan collapse. The process was highlighted by the reconvention of the Louvanium Parliament (August 1961), and the recognition by most, though not by all, Congolese factions of Cyrille Adoula as premier. Afterwards Adoula was able laboriously to reconstruct a 'national' political framework, based not least on a redefinition of provincial units in line with political realities; this progress, however, was secured above all by the success of General Joseph Mobutu in imposing his own authority on the army and rewelding it into an effective institution. Nevertheless, much of what happened at this time is hidden to the historian's naked eye. For example, there is no doubt that the Americans used all their influence to ensure that the Adoula regime survived. They did so because they feared that a balkanized central Africa would maximize the chances of a successful Russian penetration into the area. Thus, if western business pressure had something to do with the Katangan secession, western strategic concerns had a great deal to do with Congolese reconsolidation. But even the Americans could not achieve this aim by the crude twisting of arms and lining of pockets. The most important factor at work was that the great majority of the Congolese cadres (political, administrative and military) realized that they had more to lose by continued fragmentation than to gain. This rapidly induced a preparedness to compromise across the whole face of Congolese issues. This convergence of political forces remained extremely fragile, and came near to breaking down altogether after mid-1964 when renewed opposition to Leopoldville's authority crystallized amongst the Soviet-oriented groups in control of Stanleyville.[23] It was amidst this final confrontation between pro-western federalists (with Tshombe, paradoxically, having replaced Adoula as premier) and secessionist radicals that the killings and atrocities in the Congo reached their peak, and it required American and Belgian assistance finally to liquidate the Stanleyville 'pocket'. Only in the last months of 1964 did the Congo regain the territorial integrity which had prevailed at independence on 30 June 1960, and the decolonization phase really come to a belated close.

The outcome of this Congolese saga allows us to isolate one important general characteristic of decolonizations: their 'self-righting' quality, often in the face of tremendous pressures, and independently of metropolitan contributions to stabilization. If the prospect of the transfer of power from alien to indigenous authority accentuated conflicts of interest between local associational groups, it also led to the recognition by contending elites – and not only among the elites, who, after all, usually survive troubles better than most – that somehow a new patchwork of unity had to be stitched together. Sometimes the first of these factors seemed to be infused with a destructive and unstoppable momentum, but invariably the latter turned out to be quite as compulsive. What was at risk for decolonizing powers was not so much 'stabilization or chaos', although this was the scenario often painted in the western press, but stabilization in a form suited to the ex-metropole or looming superpower. The fact that the age of European decolonization was, on the whole, marked by a relative continuity of institutional and social frameworks, was not a reflection of the tactical skills (for good or ill) of metropolitan overseers, but it was proof of the cohering dynamic at work amongst the peoples concerned. Ironically, although the decolonization rhetoric amongst western officialdom as to the making of new societies was largely an attempt at expedient myth-making, the reality was often (if a moment of benign optimism may be allowed to punctuate an often grim story) not completely wide of the mark.

7. Britain: the End of Imperial Statehood

It is one of the central themes of this study that European decolonizations after 1945, particularly in their African dimension after 1956, arose more directly from changing conditions *within* the metropoles than they did from any metamorphosis at the periphery. Somewhat gradually and partially in the initial post-war years, accelerating after 1950 and climaxing towards the end of that decade, metropolitan societies became uncoupled from imperial routines and assumptions, and, as we shall see, ultimately became actively hostile towards their residual traces. The motives in this process were very mixed, and the trajectory of experience on the part of the relevant European powers distinctively different. We have already seen how it was de Gaulle's grasp of the distorting effects of colonial obligations which detonated French decolonization in sub-Saharan and North Africa. But it is the British case of this subtle revolution in the mores of west European power which is most suggestive, since it was this country whose traditions and reflexes had been so quintessentially 'imperial'. To do full justice to this chameleon-like change would really require a full-length study on its own. This chapter, however, will seek to elucidate the fundamental shifts at work by a short treatment of the Suez crisis of 1956, followed by a commentary on the changing context and revisionist consequences of that dramatic Anglo-French démarche.

I SUEZ 1956: THE TURNING POINT

The Suez crisis, inaugurated by Gamal Abdul Nasser's nationalization of the Canal Company on 26 July 1956 and brought to an end by the final withdrawal of the Anglo-French invasion forces in late

December, was probably the most decisive event in British foreign policy during the 1950s.[1] It can broadly, if crudely, be argued that the crisis concerned the UK's ability to operate as a world power whose claims to that status were uniquely geared to its role in the underdeveloped world, and that this crisis was resolved only when the British Government recognized that this status, given existing constraints, was too grandly conceived and had to be scaled down. Most significantly, recent research has shown that the unwinding of the Suez imbroglio involved unprecedented American involvement in the transfer of prime ministerial authority from Anthony Eden to Harold Macmillan (see above p. 199). A nation whose selection of leader was subject to effective intervention from Washington was obviously in no position to play the great-power game in quite the way it had been accustomed, and subsequent decolonizations in Africa and the Mediterranean were simply one aspect of an adaptation of British statecraft which flowed from this recognition. We must therefore begin this section by explaining why Nasser nationalized the Suez Canal Company, and why the British and the French came to see this as a *casus belli*.

In October 1954 Britain and Egypt had negotiated the terms and time-table for British withdrawal from the Suez Base and this seemed likely to *improve* the political relations of the two countries.[2] The UK was finally to evacuate its troops from Egyptian territory, while Nasser indicated a tentative willingness to cooperate on matters of regional strategy. In this context it was especially relevant that the Egyptian authorities yielded their old claim that sovereignty over the Sudan should revert to them once the existing Anglo-Egyptian condominium expired. Nevertheless, during 1955 Nasser's relationship with the western powers in general deteriorated sharply. Three main aspects of Egyptian policy accounted for this fact. First, Nasserite agencies consistently probed the weaknesses of the UK's remaining sphere of influence in the Middle East – particularly in Jordan. Second, the Cairo regime funnelled support to the Algerian opponents of the French Fourth Republic, and especially to the exiled revolutionary leadership in Tunis. Third, the Egyptian Government refused to be drawn into Washington's frantic efforts to construct an anti-Communist bloc in the Middle East, and nothing symbolized Nasser's determination to remain independent of American regional diplomacy more forcefully than his arms deal with

Czechoslovakia (and, thereby, with the Soviet Union) in September 1955.

In striking such postures, the Egyptian leader was risking a formidable coalition being brought to bear against him. The British could certainly bring Iraq into an anti-Nasserite alliance, and *almost* certainly Jordan, the latter's Hashemite rulers having owed their position to the British ever since 1921; the Americans looked increasingly able to steer the Saudis in whichever direction they wished; and although France had lost her old satellites in the area, her traditional influence still found echoes in various quarters, not least in the Lebanon and Israel. If Egypt could be caught in this diplomatic nutcracker, Nasser might find his domestic support evaporating very rapidly. In retrospect, it is easy to see that Anthony Eden (who had succeeded Winston Churchill as British Prime Minister in April 1955) should have been content to let such a situation develop gradually and, most significantly, under US auspices. But for the British there were costs in hewing to an American line in the Middle East. In general, as we have seen already, the UK and US had long been Middle Eastern rivals – ever since the 1920s. More especially, however, the question of an anti-Nasserite strategy brought out some basic differences between the two Anglo-Saxon powers. The Washington policy-makers were adamant that the Saudis would play an active part only if they gained sweeping concessions (on frontier demarcation, for example) in the Persian Gulf. In effect, the Americans expected the UK Government to 'buy' Nasser's downfall by yielding to the Saudis its own, long-cherished pre-eminence in the Gulf. Eden's indignation at this pressure from across the Atlantic was deep and sincere; he belonged to a Whitehall generation, indeed, which felt that the endless stream of British concessions to the US since the 1921 Anglo-Irish Treaty had, on balance, gone unrequited – a sentiment which even the great wartime alliance had not completely dispelled.

Nasser recognized that his survival depended on exploiting these Middle Eastern gaps in Anglo-American understanding. Above all, he set out to identify Nasserism with the cause of anti-colonialism in general and Arab nationalism in particular. This was the message which Cairo Radio drummed out ceaselessly from late 1955 onwards; its purpose was to make any American move aimed at Nasser's downfall appear as a capitulation to old-fashioned British imperia-

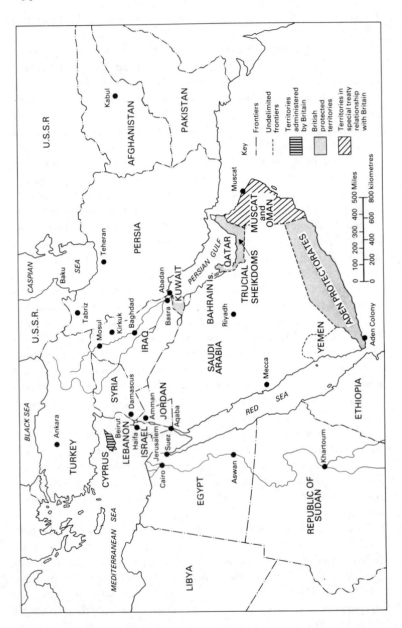

MAP 7   The Middle East in 1956

lism, and, as such, not likely to win favour amongst large sections of the US public. But it was not enough for Nasser to manoeuvre the Americans into a public relations dilemma both at home and internationally. He needed to execute some regional coup capable of convincing President Eisenhower that British influence in the Middle East was a rotted shell, and that the real initiative lay with those who carried credibility as Arab nationalists; in other words, that Nasserism was a reality which Washington had to learn to live with. It was with this latter aim in mind that Nasser orchestrated pro-nationalist riots in Amman which forced King Hussein in March 1956 to dismiss General Glubb, his long-standing military adviser and a key element in Britain's hold over the Kingdom.[3] This Egyptian thrust was perfectly chosen, for if the UK Government could no longer be perceived in Washington as determining the course of Jordanian affairs, then its capacity to do the same in Iraq also became distinctly questionable. Eden's decision to 'get' Nasser, with or without American connivance, dated from the moment that Glubb was hustled ignominiously on to an aircraft to fly him out of Amman.

Knit into these complex manoeuvres were the tangled negotiations over the Aswan Dam. This prospective scheme was commonly agreed to hold a solution for Egypt's endemic poverty. Given its enormous economic significance for the Egyptian masses, it would have been logical if the Aswan Dam had proved the touchstone of relations between Nasser and the western powers. Indeed, because Nasser's nationalization of the Suez Canal Company followed the final US rejection of the Dam proposal, this appears to have been the case. But the appearance was illusory: the Dam was always little more than a pawn in the regional struggle for power. The Americans and the British saw their veto on the project (a veto arising from their respective World Bank voting rights) as a vital element in the ring they wished to draw around Nasser, and they insisted that the construction programme, which would clearly dominate Egyptian economic management in the years ahead, should not be locally controlled. From Nasser's perspective, however, the immense economic advantages of the scheme were completely outweighed if this meant giving his Anglo-American enemies a handle within Cairo politics. The negotiations stalled. However, at this point British and American ideas on how the inevitable project cancellation should be implemented diverged. The UK Government wanted cancellation held up until it could be coordinated with a broader anti-Nasser strategy; the US Government wished instead to use cancellation as a single 'warning shot' across the Egyptian bows. In fact the date of cancellation was finally dictated by Nasser himself. By tripping the Americans into an early pull-out from the project negotiations, Nasser saw an opportunity to portray himself as a representative of the thwarted aspirations of underdeveloped countries (thus making further American machinations against him rather difficult, at least in the short term) and then to exploit the vacuum this opened up by aiming a crippling and final blow at British prestige in the region. Thus, by demanding a final decision on the Aswan scheme, Nasser pushed the US Secretary of State, John Foster Dulles, into announcing on 19 July 1956 that the administration in Washington no longer regarded the project as viable.[4] Cairo Radio was then able to stimulate Egyptian opinion to new heights of anti-western sentiment; and one week later Nasser nationalized the Canal Company.

The British Government's response was to call up 20,000 reservists and to start planning an invasion of Egypt, using Malta and Cyprus as jumping-off points. But these preparations were almost certainly still purely contingent in nature, since Eden and his Cabinet continued to expect that the Eisenhower administration would bring enough pressure to bear to make Nasser disgorge his nationalization, and that this humiliation would break him at home. Much of the British sabre-rattling at this stage had as its main purpose that of panicking the Americans into action to prevent the sight of their chief NATO partner being forced to act alone to protect its interests. Why did British Government circles believe so far into the crisis that their US counterparts would either associate themselves with or, at the least, turn a blind eye to, London's manoeuvres designed (if necessary by invasion) to topple Nasser? The reason is embedded in the unspoken assumption of British foreign policy after 1945 that, providing Whitehall always chose its ground intelligently, the Washington authorities had little option but to back up British actions in regions where any vacuum might be filled by a veritable swarm of anti-western forces. Thus after Nasser's appropriation of the Suez assets, the British joined in the motions of a reasoned internationalism primarily as a gesture to Congressional sensitivities: the UK hosted a Conference of Maritime Nations in London between 16 and 23 August which discussed the possible internationalization of the Canal, cooperated in the abortive Menzies Mission to Cairo, participated in the Suez Canal Users' Association (SCUA) talks between 19 and 22 September, and authorized the Foreign Secretary, Selwyn Lloyd, to negotiate a provisional solution with his Egyptian counterpart at the United Nations, Mahmud Fawzi. The latter initiative, in particular, seemed to make some real headway in clearing the obstacles to Egyptian sovereignty over the Canal by stressing the principle of non-discriminatory obligations to users. But far from the US administration being drawn into support of Britain's position during this essentially declaratory phase, Eisenhower and Dulles steadily distanced themselves from it, climaxing in the Secretary of State's statement at a press conference on 2 October that he envisaged no sanctions emerging from the SCUA deliberations, and that the US had no intention of complicity in 'colonialism'. Eden's subsequent decisions, and his ability to carry his Cabinet with him, derived not least from the profound shock that this evaporation of American support had within the British political system.

The impact of that shock at first threatened to force Eden from the premiership. On the Tory backbenches there had been for several years a 'Suez Group' dedicated to attacking any government moves which seemed to appease anti-British nationalism in various parts of the world.[5] The leverage of this group arose not from its rather small numbers, but from the fact that it gave voice to a widely felt sentiment liable, under certain circumstances, to become politically dominant. Eden had striven to keep these rightist elements at bay, casting them the odd gift, such as Archbishop Makarios' deportation to the Seychelles in early March 1956. But as the Americans cleaved to a position through August and September which was increasingly unsympathetic from a British vantage point, Tory backbench support for a reassertion of UK unilateralism grew apace. Equally important, furthermore, was the fact that this view had gained a key Cabinet supporter in the Chancellor of the Exchequer, Harold Macmillan. The chauvinist mood of the Conservative Party Conference at Llandudno during the second week of October confirmed Eden's fear that a revolt against his leadership was inevitable unless he took decisive action, and that such action should be in cooperation with the French Government, whose animosity towards Nasser had reached a pitch equal to that prevailing in London.

The French strategy, into which the British were now fitted, emerged during visits by French ministers and officials to London on 14 October, and subsequently at secret conclaves in the environs of Paris. These plans involved an Israeli attack on Egypt and subse-

quent Anglo-French intervention, ostensibly to separate the combatants and protect the Canal, but actually to depose Nasser. It was an
integral part of this plan that it should be made operational *before* the
US presidential elections on 6 November, so that Eisenhower's
response would be conditioned by his unwillingness to alienate Jewish
voters at home. Whatever the risks in such collusion between London,
Paris and Tel Aviv, the Israelis had provided Eden and Mollet with
the vital 'cover' for a successful strike. But because Eden faced
intense opposition to his general Egyptian policy from the Labour
Opposition, from within the Foreign Office and even within his own
Cabinet, the Prime Minister could not allow the extent of this
trilateral cooperation to be known outside a narrow circle. In the
debate which followed it was Eden's understandable omission to
stitch more of Whitehall's policy-forming mass into the collusive
pattern which made him so vulnerable to a party coup.

On 27 October the Israelis mobilized and two days later invaded
Egypt. The British and French sent a twelve-hour ultimatum to the
combatants (effectively, of course, to Egypt) calling for a ceasefire
and a withdrawal behind a ten-mile radius along the Canal – a
'freezing' of positions very much in Israel's favour. When Nasser did
not respond the Anglo-French intervention was set in motion, and on
the night of 31 October/1 November the Royal Air Force bombed
Egyptian airfields to prevent any counter-strike against Israeli cities.
During these crucial days the British authorities evaded all American
enquiries as to what was happening 'on the ground'; this blow to the
self-image of the Washington coteries as the arbitrators of events in
the non-Communist world evoked profound resentment. Eisenhower
and Dulles moved quickly to regather control of the crisis into their
own hands. On the evening of 1 November Dulles delivered an
impassioned speech at the Security Council of the UN calling for an
abstention from military activity on *all* sides, and gained virtually
unanimous support (only Australia and New Zealand supported the
British position). Meanwhile the governments in London and Paris
continued to hope that once they had succeeded in entrenching a
sufficient number of troops along the Canal, the Americans would
accept the *fait accompli* and modify their stance. Hence infantry units
were parachuted into Egypt from Cyprus on 5 November, and the
bulk of the seaborne force disembarked the following day. But by this
stage the US administration was exploiting the chief weakness in the
British position: the fragile condition of sterling on world money

markets. To what extent currency pressures at this stage were sedulously cultivated by the US monetary authorities is not clear. But by refusing to support the pound as downward influences got to work, Eisenhower was facing the UK Cabinet with a choice which the latter had never expected to face: either to continue with the attempt to topple Nasser at the cost of inducing a drastic curtailment of British living standards, or to withdraw from the venture with whatever dignity could be mustered. But this was really no choice at all, since Eden had no illusions that the UK electorate cared sufficiently about who ruled Egypt to tolerate a financial squeeze. He therefore had little option but to inform the French that British involvement was at an end, and to authorize the evacuation of the UK forces from the Canal; Mollet, who probably felt that Nasser had already received an adequate check to his Algerian machinations, promptly fell into line with this decision. With the Anglo-French withdrawal under way, Eden, who had for some time been suffering from a liver complaint, departed for a recuperative holiday in Jamaica, leaving his Cabinet colleagues to face the parliamentary grilling which followed.

The most telling aspect of the Suez aftermath, however, lay in the US administration's tacit intervention in domestic British politics.[6] It can be fairly surmised that during the Egyptian crisis the advisers closest to Eisenhower had determined to force Eden from Downing Street. It was their pressure which led the President to refuse to receive Eden for talks in Washington once the withdrawal from Suez had been completed, although he had initially expressed a willingness to do so, and the manner in which the British Prime Minister was afterwards 'blackballed' from any high-ranking contact with US officialdom was an unprecedented signal that Washington wished to see a change of leadership in the UK. Meanwhile American embassy personnel in London were having private talks with Cabinet Ministers, amongst whom the Chancellor of the Exchequer, Harold Macmillan, was prominent. The substance of these meetings can only be guessed at. The American case was (almost certainly) that the US Government would assist the reconstruction of British economic and diplomatic prestige only if Eden was replaced by a new Prime Minister prepared to align himself more closely with Washington than had been characteristic of UK foreign policy during the first half of the 1950s. This was a bitter pill to swallow for a Whitehall establishment which ever since 1945 had yearned, above all, to create for itself some freedom of movement in world affairs; but under post-Suez conditions only a more intimate and binding linkage with American power seemed likely to fend off a truly precipitate decline in Britain's international position, and with it, perhaps, that of the Conservative Party. In January 1957, therefore, the Tory machine, wielding the silver dagger draped in velvet for which it was renowned when it came to changes in the leadership, obtained Eden's resignation and the succession to the premiership of Harold Macmillan. Macmillan therefore came to power with an agenda that had, in its general outlines, already been framed; above all, he was confronted with the task of exploring new techniques of operating Britain's 'middle-power' capacities in a world which had changed radically since the Tories had returned to office in 1951. His impatience with the detritus of empire, and his early determination to force the pace of decolonization, was just one aspect of that Whiggish adaptation of the UK's national life which marked Macmillan's leadership. It is this wider theme of Britain's changing political economy in the late colonial period which now claims our attention.

II   THE CHANGING METROPOLE

Britain's post-Second World War dilemmas were almost all, to a greater or lesser extent, connected with her transatlantic relationships. To explain this situation some preliminary comment is necessary on the character of Anglo-American interactions during the first half of the twentieth century. Attitudes in Whitehall towards the United States in the three decades prior to 1939 were deeply paradoxical. On the one hand there was a consistent hankering after an 'Anglo-Saxon' front in world affairs, so that American resources could be brought into play to help reduce the gap between liabilities and capacity which was bedevilling British foreign policy. Certainly in the aftermath of the 1914-18 conflict the British Government showed a willingness to make big sacrifices (over the questions of Ireland, war debts and the alliance with Japan) in order to secure American goodwill – largely unavailingly. On the other hand, however, official opinion in London concurrently came to resent an emerging US veto over British actions, and to emphasize the need to protect 'national independence' in high-level decision-making. These clashing approaches *would* have constituted a major 'issue' in British foreign policy had successive US administrations not settled matters themselves by adopting an isolationist posture through the 1920s and 1930s. Broadly, it was the grip of isolationism on American society in these decades which critically inflated the appeal of 'Commonwealth' in British minds, since the UK had no other framework within which to order its responses amidst a deteriorating international situation.

Britain's problem with the United States was transformed after the latter's entry into the Second World War during 1941. If old diplomatic hands in Whitehall had previously hoped that the passing of the isolationist school in Washington would produce a malleable alternative eager to enter into an equal partnership with the UK, they were to be acutely disappointed. Thus if America's pre-war isolationism was unilateral, so was her subsequent drive towards 'world leadership'. The discomfiture this caused in London was ameliorated between 1941 and 1945 by the integrated structure of wartime cooperation, epitomized by Anglo-American dominance of the Allied Combined Boards which allocated physical resources. With the end of the war, however, the Truman Administration had no intention of admitting the British into a sort of condominium in reshaping the international order; the latter found themselves 'frozen out' from the inner circles of Washington. Suggestively, in 1946 the US ceased to share its atomic secrets with Britain. Just as galling to the UK was Washington's clear determination that the British future lay in a closer economic and political attachment to their continental neighbours. This pressure was powerfully stepped up after the unveiling of the Marshall Plan in mid-1947. Britain's enhanced commitment to its colonies and Dominions (minus India and Palestine) during the post-war years, symbolized by development expenditures, renewed capital flows and Sterling Area management, was a response to such pressures emanating from across the Atlantic.

One of the persistent themes in British policy after 1945 was the attempt to evade absorption into any west European grouping. In retrospect, this has come to be seen as a disastrous error, which it may well have been (although a final answer to this depends on the effectiveness of the EEC in the remaining years of the twentieth century). Certainly in the immediate post-war years a very reticent approach to west European 'unification' was, from a British vantage point, quite sensible. It was, after all, the British who would have had to shoulder most of the military burdens of such a grouping (the French army was hardly yet in a position to do so) and whose industry had most to lose from exposure to the full blast of German competition (the French, without a franc zone on the scale of their sterling counterpart, had much less choice in this matter). But if the British policy towards western Europe was rational, it was not easy to sustain. The formation of the North Atlantic Treaty Organization (NATO) in 1949, while clearly in the UK's overall interest given the burgeoning Soviet threat, accentuated this difficulty, since the Americans were bound to use the new alliance mechanism to push Britain towards closer cooperation with its continental neighbours. In this milieu the shape of UK foreign policy after 1951 – its adumbration of Britain's continuing role in the Middle East, Asia and Africa, its distancing from pan-European initiatives and its refusal to become excessively constricted into NATO's anti-Communist structures – made sense. Anthony Eden, who ran this foreign policy as Churchill's Foreign Secretary and then as Prime Minister, epitomized Whitehall's eagerness to maintain a zone of British unilateralism in world affairs, and its perception that this involved a special relationship with the underdeveloped world. Ironically, Eden, whose personal knowledge of the colonial world was distinctly limited, and who felt much more at home in Rome or Paris than in Delhi or Dar-es-Salaam, was constantly emphasizing the extra-European and extra-NATO dimensions to British interests. In doing so, he blocked the US administration's objective of shaping western power in its own exclusive image; the Suez crisis of 1956 was only the climax of an antagonism between Eden and Dulles which had already been strongly conditioned by Anglo-American differences over the future of Indo-China. The enormous resources which the UK Government were prepared to devote to fighting anti-colonial insurgents in Kenya, Malaya and Cyprus during much of the decade have, therefore, to be seen against the backdrop of these much larger international rivalries.[7]

Britain's retreat from Suez and Eden's enforced resignation signified that the attempt to extend the ambit of an independent foreign policy had failed. It was implicit in Macmillan's elevation to the premiership that his concept of national interest had to be honed much more precisely to NATO objectives as defined in the White House, and it was inevitable that the priority attached to African and Asian commitments in London should be thrust lower down the pecking order. This did not mean, of course, that these commitments were to be thrown completely overboard, but it did mean that there were strict limits to the resources the British authorities would expend in supervising local change. Macmillan was fortunate, however, that events after his arrival in power enhanced his bargaining position with the Americans. In the Middle East, for example, the Lebanese crisis of 1958 – in which the British and Americans intervened together to prevent civil war – and the Iraqi revolution – when the pro-western monarchy was destroyed – which occurred simultaneously impressed on the US administration the risks of the post-imperial age, and the advantages of helping Britain to maintain its influence in at least some of its old colonial haunts.[8] More broadly, the Soviet success in launching the first space vehicle (Sputnik I) in October 1957 shattered American confidence in its own strategic invulnerability, and underlined its need for reliable alliance partners: Britain – Anglo-Saxon, socially stable and with a governing orthodoxy geared to the maintenance of a strong military arm – fitted this requirement perfectly. Thus during the late 1950s and early 1960s Britain and the US settled down to a period of renewed intimacy, encapsulated in the much vaunted friendship between the youthful new President of 1960, John F. Kennedy, and the worldly-wise British statesman, Harold Macmillan; their friendship, indeed, throve with each blast of invective that de Gaulle directed at what he dramatized as an Anglo-American 'front'. More by luck than judgement, the Whitehall establishment seemed to have hit upon a formula which guaranteed it star international status. This formula, however, had a lot to do with British involvement in superpower rivalry, and very little to do with the vestiges of empire. Thus it was, after 1960, that UK dependencies found themselves hustled towards independence as if the old concerns with 'viable' statehood had never existed.

The successive mutations of the Anglo-American relationship served to dictate the changing values which British governments ascribed to colonies. But knit into this shifting concatenation was one factor we have yet to mention: the advent of British nuclear weaponry. Suggestively, one of the earliest post-war indications that the Truman administration had no intention of an exclusive Anglo-American partnership was its decision in 1946 to cease sharing its nuclear research findings with British scientists. The Labour Government of 1945–51 clearly did not have the available finance to make up for this deficiency, although the UK nuclear development teams were kept intact.[9] However, at this stage it was not at all clear that the investment in an independent nuclear capacity would prove worthwhile. The Soviet military threat in Europe was conventional in nature; when the Korean emergency erupted in 1950–1, it was shortfalls in this area of procurement that had to be made up at enormous cost to the British economy. Nevertheless, the risks of losing touch with nuclear technology were too great for the challenge to be evaded altogether, and Churchill, after his re-election in 1951, ensured that more cash was made available for the bomb programme, since he felt that the Americans would only accept Britain as something more than a west European power once it was equipped with a nuclear infrastructure. Thus in October 1952 Britain exploded its first atomic device at Monte Bello, Australia; less than five years later she successfully experimented with a thermonuclear version. By the time of Macmillan's succession to power Britain was within sight of bracketing itself with the US and the USSR as members of the select club of nuclear warriors, although clearly its technology in this respect was much inferior to that of the two superpowers.

Macmillan was quick to grasp that Britain's post-Suez condition required a much more dramatic shift from conventional to nuclear defence spending than had yet been contemplated in Whitehall. Expensive anti-insurgency campaigns, with the complex logistics they entailed, now had a much reduced relevance to British interests; the nuclear mode was commensurately more important, not least because it would augment the UK's leverage where it really mattered – in Washington. The 1957 Defence Review enshrined this altered priority, and opened the way to the ending of conscription in 1960. Macmillan's decision to give up the task of any systematic 'policing' of African nationalism (in Nyasaland, for example) arose logically from this strategic reorientation. The strategy embarked upon, however, was fenced in by high risks, since the moving staircase of nuclear technology made it impossible that Britain could achieve a credible deterrent without American assistance; even if the UK defence industries could produce a modern atomic warhead, the collapse of the Blue Streak project in early 1960 underlined the lack of a credible delivery system. This was the greatest external challenge which faced Macmillan's administration after 1960: to convince the US Government that the western alliance would be best served by setting its British ally up in the nuclear style to which it was determined to become accustomed. This objective was finally achieved at the Nassau Conference between Macmillan and Kennedy in December 1962, when the latter agreed to the provision of the missiles for the 'independent' British Polaris programme. This deterrent had a technical life-span stretching into the mid-1970s; at no other point in the twentieth century, probably, had British national security attained such an apotheosis. It is hardly surprising, amidst these developments, that within Whitehall colonies had become a tiresome disturbance to be sloughed off into independence as soon as possible. The comings and goings of assorted nationalists at Lancaster House made colourful copy for the British press, very necessary at a time when circulation wars in Fleet Street were even more bitter than usual, but they had become marginal to the realities of British power under contemporary circumstances.

The thrust of our argument is therefore that in the diplomatic and military fields colonialism after 1957 became dysfunctional to the operational necessities of the metropole. A similar pattern can be discerned in the economic sphere. But before outlining the reasons for this latter disjuncture, it is necessary to comment on the surprising vitality of Britain's economic relationship with the underdeveloped world in the decade after 1945. We noted earlier a prime reason for this: colonial development appealed to UK economic interests as a necessary cushion against American dominance of world markets. Certainly the trade and currency pressures which ensued in the later 1940s bound the Sterling Area together and provided a 'hedge' against Britain's progressive loss of competitiveness in relation to other industrial exporters.[10] Even the easing of economic pressures after 1950, however, did not lead UK policy-makers to question Britain's commercial orientation towards its Commonwealth and colonial partners. There were several reasons for this. First, the alternative was a closer alignment with the integrationist developments in western Europe; British interests, however, had little faith that these would succeed, while the prospect of living in a free market with Germany (however truncated) was anathema to them. Second, it seemed quite likely that in any sustained, US-led boom the world's primary producers would be key beneficiaries, and UK business could be kept busy mopping up purchasing power in this sector of the world economy with which it had strong institutional and political linkages. Third, in the early 1950s the fear remained that, as after the First World War, recovery would ultimately be followed by a relapse into deep depression, and as long as this possibility remained it was considered foolhardy to reshape traditional alliances which, for all their limitations, had been tried and tested over decades. Therefore, at the time of the Suez adventure Britain's marked economic orientation towards the world's agricultural nations, many of them colonies, was still pronounced.

After 1955, however, the 'long boom' of the post-war period did not falter. There were cyclical 'blips' (the 1957–8 dip in US markets was reflected in European growth-rates) but the consolidation of business confidence was not affected, with the result that investments continued at a high level. As long as their prosperity was so visibly connected to American economic expansion, west European countries were in no position to snub US diplomatic leadership, however vexed governing elites may have been by their subordination. Most importantly, it was the sustained stimulus to world trade through the 1950s which explained the surprising success of west European integration, culminating in the establishment of the Common Market by the Treaty of Rome in March 1957; had recession intervened, the French would almost certainly have recoiled from a process which involved opening up their domestic economy to German competition. In fact, by the end of the 1950s France was in a peculiarly favourable position, well-placed to influence the shape of the European Economic Community (EEC) and, with it, the direction of the west European heartland. De Gaulle, when he came to power in 1958, was thus in a position about which Poincaré in the 1920s, for example, could only have dreamed. It was the confidence arising from this, and the clinical determination to bend French efforts to this crucial challenge, which led the general to scale down French colonial commitments. Meanwhile British government and business became conscious of a glacial isolation. The crux of this isolation was not so much political at first, as economic; the principal gains in international trade were occurring in exchanges within industrial blocs such as the EEC, and thus passed by the world's primary-producing sector into which British interests were so deeply splayed. Furthermore, the productivity of British industry, cushioned for so long behind the Sterling Area, fell increasingly behind that of its continental competitors. Not surprisingly, Macmillan concluded after 1957 that the UK had to seek what previously she had disdained: a place in the EEC sun.[11] Only in this way, it seemed, could British trade be reshaped in ways conducive to growth, and British society as a whole exposed to the disciplines of modern commercial competition. If, in these contexts, de Gaulle's decolonizations were acts of supreme self-assurance, those of Macmillan were executed in a spirit of questing anxiety as to the UK's placement in the world system. In either instance, however, economic developments in the decade after 1955 had made the old concerns with imperial tariffs and trade, and colonial development in general, seem a fragment of dead history.

Structural changes in trading patterns were thus a factor making for decolonization. But there is one individual strand in this metropolitan economic revisionism which needs to be isolated: the growing pessimism regarding the growth prospects of underdeveloped countries, and the fear that too intimate a link with these economies – especially if that link were colonial – could prove disastrously burdensome.[12] In the late 1940s and early 1950s it had been assumed that, once poor economies received initial injections of development monies, their expansion would be self-generating. In the mid-1950s, however, it was clear that pumping investment into these societies had minimal growth effects. Meanwhile, however, their demand for metropolitan aid was multiplying: seemingly ever-increasing flows of cash were required to maintain the infrastructures which had been slotted into place, and to satisfy the local interest groups congealing around them. The British Treasury was gripped by a panic-vision of the UK economy not only being by-passed by west European prosperity, but meanwhile being milched by parasitic dependents in Africa and the Caribbean. In Whitehall, therefore, the door was increasingly being slammed in the face of colonial borrowers after 1955/6, and private institutional investors were quite adamant, when pressed, that they were not going to plug the gap by risking funds in areas where future profitability seemed to have poor prospects.[13] Harold Macmillan, as Chancellor of the Exchequer between December 1955 and January 1957 was fully exposed to a fiscal critique which was shot through with a new contempt for government spending in the colonies; a contempt which did not take long to ripen into a desire to rid the UK economy of its residual responsibilities as soon as possible. It was therefore quite logical that, when Macmillan became Prime Minister, one of his first acts was to set up a cost/benefit review of the colonial position.[14] The conclusions of this review (though not yet accessible to historians) can, however, be discerned. If Macmillan's decision to accelerate decolonization in Africa did not become overt until late in 1959, the basic attitude from which this approach sprang can thus be seen taking firm shape in the preceding three years.

So far in this section we have stressed the changing military, diplomatic and economic milieu in which British decolonization took place. It is necessary to mesh party political factors into this discussion, although their overall importance was probably quite limited. The traditional bipartisanship on colonial issues in British politics broke down after 1951: events in Central Africa, Cyprus and Egypt gave the Labour Party considerable scope for publicizing their differences with the policies of Conservative Governments. Oliver Lyttelton, Colonial Secretary between October 1951 and July 1954, attributed this shift by the Labour Opposition to pure opportunism. Certainly a sudden conversion to an undiluted anti-colonialism served Labour Party purposes quite well at the time. Opposition politicians could hardly get much mileage out of attacking government economic policies when the Tories were rolling back post-war austerity; neither could they make a frontal assault on the foreign policy front without provoking public mistrust of their own wider loyalties. The colonial question was the one area of public policy in which Labour could hope to make a clear contrast between the Conservatives' incorrigible reaction and their own progressive virtues. Their efforts along these lines did them little good, as the 1959 election result showed; the British public was not to be moved by the 'condition of Africa' question even when it was perorated upon from the Labour benches.

Nevertheless, the question remains as to whether the Labour Party's criticisms on colonial matters did affect the Conservative Government's calculations in a way that contributed to decolonization? The most careful study which has been carried out in this area concludes that the Labour Party was effective in setting parameters within which the debate over colonial policy took place. 'Though it was seldom if ever able to force dramatic and visible changes in government policy', David Goldsworthy has written, 'Labour was consistently able to . . . effect the political climate within which both Government and colonial leaders had to operate.'[15] This is no doubt true. But the whole discussion of the relationship between party politics and late-colonialism remains shallow unless it is related to the changing social currents in the UK. The outstanding fact about British life in the 1950s was the emergence of a new middle class. Because it was new, and because it was much larger than the old-established bourgeoisie, this group did not have the resources to finance house purchases and higher education for its offspring; increasingly the state was expected to subsidize such acquisitions through tax reliefs and grants, and any diversion of resources for colonial purposes (to defeat Mau Mau insurgents, for example, or to improve Tanganyikan land-use) became increasingly resented. In this way the contemporary usage of the term 'progressive' was shaped; it meant being sensitive to the special needs of new and aspirant metropolitan classes for whom imperial values had never been a significant political emotion. These were the 'floating voters' whom Harold Macmillan knew that the Tory party had to win to its standard if it was to survive electorally, and his new-model Conservatism was shaped in their image. Pushing colonies across the independence threshold to face their own uncertain future, and knocking politely at the door of the EEC to request belated membership, were just part of a broad reappraisal of national policy in the light of these social and factional dynamics.

Finally, this account of the changing metropole has been overwhelmingly skewed towards considerations of material self-interest, sometimes measured in hard cash and sometimes in political leverage. But was not decolonization also the result of a moral revolution (whereby colonialism came to be seen as plain wrong) marking western European civilization as a whole after 1945, but particularly evident, perhaps, in that liberal nation *par excellence*, Great Britain? Should we not, in other words, perceive the demission of empire as one element in a progressive mentality which came gradually to embrace the welfare state in western Europe's social arrangements, redistributive justice in its fiscal systems, ecumenicalism in its religious philosophy and remedies for the law's statutory oppression of homosexuals? It would be easy to indulge in cheap jokes at the expense of such a beneficent interpretation. One problem, as always, is that morality and self-interest overlap so closely. Thus one reason why colonies were hustled towards independence, as we have seen, was precisely to release west European resources for domestic welfare spending; the consistency here was more that of the accountant than the philanthropist. Still, even a commentator given, on the whole, to cheerful cynicism might grant that the fifteen years after 1950 witnessed, in the capitalist world at least, a genuine and widely diffused advance in the mores of human society. In western Europe it was as if the various nations suddenly dusted off the filth of two world wars, one great depression and, more recently, sustained austerity, realized that, after all, hope and prosperity had not been entirely extinguished and set off once more down the broad avenues of social betterment. The origins of the EEC may be seen in this happy light, before the gourmet-bureaucrats got to work on their own behalf, distorting and trivializing its ideals, until it became the sad, twisted (if not yet entirely unreformable) institution of the mid-1980s. Nor should this post-1950 Enlightenment be seen in purely western European terms. Perhaps its greatest moment, the epitome of what was best in a whole generation, took place in the United States: Martin Luther King's civil rights movement climaxing in the march on Washington in August 1963. The moment did not last. In North America and western Europe the rot had set in by the mid-1960s, as political entrepreneurs, machine-bureaucrats, media-aristocrats and windbag-academics clambered aboard the progressive movement, turning it in directions of their own choosing, defining its aims in terms of power rather than pragmatic justice and replanting its roots in the arid soil of particular interest groups. In this way 'liberation' could be shunted from its spiritual moorings towards an off-the-peg rationalization for indiscriminate killings, and still rate an applause on the campuses of western universities. Here, of course, we have gone well outside the proper ambit of European decolonization. Nevertheless, ultimately any complex understanding of this subject will have to be set in the context of moral and intellectual, as well as politico-economic, change. The former, however, is even more set about with traps and ambiguities than the latter, and the reader can only be forewarned against coming to easy conclusions.

8. The Climax of British Decolonization in Africa

IN this chapter we will be concerned with the classical phase of decolonization in British Africa between 1954 and 1965, and in particular with the three case-studies defined in Chapter 5: the Gold Coast, the Central African Federation and Kenya. It was stressed earlier that in the first years of the 1950s these regions appeared to be pointing in critically different directions. After 1951 the Gold Coast was headed towards a variant of political reform which involved the progressive expansion of African authority; self-government had been put on the real, as opposed to the mythical, agenda drawn up by the responsible power. In British Central Africa the establishment of the Federation marked a barely concealed attempt to order the future of the area within the norms set by white-settler supremacy, even for those Crown Colonies involved – Nyasaland and Northern Rhodesia – which their British overseers had hitherto regarded as 'native states' (that is, political units within which white-settler interests were to be kept within certain constraints). In Kenya the emerging pattern of events was much more finely poised in terms of the racial balance of power. During the later 1940s the European community had extended the leverage within the colony which they had acquired during the Second World War years, but by 1952 black African resistance to this process had gained a momentum of its own – most dramatically, in the outbreak of the Mau Mau revolt. During the course of the decade which followed, these directional polarities moved into a closer alignment with each other. In the Gold Coast political developments proved not quite as fast-moving as seemed possible in 1951, as local oppositions to Kwame Nkrumah's Convention People's Party (CPP) crystallized; in British Central Africa the

Federation proved unsustainable, and the status of Northern Rhodesia and Nyasaland as black African states was finally reasserted; in Kenya the white-settler lobby was progressively dislodged from its pivotal place in colonial society, and African leaderships inducted into the constitution-making dialogue. In the end, therefore, the compressed and frenetic pattern of British decolonization in Africa, climaxing in the early 1960s, assumed (for all the distinctiveness of individual cases) a more standardized format than might earlier have been predicted. In 1965, however, this experience was contradicted by one outstanding colonial exception, that of Southern Rhodesia, and one immutable fact: the continued regional primacy of the apartheid regime in South Africa.

I GHANA: EXEMPLARY DECOLONIZATION AND POLITICAL MYTH

We have previously described how by February 1951, following the resounding victory of Nkrumah's Convention People's Party (CPP) in the Gold Coast elections, the British Government accepted the logic of accelerated political change in West Africa. It was natural that such a demission of power by Britain should first be accomplished in the western part of the African continent since the absence of white settlers made the exercise much more manageable. Neither is it surprising that the move to independence should have first taken place in the Gold Coast rather than neighbouring Nigeria.[1] The Gold Coast suited Whitehall's need for a 'model' African decolonization, and one not likely to go off the rails in the immediately foreseeable future, on several grounds: it was less ethnically segmented than Nigeria, it appeared to have a relatively resilient economy and it had, in Kwame Nkrumah, a nationalist leader capable (in a way that Chief Awolowo in Nigeria, for example, was not) of reconciling divergent elements within his own highly individualistic persona. In retrospect, British decolonization in the Gold Coast, which culminated in the independence of Ghana in March 1957, was a timely success. At their first attempt the British seemed to have pulled off the trick of transforming a patchwork African colony into a stable, modernizing and self-governing state. This achievement, following the UK's debacle in the Suez crisis the previous year, was instrumental in encouraging Whitehall policy-makers to see blanket decolonizations elsewhere as one of the chief means whereby Britain's international standing could be restored. Looked at more closely, however, the Gold Coast transition between 1951 and 1957 was not entirely smooth: the calculations were finely poised, the political symmetry mostly cosmetic; and if it was a *tour de force* in imperial withdrawal, it was never a convincing exercise in the making of a new state.

Nkrumah's position following the 1951 elections appeared very secure; it was this apparent local impregnability (based mainly on the loyalty of the southern coastal population) which made him so attractive to the colonial authorities as a partner-in-change. Admittedly, the CPP did not possess a solid majority in the legislature because the indirectly elected members, especially those from the north, could not be considered automatic supporters of the new 'quasi' government. But the Assembly opposition was fragmented, and non-CPP members were still, at this stage, instinctively deferential to 'government', even if this was an unfamiliar government with a black southern face. Nkrumah had brilliantly succeeded in identifying his own personal leadership with the national and material aspirations of the Gold Coast masses, and this asset was not easily squandered. 'Until independence', he told a visiting group of journalists, 'there is only one political platform – that is independence – and I happen to be occupying it.' However, Nkrumah did not omit further reinforcing his position by the use of patronage, so that Africanization of the public service and the allocation of development monies were used to entrench CPP influence. The prosperity based on rising cocoa prices which set in after 1950 also came just at the right moment to create a popular mood of optimism and to lubricate the institutionalization of Nkrumah's CPP hegemony.

Despite all these political advantages, however, there was one other absolute precondition for Nkrumah's success after 1951: the support of the British administration and, above all, the personal favour of the Governor, Arden-Clarke. This is not to imply that Arden-Clarke had it in his power to break the nationalist movement had he wished, but he did have the capacity to break any particular nationalist leader – which, when the metropole was already bent on devolving power, was the vital issue. Thus if the Governor chose to signal that further movement to independence depended on the CPP stumping up a new popular figure-head, a stampede for Nkrumah's succession would immediately be set in motion. Nkrumah was well aware of this chink in his personal armour, and the texture of his relationship with Arden-Clarke indicated an almost demure subservience. It was because Governor and Government Leader understood their mutual positions, and what gifts each could extend to the other, that their political friendship warmed from the beginning. It was this unarticulated but profound alliance which was to carry Nkrumah through to the dream of independence, even when other factors had turned against him.

Between 1951 and 1954 a full-blown opposition movement emerged to challenge Nkrumah's position. This dissidence originated both inside and outside CPP ranks. Initially the overwhelming bulk of party activists had accepted Nkrumah's switch from 'Positive' to 'Tactical' Action, through which the Leader of Government Business (elevated to 'Prime Minister' by Arden-Clarke in February 1952) transmuted his confrontationist, anti-British rhetoric into the softer murmurings of negotiated cooperation. But the government had only limited resources to reward its loyalists. Many individuals were therefore left out in the cold following the Tactical Action share-out, and they came to resent the conspicuous luxury increasingly displayed by ministers and their friends. In time these aggrieved elements coagulated into loosely bound networks. Meanwhile, disaffection became even more sharply defined in those regions where the CPP had never been very strong. One factor here was Nkrumah's need to prove to Arden-Clarke his 'fitness to govern', leading him to cultivate an image of efficiency wherever possible, and since cracking down on ministerial corruption was too dangerous politically, Nkrumah instead resumed the cutting-out of diseased cocoa trees, the growers of which lay largely outside the southern CPP heartlands. Anti-Nkrumah sentiments were therefore widespread in the cocoa districts from 1953 onwards. All too easily the imposition of Nkrumah's authority in the north and east of the country appeared in those areas as little more than carpetbagging by southern opportunists, and once this perception became generalized it was inevitable that an institutional opposition would emerge.

There was always one ploy, however, which Nkrumah could use to stifle criticism: the stepping-up of agitation for a further move towards a fully independent constitution. In effect, this meant squeezing every morsel of advantage out of the independence platform, which in 1951 had made Nkrumah a landslide winner of the post-Coussey elections. In September 1953 the Prime Minister demanded that the British Government set a date for the transfer of power. The Whitehall authorities were happy to go at least part of the way required to restore the position of their chosen local ally, and the new constitution of early 1954 allowed for an all-elected Legislative Assembly, and a totally Africanized cabinet appointed on the advice of the main party leader. But this complex interaction of political tactics and constitution-mongering served only still more to alert the regions outside the south that a centralized polity run by the CPP elites was imminent. Two regional parties now emerged to challenge Nkrumah for the post-colonial succession. These were the Northern People's Party (NPP), established in April 1954, and the Togoland Congress, largely composed of the Ewe-speaking peoples in the east. These developments put the British in a dilemma. On the one hand it was desirable to hand power to Nkrumah *before* such splinterings of Gold Coast politics made decolonization even more messy and dangerous; on the other hand, it was necessary to legitimate this transfer of power by making the Prime Minister go through another (and supposedly final) electoral test before independence could be granted on the basis of the 1954 constitution.

From the start of the election campaign Nkrumah found that his old supremacy had been dented. The most evident sign of this was the sporadic breakdown of CPP discipline and the proliferation of independent candidates in the south. Aspirants to political office of any kind knew that the pre-independence election was the last chance to join the gravy-train, and those who failed to be officially selected put themselves up as independent candidates as a last resort. Meanwhile in the north the NPP demanded a separate £8m development programme, protested against endemic infractions of chieftainly prestige and lambasted the graft in Accra government circles; while in Togoland the Congress fanned the embers of Ewe nationalism. These disparate forces were not capable of actually displacing Nkrumah. The CPP could still portray him as the 'Hero' who embodied popular dreams of freedom and prosperity. Furthermore, that party still had a sufficient presence outside the south to deny the NPP, for example, a monopoly of seats in its home area. When the election was held in June 1954, the CPP won 72 seats out of a total of 104. But although this was a workable majority, Nkrumah's position had been impaired in a number of ways. The CPP had won less seats than the NPP in the north; many CPP seats were held only by thin majorities; and Nkrumah's own grip on the CPP machine had been loosened.

Because in the final phase of any decolonization the spoils of power were at stake to a unique degree, local politicians could not afford to be on the losing side, and any nationalist party which failed to keep its momentum going right up to the independence finishing line was bound to find its support flaking away as uncertainties mounted. This was the case in the Gold Coast after 1954 when remarkably rapidly the CPP was confronted with an opponent – the National Liberation Movement (NLM) – which integrated the hitherto discrete oppositions to Nkrumah's mastery. What was most potent about the NLM was its place of origin: Kumasi, capital of the ancient kingdom of Ashanti. As long as anti-CPP elements had been isolated in the northern and Ewe districts the British could afford to treat such signs of discontent lightly. But once the Ashanti politicians, centrally situated and at the heart of the cocoa economy, began to strike out in a direction of their own, a more fissile situation arose. The origins of the NLM lay in the farmers' militancy, triggered by Nkrumah's decision to fix the government buying price for cocoa at less than the world price, the local exchequer pocketing the difference. But grower-grievances in the Kumasi area merged into a more pervasive notion that the Ashanti 'nation' had to bestir itself against the threat from the south. The NLM leaders knew that the real deciders of the Gold Coast future were in London, so that from the start they concentrated their efforts on lobbying the Colonial Office to the effect that only a federal constitution could provide long-term stability. Just how long the London policy-makers could ignore these imprecations depended on Nkrumah's success in limiting the opposition's noise level so that power transfer could be effected before a more complex, and therefore less stable, pattern of decolonization became inescapable.

Nkrumah's first response to the NLM challenge was to lambast its leaders as 'stooges', 'arch-reactionaries' and 'imperialist agents', while developing a new theme of Pan-African unity which, by utilizing vast continental resources, would make all things possible, beginning, conveniently enough, in an independent Gold Coast. But such verbiage apart, Nkrumah was intent on using police and security organs to crack down on the Kumasi politicians, and he was furious when Arden-Clarke refused him permission; after all, British complicity in the strong-arming of a colonial opposition could prove intensely embarrassing should the world's press get hold of the story. The Prime Minister was then forced back on a two-pronged strategy. The first option involved linking up with the three main groups within Ashanti who were also opposed to the NLM: the educated cadres who feared the NLM as a chiefs' conspiracy, the non-Ashanti immigrants, and the Brong chieftancies bordering Kumasi who were locked into territorial disputes with the Ashanti paramount authorities. Nkrumah's second tactic was to try and tempt the NLM into a compromise negotiation – largely on his own terms. But the NLM refused these approaches, and Nkrumah appealed to the Colonial Office to send out a constitutional arbitrator – a suggestive comment on whom Nkrumah felt to be his real friends in this crisis of his career. A legal expert, Sir Frederick Bourne, was sent out by the British Government to recommend a possible solution, but the Kumasi opposition boycotted these deliberations as well. The NLM leaders were convinced that only by rejecting all formulae short of federation could they constrain the British into re-evaluating their own commitment to Nkrumah as the untrammelled heir of colonial rule in the Gold Coast.

The NLM had been encouraged in this end-game strategy by the divisions within the ranks of British officialdom, and particularly between the district officials in Ashanti and those in the Accra secretariat. The Ashanti officials deluged Arden-Clarke with complaints as to CPP bully-boy behaviour in Kumasi, and protested against parliamentary legislation which upset established local rights. Indeed, there is evidence that some British administrators close to Arden-Clarke in the capital found the extravagant pro-Nkrumah stance of the Governor overdone. But Arden-Clarke was not to be moved. He built up a strong police presence in Ashanti to ensure control if a breakdown occurred and meanwhile plied London with the merits of 'his' Prime Minister. Here was the classic case of a nationalist leader–governor–Colonial Office axis determined to see that power was transferred quietly, efficiently and in as undiluted a state as possible. Such a powerful and ruthless trio could shrug off criticisms from up-country administrators whose relevance was rapidly ebbing. These field officers, however, still had useful contacts with the (mainly Conservative) UK press, and the attention of British journalists was further drawn by the despatch of Sir Frederick Bourne to the Gold Coast. Such hasty embarkations usually meant that Whitehall was attempting to stifle something somewhere. Both the *Daily Telegraph* and the *Observer* soon carried articles on the intimidation being practised by Nkrumah's henchmen in Kumasi, and *The Times* called for a third general election to test the issue of Nkrumah's national popularity. This was the nightmare which the Colonial Office had always feared: press revelations which laid bare the myth that decolonization was about the delicate assemblage of constitutions and exposed the realities of covert agreements, political threats and bouts of back-alley violence. When a UK parliamentary delegation visited the Gold Coast to solicit NLM views on the Bourne proposals, decolonization in the Gold Coast, far from being the model exercise so keenly required by Whitehall at this stage, seemed on the verge of stalling badly.

The Colonial Office feared that a third election test in the Gold Coast might so fragment local groupings as to make an ordered transfer of power almost impossible. The worst, but by no means impossible, scenario was that the British Government might have to send troops to 'hold the ring' while some new semblance of stability was patched up, and this expensive and risky procedure might have to be repeated *ad nauseam* as other colonies moved towards independence. Similarly, Nkrumah and his ministers feared that another election campaign might raise the high-jump bar of decolonization fractionally beyond their ability to clear. It was at this point that Arden-Clarke played perhaps his most vital part. He urged on the Colonial Office that if independence could be made dependent on Nkrumah obtaining a 'reasonable' majority, the latter could be relied on to get the better of the dissidents once transfer had taken place; the Governor simultaneously convinced Nkrumah that an immediate election was his last chance of scotching the opposition and that Whitehall would, in his case, interpret what constituted a 'reasonable' majority as favourably as possible. Arden-Clarke got his way, and his Prime Ministerial cock was promptly put into the electoral pit to do battle with its rivals.

The third and final Gold Coast election prior to independence took place on 17 July 1956. The knowledge that the winner of this contest would, without doubt, scoop the independence trophy almost immediately drove the CPP and NLM to campaign vigorously in each other's preserves. The former's relative maturity as an organization, however, meant that it was better placed to garner votes on a nationwide basis. When the results were announced the CPP had won 71 out of 104 seats and had even obtained 40 per cent of the representation in Ashanti and the north. Nkrumah had given the Colonial Office its 'reasonable' majority and unlocked the gate to independence. There was, however, one last precondition on which the Colonial Secretary, Lennox-Boyd, insisted: that the opposition be appeased with the promise of Regional Assemblies as a safeguard for their future. Promises of this kind, revocable at will after independence, cost Nkrumah nothing, and such Assemblies therefore featured in the 1957 constitution, although, like much else, they did not long survive in modern Ghana. Thus it was that on 6 March 1957 Kwame Nkrumah became the first black African nationalist to lead his country to full self-government, although, in truth, it had been as much Arden-Clarke's achievement as his own.

The construction of independent Ghana, therefore, seemed to provide that exemplary case of a stable, prosperous and decolonized African polity of which British policy-makers had such an urgent need after 1956. It was especially important that the virtues of this much-trumpeted Ghanaian model should retain their glossy sheen over the following years while the formula was applied elsewhere in British-ruled Africa. On the whole, Ghana served Whitehall reasonably well in this respect up until the mid-1960s. Nkrumah's shift to a virulently anti-capitalist and anti-western 'line' right at the end of the 1950s was indeed embarrassing to the British, and was probably one subsidiary factor accelerating decolonization time-tables elsewhere. But the Ghana showcase continued to exert a curious attraction, such that shoals of western academics, not least veritable swarms of Anglo-American sociologists, climbed on for the ride, outlining – in prose of deep analytical seriousness – the crystallization of a new legitimacy under the aegis of Nkrumah's charisma. By the end of the 1960s, and progressively thereafter, the political and economic myths of this archetypal 'new state' became painfully obvious, but by then the sociologists had moved on to greener pastures.

Before taking final leave of decolonization in the Gold Coast/Ghana, however, it is perhaps appropriate at this point to add one further qualifying remark. It is easy to portray the move to self-government in western Europe's African dependencies, simple-mindedly, as essentially composed of various 'deals' between the key participants. From such a vantage point, the striking of these deals may be seen as throwing off sparks in many directions, but before long the politicians and vested interests (both local and metropolitan)

settle down to a rough but workable harmony. In this manner
decolonization may be reduced to what could be described as the
'political economy of deals', and by sticking to this glib approach the
fundamental differences between marxist and non-marxist interpreters can be suitably glossed over. Naturally such rigging of the
political market-place *was* a central feature of decolonization, and it
is a recurrent phenomenon in these pages. But an account which is
framed wholly in these terms cannot, as we shall emphasize again
later, be satisfactory. Thus politicians could sometimes misread what
was actually happening around them and, even when they understood the broad nature of developments, they frequently made
mistakes in selecting partners with whom to negotiate local alliances.
After all, colonial political life was in such a state of flux that faction
leaders could not hope to be foot-perfect in their response to events;
yet with so much at stake wrong choices were often politically fatal.
In short, the late-colonial world, in all its diverse parts, was much too
complex and mobile a situation to be successfully manipulated as
part of an overarching deal (or set of deals). Of course, to the losers in
the local struggle for power, or to outside critics comfortably
ensconced in the senior common room of some western university, it
seemed that such incisive bargains had been the sole measuring-rod
of decolonization. The latter commentators, for example, found this
very convenient, since it made teaching so much easier, and reduced
the amount of reading required to aspire to some meretricious
professional credibility. The real world in which power was transferred from European states to local polities, however, was always
more complicated, uncertain and riddled with ambiguous outcomes
than such simplistic world views allowed for.

II   BRITISH CENTRAL AFRICA:
THE UNRAVELLING OF FEDERATION

While the British Government was intent on devolving power to
black politicians in West Africa after the early 1950s, in Central
Africa contemporary experimentation had taken the form of a white-
dominated Federation of the Rhodesias and Nyasaland, and between
1953 and 1956 the Central African Federation (CAF) got off to a
reasonably satisfactory start. The rate of economic growth may not
have improved on the boom of the late 1940s and early 1950s, but

investment and incomes continued to move ahead. African wages, in particular, rose more sharply than hourly rates for Europeans. It was this fact which pacified political grievances in the African townships, and stimulated an emergent black bourgeoisie disposed to accept the new dispensation. From the start, the Federal Government's commitment to industrialization favoured Southern Rhodesia's interests within the Federation setting. Much more than Northern Rhodesia or Nyasaland, it came to resemble a modern state with its extensive road and rail systems, its big-city developments in Salisbury and its general level of public amenities. This infrastructural growth was crucial to Southern Rhodesia's ability to absorb a large influx of European (largely British) immigrants. In demographic, economic and political terms, the prospect in 1956 seemed to be of a further entrenchment of European authority, based on the dynamic growth of Southern Rhodesia and mediated through the surrounding region by the Federal mechanism.

White politicians in the Federation, however, were not so sanguine about the future. If the new constitutional arrangements were indeed to be a stepping-stone to independence from London control, then they were convinced that further advance down this road had to be made *before* the 1960 Review Conference prescribed in the 1953 legislation; they were confirmed in this belief by the disturbing signs elsewhere (in the Gold Coast, for example) that the UK was not 'safe' on the race issue. However, Sir Roy Welensky, who had succeeded Huggins as Federal Prime Minister in November 1956, was also aware that, if the CAF was to acquire self-government, the local Europeans had to show the London authorities some proof that African political rights would not thereby be permanently 'frozen'. This was the complex problem to which Welensky applied himself in recasting the Federal franchise during 1957.[2] The new electorate was divided into two rolls which, in principle, were common to all races, but which in practice kept Europeans and Africans apart. At the same time the legislature was to be increased in size from thirty-six to sixty seats, with the additional members being assigned to what were essentially white constituencies. To Northern Rhodesian and Nyasaland blacks, Welensky's franchise reform appeared as a means of extending Southern Rhodesian practices to them, and as the first stage in a drive to create a segregationist *fait accompli* before 1960. The lesson they drew from this was logical enough: northern Africans in the Federation had only a short period left in which they could impress on the British Government and public that the direction of change being engineered from Salisbury was unacceptable to them. The crystallization of black nationalism in CAF between 1957 and 1959 was, therefore, partly 'spontaneous', but was not least a response to the evolving tactics of white Federal politicians.

While inter-racial tensions were sharpening in the Federation as a whole, some basic contradictions within European political ranks were working themselves out in Southern Rhodesia. When Huggins had vacated the Southern Rhodesian premiership for the Federal arena, he had been succeeded in August 1953 by Garfield Todd. Todd's record was that of a cautious liberal – in a colony where white liberalism of any kind was rare.[3] Furthermore, Todd's political attitudes were framed by his own sense of tactical necessities under Southern Rhodesian conditions: namely, that the position of the African majority had to be made to converge with that pertaining in its Federal partners before the joint state would be ushered by the British into independence. In this sense Welensky and Todd, although they were not particularly sympathetic to each other, were complementary: the former consolidating white leadership at the Federal level, the latter softening racial polarities where they were at their sharpest and most brittle. The details of Todd's programmes need not detain us: on the issues of educational provision, liquor consumption and the territorial franchise he sought to go at least some of the way towards meeting African demands. What was most significant about Todd, however, was his style of governing: he cultivated the image of a white politician who wanted a direct and dialectical relationship with black opinion. This cut right across the European consensus that a Southern Rhodesian premier was 'responsible' only to whites, and dealt with Africans purely through the bureaucracy. Once this assumption was upset, it seemed to most Europeans that the process of colonial rule would become unsustainable as the weight of African numbers asserted itself. Fearful that Todd's leadership would prompt white voters to switch their loyalties to 'purist' right-wing alternatives, the United Federal Party (UFP) ousted him from the leadership by caucus in February 1959 and installed Sir Edgar Whitehead as premier. At the general election which soon followed, the UFP retained a mere 5-seat majority, while the conservative Dominion Party actually won more of the popular vote. The widespread surprise at the suddenness of this anti-Todd coup in Salisbury was instrumental in impressing upon blacks throughout the Federation that time was not on their side.

By 1958 the bulk of African opinion had become convinced that it was the local white leaderships, not the British Government and its Central African representatives, who were effectively shaping Federal realities, and that nationalism was the only instrumentality by which this slippage in their position could be arrested. For black politicians this mass insecurity presented them with a welcome opportunity to sell their wares, but responding to it stretched their organizational resources. It was to meet these pressures that the ramshackle Nyasaland African Congress called Hastings Banda back from his London medical practice to assume the leadership. The success Banda enjoyed over the following months in projecting himself as the representative figure of Nyasa anti-colonialism is easily explicable: he was operating in a much easier environment than that facing his counterparts in the two Rhodesias, where the bonds of European control were tighter, while the Africans of Nyasaland had a tradition of 'political' consciousness which gave edge to the outburst of anti-Federation sentiment. Paradoxically, Banda's progress had disturbing implications for Africans in the other two territories, since any British agreement to Nyasaland's secession from the Federation might all too conveniently be offset by further concessions to European demands for freedom from imperial supervision in the two Rhodesias. Black Rhodesian nationalists therefore could not afford to be 'left behind' by the Nyasaland Congress, and so stepped up their own level of political activity. In this way an inner panic linked together African politics throughout the region.

In January 1959 widespread disturbances broke out in Nyasaland, and towards the end of the month Banda hosted a meeting of Congress activists in a rural location close to the capital, Blantyre.[4] Rumour spread that this was the prelude to an African coup in which the lives of Europeans would be in jeopardy. In fact it is hardly conceivable that Banda would have risked any such debacle certain to drive London and Salisbury closer together. Much more convincing is the thesis that he was simply trying to maintain a sense of political crisis so that Federation arrived at the 1960 Review Conference in a bedraggled and discredited condition. Nevertheless, Welensky saw an opportunity to assert that law and order was a Federal, not metropolitan, responsibility, and, more particularly, to flash a message to Nyasaland and Northern Rhodesian whites that their security was assured by Salisbury, not by London. On 21 February he announced that Federal troops were en route to Blantyre to assist the civil power; five days later Whitehead declared a state of emergency in Southern Rhodesia and arrested 500 African National Congress (ANC) leaders. The British colonial administrations in the two northern territories were thus put in a deeply equivocal position: any failure to crack down on the nationalists would lead local whites to contrast their own passivity with the vigour of Welensky and Whitehead, while to allow themselves to be 'bumped' by Salisbury into repression would (as Welensky had intended) break their already tenuous relationship with the African politicians. It was the first of these eventualities which the colonial governments opted to avoid, so that on 3 March the Governor of Nyasaland, Sir Robert Armitage, declared a state of emergency in his own territory, while Banda and other Congress leaders were arrested and flown to detention centres in Southern Rhodesia; one week later the British authorities in Northern Rhodesia banned the Zambian African National Congress and similarly incarcerated its leader, Kenneth Kaunda. With what degree of prior collusion is unclear, Welensky and Whitehead had coerced British colonial governments into snapping shut the lid on African political protest in Central Africa.

  The reasoning which had led the Federal and Southern Rhodesian premiers into this strong-arm, high-risk strategy, however, merits further comment. At this point in the CAF's development there was only one year left before the review conference had to be convened. Welensky and Whitehead were both convinced that in the interim period the nationalists had to be kept on the defensive and made to appear as only marginal factors, thus allowing the British Government to yield full self-government to the white-dominated Federation without attracting international (especially American) criticism. But the securing of African quiescence required the 'clearing out' of ANC leaders in all three territories, beginning with Banda; while the British colonial administrations in the north had to be muscled into cooperation by a carefully staged crisis over white security. In this they succeeded. With Banda, Kaunda and the bulk of the Southern Rhodesian ANC activists locked up, Welensky and Whitehead could look forward to the crucial twelve months of apparent serenity so vital to their calculations. But they had, nevertheless, taken the risk that the orchestration of 'emergency' conditions in

Central Africa might cause a shift in Whitehall's thinking that was actually contrary to their own interests. Indeed, the British Government, seeing that the local white politicians in Salisbury had made such a crude shove towards the driving seat, might decide to reaffirm its own power to decide in which direction the rickety colonial vehicle was headed.

This is, in fact, what happened. In the UK Parliament the Conservatives were already vulnerable to Labour criticisms of their complicity in the machinations of white minorities in Africa, and above all in the CAF. The danger this held for Tory electoral prospects was something which, as we shall shortly see, was causing Harold Macmillan (who had succeeded Eden as Prime Minister in early 1957) some concern by 1959. But larger considerations than party advantage were at work here. If the British Government let Rhodesian and Nyasaland affairs slip from its effective supervision, the broader strategy of African decolonization, not least in the east of the continent, could break up – and the resulting clatter might prove the final blow to that British prestige which Macmillan was bent on restoring following the Suez disaster of 1956. It was with these risks brought into play that Macmillan came to give his personal attention to the central thrust of African policy, and that the British establishment (Parliament, bureaucracy and press) effectively commenced its own review of the Federation's future. The first sign of this sea-change was the appointment of the Devlin Royal Commission into the Nyasaland Emergency, which concluded that local colonial administrations had needed to preserve security under the circumstances, but which also stressed that Nyasaland, in consequence, had been made into a 'police state'. Devlin had put the fly gently into the Central African ointment: for how long, it was implicitly asked, could Britain be seen using South African-style repression in an African-majority colony without invalidating its posture as a liberal world power – a posture already critically undermined by Eden's Egyptian bondage? Welensky and Whitehead had 'tidied up' Federal politics to suit their own conception of tactical necessities, but they had unwittingly unleashed forces which ultimately destroyed Federation altogether.

The Central African swell of early 1959 had impressed on Macmillan that a British plan for the Federation had to be slotted firmly into place *before* 1960 arrived, and with this in mind he decided on the establishment of a fresh Royal Commission. It was essential that the

Federal and Southern Rhodesian Governments be represented on this body (and hence implicated in its conclusions), and infintely preferable that the British Labour Party also provide a representative. Welensky and Whitehead were both profoundly suspicious of Macmillan's motives. But the latter was in a position to force them into participation by threatening that otherwise a UK parliamentary committee might be let loose on the Federation question, with gravely unpredictable consequences. The British Prime Minister, however, had no comparable leverage over the Labour Opposition at Westminster. The Labour leader, Hugh Gaitskell, insisted that the Royal Commission be *explicitly* charged to consider the option of secession from the Federation by any territory, and when this was refused he withdrew his party's cooperation. Nevertheless, Macmillan had to ensure that the investigating body retained some credibility with left-of-centre sentiment in Britain, and he did this by settling on ambiguous terms of reference whereby the Royal Commission, while centrally concerned with making the Federation a success in future, was necessarily at liberty to conclude that the experiment had already failed. It was the sharp divergence over the ambit of what became known as the Monckton Commission which marked the beginning of a massive and irreversible alienation between the political establishments in London and Salisbury.

The Monckton Commission arrived in Southern Rhodesia in February 1960. Its proceedings, however, were overshadowed by Harold Macmillan's own official visit to Africa which, in retrospect, can be seen as a carefully planned overture to a shift in the UK's conception of the character and timing for decolonization.[5] The British premier went first to West Africa, and then flew to South Africa where he delivered a set-piece (and subsequently renowned) speech to the Parliament in Cape Town in which he perorated on '. . . the wind of change . . . blowing through this continent.' Macmillan clearly understood that decolonizations which had the approval (however grudging) of the government in Pretoria would be much less susceptible to mid-course errors than those which did not; although whether he quite grasped how deep the Anglo-South African divide had become by early 1960 is, for the present, unknowable. After his efforts to form some kind of consensus between the UK and South Africa, Macmillan travelled to the Rhodesias, and then to Nyasaland. At this stage his principal interest lay in judging whether, in the long term, Federation could 'carry' a large enough block of African opinion with it, and by the time he had tested the atmosphere in Nyasaland the Prime Minister was convinced that it could not. In particular, while there might be legitimate doubts about the representative claims of black nationalists in Southern Rhodesia such as Joshua Nkomo, there could be no similar question mark hanging over Banda's popularity in Nyasaland. The issue therefore arose as to whether the Monckton Commission could discharge its functions without taking evidence from the leader of the Nyasaland ANC? And if Banda was indeed to be interviewed, did he not have to be freed from jail for this to take place under uncompromising circumstances? It is quite likely that the British decision to release Banda was taken while Macmillan was actually in Blantyre, and was inspired by the determination, not only to facilitate the Monckton Commission's work, but to begin stuffing the genie of white hegemony back into the Central African bottle from which it had escaped under cover of the emergencies. Certainly Whitehall was deeply split over Banda's release, with the Colonial Office favouring the move and the Commonwealth Relations Office very much opposed to it. If Macmillan did continue to prevaricate after his return to London, then the matter was decided by the forceful persuasions of the Colonial Secretary, Iain Macleod. Banda was freed in April 1960. In effect, the British, by giving the Nyasaland ANC the green light to resume their operations, were signalling that the demand for secession from the CAF was negotiable.

What factors explain these shifts of position by the British Government? Obviously any answer to this must embrace the broad sweep of Britain's international position, which we have already discussed. But some comment is also needed on Iain Macleod's statement that the British approach to African problems underwent a metamorphosis in the latter months of 1959.[6] The key to this partly lies in Macmillan's belief, confirmed by his election win in the early part of that year, that the Conservative Party could only sustain itself in power by developing a modern and progressive profile. Meanwhile Labour strategists sought for some litmus test by which the reactionary character of Toryism could be 'proved', and they had found this, they felt, in the colonial issue in general, and the CAF in particular. Facing epochal and profoundly contentious decisions on policies towards Europe and nuclear deterrence, Macmillan was ruthlessly determined to shed the colonial albatross which his opponents were striving to clamp around his neck. His African trip in early 1960 was a skilled reconnaissance prior to a clinical act of disengagement, and Banda's release was the perfect means of communicating a change of mood within the Tory ethos.

While Macmillan was totting up the British electoral arithmetic in this way, events in South Africa and the Congo were gouging-out further divisions between the UK and white minorities in the CAF. In the Union a rash of racial unrest had climaxed in the Sharpeville massacre on 21 March 1960; South African police had opened fire on an African crowd, killing 69 people. The international exposure that this received, especially through the medium of television, marked a watershed; South African apartheid began to be perceived in the western world not just as a harsh form of colonial security, but as an essentially deviant means of race-domination. The British Government was driven to distance itself from its South African connection, and ultimately to accept the logic of South Africa's exit from the Commonwealth in May 1961.[7] But white Rhodesian opinion moved inexorably in the opposite direction. Whatever Central African Europeans had disliked about their Afrikaner neighbours in the past, they now discerned a fundamental community of mind. Indeed, during 1960 Southern Rhodesian blacks had themselves taken to the streets in large numbers and the Whitehead government had passed security legislation very much in the South African mould. In the post-Sharpeville world, British and white Rhodesian political cultures sheared decisively apart.

This embittered disaffection was enhanced by the unfolding of Belgian decolonization in the neighbouring Congo. At first the dramatic Belgian decision to quit its 'model' colony caused consternation amongst Central African whites. But this attitude changed when the prospect emerged of a Katangan secession from the new Congolese Federation, for the possible linkage of that rich mining province (straddling, as it did, the Northern Rhodesian border) and its powerful business corporations with the CAF promised to rework the regional odds in favour of continued European supremacy. There is no doubt, Welensky's denials at the time notwithstanding, that the regime of Moise Tshombe centred on Elisabethville in Katanga was funnelled essential supplies from Northern Rhodesia. But Welensky, and whites generally, knew that CAF support could not shore up the Katangan secession for long; they were convinced, however, that British intervention could dictate Congolese outcomes in 1960, and accordingly lobbied London hard. In this instance, as in so many others, local Europeans grossly misunderstood big-power realities and their implications for Africa: the United States, in fact, had decided to squash Tshombe and there was no way that Britain could offend Washington to please Salisbury. Nevertheless, by assisting (if only passively) in Tshombe's defeat in Katanga, which was complete by early 1963, Rhodesian whites felt that the UK Government had lost them a remarkable opportunity of securing guarantees of white survival, and acute distrust began to ripen into Anglophobia.

Meanwhile the Monckton Report on the CAF had been published in October 1960. Its conclusions called for an extension to the African franchise and reform of the colour bar, while its most suggestive remarks concerned the right of individual territories to reconsider their membership of the Federation. But as with many Royal Commissions, the issue with which Monckton was concerned had changed its form (and, in a sense, disappeared) before the Report ever emerged. Thus in July 1960 the UK Government had authorized a new territorial constitution for Nyasaland which, by according Africans a majority on the Legislative Council, made secession from the Federation and prompt independence inevitable. Indeed, by the autumn of 1960 it may be said that the Central African issue did not now concern the Federation's future so much as the post-Federation settlement. This in itself caused Southern Rhodesian whites no great pain; they had never regarded Nyasaland as a vital part of the regional jig-saw, and had felt little real commitment to Federal institutions. It was the outcome of the negotiations on revised territorial constitutions for both Southern and Northern Rhodesia which was bound to determine the Europeans' place in Central Africa, so that when the long-awaited Review Conference was finally convened in London on 5 December 1960 it was, ironically, almost immediately adjourned while the prior issues were decided.

Whatever the impasse between the political establishments in London and Salisbury, it was by no means impossible that the British and Southern Rhodesian Governments could come to an understanding regarding the future of the latter territory. Indeed, sophisticates on both sides grasped that, amidst the clanking sounds of the Federation's dismemberment, some discreet and lasting deals might be made. To these observers it therefore came as no surprise when the British and Southern Rhodesian negotiators settled on a new constitutional framework in February 1961. The British Government accepted the whittling down of most of its traditional 'reserve' powers in the colony, while the Southern Rhodesian Government accepted an electoral formula which at some still distant point would lead to black majority rule as Africans attained the prescribed educational and property qualifications. Neither side was conceding very much on this basis. The British were only too pleased to divest themselves of 'reserve' powers as a general move towards disengagement; Southern Rhodesian Ministers knew that paying obeisance to African political rights was a precondition of Britain yielding on self-government. The real question, however, concerned the acceptability of such a compromise (the shape of which was only gradually becoming distinct) to the respective majorities of the two main racial blocks in Southern Rhodesia. Nevertheless, the answer to this seemed at first affirmative, since Joshua Nkomo, speaking for the nationalist New Democratic Party, at first welcomed the February terms, and the existing white electorate approved them in a referendum five months later.

The focus of Central African affairs at this stage, however, lay in Northern Rhodesia. In other words, an African-ruled Nyasaland did not constitute a critical weakening of the European position in the region, but an African-ruled Northern Rhodesia, with its great Copperbelt, would affect the overall balance of racial power. It was on this issue that the differences between London and Salisbury intensified. Without access to the records, of course, it is impossible to define with certainty the participants' thinking. But the British clearly felt that the Northern Rhodesian blacks, with their over-whelming numerical majority in the territory, could not be refused similar constitutional rights to those already secured in Nyasaland. Furthermore, the calculation being made in London was almost certainly that, once the Southern Rhodesian whites were isolated, they would face up to the imperatives of reconciliation with the African nationalists in their midst. In forcing through this position the UK Government was in a strong position, because neither the Federal nor the Southern Rhodesian Governments had any *locus standi* in the constitutional discussions pertaining to Northern Rhodesia. Nevertheless, Welensky, striving to keep some kind of quasi-Federation alive, pressurized London policy-makers by hinting that any 'sell-out' to Northern Rhodesian nationalists would spark a coup by the Federal power in that territory and thereby a European declaration of independence from London throughout the region. Macmillan, however, was well enough aware that while Southern

Rhodesian whites might risk all to protect their own homes, they were not likely to do so for the sake of their Northern Rhodesian cousins. This episode revealed the hollowness of Welensky's position. Neither, meanwhile, was the British Prime Minister prepared to be shoved off course by the right-wing campaign which the Northern Rhodesian question brought about in the UK, largely orchestrated from the House of Lords. Macmillan knew that a sop was called for, and in October 1961, as part of a larger Cabinet reshuffle, Macleod was moved from the Colonial Secretaryship. But no further concessions were forthcoming. In February 1962 the new Northern Rhodesian constitution was finalized along the lines of that in Nyasaland, and after territorial elections in the following October an African majority was installed in the Legislative Council.[8] Here, too, full independence on something approaching one-man, one-vote was only a matter of time and tactics, and the great mining interests set out to establish a working relationship with Kenneth Kaunda as if the Federation had been a transient aberration.

Even the 'loss' of Northern Rhodesia held out possibilities for Southern Rhodesian whites, however, since if the two northern territories were guaranteed independence on the basis of *their* new constitutions, it could be logically argued that Southern Rhodesia, too, should be accorded such status on the basis of the February 1961 settlement currently in operation. Indeed, the dominant refrain of Salisbury politicians henceforth was that the British had promised that the 1961 constitution would prove a suitable foundation for full independence, despite the fact that it enfranchised only a small percentage of adult Africans. However, the Southern Rhodesian premier, Whitehead, knew very well that the British could not accede to this pressure unless it was coupled with a genuine improvement in Africans' social and political rights which could be successfully hawked around the world's press. Moreover, he was aware that such a reform programme had to be implemented rapidly so that Southern Rhodesia could advance to self-government roughly at the same time as neighbouring African states – and as if there were little real difference between these various decolonizations. Whitehead therefore quickly promoted a legislative package which accorded Africans universal elementary education, greater access to agricultural land and a progressive increase in political representation. But like Garfield Todd before him, and driven by a not dissimilar pragmatism, Whitehead risked alienating white voters from his United Federal

Party (UFP). Indeed, a new ultra-conservative party, the Rhodesian Front (RF), emerged in March 1962 to expound the view that Whitehead had been manoeuvred by the British into a sell-out, not only in the north, but within Southern Rhodesia itself. Nevertheless, Whitehead relied on two factors to carry him through the December 1962 territorial elections. The first was the longstanding loyalty of the Europeans to the UFP; the second was the African vote under the February 1961 terms which he expected to rally to the UFP in order to keep the RF out of power. On both these points Whitehead was disappointed. Europeans' attachment to the UFP broke under its opponents' orchestration of the 'Southern Rhodesia in danger' cry. Perhaps more surprisingly, Nkomo and the New Democratic Party nationalists used every available method, including widespread intimidation, to prevent qualified blacks from registering as voters. It is alleged that Nkomo was forced into this ploy by 'outside forces' which threatened to cut off his funding. Perhaps, also, Nkomo reckoned that if the February 1961 constitution could be shown to be unworkable, the imperial government would intervene at last to impose a solution more along Northern Rhodesian-cum-Nyasaland lines. When the results were in, the RF, led by Winston Field, had won thirty-five seats against Whitehead's twenty-nine, and proceeded to form a new government. If Nkomo thought this a neat and clever way to approach black majority rule in Southern Rhodesia, he, too, was about to be gravely disappointed.

The British Government had not wanted to announce the prospective break-up of Federation during the Southern Rhodesian elections, for fear of further undermining Whitehead's position, or to do so immediately after Field's victory, since that would have smacked of a gratuitous 'punishment' of the existing electorate for voting as it had. The statement was therefore delayed until 28 March 1963, by which time Federation had long been discounted by all the actors in the drama. Welensky, in London at the time for talks, evinced shock and dismay, but these were programmed responses, and the Federal premier subsequently had only a bit-part to perform (Federation itself formally dissolved on 1 January 1964).[9] The spotlight was now firmly on Field, and in particular on whether he would agree to attend the dissolution conference which the UK Government intended to convene at Victoria Falls in June 1963. It is held by some commentators that at this point Field could have refused all cooperation until the British had given a written promise of independence for Southern Rhodesia. But there was a real danger that, had he done so, Britain would simply have gone ahead with the unilateral division of the Federal assets, and it was to prevent this that Field agreed to attend. He took with him his Treasury Minister, Ian Smith. Both Field and Smith are on record as claiming that at this stage they received a British assurance that Southern Rhodesia would be allowed to move to self-government at the same time as Northern Rhodesia and Nyasaland. In fact it is hardly credible that the British negotiators would have so undermined their own bargaining position by giving such guarantees.[10] The compliance of Field and Smith with the dissolution scheme is quite adequately explained by the fact that Southern Rhodesia was accorded the Federation's military assets. This is what really mattered to them, because it put the RF leadership in a position to threaten a unilateral declaration of independence (UDI) – and without *this* particular form of credibility the party would have remained something of a joker's card in the Southern Rhodesia pack. Furthermore, it is vital to understand that the British were privately content to see Field brandishing the UDI stick, since the grim shadow it threw might induce black nationalists into a spirit of resigned compromise. The threat of illegal independence may have been first and foremost a mode of leverage which the RF leaders sought to impose over the UK, but in a subtle way it allowed the British to push African politicians towards settling for something less than one-man, one-vote.

What the British Government had perhaps not fully anticipated, however, was the effect that the military feasibility of UDI would have on the internal politics of the RF. It had seemed from London that Field was not vulnerable to a rightist coup within his own Cabinet. This miscalculation had several causes. The British had never quite grasped the 'white populist' basis of the RF which put any leader who sought a compromise automatically in danger. Neither did they see how external events such as Northern Rhodesia's sustained advance to self-government under black majority rule galled Southern Rhodesian whites and drove them temperamentally towards extremism. But above all the British Government only realized very late in the day that for some prominent RF leaders UDI had never been a mere gambling chip, but was, on the contrary, a consistent goal. This clarified only during Field's trip to London in January 1964 for talks with Alec Douglas-Home, who had replaced Harold Macmillan as Prime Minister the previous October. When

Field lodged an official request for independence on the basis of the existing franchise, he was raising the stakes in a way that Whitehall had not expected; implicit in Field's statement was the fact that the UK had now to decide either to yield self-government or face UDI. This was the point at which veiled antagonisms blossomed into open hostility and which allowed the RF power-brokers to dispense with Field, who had never been anything other than a figurehead, and replace him with Ian Smith on 3 April 1964.

Why, then, did Ian Smith not declare UDI immediately he gained power in Salisbury? His restraint can largely be ascribed to the need for a breathing space during which the security apparatus could be perfected and economic preparations completed before the leap into the illegal dark was taken. These were the matters to which Smith had to devote his early days as Southern Rhodesian premier. Indeed, all subsequent Anglo-Rhodesian talks were really concerned with the cultivation of images for media presentation, since the two sides were too far apart for a real agreement to be practicable. This was true of Smith's 'offer' in September to test the acceptability of the existing franchise as a basis for independence by, firstly, an *Indaba* of chiefs and headmen to elicit African opinion, and secondly, a referendum of the present electorate.[11] This was little more than a crude attempt to drive a deeper wedge between white Rhodesian and British opinion, since it was quite evident what a mockery the British press and television networks would make of the feathered fineries of chiefly ceremonial supervised by RF agents. It suited Smith that the anti-settler left should be given such ammunition in Britain, since their critiques would only prove to the mass of Southern Rhodesian whites (for whom UDI was always a mixed prospect at best) that nothing now could be had from negotiating with the UK. He was not therefore discomposed, one can surmise, when at the British general election on 15 October 1964 the Labour Party won a majority and Harold Wilson became Prime Minister.

Was this change of administration in Britain in late 1964, in any sense, a decisive factor in the Anglo-Rhodesian break which was to follow? Would the Conservatives, for example have proved more susceptible to concession-building as the crisis gathered pace in 1965 than Wilson proved to be? Certainly Alec Douglas-Home, true to the traditions of great Scottish landowners, felt greater moral qualms than, say, Macmillan would ever have done, about ditching white-settler societies for reasons of state. Perhaps, too, if Home and his

Tory colleagues had foreseen the future fragmentations of African politics they might have plumped for a deal with Field or Smith. But such foresight was not possible. Fundamentally, during the early 1960s Conservative governments put too much store by the Commonwealth as a new vehicle for British influence in Africa and Asia to jeopardize it by alienating what appeared to be the immutable forces of black and Third World nationalism. Furthermore, if it is highly improbable that Home would have yielded to Smith's shotgun pressure in 1965, it was equally clear that Wilson would not go so far as to retaliate against UDI by force. No UK Government, of whatever hue, could send British troops to manhandle Southern Rhodesian whites into handing over power to black Africans. Not only would this offend much of the metropolitan working class, but it risked an eventuality which Whitehall is ever conscious of avoiding – a covert rebellion of the army against the instructions of the civil power. Furthermore, even if these fundamental political constraints had not existed, the logistical difficulties facing a British invasion would have been daunting. However differently the Conservative and Labour leaderships felt about Rhodesian developments, it is virtually certain that under the circumstances their practical actions would not have markedly diverged.

The final moves towards Smith's declaration of UDI can be briefly outlined.[12] In late 1964 the Southern Rhodesian Government went through the motions of organizing an *Indaba*-plus-referendum which predictably 'approved' the acceptability of the existing franchise. In May 1964 Smith called a general election and obtained an overwhelming majority, and in early October he visited London largely in order to launch an appeal over Wilson's head to the British public. Wilson acted to limit Smith's access to the broadcasting networks. But the real significance of these months is hidden from our gaze, since what really mattered was Smith's drive to forge access to oil and other raw materials for a post-UDI regime. Whether Wilson's own visit to Salisbury in late October was designed for media attention, to show the British public that he really had exhausted all avenues of reconciliation, or whether the British Prime Minister still thought some settlement was practicable, is impossible to determine, although the odds must favour the former. What is clear is that by early November Smith was ready to press the UDI button, and on the 11th of that month he duly did so with an antique statement based on the American version of 1776.

III KENYA: THE STRUGGLE FOR STABILIZATION

It is ironic that Southern Rhodesia should have proved the Achilles heel of British decolonization, since in the preceding decades it was invariably Kenya which appeared likely to prove the source of future African embarrassments. Certainly from the late 1940s onwards it was this East African territory which attracted the most anxious attention of the London policy-makers. Kenya was the 'swing state' of political transition in British colonial Africa: any loss of control there to the 'forces of disorder' would inevitably have reacted throughout the eastern part of the continent, and reverberated on the careful balances being struck in West and Southern Africa. It was for this reason that from the outbreak of the Mau Mau troubles to independence in 1963, the British Government was consistently prepared to commit the resources required to stabilize and shape Kenyan politics – although in the final years the odds were allowed to become distinctly marginal. Above all, for much of this period it remained vital to the authorities in London that in Kenya the newly honed ideal of 'multi-racialism', in which the interests of European settlers and African entrepreneurs might mesh, should be shown to be operable, and the chances of the formula's application in south-central Africa thereby heightened. It was only after 1960 – and possibly not until 1962, when it became clear that a federal constitution was unattainable – that the theme of multi-racialism finally disappeared from British thinking, and a less modulated exit from Kenyan affairs was adopted.[13] Thus decolonization in Kenya was of a more penetrative and determined kind than that which prevailed in the neighbouring territories of Uganda and Tanganyika, because the stakes were higher and the pressures more intense.

The causes of the Mau Mau revolt were, in an earlier section, located in a breakdown of Afro-European relationships. After 1952, however, Mau Mau also constituted a bitter civil war within the African community. This internal fragmentation amongst Africans ran along two main fault-lines. First, the Mau Mau movement marked an attempt to forge a coalition of Kikuyu, Meru and Kamba peoples against other tribes, such as the Masai and Kalenjin, whose relationship with the administration was traditionally more stable. One of the reasons for the failure of Mau Mau was that the Kikuyu activists were never able to secure support outside their core areas (above all, in Central Province) to stretch the government's military resources to breaking point. Second, Mau Mau embraced a struggle within the Kikuyu heartland itself. Thus the colonial authorities proved able to shore up Kikuyu 'loyalists', thereby isolating the Mau Mau fighters and allowing the security forces to wear down their resistance. But whatever the sectional divisions amongst Kenyan blacks, it should not be supposed that anti-Mau Mau 'loyalism' involved a commitment to the colonial status quo. When the new Governor, Sir Evelyn Baring, toured the Central Province in October 1952 he found a uniform mood of anti-Government hostility *through-out* the villages.[14] For most Africans, the overarching virtue of European rule had been its provision of a stable political environment; once colonialism ceased to provide that at the end of the 1940s, all that remained were its corollaries of economic imposition and racial humiliation, and so it began to be despised, even by those Africans who had no illusions about Mau Mau opportunism. Although the government in Nairobi was able after 1952 to exploit the weaknesses of its Mau Mau enemy, the collaborative consensus on which colonial rule was based had rotted from within.

The Emergency not only signalled to Africans that the colonial administration could not perform its traditional functions: it also shifted the balance of power between local European authority and Whitehall supervision in favour of the latter. The white settlers had been forced to call on metropolitan resources to defeat rebellion, but in doing so they had provided proof to the UK Government that its collaborative relationships in Kenya needed to be diversified before stabilization could be attained. Thus one of the hallmarks of the period was the growing suspicion of the settlers towards the intrusions of metropolitan power, and the flavour of the times is communicated by the semi-comic episode in which white protestors besieged Governor Baring in Government House. Settler fears on this score were well grounded. As the British military presence expanded to meet the threat of Mau Mau, arrangements were installed by which the local settler-influenced government remained responsible in the civil sphere, but the British Army Commander-in-Chief in Kenya, General Erskine, not only possessed full control over security matters, but had the right (discreetly kept secret) to assume civil power if he ever felt it necessary. Moreover, Erskine loathed white Kenyans. He saw them, and in this he reflected a significant shift in contemporary British moods, not least in establishment circles, as selfish parasites, or, to use his own expression, 'middle-class sluts'; defeating Mau Mau in Erskine's mind was only the prelude to the construction of a Kenyan polity in which privileges could not be held as of racial 'right'. It was because local whites sensed this sea change in their position that the creeping successes of the security forces after 1954 did little to soothe their political anxieties.

Settler–army relations were not made easier by the counter-insurgency tactics which were adopted. White farmers in isolated districts were naturally concerned that their protection should be the top priority, whereas Erskine's strategy was to concentrate resources in policing the Kikuyu heartlands where few Europeans resided. Indeed, the security forces revolutionized the patterns of Kikuyu life, forming 'loyalists' into a Home Guard and bunching settlement into nodal villages. But the army command was well aware that the key to anti-insurgency success lay in Nairobi, since it was from the capital that Mau Mau fighters in the Aberdare Forests were supplied and directed. Once they had staunched Mau Mau penetration into rural Kikuyuland by early 1954, operation 'Anvil' was unleashed in which 11,000 Mau Mau suspects in Nairobi were arrested and a complex process of 'screening' and rehabilitation begun. Subsequently a network of camps operated which constituted a 'pipeline' down which detainees passed, or did not pass, depending on the degree to which they exhibited conversion to anti-Mau Mau sentiments.[15] The Malayan precedent for such a 'squeeze' of anti-European radicals was invaluable. The pipeline was a process by which the British were able to filter-out hard-core antagonists and construct cadres whose nationalism was of a more malleable sort. In security terms this exercise enjoyed considerable success by the end of the decade. But it inevitably involved harsh treatment of many thousands of people whose implication in Mau Mau had never been anything more than marginal, so that a complicated psychology resulted in which re-nunciations of Mau Mau mingled with a deepened hostility to continued European rule. But such side-effects, providing they were kept within limits, were of little concern to the military authorities who, as we have seen, did not confuse their aim of smashing Mau Mau with making Kenya safe for a resumed settler-supremacy.

By the end of 1956 Mau Mau activity had been effectively broken. The Emergency ordinances, however, remained in operation until 1960, so that pressure could be maintained on Kikuyu society while the colonial authorities experimented on two other fronts: agrarian reform and constitutional innovation. Changes in these spheres had begun in the first two years of Baring's governorship, but had been overshadowed by the military effort. Nevertheless, it was the erosion of settler power which had allowed the administration to switch resources towards the advancement of African farming on a much bigger scale than hitherto. This reappraisal of Kenyan economic development was spearheaded by the Swynnerton Plan. Introduced in 1954, and based on the recent findings of the East African Royal Commission, this plan was designed to create a class of African smallholders on consolidated farms. The encouragement of a free land market had to be carefully managed, since it necessarily entailed the emergence of a landless class whose future was to be that of paid workers on African-owned farms. Tact was also required because the administration focused its programmes on Kikuyuland, leading to resentments amongst other tribal groups that their loyalism had evidently not averted a British-Kikuyu axis on which political change (and ultimately decolonization) would be made to turn. By the end of the 1950s, however, the policy had gone far towards nurturing a prosperous market-oriented elite in the Kikuyu heartlands which, while still eager for the colonialists to depart, now had a critical interest in ensuring that the transition should be peaceful and graduated. But the strategy of stimulating rural African capitalism meant logically moving towards the right of land purchase by blacks in the White Highlands. For most white farmers, this marked the crucial wedge into their established privileges; for the administration it was the necessary means of dissipating the 'lost lands' tradition which was the chief underpinning of racial animosity in Kenyan African nationalism. Consequently the government moved gingerly on this question and waited until October 1959 before the ordinances banning African landownership within the White Highlands were amended. By then British officials were increasingly prepared to 'bounce' hardline settlers into whatever reforms were required to open up new economic and political balances between the racial communities in the colony.

Parallel with this reconstruction of African consciousness along economic, rather than racial, lines was the attempt to induct African representatives into 'national' political life, but on terms which ensured cooperative behaviour. With the Emergency ordinances still in place as a deterrent to any post-Mau Mau generation of radicals, late-colonial Kenya is a classical example of how the imperial power used 'constitutional progress' ruthlessly to bait nationalist leaders into playing the decolonization game by western rules. This drive to constitutionalism really dated from March 1954, when Oliver Lyttelton flew into Nairobi and virtually imposed a new constitution which, for the first time, gave non-Europeans an established role in government.[16] Lyttelton's initiative derived from the Westminster view that the British public would not accept the financial burdens of defeating Mau Mau unless the white settlers, too, were seen to pay a price for their own security. Inevitably, the space which Lyttelton negotiated for non-Europeans in the political system remained very limited. There was to be a new ministerial system in which Asians held two portfolios, and the Africans one (that of Community Development); ministerial under-representation for Africans was to be offset by the appointment of African under-secretaries in the civil service; and in 1956 the question of electing Africans to the Legislative Council was to be reviewed. Not surprisingly, as long as the Lyttelton constitution survived it was attacked by African members of the Legislative Council as a mere cosmetic device. Nonetheless, gradually African politicians were brought round, not least by their friendly contacts in the British Labour Party, to the belief that the government in London *was* prepared to sell off constitutional job-lots in return for political understandings. The settlers could feel this trap-door giving way beneath them, too, which was why the internal cleavages in that community between bitter-end conservatives and liberal pragmatists also commenced at this stage.

The first general African elections under the Lyttelton constitution took place in May 1957. The stance adopted by the African members who subsequently entered the Legislative Council – refusing participation in its work unless some nearer approximation to one-man, one-vote was introduced – would, quite probably, have made further reform inevitable sooner rather than later. But by the late summer the British had their own reasons for wishing to reshape the representative system. With African political parties still banned, popular activism had shifted towards trade unions. The Kenyan Federation of Labour, led by Tom Mboya,[17] and building on a tradition in local African politics going back to Harry Thuku's Young Kikuyu Association in the 1920s, had established a wide constituency, and Mboya received considerable media attention and financial support during a trip to the United States. With the Emergency effectively surmounted, the British were eager to fend off American criticisms of their continued colonialism, and much more important, to redirect

African politics into the legislature where new collaborative partner-
ships might more easily be negotiated and the possibility of a revived
insurgency in countryside and townships averted. In October 1957
Alan Lennox-Boyd, the new Colonial Secretary, followed in Lyttelton's footsteps to Nairobi and thrashed out another constitutional
formula. Africans were now to be accorded an extra ministerial seat,
and six elected members in the Legislative Council. The effect of this
was to equalize the communal representation of Africans and Europeans. Furthermore, the Lennox-Boyd constitution affirmed that
future electoral enlargements would not be communal at all, but
would be effected through a common voters' roll. As a first step
towards the latter, there was also to be a category of Specially Elected
Members, selected by the Legislative Council, sitting as a collegial
body in which successful candidates were required to draw votes
from across the racial boundaries. By introducing the common roll
element, Lennox-Boyd was declaring that an African-majority
government had become a real constitutional possibility, but that
progress towards this ideal would depend on convincing evidence that
such a government would operate on non-racial principles.

If leading African politicians, such as Oginga Odinga, had been
certain that the Lennox-Boyd constitution marked a 'sticking point'
beyond which the British Government could not be pushed, it is quite
likely that they would have attempted to work its provisions to their
advantage. But that constitution, even more than its predecessor, had
the misfortune to begin life just when external conditions – in
Nyasaland, in the Congo, and with Iain Macleod's appointment as
Colonial Secretary in October 1959, in London – made it unlikely
that African majorities could be denied a legislative primacy without
appearing grossly out of step with developments elsewhere. Sensing
this dramatic shift of possibilities, elected African members immediately boycotted the newly convened Legislative Council, while Oginga
Odinga, by fulsome references to the imprisoned and now patriarchal Kenyatta, implicitly threatened a renewal of Kikuyu anti-
colonial populism. Those Africans who had taken up assignments
within the Lennox-Boyd framework (essentially the black Specially
Elected Members) were thus isolated and subject to vilification. This
deadlock was broken only when in December 1959, with Harold
Macmillan about to set off on his African tour, the British Government announced that a Kenyan Constitutional Conference would be
convened in which the various racial groups would, for the first time,

be brought face to face in a negotiation to establish commonly agreed forms of government.

Before describing the outcome of what became the First Lancaster House Conference, we must pause and consider the general shift in Kenyan affairs at this stage. Why, in particular, had Macmillan and Macleod in late 1959 given up the Lyttelton–Lennox-Boyd process which lent itself to the careful modulation of change, and set off down the road of a 'caucus constitutionalism' which, whatever the physical comforts of Lancaster House, was bound to prove a bumpy and unpredictable ride? It has already been suggested, with reference to Central African developments, that Macmillan saw revisions of African policy as a means of modernizing the Conservative Party image. Indeed, this revolution was, in no small part, simply the knock-on effect of a redrawing of the UK's world stance by a highly supple and singleminded Prime Minister.[18] These quintessentially metropolitan impulses lay at the heart of British decolonization. But this is not to say that Macmillan and Macleod saw the technique of the 'all-in' conference, Lancaster House-style, as foreshadowing a necessarily *rapid* move to independence. British imperial experience was that such a widening of the dialogue was apt in the first instance to immobilize change by splitting nationalist forces into warring factions, usually expressed in ethnic terms. Such initiatives had usually put the metropole into a better bargaining position (as it had, for example, in India) as the arch-arbitrator of the post-colonial succession. Kenya provided excellent ground for such staggered decolonization because of the deep divisions between its peoples. In calling the Lancaster House Conference, the British were not so much hastening the end of the colonial poker game in Kenya – although that possibility was certainly inherent in it – as equipping themselves with a new set of cards for the next phase in the contest.

If the Macmillan–Macleod tactics hinged on dividing black natio- nalism into multiple factions, they also hinged on hammering apart the monolith of settler conservatism. The decision to convene a constitutional conference, indeed, derived from the observation that *both* these tendencies were now strongly at work. Michael Blundell, a longstanding member of the Legislative Council who had subse- quently served as a minister, resigned his portfolio in April 1959 and established the New Kenya Group (NKG).[19] This had served as convincing proof that the different economic interest groups within the European community were flaking apart. Blundell's new grouping was composed of the commercial, industrial and professional classes whose role within the modern sector of the economy had grown considerably during the 1950s in relation to the traditional core of white proprietary farmers. The former felt sufficiently confident of their economic viability to negotiate their place in a new, Africanized order; the latter were convinced that they could survive only in a European-dominated polity. Macmillan, Macleod and Blundell shared the vision of a multiple-party Kenya in which whites, numerically few but economically strong, could bargain their way into the reformed status quo. They accepted that the 'marginal' white farmers would be squeezed out of Kenya, suitably compensated, but it was important, too, that efficient white agriculturalists should stay and bolster the European position. It was for this reason that London policy-makers and the NKG leaders were opposed to any outstandingly generous compensatory deal which would lead to an indiscriminate white stampede from the estates; their objective was to oversee an entrenchment of proprietary rights likely to encourage capital-owning European farmers to remain. The First Lancaster House Conference of January 1960 was the point at which the constitutional issue and that of the proprietary farmers were joined ineluctably together.

The British aim was to lock liberal Kenyan Europeans and moderate black nationalists together, and at the January conference much of the bargaining was done in private session by Blundell and Ronald Ngala, a leading non-Kikuyu member of the Legislative Council who had already expressed misgivings as to the future distribution of power between the different components of African society. The overall outcome was agreement on a new legislature in which Africans would enjoy an absolute majority. That majority, however, would be tempered by three safeguards: a block of twenty seats would be reserved for minority communities; there would be twelve Specially Elected Members who would continue to require inter-racial support to gain election; the governor retained the right to nominate enough official members to gain a majority if an emergency required such intervention. Voting qualifications for all communities were substantially lowered, but this democratization was not yet to underpin 'responsible' self-government. The British made it plain that this final jump – from a popular, Africanized legislature to a majority-dominated government – hinged on assurances that the political transition would not affect established rights in land. But no African politician could risk giving such blanket assurances since his rivals would take the opportunity of portraying him at home as the man who had bought power for himself by giving way on the 'lost lands'. Serious bargaining by the Africans had to await the formation of national political parties, since individual negotiators could then operate behind the protection of their collective structures. With no consensus on proprietary rights, the Lancaster House proceedings came to an inconclusive end. The British had pushed the ball firmly into the nationalist court, and hinted broadly that the African return had to fall between carefully marked lines if the decolonization match was to proceed further.

The immediate post-conference period was dominated by the emergence of the two parties which were to monopolize the approach to independence. Their respective compositions reflected tribal coalition-making. The Kenya African National Union (KANU) represented a Kikuyu-led alliance which embraced related groups such as the Meru and the Kamba, while the Kenya African Democratic Union (KADU) arose from the meshing of minority peoples, such as the Masai and Kalenjin, who had come to fear that their interests might be threatened in a successor-state in which the British no longer 'held the ring' for competing groups. These institutional-cum-tribal divergences were conditioned by the contrasting economic environments of Kenyan regions. Thus overcrowding was endemic in the Kikuyu reserves, and they therefore laid claim to the bulk of land which the expected European exodus would make available for redistribution, but to those indigenous masses who lived in areas only marginally affected by land-hunger, these Kikuyu demands seemed an attempt to hog the benefits of decolonization. The colonial government, liberal-pragmatic Europeans and KADU clearly shared one common objective: to ensure that KANU was not driven by its own, often impoverished, constituents into illegal take-overs of vacated property, since this would critically destabilize the economy and possibly unleash ethnic disorders in which minorities of all kinds would be at risk.

At the elections during February 1961 KANU won a decisive majority. But the KANU leadership made their entrance into the ministries dependent on the prior release of Kenyatta, the man whom the British had made into a hero by his long imprisonment in the distant northern province of Turkana. In fact KADU was also pressing for an end to Kenyatta's incarceration, but it was not a precondition of the party's acceptance of government portfolios; the new administration was therefore dominated by KADU nominees. Why had KANU proved so abstemious at this stage, despite the fact that post-Mau Mau radicals such as Oginga Odinga and Tom Mboya had no close personal relationship with Kenyatta, and had (as the future might be said to prove) something to fear from his return to centre-stage? The answer is probably to be found in the deteriorating situation in the countryside. Already by late 1960 the Kenyan economy was seizing up. External capital was ceasing to flow into the territory, while white farmers put a stop to the reinvestment of agricultural profits. African workers made redundant in the White Highlands remigrated to their home districts, only to find that land consolidation had gone so far that they could not establish themselves on communal estates, and that their only alternative was to seek wage-labour under African landlords; for such individuals this swapping of white bosses for black bosses came as a painful insight into the downside risks which accompanied rapid political change. These pressures were experienced with peculiar intensity in Kikuyu-land, and there were manifold signs that the KANU structure was bifurcating into rival sections representing 'haves' and 'have-nots'. The swearing of oaths was renewed, local politicians rashly promised the distribution of free land at independence, and a breakdown of law and order seemed a real possibility. Had KANU entered government at this stage it would have needed to discipline expectations by making it clear that a free hand-out of land was impossible, and such action might have broken the party altogether. The KANU leadership's elevation of the question of Kenyatta's release into a precondition of their cooperation with the British was thus partly an evasion of these dilemmas. But it also arose from the knowledge that only Kenyatta had the popular stature which might allow a future KANU government to preside over a stable land market without provoking massive unrest in the villages.

Under these conditions, British and Kenyan government officials set out to identify methods of resettlement capable of reducing village pressures as a prelude to independence. At first concern with economic efficiency led them to think in terms of designing land-transfers to favour a prosperous class of 'yeomanry' capable of integrating with large-scale European agriculture. But the deteriorating security situation in the Kikuyu localities led to essentially political priorities and the predominance of programmes geared to incorporating much larger numbers of peasant smallholders operating only marginally above subsistence level. It was while the colonial authorities, both in London and Nairobi, were tussling with these conflicting pressures that the preoccupation with the survival of European farmers in rural Kenya gave way to a gritty determination to shore up land values sufficiently long to get those Europeans who wished to leave (which meant the great majority) out with cash in their pockets.

To achieve this end the British had to prevent tribal competition sliding into occupation and counter-occupation of lands, and money had to be found to finance transfers of estates just when the prospects of long-term repayment were becoming increasingly slim. The problem of maintaining order led the British Government to accept the organization of resettlement along regional lines, so that ethnic groups were assured of prior access to vacated estates in their own areas. The metropolitan decolonizers only reluctantly accepted this particular departure, since they instinctively favoured strong, central authority on this matter, but under the circumstances it was the only means of containing conflicts. The problem of funding was met by inducting the World Bank into Kenyan affairs, and by persuading the UK Treasury to dig deeper into its purse than it had previously been prepared to do.[20] The World Bank involvement is instructive because it shows how the link between African politics and international financial institutions was made at the foetal stage of the post-colonial polity; while the infusion of dollars also indicated one way in which the Americans were acting to help the UK disentangle itself from imperial constraints in the early 1960s. But the actual timing of independence was more intimately connected with thinking inside the British Treasury. Throughout 1961 the latter body became increasingly worried that the longer the decolonization process was spun out, the bigger the resettlement bill that the UK exchequer would have to face. The Treasury therefore now expressed a willingness to find the sums required to finance a final rush of land-transfers provided that the independence time-table was at last set. But if the colonial authorities were to preside over a short but bumpy dash to independence, it was vital that KANU should prove strong enough to keep the aggrieved sections of Kikuyu society 'in line'. Given constraints of time, there was only one way to achieve this: release Kenyatta and gamble that he would put his prestige behind a stable transition to complete self-government. Ironically, Jomo Kenyatta, the man whom the current Governor, Sir Patrick Renison, had as recently as May 1960 described as 'the leader to darkness and death', had become the final resort of British colonialism in Kenya.[21] Whitehall's new-found faith in the (alleged) moving spirit of Mau Mauism was not to be misplaced.

The new British emphasis on the speedy completion of decolonization, and the critical presence of Kenyatta, meant that a constitution-and-land package could be concluded at the Second Lancaster House Conference in February 1962. By this point a joint interim KANU–KADU administration had been formed, since with the time-table clearly being advanced behind the scenes, the former party could no longer afford to sit on the side-lines, however great were the risks of accepting 'responsibility' for decisions likely to be gravely unpopular with large sections of the population. The new Lancaster House Conference did not firmly fix a date for independence, although it was implicit in its arrangements that self-government was now close. What it did do was to define constitutional principles striking a middle course between KADU's devolutionary inclinations and KANU's centralist beliefs. Just how much faith the British retained in KADU as their 'preferred partner' in Kenya by this stage is unclear. It seems likely that many UK officials had ceased to peer into the increasingly murky depths of Kenyan politics, and were simply intent on maintaining the twin necessities of civil order and regulated resettlement until full responsibility could be thrown thankfully on to black shoulders; in this sense British demission of power in Kenya had a canny likeness to India in 1947. Nevertheless, there was at least a residual conviction that, from a metropolitan perspective, the success of decolonization in Kenya depended on the entrenchment of a federal constitution in the territory, and it was only when there was local agreement on such provisions in March 1963 that an independence date was finally set for the following December. With the time-table at last established, however, the constitutional consensus almost immediately began to unravel, and with it the likelihood of a post-colonial polity sensitively attuned to the various regional interests. Press speculation in the run-up to the elections of June 1963 focused on the possibility that KANU's fragile internal unity would break apart as class differences amongst its supporters asserted themselves. In fact KANU, although it remained, at heart, a vehicle for the ambitions of a disparate Kikuyu bourgeoisie, was more successful at maintaining the delicate balances of cross-tribal, cross-class support than the British had anticipated, and than was the case amongst most other nationalist parties in Africa. This was due partly, but no means wholly, to the role of Kenyatta as a truly 'national' figure who, after his release from prison, had become KANU's leading light. It was therefore this enigmatic figure who, on 12 December 1963, became the first African Prime Minister of the independent state of Kenya. As a man whose career had been touched by violence and whose language was couched in terms of anti-colonialism, but whose instincts were fundamentally cautious and governed by the pitfalls surrounding him, Kenyatta epitomized much African nationalist leadership during the decolonization era, albeit in shrewder form than most.

9. British Decolonization in the Mediterranean

LOOKING back from the vantage point of the 1980s, the Mediterranean dimension of British decolonization after 1950 seems much more dated than its African counterpart. Thus the Mau Mau revolt in Kenya seems to retain something of a contemporary ambience, whereas recollections of British troops patrolling the streets of the Cypriot capital, Nicosia, have about them the musty bouquet of a dead age. The reasons for this are simple enough: the colonial issue in African politics was sustained through the 1960s and 1970s because white-settler power remained entrenched in certain territories through these years. In contrast, British colonialism in the Mediterranean quickly shed its rationale after the Suez fiasco in 1956, and had essentially disappeared by 1965. Admittedly, Gibraltar remained a UK possession, but the forces making for Anglo-Spanish understanding were too powerful to allow this to emerge other than fitfully as an 'issue'. But if Britain's African decolonizations loom with greater clarity within the metropolitan folk memory, its Mediterranean decolonizations were, in the crucial phase of the 1950s, often more dramatically significant. Even after Indian independence in 1947, Cyprus and Malta remained of critical relevance to imperial interests because of their location on the sea lanes to the east. It was this general strategic consideration which made the Cypriot and Maltese stakes so high, and it was the shift in the assumptions underlying this thinking which suddenly lifted the imperial blockage to change in the latter part of the decade. In the interim, however, this blockage had intersected with a plethora of clerical, factional and communal factors to distort these small societies on the eve of their 'liberation' from British suzerainty. In the process Cypriot affairs were traumatized to a much greater degree than was the case in Malta, and the post-colonial partition of the former island was foreshadowed (if not made inevitable) by the particular dynamics of decolonization which prevailed. In Malta, too, however, the divisive texture of its political life after 1964 arose from the internal conflicts which had been branded upon the colonial end-game. On both these balmy islands it was the aspiration of the populace for social peace and a heightened prosperity, not the phenomenon of British power, which was the real victim of events.

I   CYPRUS: THE FATAL NEXUS – STRATEGY, CLERICALISM AND COMMUNALISM

The dominating figure of the Cypriots' stormy and divisive passage to independence was Archbishop Makarios, the leader of the Greek Orthodox Church on an island which, while possessing a clear Greek majority, also encompassed a substantial Turkish minority. During the Cypriot 'revolt' of the 1950s, which was really a revolt amongst a segment of the Greek community, this black-garbed patriarch came to symbolize for much of the British public the sinister forces of Anglophobia, working under the guise of anti-colonialism, which had suddenly become such a feature of the contemporary world; in this respect Makarios was outstripped only by Nasser. But Makarios' British (and largely sympathetic) biographer, Stanley Mayes, has concluded that the Archbishop's political career can, in retrospect, be seen only as a failure.[1] His approach to decolonization meant that at the point of independence in 1960 Greek-Turkish relations in Cyprus were deeply embittered; within fourteen years a Turkish invasion confirmed the *de facto* partition of the island; finally, in 1983 the Turkish 'republic' in the northern part of the island declared itself to be constitutionally independent from the Greek south. Most of this narrative lies outside our present scope. The Cypriot story between 1952 and 1960 attracts our attention because of its bearing on that break-up of British power in the Mediterranean which, as we have noted, was such a crucial facet of the broad splay of decolonization. It is also, however, a fascinating example of how a nationalist leader could become the victim of his own tactics, which, however successful they were in their initial purpose of forcing metropolitan authority on to the defensive, also carried with them unintended and destructive effects.

Makarios' nationalism took the form, not of a vision of an

independent Cypriot island-state, but rather of Cypriot union with Greece (a goal which was termed *Enosis*). This was hardly a political doctrine designed to appeal to the Turkish minority, or to reassure them as to their future prospects under any new dispensation. But in adopting the formula of *Enosis*, Makarios was not driven by a crude and self-justifying communalism. His dominating concern was always to preserve the leading role of his church in Cypriot life. In the early 1950s, however, it seemed likely that political change supervised by the British would militate against this. In particular, the likelihood was that the colonial power would conceive of the future Cypriot state as a secular entity; the Orthodox patriarchate would find itself pushed into the background as a piece of historical lumber, and the political initiative amongst the majority Greek community (and even amongst parts of the Turkish community) would pass to AKEL, the Communist-led Left party which had its base in the trade unions. The appeal of *Enosis* for Makarios is therefore plain enough: by ensuring that the end of British sovereignty was followed by integration into the monarchical and clerical forms of Greek conservatism as they existed on the mainland, the Orthodox institutions in Cyprus to which he was devoted would be able to survive the decolonization experience relatively unscathed. Whatever antagonism the AKEL leaders felt about Makarios' ecclesiastical traditionalism, they could not risk openly opposing the head of a church which continued to monopolize peasant loyalties. Makarios' orchestration of a campaign for *Enosis*, however, understandably aroused an even greater sense of anxiety, and with it a heightened communal consciousness, amongst the mass of Turkish-Cypriots. It was this communalization of Cypriot politics, not in itself an aspect of Makarios' thinking, which was to bedevil his own future and that of his country.

Between 1950 and 1954 Makarios glimpsed an opportunity to secure his objectives by purely political means. Unofficial delegations calling for Cypriot 'freedom' under the colours of *Enosis* were despatched to the United Nations. This was, however, more subtle than a simple appeal to 'world opinion'. Makarios aimed to engage the support of the US Government by prompting the thought that a Cyprus which continued to be dominated by the Orthodox Church would prove a reliable bulwark against Communism in the eastern Mediterranean. The archbishop, whose seminary training had included an eighteen-month sojourn at a Methodist institution in Boston, enjoyed excellent access to the American media, of which he made full use. His optimism at this stage also arose from the prospect that the British might shortly vacate Cyprus as part of a more general withdrawal from the Middle East. But Makarios' hopes for such a painless transition were dashed. In fact the momentum of the Cold War made Turkish friendship a much more important consideration for the NATO powers than anything Makarios had to offer; this was later confirmed by the Baghdad Pact of early 1955, which slotted Turkey into a strategic understanding with the Anglo-Americans.[2] Furthermore the British had already drawn the conclusion from their difficulties in Egypt that a continued presence in Cyprus was more, not less, vital in strategic terms. It was for this reason that on 28 July 1954, when the UK Government announced the forthcoming evacuation of British troops from the Suez base, a minister appeared to use the term 'never' (admittedly in a rather ambiguous sense) in reference to Cypriot independence when quizzed, during the course of debate,[3] on the prospects of such an eventuality. It was this die-hard statement which contributed to the outbreak of that violence and counter-violence which was shortly to grip Cypriot affairs.

The constraints on Makarios' position had become palpable by 1954. In Cyprus the Turkish minority was bound actively to oppose *Enosis* if any attempt was made to implement it, and some Greek leftists would do so covertly. The British and Americans, for different but overlapping reasons, both felt that strategic circumstances made any alteration in the status of Cyprus inopportune. Meanwhile the Greek Government remained so indebted to both London and Washington for the defeat of the mainland Communists in the late 1940s (and might be in need of such assistance in the future) that it was not likely to risk any diplomatic ruptures over the Cyprus question. Blocked by these interlocking considerations, Makarios, as we shall see, became the prisoner of extremist and inchoate forces which he could not control. He encouraged the establishment of Orthodox youth groups (such as the Pancyprian National Youth Organization, or PEON) whose enthusiasm for *Enosis* became impregnated with anti-British sentiment; one of the features of the subsequent conflict was the commitment to *Enosis*-by-violence evinced by young Greek Cypriots in the towns, particularly in the capital, Nicosia. These aggressive responses were understandable. Here was a new post-war generation, European by race and culture, appalled at the prospect that the benefits of a post-colonial age might pass them by, even when they were being successfully laid hold of by their Asian counterparts. The combination of Orthodox chauvinism and youthful aspiration was to prove a heady but erratic mixture.

It was Makarios' trawling for support in mainland Greece, however, which was, above all, fatefully to set the course of his career. Indeed, it was only by acquiring leverage over the politicians in Athens that the archbishop could hope to neutralize metropolitan Turkey's opposition to *Enosis*. He had friends amongst the Orthodox establishment who sympathized with his aims, including the Greek primate himself, and *Enosis* was also espoused by some discontented members of the government led by Constantine Karamanlis. But Makarios found his most unqualified allies in the shadowy world of the monarcho-fascist right. The outstanding figure among these was Colonel George Grivas, who saw *Enosis* as a means of shaping Greek politics according to an authoritarian, militarist romanticism.[4] The union of Cyprus with Greece, *per se*, was of little direct relevance to Grivas' embittered politics; but an *Enosis* which involved a guerrilla campaign against the British, and which identified his own brand of conservative extremism with anti-colonial nationalism, held great possibilities as a mobilizing force. From mid-1951 Grivas built up his contacts with Cyprus and planned for the logistical support of his nascent organization, the National Organization of Cypriot Fighters (EOKA). From the beginning of his relationship with Grivas, Makarios apprehended the risk that the Greek colonel might in the end prevent his being able to negotiate a compromise of any kind with the British, and he impressed on Grivas that selective sabotage, not outright terrorism, had to be the hallmark of EOKA operations. Indeed, if at the crucial juncture of mid-1954 Makarios had received some solid evidence that the British Government might be susceptible to an 'understanding' on future policy, it is not unlikely that he would have acted more decisively to keep EOKA in check, even at the risk of offending Grivas. But the July 1954 statement ('never') in the House of Commons made any such meeting of minds impossible. In effect, Makarios had come to need Grivas as much as Grivas needed him, and on 1 April 1955 EOKA agents exploded a number of bombs in central Nicosia to mark the commencement of a 'terror' campaign. Like Kenyatta in Kenya, the archbishop was very careful to distance himself from all violence, but he refrained, too, from any outright condemnation of EOKA; and unlike as with Kenyatta, the British authorities could not lightly take retaliatory action (such as imprison-ment or deportation) because Makarios was 'covered' by his headship of the most deeply rooted institution of Cypriot life, the Church.

However, if EOKA bomb outrages put pressure on the British Government, they also indirectly put pressure on Makarios. Each incident emphasized that the archbishop had to develop a strategy of his own, independent of Grivas; otherwise, when *Enosis* finally arrived, it would be seen by the masses as coming out of the barrel of the colonel's gun, not as a consequence of the Church's pastoral concern for the faithful. Once again Makarios sought to promote his own effective and distinctive leadership by turning to international diplomacy. In April 1955 he attended the Non-Aligned Conference in Bandung, Indonesia, where Makarios made an impressive – and much photographed – sight in his severe patriarchal splendour alongside Sukarno, Nasser and Chou En-Lai.[5] Quite why a represen-tative from tiny Cyprus should be accorded such prominence along-side the nationalist giants of Indonesia, Egypt and China may seem puzzling, but the presence of a Greek Orthodox primate invested the Bandung proceedings with an element of ancient kudos. The arch-bishop's real message at Bandung, however, was directed to the Americans and the British: if forced to do so, the cause of *Enosis* was in a position to find patrons in the non-western camp.

By raising the stakes of the Cypriot game in this way, however, the archbishop was running the risk that the British might play the diplomatic trump card in their own hand: granting metropolitan Turkey a *locus standi* on Cyprus' future, a move which would stymie any chance of the whole island being integrated into Greece. This gambit had disadvantages from London's viewpoint since, by raising the spectre of a future partition of the island between Greece and Turkey as the only way out of the impasse, it threatened to produce the kind of fractured decolonization which the British instinctively abhorred. But by the summer of 1955 the UK Government had become so preoccupied with eastern Mediterranean affairs that it was prepared to take risks to put some check on Makarios; to this end it called a tripartite conference in London between the British, Greek and Turkish Governments in late August. However, the British were mistaken in thinking that the Turkish presence could be easily manipulated to shape a Cypriot settlement along the lines favoured in London. Halfway through the conference massive riots erupted in Istanbul aimed at the large Greek community in the Turkish capital.

After this, the tripartite conference broke up in disarray. The fateful heightening of Turkey's involvement in the determination of the island's future status, and the domestic instability which led the Ankara regime to indulge in belligerent postures whenever possible, may have put a road-block in front of *Enosis*, but it also threatened to polarize communal relations within Cyprus and so make any settlement inherently unstable. Already the security situation on the island had deteriorated to the point where the British Government had appointed a new military governor, Sir John Harding, whose anti-Mau Mau experience clearly recommended him for the position.

In Cyprus, as in Kenya and Malaya, the ensuing British strategy was one of a military build-up allied to an attempt at locating a new political consensus. In this instance the intention was to 'reconstruct' Makarios by offering him a leading role in a unitary Cypriot state while disengaging him from EOKA and *Enosis*. Harding had several private meetings with the archbishop when this general formula was, it can be surmised, outlined; and in February 1956 the Colonial Secretary, Alan Lennox-Boyd, flew to Nicosia to provide Makarios with guarantees at the highest level. But the latter remained impassive in the face of these offers. Suggestively, EOKA maintained a high incident rate throughout this period, as a signal that it could not be left out of a settlement, and the archbishop probably calculated that once he broke with EOKA, the British would cease to treat him seriously. With their attempts at negotiation foiled, the colonial authorities recognized that no progress could be made until EOKA's credibility had been decisively broken, and it was to clear the way for an anti-terrorist drive that on 9 March 1956 the archbishop was arrested and exiled to the Seychelles. In retrospect, this was not an unlucky turn of events for Makarios; in the ensuing months he was able to gain all the aura of nationalist exile, while evading the daily dilemmas of what had become a bloody civil, as well as anti-colonial, conflict.

During the summer of 1956 the colonial government in Cyprus proceeded to implement the twin-prong strategy of military pacification and constitutional reform. On the military front British troop reinforcements attempted to root out EOKA 'cells' from their hideouts in the Troodos mountains; on the constitutional front an eminent jurist, Lord Radcliffe, was despatched to Cyprus to establish the outlines of a political solution. But whereas in Malaya and Kenya these tactics had been pursued relatively free of external conditions, in Cyprus they were cut across by a major international crisis: the Anglo-French invasion of Egypt, focusing on the Suez Canal, in 1956, and for which Cyprus was the major jumping-off point. The Suez episode had two effects on the Cypriot situation, both of which enhanced the chances of a settlement. First, the military build-up in the Mediterranean meant that Harding had a considerably aug-mented body of troops available to him, and from this time on there were signs that EOKA was struggling to survive. Second, and even more crucially, the imperial presence in Cyprus was inevitably caught up in the reappraisal of UK strategy which followed the Suez debacle and Harold Macmillan's elevation to the premiership in January 1957.

In December 1956, while these shifts were under way in their respective spheres, Radcliffe published his constitutional proposals. In calling for an immediate move to independence, it can be supposed that this judicial (and judicious) gentleman did not move far from the desiderata which he knew to be in the minds of those in London who appointed him. The Radcliffe formula did not embrace a rigid federation of Cyprus into its Greek and Turkish parts, but included a network of safeguards which not only protected the civil rights of the chief minority community but also put them in a position to block *Enosis* at any future point. Nevertheless, it was clear that in a Radcliffe-designed Cyprus, the Greek majority would be the dominating force, and the British contention (in retrospect, quite accurate) was that the Greek Cypriot politicians should grab this option while it was available, because it was the best offer they would ever have made to them. It was to persuade them into such acceptance that Makarios was now released and shortly allowed to return to the island, despite the bitter resistance put up by right-wing Conservatives in the UK. Indeed, when the decision was announced in March 1957, a leading UK Cabinet Minister, Lord Salisbury, resigned, making no secret of his reason for doing so; this was the only example of such a ministerial crisis triggered by British decoloniza-tion.[6] By this point, however, Macmillan was determined to accept high risks in order to cut free from the Cypriot entanglement.

The fact that the British were ready to 'settle' on certain terms, however, meant little as long as the Greek and Turkish Cypriots showed no signs of moving towards a mutual consensus. The UK Government tried to encourage such a trend by re-establishing a civil government under Sir Hugh Foot.[7] At one level this was an attempt to 'lift the atmosphere'; Foot mingled with villagers without the security paraphernalia which had previously surrounded Sir John Harding, and EOKA suspects were paroled. This move, however, also constituted a veiled British statement that if the Cypriots (Greek and Turkish) wanted an all-out civil war, the UK was not going to waste men and money getting in-between the combatants. European decolonizations were shot through with this sort of double-code. In fact the growing evidence that the British desire to maintain its colonial hold on Cyprus had finally broken served only, ironically, to heighten Turkish fears about the future, since Radcliffe-type safeguards were not convincing to them. Hitherto EOKA murder victims had largely been Britishers, or, more often still, Greek-Cypriots employed by the government (usually as policemen and civil servants), but by early 1958 Turks began to fear that independence, however constitutionally framed, would soon be followed by EOKA action against their own community as a new phase of a continuing campaign for *Enosis*, and they therefore set about acquiring small arms, of which the eastern Mediterranean had a ready supply in the later 1950s. The effect of these anxieties and procurements was seen on 7 June 1958 when, after Turkey's information office in Nicosia had been bombed, Turkish-Cypriots rioted in the city, destroying Greek-owned property in the Turkish-majority districts. These disturbances quickly spread to the countryside, leaving many casualties in their wake. This breakdown of law and order caught the local British administration by surprise, and was deeply embarrassing internationally. Macmillan responded by floating a new proposal for transition to independence in which sovereignty was temporarily shared between the British, Greek and Turkish governments while communal tensions cooled off; entitled 'an adventure in partnership' while race mobs were charging through Cypriot towns and villages, this was a picturesque example of that split image of constitutional jargon superimposed upon sectarian atrocities typical of European decolonizations. In fact no 'paper' constitutions drawn up by British authority could, at this stage, stabilize Cypriot affairs. Only a démarche between the governments in Athens and Ankara – each acting to check its own local allies – could do that. This, however, is precisely what happened. In late 1958 the Greek and Turkish representatives in the UN agreed to informal talks; these took place in Zurich in early February 1959, and later that month a formal conference of interested parties gathered at Lancaster House in

London. Cyprus had been put back on the tracks of caucus-decolonization, which was always the idealized British conception of what transfers of power should be.

The combination of forces which had produced a new, if purely temporary, equilibrium in Cyprus and so opened the way to independence in 1960 had little to do with skilled British negotiation and a lot to do with the crude impact of the communal clashes in 1958. Prior to these events the Cypriot issue had been a convenient opportunity for Turkey to assert its claims as an Aegean power, but once a real off-shore civil war loomed, that country became much more amenable to a compromise. Similarly, the Greek Government became frightened at the prospect that a major confrontation in Cyprus would be exploited by its own rightist opponents at home and possibly lead to a coup in Athens. It is also quite probable that, in bringing about such a rare instance of Graeco-Turkish conciliation, US pressure had a significant part to play, since this was an area where NATO strategists felt that local instabilities could damage its interests; if so, this was one more example of how after 1956 discreet American interventions often eased the path of British decolonizations. This forging of an 'international' consensus, however, would have meant little if it had not been paralleled by shifts within local Cypriot politics.

The starting-point of this internal refiguration was probably the success of the British security apparatus in breaking EOKA morale. This reduced Grivas' ability to force on his own cadres in the face of mounting losses, and by the same token convinced Makarios that he could begin to negotiate compromises without forfeiting prestige within his community. Above all, the archbishop was able to assert his own leadership by promising EOKA veterans prominent places in a self-governing state. Meanwhile, if Grivas had failed to achieve his goal of *Enosis*-by-violence, he was satisfied with the plaudits of 'resistance-hero' which Makarios was careful to see heaped upon him. The cease-fire which operated from March 1959, and which included a safe-conduct from the British military authorities for Grivas' return to Athens, then allowed two sets of negotiations to get under the way. The first of these concerned the balance of power between Greeks and Turks within an independent, unitary Cyprus. Fearful of renewed hostilities, the local Turkish politicians were prepared to settle for constitutional arrangements under which, although Greek-Cypriots were bound to dominate much of political life, nonetheless the Turkish population was assured of substantive representation in the legislature and leading government positions were reserved for members of that community – including a permanent lien on the Vice-Presidency. Most important, any future proposal for *Enosis* would not be able to be carried without securing a separate majority amongst the Turkish electorate – which meant never. The second set of negotiations revolved around the British demand to retain sovereignty over base areas on the island. These talks were set in train by the presidential elections of December 1959, in which Makarios won an overwhelming victory. Much sound and fury surrounded these discussions, if only because the archbishop had to be seen apparently driving very hard bargains with the old colonial power. But in fact the differences of opinion concerned the physical extent of these base areas, not the principle of their existence. Indeed, the main Cypriot factions were all only too pleased to accept a continuing British military presence, partly because it was a source of much needed foreign exchange, but also because it provided some guarantee against opportunist opponents of the emerging regime who might seek to promote destabilization. It was this exhausted and nervous equilibrium which thus characterized Cypriot politics and society when formal self-government, under the ecclesiastic leadership of Makarios, commenced on 16 August 1960.

Perhaps the most suggestive facet of the Cypriot experience in the 1950s was how a question, which seemed so quintessentially 'imperial' in the first half of the decade, ceased quite suddenly to be so after 1957; the constraints and divisions did not disappear, but came to be rooted in different realities. From a metropolitan perspective, an island possession in the eastern Mediterranean which seemed so inalienable in 1954, became largely dispensable only a few years later. Many, if by no means all, of those who lost their lives in the course of the Cyprus revolt may therefore be seen as victims of Whitehall's delayed adaptation to changing strategic circumstances, an adaptation which, in the end, was enforced only by the Suez disaster. But if these individual tragedies may be partly ascribed to the distorting effects of imperial strategy and diplomacy as they impinged upon a small island society, they also arose from the ecclesiastic priorities which drove Makarios to adopt the 'impossibilist' goal of *Enosis*. By choosing this instrument to shape the transition to post-colonialism in his own image, the archbishop ensured that self-government was secured only after communal relations had already been profoundly disorientated. In 1960 it was still hoped that the politics of independent Cyprus would settle down to more tolerant and pluralist forms; this was an optimism, however, like many optimisms of the age, which was to prove illusory.

II MALTA: FROM GEORGE CROSS ISLAND TO THIRD WORLDISM

Politics in Malta before and after the Second World War bore little resemblance to each other, except in one vital respect: the underlying issue remained the primacy of the Catholic Church within the national polity.[8] Prior to 1939 the Nationalist Party, the only organized political faction and in intimate alliance with the Catholic hierarchy, had been continuously at odds with the British administration, so that in 1922 and 1933 the government had suspended the constitution and resumed direct rule. Superficially, it was the question of language rights which lay at the heart of this controversy since the Nationalists, dominated by the bourgeois and professional classes of the capital, Valletta, were determined to make Italian the official language of the island, before it was finally overwhelmed by the spreading use of English amongst the Maltese masses.[9] Secreted within the language issue, however, was the even more explosive matter of the Church's ancient but often contentious leadership in a society where colonialism and secularism had long shown tendencies of locking tightly together.

After 1945, however, the forms of Maltese political life shifted; in particular, the Nationalists had to turn their fire-power on a new and more dangerous enemy, the Malta Labour Party (MLP). MLP drew the bulk of its support from the great Admiralty dockyards of Valletta, which had been greatly expanded during the war. The party was, naturally, proletarian in spirit; but it was also secular and, since English was the language of dock labour, deeply anti-Nationalist. This post-war constellation was advantageous to the colonial power, since bourgeois anti-colonialism had evidently been stopped dead in its tracks. In 1947 the British administration was therefore able to introduce a new representative constitution and set about establishing a new local equilibrium in which the chastened Nationalists might prove more pliable.

The party conflicts of the 1947–55 period need not detain us here.[10] But it was during this period that the MLP leader, Dominic Mintoff, came to visualize Malta's future in integration with the United Kingdom. That the leader of a populist political party in a colony (especially a leader who later veered sharply towards an intense Anglophobia) should have thought in these terms appears somewhat piquant, but it was a logical reflection of Maltese circumstances in the early and mid-1950s as seen through MLP eyes. The touchstone of Maltese affairs at this time was that independence, *pur et simple*, was impossible and undesirable: the island (like Cyprus) was too strategically significant for the UK Government to contemplate decolonization, and the economy (to a greater extent than Cyprus) was acutely dependent on the British military presence, and especially on the Admiralty dockyards. Nevertheless, it was profoundly embarrassing for a mass party simply to support the *status quo*, when many other colonies were being kitted out for an independence which, if not imminent in many cases, at least was now foreseeable. Even so, to opt for integration with, not separation from, the metropole appears as a paradoxical solution to this tactical dilemma. But the MLP's chief opponent was the Church, and it was as a weapon to break the social power of that institution that integration with a Protestant motherland held its real attraction for Mintoff. Thus when he became Prime Minister following the elections of February 1955 he promptly tabled outline proposals under which Malta would become a part of the United Kingdom – a variant of the Jersey model, but one situated in mid-Mediterranean.

Why did the British Government so unprecedentedly consider, and at the Round Table Conference of December 1955 accept, subject to local referendum, Mintoff's plan? One factor was the unique aura which surrounded Malta in British opinion following the heroic defence of that island during the Second World War, for which the whole population had been collectively awarded the George Cross medal. Subsequently there was an intimate conception of Anglo-Maltese relations which had no parallel, for example, in the Anglo-Cypriot case. Integration, too, had a strong economic rationale, since there seemed no possibility that any Maltese government would be able to develop sufficient revenues other than those arising from the connection with the British Admiralty on which to base 'independence'. But the most powerful factor which made the integration formula palatable in Whitehall related, predictably, to the wider Mediterranean position whereby Nasser had negotiated British troops out of the Suez Canal zone in 1954 and EOKA, shortly after, began to try bombing them out of Cyprus. Amidst all these uncertainties, the prospect of making Valletta – the finest natural harbour in Southern Europe suitable for military purposes – into a 'home' port on a permanent basis held clear-cut appeal. At this point Anthony Eden's determination to respond effectively to Nasserism in the eastern Mediterranean, and Mintoff's determination to dish his ecclesiastic enemies, came conveniently together.

This mutual regard between Whitehall and the MLP leader did not survive the integration referendum in Malta. During the campaign the Nationalists and the Catholic hierarchy played forcefully on the religious emotions of the electorate. They did not attack integration directly, since it clearly had economic benefits which Mintoff's opponents could not allow themselves to be seen abandoning. Instead, the Nationalist leader, Borg Olivier, and the Maltese Archbishop, Monsignor Gonzi, campaigned on a platform of full guarantees for Catholic rights, and they made little pretence that to vote for integration under Mintoff's premiership amounted to an act of religious disloyalty. Most lay Catholics therefore felt themselves to be pinioned between economic self-interest and the old faith; their response was to abstain in large numbers. The referendum of February 1956 thus produced a majority in favour of integration of those who voted, but the abstention rate meant that this plurality was a minority of the total electorate. Mintoff blamed this disappointing outcome on the British Government for not making the terms of integration sufficiently attractive to outweigh ecclesiastic intervention; the British Government, on the other hand, saw the result as proof that Mintoff could not 'deliver' his side of the Maltese bargain, and immediately downgraded him as a likely local partner for the future. Disaffection rapidly set in on both sides and soon made the integration episode appear curiously dated.

The Suez debacle cut across the darkening scene of Anglo-Maltese relations just as it did in Cyprus. Mintoff shifted his ground from integrationist enthusiasm to zealous anti-colonialism. He did so on two main grounds. First, with the British world position so badly affected, it seemed possible that an independent Malta might be able to bargain effectively with a British Government desperate to 'buy' friends and facilities in strategically vital areas. Second, Mintoff had previously feared independence because of the dominant local position enjoyed by the Church, but the political fashion of the later

1950s was tending towards a radical secularism which made MLP more confident of facing an out-and-out struggle with the clericalists. Mintoff – whose own remarkably volatile temperament was obviously a factor in these sudden shifts of position – therefore restyled himself as an anti-colonial politician of Third World stamp, especially courting the friendship of Nasser. But in this context it was a distinct disadvantage to be Prime Minister, and so tarred with the imperialist brush. Mintoff therefore engineered his own dismissal during April 1958 by refusing to authorize the police actions to control MLP-instigated riots in Valletta, leaving the Governor little choice but to revert to direct rule.[11] From that point on Mintoff's hope was that the British would finally tire of this constitutional impasse, and turn to him, however reluctantly, as a decolonizing partner; the result would be an independence settlement in which the Nationalists and clericalists were accorded a minor (and henceforth extremely vulnerable) role. He was to be disappointed.

Meanwhile, if Mintoff was turning to anti-colonialism, so too, as we have already seen, were the British. The hostile sentiment building up in Whitehall against costly external entanglements clearly had implications for the Maltese situation. Thus it is feasible that the UK Treasury would have used all its influence to block the implementation of integration, subsidies and all, even if the governmental proposals had been carried decisively in the Maltese referendum of 1956. Such financial parsimony, critically combined with post-Suez military reform, greatly reduced the significance of the Valletta dockyards in British thinking. In mid-1960 an accelerated rundown of the Admiralty infrastructure and personel in the dockyards was announced by the British Government. This was a slap in the face for Mintoff, and proof that the real leverage in the situation lay with the London authorities. The Admiralty cuts fed anti-British sentiment amongst Maltese dockers, but amongst island opinion more generally a fear developed that Mintoffian bombast concealed a complete absence of any coherent economic programme for an independent Malta bereft of British friendship. At the general election of February 1962, therefore, the Nationalist Party of Borg Olivier won a majority of seats, and so it was with its old pre-1939 opponents (but for whom Rome, not Cairo, remained an inspiration) that the UK Government moved to effect a speedy independence settlement.

The sequence of events which fanned out until Malta's formal independence in September 1964 will not be recounted here. The

chief irony to note, however, is that whereas during the period of
integration negotiations in the mid-1950s it was the Church which had
been forced to seek written guarantees for its existing rights in the
proposed arrangements, between 1962 and 1964 it was the MLP
which sought the entrenchment of civil and religious freedom in the
new constitution. Angered by the clear intention of the constitution-
makers to recognize Catholic primacy in the state, the MLP boycotted the Round Table Conference of July 1963, only to find that the
British Government (again uniquely in its decolonization record)
simply went ahead and agreed to a schedule for the transfer of power
without bothering to ensure that enough concessions were proffered
to the main opposition party to draw them into a consensus. Thus by
identifying himself with anti-western forces Mintoff had miscalcu-
lated; instead of forcing the British to cooperate on *his* terms, the
MLP leader had been shunted on to the side-lines. Looking beyond
Maltese independence, of course, it might be argued that this was
only a temporary check to the realization of Mintoff's objectives. He
went on to dominate Maltese politics, and used his long years of
power to set about dislodging the old clerical supremacy. But this was
a second-best outcome. In effect, Mintoff spent two decades chipping
away at Maltese institutions which a differently shaped decolonization might have weakened at a stroke; as the independence agreement
had stipulated, British servicemen did not finally disappear from the
island until 1974, while, most importantly, the sustained onslaught
against the Church during the later 1960s and 1970s meant that
economic issues were badly neglected. In Malta the final tally of
decolonization shows that the metropole was able to win on points
against those nationalists who had opted for the radical road to
power.

Finally, this chapter's survey of developments in two Mediterranean
contexts illustrates the essential obliqueness of decolonization as an
aperture through which to observe the societies concerned. In other
words, what was fundamentally at stake in these islands was the place
of the clergy in their political and social arrangements (Catholicism
in Malta, Orthodoxy in Cyprus). The impending departure of the
British took its significance from the way it cut across this dominating
question. It was because metropolitan policy-makers and publics had
little grasp of these complexities that decolonization held so many
nasty surprises for them. Historians (of various hues) often make the

same mistake, identifying only a breaking of the British 'will to rule' and the scramble for power amongst local groups which this unleashed. The reality was always more complex, subtle and rooted in the particularities of the past. It is for these reasons, by extension, that any account of decolonization can encompass only a slice of the recent experience of colonial peoples caught up, for a brief but usually dramatic moment, in the dilemmas arising from European withdrawal.

PART V   1965–81

10. The Assertion of a Post-colonial Age

As a broad generalization, it can be said that by 1964 the great age of European decolonization had already passed its peak. The outstanding exceptions to this statement lay in southern Africa, where the entrenchment of white-settler society imposed a different time-scale on events. In the final section of this volume, therefore, the tangled story of Southern Rhodesia, and the final collapse of Portuguese rule in Africa after its long isolation from the mainstream of continental development, will be outlined. An exhaustive catalogue of transfers of power during the 1960s, however, with the seemingly endless succession of flag ceremonies set in dusty squares and presided over by some eminent (usually royal) metropolitan personage, will not be attempted. These were simply the motions of those decisions taken in the late 1950s and early 1960s whose origins and nature have already been explored. Even where the British still showed a tendency to cling to traditional relationships after 1960, as they did in parts of the Arabian peninsula, the reason for this tenacity had less to do with pressures emanating from the past and more to do with a new set of contemporary circumstances; we shall see later that even here – in Aden and the Gulf – the British finally decided to cut their losses and vacate.[1] It is nicely ironic that in the latter of these instances the British departure ran *against* the wishes of the indigenous ruling elite; by the early 1970s the golden years of Anglophobia in the Middle East had long passed.

The quintessential problem of the post-1964 period was no longer (except in certain outstanding instances) that of whether and how to decolonize, but rather how to graft the plethora of 'new' underdeveloped states into western interests. If the context of this challenge was novel, the principle determining responses to it was not; it involved a drive towards an appropriate set of collaborative devices by which the leading interests of western and Afro-Asian societies could be brought into a stable equilibrium. The methods employed were hoary with age; they were those of strategic protection (so that the UK ensured Malaysian friendship by acting as its shield against Indonesian aggression) and economic patronage (through the network of development aid carefully put into place during the mid-1960s). It was the apparent underlying changelessness of this situation, regardless of how constitutional forms had been broken up and recast, which gave a superficial cogency to concepts of 'neo-colonialism'; that is, the contention so prevalent in liberal-leftist circles that European decolonizations were merely the induction of another, and more modern, means of appropriating the resources of the Third World for the needs of advanced (but crisis-wracked) capitalism. This was a theoretical model chiefly fashioned around the pervasive, world-wide corporatism of the great multinationals.[2] By ascribing an aggressively creative quality to big business strategies this interpretation, in its characteristic formulations, invariably fails to grasp the damage-limitation approach which characterized western commerce as it was buffeted by African decolonizations; 'get your head down and don't get hurt' was the brisk but defensive maxim which guided expatriate business thinking in late-colonial situations as diverse as Nigeria, Kenya and the Belgian Congo. The reality for the teeming un- and under-employed millions of Afro-Asian nations was somewhat more perturbing than that held out by the interpreters of neo-colonialism; the utilization of Third World resources seemed to be less, not more, necessary to the raising of living standards in Europe and North America.

In reacting to the effusions of radical theorists, the more cynical western liberals have sometimes been piqued into the observation that if there is one thing worse for the Third World than being exploited by the West it is not being exploited, and as with the conventional radical theories themselves, this trite comment at least touches on part of the truth. Certainly the shattered aspirations which followed the arrival of independence in many new states may, in general, be ascribed not to their more intensive integration within open market processes, but rather to the manner in which the operation of those processes was blunted and then deformed. This blockage had both internal and external causes. Internally, bureaucratic and urban elites used their acquisition of sovereign political power to monopolize the one source of financial surplus within their

societies, that of the cash-crop farmers. Externally, and most suggestively from the viewpoint of this study, western Europe increasingly
retreated from participation in world agricultural markets. It did so
through the mechanism of the EEC's Common Agricultural Policy,
which was put into formal operation during 1964, and the in-built
dynamics of which ensured that Europe's food demand would
progressively be met by home producers. These pressures working
against the economic prospects of the underdeveloped nations were
all the more deleterious against a background of continued population growth, to which the new states were even less able than their
colonial predecessors to devise meaningful responses. It is only by
ignoring these larger developments, and by concocting a mythical
world in which the small change of bilateral aid and World Bank
financings are accorded centre-stage, that a voracious capitalism
might be portrayed struggling to perpetuate itself through the agency
of the Third World. Capitalism, like all economic systems, is by its
nature voracious, but what is significant about the post-1960 period is
the partial disengagement of Europe and the underdeveloped world
in the strategic realms of economic policy, regardless of the inflated
publicity which enveloped the inauguration of western aid programmes.

The period from 1964 to 1968 in Britain requires some special
mention because it was marked by a final acceleration of that process,
aptly referred to by one scholar as 'disimperialism',[3] whose previous
peaks had been 1946–7 and 1957–60. The uncouplings in this third
crisis phase were obscured at the time by Harold Wilson's 'east of
Suez' rhetoric on becoming Prime Minister of a Labour Government
in October 1964, by the skilful promotion of the Commonwealth
organism (newly equipped with its own Secretariat) and by the
drama of Southern Rhodesia, all of which, in different ways,
distracted attention from a fundamental reshaping of British political
economy. The real British spirit of the times, however, was revealed
by the manner in which a cluster of colonial remnants, which even in
the early 1960s would have been judged unready for the shock of self-
rule, were now hustled rudely into independence – during 1966
British Guiana had this status draped upon it in May, Basutoland in
September, Bechuanaland in October and Barbados in November –
and by the sudden decision to devalue the pound sterling in
November 1967. It was the latter of these moves which was the litmus
test *par excellence* of British attitudes. Up until that point recent British

Governments, and especially the Wilson administration, had been deeply committed to maintaining sterling's parity at $2.80. That parity, both technically and symbolically, was held to underpin the fact that the UK's withdrawal from its dependent empire did not mean that her placement in the western system of power was affected in any substantive way. British Governments were so determined to maintain this 'signal' that they accepted the implicit cost of nailing the domestic economy to the prevailing dollar exchange-rate. Interestingly, it was yet another Middle Eastern conflict, the June 1967 Arab-Israeli war, which generated 'hot' money flows on a scale beyond the capacity of the Bank of England to control. But implicit, too, in the caving-in of Wilson's Cabinet to pressures for devaluation was the definition of a new governmental assumption: not only that Whitehall was prepared to make adjustments 'at the fringes' in order to cut a path towards national stabilization (which was the spirit of Macmillan's decolonizations, for example) but that by 1968 it had been harried into accepting a basic alteration in Britain's relationship to the western order. This was a point which went far beyond the ambit of colonies, wherever they might still be, but, amongst its other significances, the events of autumn 1967 can be taken as the point at which the last elements of imperial statehood finally burnt away into the atmosphere.

Thus, when the UK finally gained entrance to the EEC in 1972, the one advanced capitalist nation with a policy-making tradition of sensitivity to the trading needs of the Third World was lost to view.[4] Part of the rationale of British entry to the EEC – that it would make the latter more sensitive to underdeveloped countries – never stood much chance of becoming reality; the Brussels bureaucracy had become much too introspective, and too penetrated by vested interests, for that to be the case. This did not seem to matter in the mid-1970s, when the balance of payments of the poorer nations appeared to be bridgeable by the endless and easy credit on offer from western banks stuffed with the recycled surplus from the Organization of Petroleum Exporting Countries (OPEC) following the oil price-hike of 1973–4. It did matter, however, by the early 1980s, when the credit dried up, and Third World countries desperately required, not the petty aid patronage dropped by some visiting French diplomat or EEC bureaucrat, but a structural adaptation of world market patterns to open up opportunities for renewed growth. But by then not only had Britain's leverage within the international trading

system slipped, but its own economic psychology had been transformed. The Thatcherite silence in the face of Third World debt
problems was deafening. There could be no more evocative testament
to the atrophy which had come to beset the commercial nervous
system which had once made for organic, if imperfect, interaction
between the advanced and the non-advanced worlds.

In striking out towards more insular forms of economic growth, it
might have been expected that western Europe would attract the
brickbats of the Third World for barring their collective way to
progress. In fact the glossy tinsel of such façades as the Lomé
Convention and the drip-feed of bilateral and multilateral aid
proved enough to appease the post-colonial elites of Afro-Asian
countries, which frequently had their own reasons for fearing open
market expansion at home since the effect might be to smash their
world of parastatal favouritism.[5] But the west Europeans were lucky,
too, in that during the 1960s (not least as a result of the Vietnam
War) anti-Americanism became the mood-music of the times. While
EEC governments built up top-heavy structures of agricultural
surpluses where a 'natural' propensity to import should have prevailed, crowds in Third World cities could often be relied on to dance
around burning the Stars and Stripes. This was – viewed from some
Picardy farmyard – a fortunate comedy, the pernicious effects of
which did not emerge until two decades after the Common Agricultural Policy had commenced operation.

The European decolonizers were also fortunate in another sense:
the years which followed their rapid evacuation from dependent
territories were marked (on the whole) by détente between the
American and Russian superpowers. If this had not been the case,
and if decolonizations had generally been cut across more deeply by
great-power rivalries, the shaky foundations of these gimcrack crea-
tions might have been exposed early on to more pressures than they
could withstand. From the perspective of the 1980s it is possible to see
how curiously advantageous the early and mid-1960s were for cutting
colonies adrift; for all the superpower tensions which surrounded the
Congolese debacle and the discovery of Russian missile-silos on Cuba,
Russo-American confrontation had not yet become sufficiently dispersed across the globe or infused with a consistent intensity to draw
European decolonization into its vortex. This was to change in the
early 1970s, but by then only southern Africa remained to be scarred
by the impact. It is, then, to these residual issues of European

colonialism between 1965 and 1981 that we finally turn: the British withdrawal from Aden and the Gulf, the protracted struggle over . Southern Rhodesia and the collapse of Portuguese authority in Guiné, Mozambique and Angola.

I EAST OF SUEZ: THE BRITISH DEPARTURE FROM ADEN AND THE GULF

Britain's abdication of its existing political and strategic role east of Suez, and more particularly in the Gulf and South Arabia, between 1963 and 1971 is usually taken to be the final death-rattle of the most predatory of all the great European colonial powers. In a sense this was so; the UK was locked by historical commitments into a 'police' function in this zone, and it was in these years that residual imperial commitments were finally dispensed with. However, the continuance of the role beyond 1963 may also be ascribed to factors disconnected with colonialism in its traditional guise; one major reason, for example, lay in the US Government's new-found desire that the UK should continue its supervisory chores in the Gulf as a contribution to western security in an area which (not for the first time) threatened to become the focus of international rivalry. It is this merging of old and new modes of power, indeed, which makes the end of empire such a shifting and complex subject of study.

At the time of the 1957 Defence Review the significance for Britain of its Aden outpost was steadily diminishing. That outpost had always had its relevance defined largely by its relationship to the Indian *Raj*; after 1947 the gradual erosion of traditional strategic doctrines detracted from Aden's importance. Ironically, however, in the few years after 1957 this trend was reversed.[6] First, once decolonization became a benchmark of British official thought, the preservation of key (and delimited) bases became all the more desirable. Certainly the British armed services in the early 1960s saw the hoarding of such bases – of which Aden would be a prize item – as one way their accustomed style of operations, including all the perquisites of overseas postings, could be continued into the post-imperial age. Second, the Americans became eager to steer their European allies, especially Britain, towards conventional, rather than nuclear, orientations in their defence expenditures. Macmillan and his successors in Downing Street, for whom a good relationship with the US administration was so vital, could not afford to be rigidly unreceptive to such pressure. The problem, therefore, was how to maintain the British presence in Aden when radical, pan-Arab politics was already undermining traditional leadership in the port, above all through large-scale strikes amongst the workforce.

The British hoped they had found the answer in the establishment during January 1963 of the Federation of South Arabia.[7] This unit was formed by meshing together Aden and those tribal states in its hinterland which had long enjoyed formal British 'protection'. The intended scenario was straightforward: it was hoped that the Federation would be controlled by the pooled political resources of traditional rulers inside and outside Aden, and that the pan-Arab radicals would be squeezed out of existence. At some point in this process the Federation could be accorded independence, and the base would be secured for British use in perpetuity. This plan might have worked if dissident forces had been effectively cut off from external support. But after September 1962 Nasser had installed an Egyptian army in North Yemen to shore up the 'revolutionary' Yemen Arab Republic in its struggle with its royalist opponents, and he proceeded to destabilize the Federation from outside; this, indeed, was hardly difficult, given the acute divisions within the indigenous order. British and Federal forces extinguished the initial guerrilla operations in the Radfan mountains, but it was clear that the status quo had become extremely fragile.

The election of a Labour Government in Britain under the leadership of Harold Wilson in October 1964 further undermined the Federation experiment. It was acutely embarrassing for a Socialist Cabinet to be seen in league with what were widely regarded as Arabian 'feudalists' against their 'progressive' opponents. The various radical-cum-terrorist factions, recognizing this opportunity, stepped up the incidence of demonstrations and killings in order to test the Labour Government's resolve; by this time two dissident organizations were emerging, the National Liberation Front (NLF) and the Front for the Liberation of South Yemen (FLOSY), both locked in a mutual competition for grass-roots support in Aden. Wilson decided to distance his government steadily from its Federation commitments. The British High Commissioner, Sir Kennedy Trevaskis, whose advice had been to make the Federation fully independent under its current constitution and in the process let the traditional elements 'off the leash' to liquidate the assortment of

Nasserists and Marxists in the guerrilla movements, was sacked towards the end of 1964. Finally, in August 1965 the Labour Government suspended Aden's constitution and, as a temporary compromise, reimposed direct rule.

It still seemed at this stage that Wilson would maintain the British presence in Aden, at least for the next few years, by a mixture of military reprisal and political brinkmanship. This conclusion could be drawn from the fact that between 1964 and 1966 Wilson's advocacy of an 'east of Suez' role reached a pitch quaintly reminiscent of backwoods Toryism.[8] For this strange, but not altogether uncharacteristic, phenomenon, several influences are accountable. Wilson wanted to appeal to the centre-ground of the British electorate as being strong on defence, while pushing the nuclear issue, on which his party activists were so sensitive, into the background. Beating the east of Suez drum was a way of causing these twain to meet. Furthermore, in its early phases the Labour Government was looking to cut down its defence commitments in western Germany, and needed to balance this by a more vigorous approach in some other quarter. It was in western Germany that big financial savings might be made by the UK Treasury, and reductions in this sphere would be particularly well received by Labour leftists who disliked the concept of a 'front line' against the Russians. Finally, and not of least importance, Wilson spoke of the east of Suez role with a glowing attachment because it was what the Americans wanted to hear, and because the Prime Minister was all too aware that the UK's deteriorating financial position after 1964 would never be corrected without American assistance in a future sterling crisis.

At some point in late 1965 or early 1966, however, this approach sank without trace. The February Defence Review introduced by the responsible minister, Dennis Healey, envisaged a severe cut in the British defence effort outside Europe, particularly east of Suez, and Aden was to be made independent by the end of 1968.[9] The precise motives for this swift change of direction are necessarily clouded. The now critical state of sterling meant that public expenditure savings were urgently required. But Wilson's salvage strategy for the British economy had two political prongs, both of which could be helped by withdrawing from east of Suez: a renewed application to join the European Common Market – the chances of success of which would be helped by evidence that the UK really had put its old imperial orientations behind it – and the transmission to Washington of the news that Britain would not shoulder alliance burdens so easily in future unless her unique currency problems received sympathetic attention from the superpower who was in a position to alleviate them if only it had the will to do so.

However, the evacuation from Aden proved a far from easy operation to carry out. The British attempts to involve the UN as an effective arbitrator got nowhere, and by early 1967 it was obvious that no clear successor-authority would emerge to whom power could be smoothly transferred. With the British Government under mounting economic pressure, they decided to move forward the date of the British departure and to do so regardless of local circumstances. A new Governor, Sir Humphrey Trevelyan, was appointed in May 1967, prepared to carry out what was a ruthless exercise of decolonization.[10] Even Nasser's defeat in the Egyptian-Israeli war of June 1967, which held out the prospect that Arab radical pressures in the region might actually be on the point of decline, did not sway the British Cabinet from this decision. Subsequently one of its key concerns was to minimize the number of British casualties in the terrorist actions which now gripped Aden and its environs, since the steady stream of news regarding army losses seemed likely to be electorally damaging. Thus the central district of the city, the Crater, was almost denuded of British security, and the NLF, FLOSY and any other contenders for power left to settle their differences by the gun. By October it was clear that the NLF had come out on top of this bloody confrontation, and at the end of that month George Brown, the Foreign Secretary, felt able to announce that his representatives would enter immediate talks with that body as a prelude to independence in November. On 29 November 1967 the last British troops left Aden, 130 years after their first arrival.

Throughout the Aden imbroglio, the British Government had sought to assure the rulers of the Gulf states, for whose defence the UK was responsible by treaty, that no change in their longstanding relationships with Britain was in prospect. Such assurances were still issuing from ministerial mouths in December 1967. This was deception in spirit, if not actually in the letter. On the preceding 18 November sterling had at last succumbed to devaluation and the Labour Government was compelled to apply to the International Monetary Fund (IMF) for a loan to lubricate the transition. It was not until early January 1968, however, that a consensus was reached within the Labour Cabinet on the distribution of the public expenditure cuts which were a precondition of IMF assistance. In the event the left-inclined members of the Cabinet swallowed welfare economies only in return for an off-setting reduction in defence spending, and the right-inclined were pleased, in this context, to sacrifice the Gulf presence rather than put in question the monies earmarked for the nuclear deterrent programme. Official messengers were then packed off to Washington and the Gulf states to break the news of this new twist to British policy, timed to take effect in March 1971.

Rulers of small Gulf states had good reason to fear the British departure, since all of them were subject to external threats. In some cases these states had claims upon each other's territory, but all were apprehensive of being trampled underfoot as the Saudis and the Iranian Shah competed with each other to establish regional dominance. The British advice was that the small states should combine into a unit capable of protecting their mutual interests, and most of the shaikhdoms did signify their intention to enter into a Federation of Arab Emirates. If this Federation was to come about, however, sustained British initiatives were required and specific promises of military aid after March 1971. The Labour Cabinet was not in any position to take such forceful action, partly because its attentions were elsewhere, and partly because the Saudis and the Shah made it clear that they would not look kindly on any British attempt to create some rickety structure designed to block their own natural ambitions. With OPEC looking well placed to exert an upward influence on oil prices, and given the Saudi and Iranian leverage within that body, these were no idle threats. The Gulf shaikhs, meanwhile, could only take refuge in the hope that the Conservative Opposition in Britain, which had lampooned Wilson's proposed scuttle from the Gulf as symbolic of his disregard for Britain's international prestige, would win the forthcoming general election.

The formation of a Conservative Government under Edward Heath did, indeed, appear at first to put Gulf policy back into the melting-pot. But it soon became plain that the Cabinet did not consider itself committed to reversing earlier decisions, even if the time-scale of their implementation had already slipped. Then, on 1 March 1971, the Foreign Secretary, Lord Home, announced in Parliament that the relevant treaties would be terminated by the end of the year and British troops withdrawn simultaneously. This eventuality had sprung from the coincidence of a decisive shift in Foreign Office evaluation of Middle Eastern politics (which itself reflected new American prejudices), and the particular foreign policy concerns within the Heath government. Thus the British Foreign Office had by 1970 become converted to the contention that western interests in the Middle East could best be guaranteed by 'working in' with Saudi and Iranian influence, and that Gulf affairs had to be ordered accordingly; while such a perspective appealed strongly to the Heath government which was bending all its efforts to force entry into the Common Market and found formal external commitments a hindrance in promoting the UK as a quintessentially European power. In effect, between March and November 1971 the British pressed the treaty-shaikhdoms into negotiating the United Arab Emirates (UAE) on terms which appeared to open the way to a Saudi-Iranian condominium (however uneasy the latter might be). It was only afterwards, when British influence had been much reduced, that the inability of either the Saudis or the Iranians to play a quasi-imperial role became transparent. After the mid-1970s the western powers began to worry about the fragile arrangements for Gulf security, and the US Government had to spend large amounts of money developing Rapid Deployment Forces for emergencies. The old subtleties of the British presence had been replaced by the looming threat of the modernized gunboat.

II   SOUTHERN RHODESIA: THE LIFE AND DEATH OF UDI

In retrospect, the extent to which Southern Rhodesian affairs dominated Britain's foreign policy concerns after UDI (Unilateral Declaration of Independence) in November 1965 appears somewhat anomalous.[11] Not only was the UK at this very point in the final throes of shedding its residual colonial responsibilities in Africa, but that continent was rapidly being reduced to a strategic backwater after a brief flurry of world attention during the Congo crisis of 1960–3. Why did Rhodesia continue to 'matter' in Westminster and Whitehall under these conditions? There are several overlapping answers to this conundrum. In reality, Rhodesia did not preoccupy the 1964–70 Labour Government quite as much as the coverage in *Hansard* or the press suggests; concern at the timing and scale of the next sterling crisis always carried a higher anxiety rating. But the passions aroused in Britain by the UDI drama were not mere shadow-play; coincidentally, Rhodesia had provided the 'ground' on which the ideological and tactical tensions between, and within, the two great political parties of the state were played out amidst the fluidities of the 1960s. Neither could any British Government have denied a continuing responsibility in Rhodesian matters without triggering a walk-out of leading African states who had previously accepted membership of the Commonwealth following their independence. With the UK excluded from the EEC, and with a British public sceptical of the Labour Government's management of foreign relations, Harold Wilson was particularly keen to keep the Commonwealth flower-stall in business, if only for appearance's sake. Finally, in the 1960s US administrations continued to expect Britain to supervise western interests in much of central Africa, so that any breakdown in that region might have soured relations between Downing Street and the White House just when the latter's co-operation in sterling stabilization was vital. It was thus the manner in which Ian Smith's breakaway crossed with other, and usually larger, issues which invested the Rhodesian question with such *gravitas*.

Wilson's Rhodesian dilemma was certainly acute. His international strategy required that he nurture a good relationship with independent black African statesmen such as Kaunda of Zambia and Nyerere of Tanzania; his domestic strategy required that he never stray far from the centre-ground of British politics, streaked as it was with nationalist and (not least amongst the working classes) racist emotions. Wilson therefore did what came naturally to him, and what any British Prime Minister would have done under the circumstances: he struck out for the centre-line between this Scylla and Charybdis. But what constitutes a centre-line depends on the angle of the viewer, and in this case Wilson's perspective was biased in favour of Ian Smith. This did not reflect the British Prime Minister's personal instincts, but arose from his judgement of the UK public's gut response to the Rhodesian problem. Therefore Wilson, on what was really the crucial issue, ruled out the use of force by Britain to crush what was clearly an unconstitutional coup in a dependent colony. This meant that if there was any fighting to be done, then the African nationalists were going to have to undertake it themselves, with fearful consequences not only for Rhodesia but also for the neighbouring states which would undoubtedly be drawn into the fray.

Britain's relationships with independent black Africa were pro-

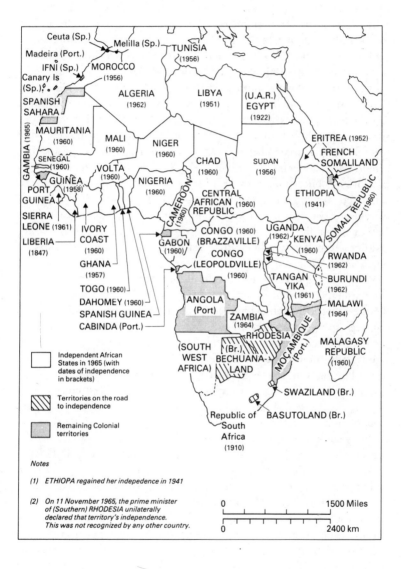

Map 8   The pattern of alien rule in Africa, 1965

foundly shaken by this decision. Wilson sought to offset the ensuing African resentments by announcing a programme of extended sanctions against the UDI regime on 1 December 1965, and in the middle of the same month escalating these to include the crucial commodity of oil. The Labour leader's chief aim in these moves was to survive the imminent, specially convened Commonwealth Conference without any embarrassing splinterings from that organization. When the Conference met in Lagos during January 1966, Wilson continued trying to pacify his African critics by assuring them that sanctions would defeat Smith in weeks rather than months, and by adopting the NIBMAR precondition for any British involvement in a settlement: No Independence Before Majority Rule. These essentially rhetorical concessions, however, were in some ways not so much designed to persuade the African leaders themselves of British good intentions, but rather to help those leaders to persuade their own agitated publics that the Smith regime was being 'dealt with'. Kaunda and Nyerere knew that British sanctions were not likely to succeed in their stated aim, and were probably a farce (which, of course, they turned out to be), but meanwhile Wilson became increasingly conscious that the Africans could not walk out of a Commonwealth club which was one forum in which an effective strategy to displace Smith might eventually emerge, and where, more generally, their diplomatic voices could be heard loud and clear – in contrast to the UN, where nobody's voice could be heard amidst the din. Throughout the years of controversy over Rhodesia, indeed, there were no 'misunderstandings' of the sort much written about by journalists; instead, there was a complex process in which all parties sought to explore the weaknesses of others.

Between the Lagos Conference and his defeat in the 1970 UK general election, Wilson shifted his ground on Rhodesia. Having ruled out a military solution in 1965/6, it had been impossible to attempt any negotiation with Smith, since this would have meant breaking altogether with 'radical' opinion both at home and overseas. After 1966 Wilson had more room for manoeuvre. This partly arose from the fact that, with the evaporation of their hopes that Smith's UDI might fail at the outset for essentially economic reasons, independent African leaders became too eager for some form of compromise settlement to undermine Wilson's efforts from the sidelines. But other events in Africa also contributed to a reduction in the leverage which could be brought to bear on Britain; most significantly, the Federal Government of Nigeria became too indebted to the British Government for military assistance during the war of Biafran secession to make much trouble over affairs elsewhere in the continent. In going for an agreement with Smith, however, Wilson could not risk a long-drawn-out negotiation without allowing his political opponents an opportunity to whip up dissatisfaction with his conduct of affairs; hence the quick-fire nature of the talks on board HMS *Tiger* in mid-Mediterranean during December 1966 and HMS *Fearless* in Gibraltar docks during October 1968. The *Tiger* negotiations ended in an early breakdown; the *Fearless* attempt yielded a package which Smith at first seemed to accept, and only rejected after (much to British annoyance) taking the terms home ; Salisbury, where his Cabinet pronounced them to be inadequate. The degree of integrity of these peace drives remains obscure. Quite possibly both these ship-borne enterprises were mere exercises in public relations in which both leaders could signal to their respective publics that they were doing all *they* could to reach a reasonable agreement on terminating UDI. Certainly after October 1968 Wilson could conveniently let Rhodesia fade once more into the British political background as a general election approached. Subsequently, Wilson's Rhodesian bondage has been treated as a gross humiliation for the Labour leader. This seems a harsh judgement. Since Wilson knew that he was in no position unilaterally to obtain a settlement, his only concern was to prevent the issue reverberating on Britain's wider international position, and in this aim he largely succeeded. In fact the dilemma of the British Government was eased by the 1969 Rhodesian constitution pushed through the legislature by Smith which instituted a republic and which definitely blocked any passage to majority rule; after that it was not possible for other nations credibly to argue that the Rhodesian question was *solely* a British problem requiring a British-supervised solution.

Meanwhile, however, the British Conservative Party had not escaped lightly from the shock-waves set up by UDI. The party was deeply split between those who felt a residual loyalty towards the white-settler fraternity, and those for whom the latter were frankly expendable. Again, it was the manner in which this division matched up with more fundamental conflicts within Toryism which gave it real force; in this case, the continuing struggle for patronage between the *grandee* faction, for whom 'colonial values' still ranked as a political virtue, and the new generation of grammar-school aspirants,

for whom colonial responsibilities smacked of an inefficient, sentimental and sinecure-ridden conservatism which they despised. As a
grammar-school product, but also as the protégé of the arch-*grandee*
Alec Douglas-Home, whom he succeeded in the party leadership
during July 1965, Edward Heath was well placed to hold these
extremes together. His strategy was to emphasize the one point – 'no
use of force' – on which a Tory consensus existed, and maintain an
equivocal posture regarding sanctions whereby he refrained from
criticizing the principle of the Labour Government's measures while
asserting that they could not ultimately gain their end without South
African cooperation – a highly unlikely eventuality in the 1960s. Like
Wilson, Heath's prime objective was simply to arrive at the next
general election without having his party crack apart beneath him on
the way there. On balance, the British political system put on a
virtuoso performance during the first (and most symbolically laden)
five years of the post-UDI crisis: the different poles of political
emotion were given impassioned parliamentary expression while the
party managers were able to ensure that Westminster business was
not disturbed by the backwash.

In fact Edward Heath's position over Rhodesia during his 1970–4
premiership was considerably easier than that of his predecessor. By
the early 1970s African questions in general, and Rhodesia in
particular, had been pushed firmly into the international background. Western nations were too absorbed by the knock-on effects of
the 1967 war in the Middle East, and especially with the instabilities
of the world monetary system, to concern themselves other than
marginally with the contortions of African states, whatever the
pigmentation of their ruling groups. After 1969, too, the UDI which
most worried the British Government was that in the Falls Road,
Belfast, not its more distant variety, although this fact was not always
accurately reflected in the coverage by UK newspapers. Heath's
scope for negotiation over Rhodesia was also distinctly broadened
after 1970 by the awful prospect that guerrilla war opened up for
Kaunda and Nyerere. These leaders, conscious of the arms from
Soviet and Chinese suppliers reaching black African exiles ensconced
in their territories, were quick to apprehend that their own regimes
were potentially threatened – and became commensurately more
sympathetic (if only in private) to any deal with Salisbury that might
prevent regional destabilization.

In November 1971, after extensive contact, the British Foreign

Secretary, Alec Douglas-Home, arrived in the Rhodesian capital with a high-level delegation which included the Attorney-General and his own permanent under-secretary. This was eloquent testimony that the British were seriously intent on an agreement. Smith's ability to bargain from strength had certainly slipped since his encounters with Wilson. After 1971 he faced intensifying guerrilla incursions over the Zambezi from Zambia, and increasingly from that portion of Mozambique controlled by the anti-Portuguese forces of FRELIMO (Front for the Liberation of Mozambique). The UK mission was able to make powerful use of the argument that this was the last chance for a political settlement. With the emergence of Soviet support for black 'liberation' movements, the cogency of this was not lost even on the most hardbitten of Rhodesia Front veterans. The result was an agreement which would extend African participation in government, and buttressed this with a justiciable Bill of Rights, but which would not have yielded majority rule in the foreseeable future. The British advocacy of this compromise was that, for all its limitations as a form of political justice for Africans, it nevertheless put Rhodesian affairs on a footing which pointed towards, rather than away from, a better material and moral future for blacks. Neither did it seem unlikely that such a conclusion might prove acceptable in Lusaka and Dar-es-Salaam as long as it foreclosed the drift to generalized breakdown in Rhodesia.

Here, indeed, was the rub: a settlement with Smith was of no use to Heath, Kaunda or Nyerere unless it was workable *within* Rhodesia. The British had therefore made the agreement hinge on its proven acceptability to the majority of Rhodesia's peoples. Subsequently it was decided in London that this 'test' of opinion was best achieved through a Royal Commission, which was set up under the chairman-ship of Lord Pearce. The choice of a Commission for this purpose was suggestive; its concern was not, in reality, with whether more heads were 'against' than 'for' the proposed new constitution, but with the more subjective issue of whether that constitution could be made operable, so that a Commission had the capacity (albeit by sleight of hand) to pronounce the terms offered as 'acceptable' to Rhodesians, even if the actual counting of numbers might marginally have given an opposite answer. Furthermore, the Commission was in a position to discount a certain percentage of opposition to the deal fixed between London and Salisbury on the grounds that it was the product of intimidation by armed radicals. The problem facing the

Pearce team during its investigation, however, was that Rhodesian blacks were *overwhelmingly* antagonistic to the terms of settlement, and to have concluded otherwise under these conditions would have meant a margin of distortion which the world's press could easily have latched on to. Once the Commission had turned in its negative findings, the Heath Government had to decide whether to push on regardless or to accept the new impasse. In fact the costs of the first option, which would have caused a howl of international outrage, mostly from those furthest from the Rhodesian scene and for whom such indignation came cheap, were too high; while the alternative – of withdrawing from all negotiations, leaving the immediate combatants to weaken each other further in a bush-war – had attractions of its own.

The war of insurgency and counter-insurgency dominated the Rhodesian scene after 1972. Indeed, African guerrilla fighters had been operating against the Smith regime since 1964, when both ZAPU (Zimbabwe African People's Union) and ZANU (Zimbabwe African National Union) had been banned and their leadership forced into exile in Lusaka. The increasing internal divisions within and between these two factions had been one factor persuading Smith against making any concessions to African politicians during the later 1960s, since it seemed that the political and military opposition to white hegemony was so friable. Bottled up in Lusaka, starved of cash and with little prospect of future spoils, it is not surprising that ZAPU and ZANU rigidified into ethnic and mutually antipathetic entities. Thus ZAPU by 1969 had become an essentially Ndebele organization, while ZANU was dominated by Shona. With the greater availability of modern small arms in the area, Kaunda ordered his security forces to impose discipline on these volatile guests, and it was to escape these constraints that ZANU, amongst whose leadership Robert Mugabe was increasingly prominent, switched its operations after 1970 to Mozambique, where its FRE-LIMO ally was controlling extensive tracts of border country. These developments were of clear concern to the Rhodesian regime, and forced Smith to begin exploring the possibility of an 'internal settlement' with African elements; thus from mid-1973 he was in sporadic dialogue with Bishop Muzorewa, a faction leader who had risen to local prominence during the period of the Pearce Commission. But before 1974 Smith could still feel that, with the military odds in his favour, there was little incentive in negotiating away white privilege. He was confident that in the end Kaunda could be bounced into destroying the Rhodesian guerrilla organizations based in and around his capital, and it was to build up pressure to this climax that Smith closed the frontier between Rhodesia and Zambia in January 1973, with enormously deleterious effects on Zambia's economy. Once the Portuguese authorities finally got a throttle-hold on FRELIMO, as was fully expected, then Smith believed that ZANU, too, would cease to be a real threat. Finally, the Rhodesian Prime Minister knew that as long as his regime retained South African support it could not be toppled, and in late 1973 there seemed no reason why Pretoria should cut off the supply-lines and withdraw the military personnel which helped to keep the illegal 'white' republic to the north afloat.

The breakdown of Portuguese rule in their African dependencies after April 1974 transformed this situation. With crushing sudden-ness, the Rhodesian economy was deprived of its most ready access to the sea via the Mozambique ports, and the perimeter of its vulnerable borders had been greatly extended. In short, it had always been probable that the Smith Government could successfully wage a one-front war across the Zambezi, but it was highly improbable that it had the resources to fight a two-front war with ZANU operating from secure and well-stocked bases in Mozambique. Furthermore, South Africa was confronted with a choice it had previously hoped would never have to be faced: either to assume a much bigger military responsibility for white Rhodesia's survival, or to accept that some form of black government in that country was inevitable and, as a consequence, therefore best arranged as quickly as possible while the process could be controlled. It was the latter approach which best fitted the *verligte* (or 'enlightened') foreign policy which the South African Prime Minister, Dr John Vorster, was currently striving to develop, involving an 'opening up' of relationships between South Africa and those of her continental neighbours prepared to accept the economic benefits he was in a position to distribute. Furthermore, the feasibility of 'managed change' in Rhodesia was simultaneously accentuated by Kaunda's desire to fix a settlement before the weight of guerrilla activity shifted to Mozambique, making it unlikely that any Zambian protégé would prove victorious in the scramble for power in Salisbury which would inevitably follow a white collapse. It was the dovetailing pressure exerted by Kaunda and Vorster which brought together a conference at Victoria Falls on 25 August 1975, attended by Smith, Muzorewa, Nkomo and Ndabaningi Sithole. No agreement resulted as to a future Rhodesian constitution, but it can be surmised that there was an understanding on one crucial point: the need to minimize the future role of Mugabe's ZANU and its Mozambique mentor. It was not, perhaps, a coincidence that the Rhodesian security forces proceeded to hit hardest against the Mozambique bases while the South Africans, Americans and British chose this moment to drive towards a political solution.

The Nixon administration in the US had begun to take a fitful interest in the Rhodesian imbroglio after 1970 as a response to growing Soviet activities in southern Africa. After the Portuguese coup, which opened up a cluster of new opportunities for Kremlin strategists in their African ambitions, this interest crystallized into a major foreign policy priority. Indeed, the Angolan debacle during 1975, when despite both American and South African efforts the pro-western elements were squeezed out of the *de facto* settlement, only highlighted the importance for the NATO powers of keeping the Rhodesian end-game under better control. The problem was that the Americans had no traditional links, or decisive economic leverage, in an area which had never figured large in Washington's mind. The US Secretary of State, Henry Kissinger, had little option but to work through the South African 'proxy'. This, in fact, did not matter at first, in so far as Kissinger's habitual method of statecraft was to attempt to fix regional stabilizations by filtering his objectives through dominant local powers whose interests had a high level of congruity with those of the US. But the method was flawed. Such proxy-tactics might have worked in previous eras for the older imperial powers when the world had been a less complicated and integrated place. But Kissinger found that proxies could break apart in American hands (as happened most dramatically later in Iran), while an entente with Pretoria was not a very auspicious means of ordering western relations in southern Africa. Nevertheless, Kissinger met Vorster in Zurich during September 1976 and together they decided on an all-party settlement in which Rhodesia's internal black leadership, especially Bishop Muzorewa, would hold the real reins of power. Smith was not in a position to resist such a US-South African diktat, and after a meeting with Kissinger in Pretoria, a package emerged figuring a two-year transition to majority rule, with an interim government headed by a black Prime Minister – who would, of course, have been Muzorewa. In effect, the Americans, the British and the South Africans were gambling that the exiled guerrillas in Zambia *and* Mozambique were sufficiently close to exhaustion to grab at a compromise which offered them some fruits of future office, but which would have subordinated them to a moderate internal coalition of black politicians who had always distanced themselves from the military struggle – and from Soviet propaganda. It was the burgeoning recognition that they were being muscled aside by these Washington-orchestrated initiatives which proceeded to drive ZANU and ZAPU together into the (highly unstable) 'Patriotic Front'; although its representatives attended the all-party Geneva Conference in December 1976 under British chairmanship, the Front ensured its break-up when the degree of 'internalization' implicit in the proposed Rhodesian settlement became clear. Kissinger's plan, based on the assumption that ZANU and ZAPU were too riven by mutual rivalries to unite against the pressures brought to bear on them, had split apart at the seams.

Between 1977 and early 1979 the focus again shifted from political to military events. Both the Rhodesian security forces and the nationalist insurgents resembled two drained and much pummelled boxers whose ability to stay in the ring became increasingly problematical, while their respective backers, unable to forge a consensus among themselves, waited to see whose knees would buckle first. By the late 1970s, however, the cards were heavily stacked against the white Rhodesian cause, for not only had they to fight a constantly extending bush war, but also to run an economy which (like all other economies) had been hit by the inflations and recessions so characteristic of the decade and which (unlike other economies) was subject to international sanctions. Knowing that time had moved against him, Smith strove to push through his own deal with internal black political factions, and in April 1979 the security apparatus stretched itself to the limit to 'screen' national elections which gave a thumping majority to Muzorewa's party. This time, indeed, the official British observers, led by Lord Boyd, approved the legitimacy of the result. For a moment it seemed all might not be lost for Smith. If the UK Government could be brought to recognize the new dispensation, regardless of the declamatory excesses this would provoke in such forums as the UN, then it was possible that the South African Government might be persuaded at long last to raise its military stake in Rhodesia; in these ways victory could still be snatched from the jaws of defeat, and ZAPU and ZANU left where they were –

vicariously living off charity in Lusaka and Maputo. In June 1979 the election of a Conservative Government led by Margaret Thatcher, with impeccable right-wing credentials, brought this scenario to apparent life.

Almost immediately following the British election, however, the Thatcher Government ditched its manifesto commitment to act on the Boyd recommendation, and in so doing doomed any purely internally arranged succession to white hegemony in Rhodesia. Several reasons can be adduced for this uncharacteristic Thatcherite backdown. Smith's security organization had only barely succeeded in policing the April elections; there was little prospect of its being able to supervise a constitutional transition in Rhodesia without strong external reinforcement. This would be expensive at a time when the British Prime Minister was battening down the public expenditure hatches; it would also be dangerous when she was intent on husbanding British prestige and when the military uncertainties in Rhodesia were so large. Simultaneously, and crucially, however, the possibilities of forcing the external guerrilla factions into a *generalized* settlement suddenly brightened; if this was not to Smith's taste, because it would create a new order which he would not be in a position to manipulate from the side-lines, it was certainly preferable to the British since it promised to be more stable in the long term than an internalized solution built on a dangerously narrow base. By 1979 the post-1973 rundown in most African states caused by oil price rises had attained crisis proportions in Zambia and, highly significantly, in Mozambique. In the latter case the Mozambique leader, Samora Machel, now had a real and urgent interest in pushing Robert Mugabe and his ZANU cohorts towards a negotiation with other parties, since this action was the vital precondition for any western banking loans to his regime. The Commonwealth Prime Ministers' Conference was scheduled for Lusaka in August 1979, and this proved an excellent venue for Mrs Thatcher to draw the threads of the Rhodesian problem into her hands. To what degree the resulting package had already been put together *before* the Lusaka proceedings began, and to what extent it was the product of conference brinkmanship with key roles played by such brokers as the Australian Prime Minister, Malcolm Fraser, cannot be known. The provisional agreement, however, clearly stipulated all-party involvement in the transitional arrangements, a fully democratic constitution with safeguards for minorities and immediate elections to be supervised by the

UK. Both Muzorewa and Mugabe expressed considerable dismay at what each saw as a *fait accompli* likely to prejudice their respective positions, but neither could refute their backers' demands that they enter a trilateral negotiation with the British Government to thrash out the details of implementation.

The apparent ease with which the new British Foreign Secretary, Lord Carrington, bludgeoned Mugabe and the ZANU radicals into cooperation on the detailed application of the Lusaka principles came as a surprise to all but the most informed observers of southern African affairs. Carrington's leverage arose from the credible threat that the British Government *might* decide to go ahead unilaterally with Muzorewa, thus leaving any non-compromisers out in the cold, and from the frailty of the Machel regime in Mozambique. But Mugabe's pliability (however much it was concealed behind vivid protestations) was also underpinned by his own confidence that he would win the independence elections which were the keystone of the proposed transition. The pressures and manoeuvres which surrounded these elections will not be treated here. Nevertheless, it is worth noting that the supposed expectation in London and other western capitals that Muzorewa's party would emerge victorious seems hard to believe. The scale of Mugabe's electoral triumph in March 1980 might not have been predicted, but the essential outcome – the leading role of ZANU in independent Zimbabwe – was almost certainly implicit in western thinking in the final stages of Rhodesian decolonization. The extent of ZANU penetration in much of the countryside was too great for any other assumption to have prevailed. The important consideration was that this leading role should be fitted into a system of constitutional, political and economic constraints. How successfully this task was actually fulfilled from the vantage point of the various participants at the Lusaka Conference will emerge only in the course of the later 1980s.

It was fitting that Britain's final disentanglement from Rhodesia should have come during the premiership of Margaret Thatcher. She represented an unbending commitment to the regearing of British society and economy to a world order which had changed profoundly over the preceding twenty years; in her reformist convictions she was reminiscent of Harold Macmillan, although fortuitously for her many of the constraints which had limited his scope for action had since dissolved. It might be argued, nevertheless, that the Falklands War of 1982, and the intensity of public emotion it aroused in the

UK, indicated that the imperial plasma was still secreted within the tissues of British society. This is probably misplaced. What the Falklands highlighted was a Britain which cared very little about what African, Asian or the rest of Latin American opinion thought on an issue where British interests were held to be at stake. By the early 1980s Britain had arrived at a point long occupied by Western Germany regarding the non-advanced world: the latter counted as suppliers and consumers, nothing more. The moral rhetoric of decolonization had given way to an implacable economic reduction-ism. Thus right-wing opinion in Britain looked on with satisfaction while the new Conservative Government scaled down overseas aid programmes; meanwhile left-wing commentators adumbrated an 'alternative economic strategy' consisting of a battery of protectionist devices, one of the chief aims of which would be to export deflation and unemployment to the newly industrializing countries of the Third World. The metropole-hinterland relationship had been trans-muted into a purely business affair, interrupted by the odd strategic flurry as great-power rivalries refracted through the outer world. The age of formalized European empire, which once seemed such a logical outcrop of 'modern' forces, and which was a blend of authoritarianism and racism on the one hand and 'responsibility' for development and stability on the other, appeared now to be a curious departure from the normative, cash-register interaction between the world's different continents.

III PORTUGAL'S AFRICAN EMPIRE: REVOLUTION FROM THE METROPOLE

The Portuguese decolonizations in Guiné, Mozambique and Angola were the inevitable consequence of the successful coup against the dictatorship of President Antonio Salazar in Lisbon during April 1974.[12] The coup itself, however, was the product of a progressive weakening of the Portuguese position in its African colonies after 1970. It was this rapid crumbling of the Portuguese presence in the region which not only sealed the fate of the UDI regime in Rhodesia, but, more broadly, triggered a struggle among interested powers for a pre-eminent position in the new southern African dispensation. Had Portuguese colonialism in Africa been drawn into line with other European transfers of power in the early 1960s, and indigenous regimes compliant with western interests slotted into place, then the Soviet Union and its clients (above all, Cuba) would not have been granted the windfall opportunity to penetrate central-southern Africa which came their way a decade later. The questions we must ask are, therefore, why did the Portuguese dictatorship succeed in maintaining its African authority through the 1960s, and why was this achievement so rapidly reversed in the first half of the 1970s?

Just when the British, French and Belgian metropoles had swung away from their colonial orientations after 1955, the Portuguese commitment to their African dependencies had been greatly reinforced. This enhanced commitment took two main forms: an increase in the numbers of white settlers (such that there were 350,000 such arrivals in Angola *after* 1960) and a build-up in the military forces 'on the ground' (such that in 1974 one in four adult Portuguese males were in the armed forces). African resistance to this accelerating penetration was feeble. The Bkonde rebellion in Angola during 1961 was bloodily but successfully crushed, and the nationalist cadres were sealed off from the masses by intensive security operations. Clearly, if a European power (even a weak one) wished to break an African nationalism after 1960, it was able to do so, at a cost.[13] Portugal's acceptance of these costs was predetermined by the nature of its domestic economy. Since Salazar had taken power in 1928, Portugal had been shielded from those modernizing tendencies (generated by depression, war and reconstruction) so evident in northern Europe. This cordoning-off of Portuguese society would not have been sustainable if their larger neighbour, Spain, had maintained its place in the mainstream of continental development, but wartime neutrality, and Francoist authoritarianism, meant that the whole Iberian peninsula was strapped into social and economic immobility. Portugal, itself in certain senses a dependency of more advanced industrial economies and effectively pushed to the margins of Europe's transforming capitalism, concentrated its stagnant pool of resources and skills on cultivating its African allotment. This connection was predicated on continuing *formal* political domination of colonies because the metropole lacked the economic magnetism necessary to make informal control a viable alternative. As Amilcar Cabral, the self-styled martyr of Portuguese decolonization, commented: 'Portugal cannot afford neo-colonialism'.

However reluctant the Portuguese political and business establishments were to break out of the old colonial nexus, it might have been expected that the other western powers would have pressed them into decolonization. Thus Portugal had been a NATO member since its inception in 1949, and by the early 1960s the US had long been determined to disengage the alliance from the taint of colonialism. In Britain, too, Harold Macmillan might logically have wished to see the Portuguese empire dismantled in Africa after 1959, since his own domestic right-wing critics, resentful of the swing in British colonial policy, were further incensed by the observation that the Portuguese were quite able to withstand the 'wind of change' which Macmillan chose to find so overwhelming. But paradoxically, the maintenance of Lisbon's authority in Africa suited other NATO powers quite well. The cost, after all, was borne entirely on the Portuguese exchequer, or, more precisely, by the Portuguese peasantry who were recruited in their hundreds of thousands for service in Africa. Since the armed services of this minor ally had no real role to play in western defence thinking, the diversion of its energies in African directions did not cause concern in Washington. Indeed, US administrations were anxious that Communist powers might fill any vacuum left by a Portuguese departure, and so accepted the status quo as the best of all possible worlds. The British shared in these American attitudes. But the continuance of Lisbon's authority in Guiné, Angola and Mozambique (especially in the latter two territories) had one particular advantage when viewed from London: it provided a kind of regional 'guarantee' which permitted British decolonizations to be pressed in southern-central Africa with a greater confidence than might otherwise have been the case. But overarching these considerations was the knowledge that any unscrambling of Portuguese colonialism in Africa would necessitate the unscrambling, too, of the Salazarist dictatorship itself. Throughout the 1960s this remained an unwelcome prospect within NATO, since renewed instabilities in the Iberian peninsula had been a scenario which western governments had been eager to stifle ever since the Spanish Civil War had ground to a halt in 1939.

After 1970, however, Portuguese resources were badly stretched by the heightened tempo of its military engagement in Africa.[14] The changing pace of events was partially caused by internal political shifts within the various dependencies. It was quite logical that large blocks of indigenous black opinion should have been mobilized as majority-rule independence seemed to have passed them by altogether, just as it had passed by Rhodesian blacks; in this way it became easier for such nationalist factions as the African Forces for the Independence of Guiné and Cape Verde (PAIGC), the Front for the Liberation of Mozambique (FRELIMO) and the Popular Movement for the Liberation of Angola (MPLA) to attract recruits. But the root cause of the altered situation in Portuguese Africa after 1970 was external: the flow of arms, munitions and specialist advisers from non-western countries transformed the guerrilla factions into credible opponents of Portuguese mastery. This intervention emanated above all from the Soviet Union and its East German and Cuban proxies; it was just one facet of the Warsaw Pact's decision at this stage to extend its global challenge to American power. Had the Americans not been embroiled in the Vietnam War it is probable that an early response would have been made to this Soviet entry into southern Africa. As it was, however, the Portuguese were left to cope with a regional escalation as best they could, hiking-up their own man- and firepower to maintain their margin of superiority over the guerrillas. But by 1975 the metropole's ability to sustain this huge military effort was beginning to crack.

If this was the crucial background to the coup of 25 April 1974 in Lisbon, it is necessary to go on and differentiate between the two main groups which ensured its success. First, there was the mass of military conscripts (middle- and junior-ranking officers, and ranks) who saw their personal aspirations being subordinated to unwinnable African wars, and who had become convinced that only a return to democracy at home offered a way out of the impasse. This opinion was organized for action in the Armed Forces Movement (AFM) and deeply overlaid with radical and proletarian sentiments. Second, there was the burgeoning consensus amongst the business and bureaucratic classes that Portugal had to reorientate itself towards integration within the EEC, a long-term goal which required as a first step the ending of domestic authoritarianism and any commitment to colonial pacification. Thus the expansion of the EEC in 1972 with the signature of the Treaty of Rome by the UK, Ireland and Denmark had opened up the whole question of southern Europe's absorption into that ambitious block; if, as Amilcar Cabral had said, Portugal could not afford neo-colonialism in the 1960s, in the 1970s it could afford even less to see Spain edge towards a re-entry into west European affairs and thus be left out in the cold on its own. It was this transient coincidence between popular protest as expressed in the AFM and the strategic calculations of metropolitan oligarchies which allowed the coup to run its course so easily and (almost) bloodlessly, placing transitional power in the hands of General Antonio de Spinola.

The 'coup consensus', however, did not mean that the moving spirits of the April revolution had identical views on what shape decolonization in Africa should take. The AFM leaders pressed for immediate settlements with the guerrilla armies, whereas establishment interests held out for a more closely controlled process in which transfers of power should be made to hinge on a non-appropriation of metropolitan-owned assets in the colonies. Spinola had constantly to bridge this gap. His original, pre-coup conception of a Lusitanian Federation (a kind of French Community-style solution) lacked credibility; Portugal did not have the power to impose such a system as France had been able to do in West Africa. Within months of coming to power, Spinola had decided to differentiate between the three African situations with which he was confronted. He gave the AFM factions in Guiné the scope to negotiate a ceasefire followed by independence, because the military situation was irretrievable and because Guiné was economically of little value. Similarly, Spinola accepted a settlement in Mozambique, since Samora Machel's FRELIMO was firmly in control of much of the country and seemed likely to prove a malleable partner after power was transferred. Angola, however, was crucially different, and it was in this territory that decolonization was to prove deeply contorted and deformed by international rivalries. In particular, the new regime in Lisbon could not allow Angola – rich in minerals, occupying a strategic position in the continent and vulnerable to external manipulation by virtue of its conflicting regional and ethnic formations – to slip into an unstable, Soviet-penetrated independence without angering those western nations on whose future favours Portugal would be dependent. Spinola therefore strove to effect a negotiated end to colonial rule in which the role of the Marxist-led MPLA was carefully buttressed by its competitors, the National Front for the Liberation of Angola (FNLA) and the National Union for the Total Independence of Angola (UNITA) whose external links lay with NATO. Finally, in January 1975 he secured a document signed by representatives from all three of these aspirant bodies providing for independence in Angola in the following November, after which free and fair elections would be held as soon as possible; the Portuguese military presence would not be completely withdrawn until February 1976. This last stipulation was not least intended to give white settlers the assurances they required to stay on in the colonies, so that their skills and production would not be forfeited just when the emerging independent states would have desperate need of their resources. But in fact, given the preparations that the MPLA, UNITA, and FLNA were each making for civil war, the January 1975 agreement was a farce; its only effectiveness probably lay in allowing Spinola to signal loud and clear that Portuguese capacities had now been exhausted, and that other (and bigger) powers would have to see to it that the Angolan dénouement was not a catastrophe for the western alliance. Sensing that their 'home' government had no stomach even for 'emergency' measures to protect its exposed nationals in Angola, and shocked by the inter-factional fighting which tore the Angolan capital, Luanda, apart during March 1975, the Portuguese settlers proceeded to stream back to Europe in a massive exodus reminiscent of the end of French Algeria. Holding the Luanda 'ring' while this migration took place, and absorbing the refugees back into metropolitan society, was really the last significant act of Portuguese colonialism.

Because the Portuguese role in subsequent Angolan events was so limited, the events which ensued really fall outside our present scope, but a brief summary would be appropriate. Henry Kissinger, who dominated foreign policy-making in President Ford's Republican administration in the US, was just as determined to prevent the MPLA scooping the Angolan pool as he was to thwart ZANU and ZAPU in Rhodesia, and in early 1975 he saw a solution to both these tangled situations in the evolution of an American-South African 'umbrella' fixed over these portions of central-southern Africa. But the rapid disintegration of the Portuguese presence by the summer of 1975 meant that this cooperation between Washington and Pretoria had to take on an explicit military form. It is quite likely that at first Kissinger felt such action to be an advantage, since a limited and successful intervention in Africa might help to staunch that post-Vietnam defeatism at home which the Secretary of State felt to be such a danger to American power at large. Thus in October 1975 a US-financed and equipped force moved south from Zaire into Angola, while South African armoured columns moved north with UNITA and FLNA units, intending to break the MPLA strongholds around Luanda. The massive Cuban counter-reinforcements which followed, however, raised the military stakes in a way the US administration had not anticipated, and to a degree which evoked the intense nervousness and caution currently dominant within the

Congress; in December 1975, with a presidential election year looming, the American commitment to Angolan operations was suddenly withdrawn. The damage done to US-South African understanding was profound and lasting, and as a result the anti-Communist powers were left without any mechanism to achieve their goals in the area. The South African Government maintained its offensive in the south so as to create as much havoc as possible within the MPLA zone, but inevitably these troops, too, drew back in the latter months of 1976, since without American back-up they could not hope to impose solutions over such a large area stretching beyond South African borders. It was therefore the MPLA and its Cuban backers whose dual authority succeeded that of Portugal over most of Angola's vast tracts, and most significantly around the Luanda 'core'. But UNITA and the FLN continued to exercise power within their own regional fiefdoms, and the South Africans evinced a readiness to reintervene to sustain that condition of confused deadlock which (under the circumstances) served their interests best. What had followed upon the Portuguese withdrawal from Angola, therefore, was not independence in any meaningful or substantive sense, but rather a field of play upon which intricate and layered patterns of conflict – national, regional and international – were branded.

If in the 1970s, therefore, the western powers succeeded (just) in keeping Rhodesian decolonization within the guide-lines of their own interests, they clearly failed to do so in Angola. The reasons for this contrast are fundamentally simple: settler-power, and western influence generally, was much more deeply entrenched in Rhodesian society than had been the case in the latter's Portuguese-ruled neighbours. But perhaps the most pertinent conclusion to draw from this narrative is how lucky or astute British, French and Belgian governments had been to drive towards blanket decolonizations in the first half of the 1960s when the Soviets had yet seriously to challenge western power in Afro-Asia. Had many of these decolonizations, especially the more complicated among them, been delayed for a decade longer, by which time the USSR had become a truly global military power, the processes of power transfer would have been infinitely more subject to international complications. The chronological pattern of decolonization after the late 1950s was therefore probably conducive to the world's peace (on essentially western terms), even if it did little for the aspirations to prosperity of the newly self-governing masses.

Postscript

Most writers (except, perhaps, the romantic novelists) approach their concluding passages with a heavy heart; it is as if a climber, clambering at last on to what he took to be a table-top peak, finds another flush-faced ridge rising startlingly above him. This weariness of spirit is felt particularly by historians of the liberal-eclectic sort who, unlike their more crystalline, ideologically inclined colleagues, have no patter of ready-made conclusions to send their readers away with the happy thought that all has finally been revealed. Indeed, any historian of decolonization must blanche at the thought of summarizing in a few, compact pages the vast array of human fates and fortunes encapsulated in that historical episode. No such brazenly ambitious task will be attempted here. Our postscript will simply delineate some of the themes which have marked this introductory study, and gloss upon their relevance for the contemporary world scene.

The demission of European empires was not a linear process; it was characterized by remissions and revivals as the calculus of inputs and outputs was altered by events. Thus in the two decades after 1919 the British became progressively less convinced of the utility of an imperial system, although its formal dismantling was not yet envisaged; the Second World War, by raising the extra-European stakes, pushed the London authorities into accepting the costs of a renewed colonial activism, and this dynamic was maintained through to the early 1950s by a mixture of economic crisis and Cold War diplomacy; but after 1955 the relationship between British interests in the wider world and the gaggle of dependencies in Africa, the Caribbean and parts of Asia fell into a new and, this time, fatal disequilibrium. The texture and timing of French 'disimperialism' was often distinctively different from the British counterpart, but the structural pattern was essentially the same.

One outstanding deduction that can be made from this is that decolonization was not simply a spin-off from the more general decline of European power within the international system. Western Europe's status and capacity relative to the United States was clearly on the wane for most of the twentieth century, and violently so after 1945, but whether that status and capacity fell in relation to Upper Volta or the Gold Coast/Ghana is very doubtful. This should be obvious enough, except that in recent years a whole literature of 'declinology' has burst into (somewhat flickering) life, so often bearing exotic subtitles along the lines of 'Illusions of Grandeur' that one can almost hear the office applause of dustjacket designers in the background. The reality was that after 1950 the pace of modernization and reform was much greater in the old metropoles – even in that most laggard of west European societies, the United Kingdom – than it was in the peripheries successively fitted out for independence. Thus in the era of classical imperialism the development of colonizer and colonized had been brought into a tense but workable harmony, but after the mid-twentieth century these sheared apart, to the detriment of the latter. This was suitably obscured by the effusions of western media and academics to the effect that 'new' Afro-Asian societies were emerging from beneath the white-colonial heel; rarely can hypocrisy, opportunism, occasional shafts of genuine idealism and an unyielding intellectual mediocrity have been so inextricably bound together than among the western intelligentsia of the 1960s.

Neo-colonial interpreters of European decolonization consistently possessed the merit of recognizing that British or French 'decline' had little direct relevance to their subject of study. Instead, they fell into an illusion of their own: that really nothing (besides the constitutional wrappings) had changed, and that the so-called 'new states' of Africa and Asia had been bound more tightly than ever into the dynamic process of western-orchestrated capitalist accumulation. There was one recurrent contradiction amongst the 'neo-colonial' school which increasingly bobbed to the surface: on the one hand it was argued that western industrial capitalism had desperate need of the markets and commodities of Third World countries, hence the intricate control system over which the multinationals in particular presided, while on the other it was pointed out that the less-developed economies had been effectively shunted to the margins of the world order. The latter was much nearer to the truth, although it posed problems for marxist scholars reared in the leninist tradition that European capitalism had long clung to colonies as a means of delaying the inevitable debacle. Colonial polities had gained their independence, not because nationalists had at last proved capable of exploiting their leverage within western economic arrangements, but because they had ceased to matter; or, rather, to matter enough to merit a retention under contemporary conditions.

This is not to contend that the processes of capital accumulation and political decolonization were unrelated, but only that the relationship cannot be described by cliché. Thus the industrial metropoles had come to seek growth and stability (that unattainable duo) by exploring the opportunities for cooperation between themselves, not by cultivating their respective relationships with Afro-Asian partners. Their vested interest in these peripheries came to be static, not dynamic; in short, the preservation of local equilibrium such that existing investments remained secure and the Russians were kept out. This objective fortuitously coincided with that of the indigenous elites thrown up by earlier waves of colonial economic change and which by the 1950s had attained a degree of social maturity. These classes now had an interest, not in accelerating the impulses to change in their environment, but in choking them off short; they were eager, in other words, to 'lock-in' a situation conducive to their own modest but vulnerable positions of power and prosperity. Thus nationalist leaders such as Kwame Nkrumah and Julius Nyerere built coalitions around social groups (not least bureaucratic cadres) whose productive utilities were often close to zero; stagnation was often the result, and a military authoritarianism designed to discipline those mass aspirations whose very existence had been antithetical to the 'command position' of the decolonizing elites of the late 1950s and early 1960s.

This branding into place of low-level equilibrium was the essence of modern European decolonization. It was the product of external and internal circumstances in (probably) about equal measure. Such a fragile construct was, however, good for something like a decade but not much more since, Alice-like, any society has after a while to run fast even to stay in approximately the same place. This was the dilemma which set in after the mid-1970s, triggered by oil price rises and world recession. Quite what the effect of the augmented crisis of the early 1980s has been on this situation is, of course, difficult to say. It seems almost certain that the enormous changes in the technological and industrial structure of the western world effected by the OPEC-induced slump will end by putting a sociological gulf between

the advanced and non-advanced world much wider than that which
has prevailed since the First World War. Some Third World countries
(those equipped with the most flexible social and political arrangements) should be able to exploit the shifting circumstances of a new
age to project themselves from the coalition of 'have-nots' into that of
the 'haves'. In general, however, one can conclude that whereas
Asian and African masses were able to gain access to such magical
inventions as the transistor radio not so many years after their
'advanced' counterparts, the petit bourgeois generation with expectations shaped by more sophisticated electronic cults is certain to be
decisively thwarted.

Notes

1 THE EUROPEAN EMPIRES IN A TRANSFORMING WORLD

1. Colin Cross, *The Fall of the British Empire* (London, 1968) pp. 15–34.

2. John Gallagher, *The Decline, Revival and Fall of the British Empire* (Cambridge, 1982) p. 74.

3. There is no comprehensive account of the impact of the 1930s depression on the colonial world. See, however, A. J. Latham, *The Depression and the Developing World, 1914–39* (London, 1981).

4. A. M. Carr-Saunders, *World Populations: Past Growth and Present Trends* (London, 1936) pp. 269, 280.

5. A spate of books dilating on the problems of Asian agricultures appeared in the 1920s and 1930s. A classic example of this literature was Sir Malcolm Darling, *The Punjab Peasant in Prosperity and Debt* (Oxford, 1925).

6. This treatment of Indo-Chinese affairs is largely based on material in Charles Robequain, *The Economic Development of French Indo-China* (Oxford, 1944).

7. For a contemporary survey of this region during the later 1930s see Virginia Thompson, *French Indo-China* (London, 1937).

8. Robequain, *The Economic Development of French Indo-China*, pp. 168–77.

9. B. B. Misra, *The Indian Middle Classes: Their Growth in Modern Times* (Oxford, 1961) pp. 213–307.

10 Eric Davis, *Challenging Colonialism: Bank Misr and Egyptian Industrialization, 1920–41* (Princeton, 1983).

11. The fullest account of this subject is Rajat K. Ray, *Industrialization in India: Growth and Conflict in the Private Corporate Sector, 1914–47* (Delhi, 1979).

12. This requires some qualification: in the 1920s parts of the European bourgeoisie *did* come to fear a relapse into personal destitution, and it was their anxieties which underpinned fascist ideologies.

13. See Victor Purcell, *The Chinese in South-East Asia* (Oxford, 1965).

14. For a sensitive study of 'independent Christianity' in an African setting see B. G. M. Sundkler, *Bantu Prophets in South Africa* (Oxford, 1961). A cruder political coverage of the same theme may be found in Robert I. Rotberg and Ali A. Mazrui, *Protest and Power in Black Africa* (Oxford, 1970) pp. 377–426.

15. Thomas D. Williams, *Malawi: The Politics of Despair* (London, 1978) pp. 110–18 and Rotberg and Mazrui, *Protest and Power in Black Africa*, pp. 337–76.

16. John F. Cady, *A History of Modern Burma* (Ithaca, 1958) pp. 309–14.

17. Ibid., pp. 231–4, 250–3.

18. Harry J. Benda, *The Crescent and the Rising Sun: Indonesian Islam and the Japanese occupation, 1942–45* (The Hague, 1958) pp. 9–99. For a general political survey of the Dutch East Indies in this period see G. M. Kahin, *Nationalism and Revolution in Indonesia* (New York, 1952) pp. 1–101.

19. A good overview of the causes and course of the Depression is Charles P. Kindleberger, *The World in Depression, 1929–1939* (London, 1973).

20. This point comes out well, if somewhat obliquely, in P. J. Vatikiotis, *Nasser and his Generation* (London, 1978) pp. 47–64.

21. R. F. Holland, 'The End of an Imperial Economy: Anglo-Canadian Disengagement in the 1930s', *Journal of Imperial and Commonwealth History*, XI (January, 1983).

22. B. R. Tomlinson, *The Political Economy of the Raj, 1914–47: The Economics of Decolonization* (London, 1979) pp. 31–4.

23. D. K. Fieldhouse, *Unilever Overseas: The Anatomy of a Multinational* (London, 1978) pp. 148–69, 558–60.

24. A. G. Hopkins, *An Economic History of West Africa* (London, 1973) pp. 237–67.

25. Michael Lipton, *Why Poor People Stay Poor: a study of urban bias in world development* (London, 1977).

26. Tomlinson, *Political Economy of the Raj*, pp. 164–5.

27. For comments on smallholder production in south-east Asia see P. T. Bauer, *The Rubber Industry: a study in competition and monopoly* (London, 1948) pp. 56–73.

28. The regulation of rubber production was perhaps the most interesting of the commodity control experiments which characterized the post-1929 Depression. See Sir A. McFadyean, *The History of Rubber Regulation, 1934–1943* (London, 1944).

29. Gavin Kitching, *Class and Economic Change in Kenya: The Making of an African Petit Bourgeoisie, 1905–1970* (Yale, 1980) pp. 57–107.

30. G. C. Allen and A. G. Donnithorne, *Western Enterprise in Indonesia and Malaya: a study in economic development* (London, 1957) pp. 57, 124, 204–6.

31. See B. R. Tomlinson, 'Colonial Firms and the Decline of Colonialism in Eastern India, 1914–47', *Modern Asian Studies*, 15, No. 3 (1981). This business cooperation across the racial divide was not, in itself, an especially novel phenomenon, but had been distinctive of an earlier phase of British rule in India. See C. Bayly, *Rulers, Townsmen and Bazaars: North Indian Society in the age of British Expansion, 1770–1870* (Cambridge, 1983).

32. This treatment of Egyptian developments during the early post-war years is largely based on John Darwin, *Britain, Egypt and the Middle East: Imperial Policy in the Aftermath of War, 1918–22* (London, 1981) pp. 49–137.

33. Viscount Wavell, *Allenby in Egypt* (London, 1943) pp. 35–47.

34. Darwin, *Britain, Egypt and the Middle East*, p. 115.

35. There is no major scholarly survey of the impact of the First World War on India. Some information may be gleaned from De Witt C. Ellinwood and S. D. Pradhan (eds), *India and World War One* (New Delhi, 1978).

36. A recent study of this subject is Gail Minault, *The Khilafat Movement: Religious Symbolism and Political Mobilization in India* (New York, 1982).

37. Judith Brown, *Gandhi's Rise to Power: Indian Politics, 1915–22* (Cambridge, 1972).

38. This analytical approach is pursued in J. Gallagher, A. Seal and G. Johnson, *Locality, Province and Nation: Essays on Indian Politics, 1870–1940* (Cambridge, 1973).

39. P. J. Robb, *The Government of India and Reform, 1916–21* (Oxford, 1976).

40. B. R. Tomlinson, *The Indian National Congress and the Raj, 1929–42: The Penultimate Phase* (London, 1976) pp. 28–31.

41. For the flavour of contemporary British discussion on India's internal political condition see George Schuster and Guy Wint, *India and Democracy* (London, 1941) pp. 133–210.

42. R. F. Holland, *Britain and the Commonwealth Alliance, 1918–39* (London, 1981) pp. 164–6.

43. For analyses of Irish Free State developments as they impinged on British Commonwealth affairs prior to the Second World War see David Harkness, *The Restless Dominion: the Irish Free State and the British Commonwealth of Nations, 1921–31*

(London, 1969); Holland, *Britain and the Commonwealth Alliance*, pp. 152–66; Ged Martin, 'The Irish Free State and the evolution of the Commonwealth, 1921–49' in Ged Martin and Ronald Hyam, *Reappraisals in British Imperial History* (London, 1975).

44. Intra-Commonwealth diplomatic dealings during the run-up to the Second World War are exhaustively covered in R. Ovendale, *'Appeasement' and the English-speaking World: Britain, the United States, the Dominions and the policy of 'appeasement', 1937–9* (London, 1975).

45. Surprisingly, there are few textbook treatments of South African affairs in the twentieth century. For political developments T. R. H. Davenport, *South Africa: A Modern History* (London, 1977) provides a broad outline. Those interested in economics may refer to D. Hobart Houghton, *The South African Economy* (Cape Town, 1964) and Jill Nattrass, *The South African Economy: its growth and change* (Cape Town, 1981).

46. Two recent studies which touch on this issue are Dan O'Meara, *Volkscapitalisme: Class, capital and ideology in the development of Afrikaner nationalism* (Cambridge, 1983) and David Yudelman, *The Emergence of Modern South Africa: State, Capital, and the Consolidation of Organized Labour on the South African Gold Fields, 1902–1939* (Westport, Connecticut, 1983).

47. For a description of migrant labouring in African social experience see Charles van Onselen, *Chibaro: African Mine Labour in Southern Rhodesia, 1900–1933* (London, 1976).

48. Clement Kadalic, *My Life and the ICU: The Autobiography of a Black Trade Unionist in South Africa* (London, 1970).

49. L. H. Gann, *A History of Southern Rhodesia: Early Days to 1934* (London, 1965) p. 247.

50. Anglo-South African relations in this period are covered in R. Hyam, *The Failure of South African Expansion, 1908 48* (London, 1972).

51. Michael Crowder, *West Africa Under Colonial Rule* (London, 1968) pp. 198–233.

52. John Iliffe, *A Modern History of Tanganyika* (Cambridge, 1979).

53. The standard account of 'trusteeship' thinking is Kenneth Robinson, *The Dilemma of Trusteeship: Aspects of British Colonial Policy Between the Wars* (London, 1965).

54. Robert G. Gregory, *India and East Africa: A History of Race Relations within the British Empire* (Oxford, 1971) pp. 177–265.

55. Holland, *Britain and the Commonwealth Alliance*, pp. 176–8.

56. It was particularly important, for example, in promoting pan-African ideals. See J. Ayodele, *Pan-Africanism and Nationalism in West Africa, 1900–45* (Oxford, 1973) pp. 327–37.

2   MOBILIZATION, REJUVENATION AND LIQUIDATION: COLONIALISM AND GLOBAL WAR

1. John Gallagher, *The Decline, Revival and Fall of the British Empire* (Cambridge, 1982) pp. 137–41.

2. Richard Storry, *Japan and the Decline of the West, 1894–1943* (London, 1979).

3. E. B. Schumpeter, *The Industrialization of Japan and Manchukuo 1930–40: Population, Raw Materials and Industry* (London, 1940).

4. For an evaluation of Japan's industrial prospects on the eve of the transformation induced by depression see John E. Orchard, *Japan's Economic Position: The Progress of Industrialization* (New York, 1929).

5. This shock is reflected in Virginia Thompson, *Post-Mortem on Malaya* (New York, 1943).

6. Jan Pluvier, *South-East Asia from Colonialism to Independence* (Kuala Lumpur, 1974) p. 300.

7. H. J. Benda, *The Crescent and the Rising Sun: Indonesian Islam and the Japanese Occupation, 1942–45* (The Hague, 1958) p. 172.

8. For Sukarno's position in Indonesian politics during the Japanese occupation see J. D. Legge, *Sukarno* (London, 1972) pp. 147–80.

9. One helpful introductory survey of Vietnamese history in the late colonial period is Ellen Hammer, *The Struggle for Indo-China* (Stanford, 1954).

10. The development of the Viet Minh in this period is traced in John T. McAlister, *Viet Nam: The Origins of Revolution* (Princeton, 1969).

11. Gavin Kitching, *Class and Economic Change in Kenya: The Making of an African Petit Bourgeoisie, 1905–1970* (Yale, 1980) pp. 108–50.

12. B. R. Tomlinson, *The Political Economy of the Raj, 1914–47: The Economics of Decolonization* (London, 1979) pp. 92–100 and Rajat K. Ray, *Industrialization in India: Growth and Conflict in the Private Corporate Sector, 1914–47* (Delhi, 1979) pp. 188–90, 256–8, 278–9.

13. Martin W. Wilmington, *The Middle East Supply Centre* (New York, 1971).

14. A. R. Prest, *War Economies of Primary Producing Countries* (Cambridge, 1948).

15. For a broad study of British war finance see R. S. Sayers, *History of the Second World War: Financial Policy, 1939–45* (London, 1956).

16. Barrie St. Clair McBride, *Farouk of Egypt: a biography* (London, 1967) pp. 103–19.

17. The two outstanding accounts are C. Thorne, *Allies of a Kind: The United States, Britain and the War against Japan, 1941–5* (Oxford, 1978) and Wm Roger Louis, *Imperialism at Bay: The United States and the Decolonization of the British Empire, 1941–45* (Oxford, 1977).

18. David Howorth, *The Desert King: The Life of Ibn Saud* (London, 1980) pp. 189–94.

19. Thorne, *Allies of a Kind*, pp. 278–80.

20. For an account of the wartime Colonial Office see J. M. Lee and M. Petter, *The Colonial Office, War and Development Policy: Organization and the Planning of a Metropolitan Initiative, 1939–45* (London, 1982).

21. Louis, *Imperialism at Bay*, pp. 515–16.

22. For a description of the Mutual Aid Agreement between the United States and Great Britain see Sayers, *Financial Policy, 1939–45*, pp. 375–427.

23. US policies in the final phases of the Second World War are delineated in Gabriel Kolko, *The Politics of War: Allied Diplomacy and the World Crisis, 1943–45* (London, 1969). Anglo-American differences in the financial and trade spheres are best discussed in R. Gardner, *Sterling–Dollar Diplomacy: Anglo-American Collaboration in the Reconstruction of Multilateral Trade* (Oxford, 1956).

24. D. J. Morgan, *The Official History of Colonial Development. Volume One: The Origins of British Aid Policy, 1924–45* (London, 1982) pp. 198–206.

25. R. J. Moore, *Churchill, Cripps and India, 1939–45* (Oxford, 1979).

26. This treatment is drawn from I. A. Talbot, 'Deserted Collaborators: The Political Background to the Rise and Fall of the Punjab Unionist Party, 1923–47', *Journal of Imperial and Commonwealth History*, XI, No. 1 (October 1982).

27. A fuller discussion of this question can be found in R. J. Moore, 'Jinnah and the Pakistan Demand', *Modern Asian Studies*, 17, No. 4 (1983).

28. A full-length, scholarly study of the Indian National Army has yet to be written. K. K. Ghosh, *The Indian National Army* (Meerut, 1969) tells the story from the conventional nationalist viewpoint.

29. See Ronald Lewin, *The Chief: Field Marshal Lord Wavell, Commander-in-Chief and Viceroy* (London, 1980).

30. R. J. Moore, *Escape from India: The Attlee Government and the Indian Problem* (Oxford, 1983) pp. 16–17, 34–55.

31. For a discussion of this issue see Nigel Hamilton, *Monty, Master of the Battlefield 1942–44* (London, 1983).

32. Kitching, *Class and Economic Change in Kenya*, pp. 108–20.

33. The Brazzaville Conference is described in Edward Mortimer, *France and the Africans, 1944–60: a political history* (London, 1969) pp. 27–49.

34. The evolution of British administrative policies in Africa after the outbreak of the Second World War is traced in R. D. Pearce, *The Turning Point in Africa: British Colonial Policy, 1938–48* (London, 1982).

35. Ronald Robinson, 'Andrew Cohen and the Transfer of Power in Tropical Africa, 1940–51' in W. H. Morris-Jones and Georges Fischer, *Decolonization and After: The British and French Experience* (London, 1980).

36. N. J. Westcott, 'Closer Union and the future of East Africa, 1939–48: A case-study in "the official mind of imperialism"', *Journal of Imperial and Commonwealth History*, x, No. 1 (October 1981).

37. Pearce, *The Turning Point in Africa*, p. 72.

3 EUROPE'S ASIAN STAKE: ADAPTATION, RESTORATION AND DESTRUCTION

1. Two recommended narratives are Penderel Moon, *Divide and Quit* (London, 1961) and H. V. Hodson, *The Great Divide: Britain–India–Pakistan* (London, 1969).

2. For an 'inside' account of the Mountbatten viceroyalty see Alan Campbell-Johnson, *Mission with Mountbatten* (New York, 1953).

3. A succinct cartoon-summary of this phenomenon appears in Paul Scott, *A Division of the Spoils* (London, 1977) pp. 414–17.

4. R. J. Moore, *Escape from India: The Attlee Government and the Indian Problem* (Oxford, 1983) pp. 183–201, 208–11.

5. Kenneth Harris, *Attlee* (London, 1982) pp. 355–88.

6. Hodson, *The Great Divide*, p. 324.

7. For a participant's view of these security dilemmas see Francis I. Tuker, *While Memory Serves* (London, 1950).

8. A judicious critique of Mountbatten's record as Viceroy by one who was there can be found in W. H. Morris-Jones, 'The Transfer of Power, 1947: A View from the Sidelines', *Modern Asian Studies*, 16, No. 1 (1982).

9. For a fuller narrative see Nicholas Mansergh, *The Commonwealth Experience. Volume Two: From British to Multiracial Commonwealth* (London, second edn, 1982) pp. 135–62.

10. F. S. V. Donnison, *History of the Second World War: British Military Administration in the Far East, 1943–1946* (London, 1956) pp. 413–35.

11. A. Arthur Schiller, *The Formation of Federal Indonesia 1945–49* (The Hague, 1955).

12. J. D. Legge, *Sukarno* (London, 1972) pp. 199–202.

13. For the Governor General's account of these events see J. H. van Mook, *The Stakes of Democracy in South-East Asia* (London, 1950).

14. Jan Pluvier, *South-East Asia from Colonialism to Independence* (Kuala Lumpur, 1974) p. 438.

15. G. M. Kahin, *Nationalism and Revolution in Indonesia* (New York, 1952) pp. 290–300.

16. The course of the controversy over West Irian is charted in Leslie Palmier, *Indonesia and the Dutch* (Oxford, 1962) pp. 111–67.

17. Donnison, *British Military Administration in the Far East, 1943–46*, pp. 401–11.

18. Recommended narratives covering the Franco–Viet Minh war are Ellen Hammer, *The Struggle for Indo-China* (Stanford, 1954); Bernard B. Fall, *Street Without*

Joy: Insurgency in Indo-China 1946–63 (Harrisberg, 1963); Phillippe Devillers, *Histoire de Viet-Nam de 1943 á 1952* (Paris, 1952).

19. While Mao Tse-tung enters the story of European decolonization only spasmo-dically in a direct sense, his figure, and the longer shadow thrown by the Chinese Revolution, looms over the period. Dick Wilson, *Mao, the people's emperor* (London, 1977) is a colourful introduction to the subject.

20. Jules Roy, *The Battle of Dien Bien Phu* (New York, 1965).

21. Phillippe Devillers and Jean Lacouture, *End of a War: Indo-China 1954* (London, 1969).

22. See A. J. Stockwell, *British Policy and Malay Politics during the Malayan Union Experiment, 1942–48* (Kuala Lumpur, 1979).

23. Ibid., pp. 73–86.

24. Lucian W. Pye, *Guerrilla Communism in Malaya: Its Social and Political Meaning* (Princeton, 1956) pp. 198–248.

25. Anthony Short, *The Communist Insurrection in Malaya, 1948–60* (London, 1975) p. 65. Short's book is the official history of the Emergency. For a contemporary British view of these events see Harry Miller, *Menace in Malaya* (London, 1954).

26. Sir Robert Thompson, *Defeating Communist Insurgency: Experience from Malaya and Vietnam* (London, 1966).

4 BRITAIN, PALESTINE AND THE MIDDLE EAST

1. The clearest introduction to this subject is Elizabeth Monroe, *Britain's Moment in the Middle East: 1914–56* (London, 1963).

2. See Christopher Sykes *Crossroads to Israel, 1917–48* (London, 1965) and John Marlowe, *The Seat of Pilate: An Account of the Palestine Mandate* (London, 1969).

3. For the United States dimension see Zvi Ganin, *Truman, American Jewry and Israel, 1945–48* (New York, 1979).

4. Bevin's entanglement in Palestinian affairs receives full coverage in Alan Bullock, *Ernest Bevin: Foreign Secretary, 1945–51* (London, 1983).

5. R. Gardner, *Sterling–Dollar Diplomacy: Anglo-American Collaboration in the Recon-struction of Multilateral Trade* (Oxford, 1956) pp. 312–25.

6. C. M. Woodhouse, *The Struggle for Greece, 1941–49* (London, 1976).

7. S. H. Longrigg, *Iraq, 1900 to 1950: A Political and Economic History* (Oxford, 1953) pp. 334–98.

8. For an introductory survey see John Marlowe, *Anglo-Egyptian Relations 1800–1956* (London, 1965).

9. For a penetrating analysis see A. Banani, *The Modernization of Iran, 1921–41* (Stanford, 1961).

10. Monroe, *Britain's Moment in the Middle East*, pp. 171–2.

5 EXPERIMENTATION, CONSOLIDATION AND DEADLOCK IN BRITISH AFRICA

1. R. Robinson and J. Gallagher, 'The Imperialism of Free Trade', *Economic History Review*, 2nd ser. VI, I (1953) 15.

2. See N. J. Westcott, 'Sterling and Empire: The British imperial economy 1939–51', Institue of Commonwealth Studies (London) Seminar Paper, January 1983.

3. The following account of events in the Gold Coast up until 1954, and that in Part IV continuing the story up to Ghana's independence in 1957, is largely based on Dennis Austin, *Politics in Ghana, 1946–60* (Oxford, 1964) and Richard Rathbone, 'The

transfer of power in Ghana, 1945–57', thesis submitted for the degree of doctor of philosophy in the University of London, 1968.

4. A recent biography is David Rooney, *Sir Charles Arden-Clarke* (London, 1982).

5. Nigerian developments in this period are excellently introduced in J. S. Coleman, *Nigeria: Background to Nationalism* (Berkeley, 1960).

6. Keith Hancock, *Smuts: The Fields of Force 1919–50* (Cambridge, 1968) pp. 492–510.

7. See Newell M. Stultz, *Afrikaner Politics in South Africa, 1934–48* (Berkeley, 1974).

8. These campaigns are outlined in Gwendolen M. Carter, *The Politics of Inequality: South Africa Since 1948* (London, 1974) pp. 302–39.

9. For the birth of the Central African Federation see Robert Blake, *A History of Rhodesia* (London, 1977) pp. 243–83 and Prosser Gifford, 'Misconceived Dominion: The Creation and Disintegration of Federation in British Central Africa' in Prosser Gifford and Wm Roger Louis (eds) *The Transfer of Power in Africa: Decolonization 1940–60* (Yale, 1982), pp. 387–426.

10. David Goldsworthy, *Colonial Issues in British Politics 1945–61: From 'Colonial Development' to 'Wind of Change'* (Oxford, 1971) pp. 208–9, 214–30, 306–10, 366–70.

11. Sir Philip Mitchell, *African Afterthoughts* (London, 1954) pp. 227–44.

12. Jeremy Murray-Brown, *Kenyatta* (London, 1972) pp. 232–3.

13. For the urban origins of Mau Mau see Rob Buijtenhuis, *Essays on Mau Mau: Contributions to Mau Mau Historiography* (Leyden, 1982).

14. This causal sequence is particularly evident in the Tanganyikan case. See G. Andrew Maguire, *Towards 'Uhuru' in Tanzania: The Politics of Participation* (Cambridge, 1969) pp. 112–59.

15. F. D. Corfield, *Historical Survey of the Origins and Growth of Mau Mau*, Cmd. 1030 (London, 1960).

16. For an informative biography see Charles Douglas-Home, *Evelyn Baring: The Last Proconsul* (London, 1978).

17. Some suggestive insights into the political culture of white settlers in Kenya may be culled from Negley Farson, *Last Chance in Africa* (London, 1949).

6 ORDER AND CHAOS: PATTERNS OF DECOLONIZATION IN FRENCH AND
   BELGIAN AFRICA

1. See W. A. E. Skurnik, 'France and Fragmentation in West Africa: 1945–60', *Journal of African History*, VIII, 2 (1967).

2. Edward Mortimer, *France and the Africans* (London, 1969) pp. 105–10.

3. Ibid., pp. 161–79.

4. For a contemporary survey of late-colonial French West Africa see Virginia Thompson and Richard Adloff, *French West Africa* (London, 1958).

5. For a discussion of FIDES see Virginia Thompson, 'French Economic Policy in tropical Africa', in Peter Duignan and L. H. Gann (eds), *Colonialism in Africa, 1870–1960. The Economics of Colonialism* (Cambridge, 1975).

6. Two examples of neo-colonial interpretations of decolonization in French West Africa are Gerard Destanne de Bernis, 'Some Aspects of the Economic Relationship between France and its Ex-colonies' and Guy Caire, 'Dependence, Independence and Interdependence in Economic Relations' in W. H. Morris-Jones and Georges Fischer, *Decolonization and After: The British and French Experience* (London, 1980).

7. Mortimer, *France and the Africans*, pp. 360–8.

8. Students interested in colonial Algeria may refer to Vincent Confer, *France and Algeria: The Problem of Civil and Political Reform, 1870–1920* (Syracuse, 1966) and Rudolf von Albertini, *European Colonial Rule 1880–1940: The Impact of the West on India, South-*

East Asia and Africa (London, 1982). The following treatment of events in Algeria after 1954 is largely based on John Talbot, *The War Without a Name: France in Algeria* (London, 1981); Alistair Horne, *A Savage War of Peace: Algeria 1954–1962* (New York, 1978); Tony Smith, *The French Stake in Algeria 1945–62* (Ithaca, 1978).

9. Lorna Hahn, *North Africa: Nationalism to Nationhood* (Washington, 1960) pp. 1–132.

10. Horne, *A Savage War of Peace*, pp. 35–6.

11. For some relevant remarks on this matter see Philip M. Williams, *Crisis and Compromise: Politics in the Fourth Republic* (London, 1972).

12. Ibid., p. 411.

13. The theme of the French Army and decolonization is pursued in George M. Kelly, *Lost Soldiers: The French Army and Empire in Crisis* (Cambridge, Mass., 1965).

14. Henry F. Jackson, *The FLN in Algeria: development in a revolutionary society* (London, 1977) bravely attempts to discuss a subject where information is decidedly sparse.

15. Rene Lemarchand, *Political Awakening in the Congo* (Berkeley, 1964) pp. 55–75.

16. Ibid., p. 75.

17. Jean Stengers, 'Precipitous Decolonization: The Case of the Belgian Congo' in Prosser Gifford and Wm Roger Louis (eds), *The Transfer of Power in Africa: Decolonization 1940–60* (Yale, 1982) p. 319.

18. Crawford Young, *Politics in the Congo: Decolonization and Independence* (Princeton, 1965) pp. 146–52.

19. Ibid., p. 267.

20. Ibid., p. 321.

21. For a biography see Joseph P. Lash, *Hammarskjöld* (London, 1962).

22. Conor Cruise O'Brien, *To Katanga and Back* (New York, 1962) is a famous account of these events by one who was closely involved.

23. Young, *Politics in the Congo*, pp. 592–601.

7 BRITAIN: THE END OF IMPERIAL STATEHOOD

1. There is a voluminous literature on the Suez crisis. A good brief account is in David Carlton, *Anthony Eden: A Biography* (London, 1981) pp. 403–65. The effects on British politics can be followed in Russell Braddon, *Suez: The Splitting of a Nation* (London, 1973) and Leon D. Epstein, *British Politics in the Suez Crisis* (London, 1964). Anthony Nutting, *No End of a Lesson* (London, 1967) and Selwyn Lloyd, *Suez 1956: A Personal Account* (London, 1978) give two differing narratives from vantage points in London. Christian Pineau, *1956: Suez* (Paris, 1976) affords a view from Paris.

2. Sir Anthony Eden, *Full Circle* (London, 1960) pp. 260–1.

3. Sir John Bagot Glubb, *Britain and the Arabs* (London, 1959) p. 301.

4. Carlton, *Anthony Eden*, pp. 403–6.

5. David Goldsworthy, *Colonial Issues in British Politics 1945–61: From 'Colonial Development' to 'Wind of Change'* (Oxford, 1971) pp. 279–316.

6. Carlton, *Anthony Eden*, pp. 458–65.

7. See R. F. Holland, 'The Imperial Factor in British Strategies from Attlee to Macmillan, 1956–63', *Journal of Imperial and Commonwealth History*, XII, No. 2 (January 1984).

8. Humphrey Trevelyan, *The Middle East in Revolution* (London, 1970) pp. 135–205.

9. For a history of the early phases in the UK nuclear programme see Margaret Gowing, *Independence and Deterrence, I: Policymaking* (London, 1974).

10. See A. R. Conan, *The Sterling Area* (London, 1952) and A. C. L. Day, *The Future of Sterling* (Oxford, 1954).

11. The story of Britain's changing attitudes to the integrationist experiment in western Europe is well told in Miriam Camps, *Britain and the European Community* (London, 1964).

12. Such pessimism, official and unofficial, was felt particularly strongly with regard to the West Indies. See D. J. Morgan, *The Official History of Colonial Development. Volume Four: Changes in British Aid Policy, 1951–1970* (London, 1980) pp. 44–7.

13. D. J. Morgan, *The Official History of Colonial Development. Volume Three: A Reassessment of British Aid Policy, 1951–65* (London, 1980) pp. 191–6.

14. D. J. Morgan, *The Official History of Colonial Development. Volume Five: Guidance Towards Self-Government in British Colonies, 1941–71* (London, 1980) pp. 96–7.

15. Goldsworthy, *Colonial Issues in British Politics*, pp. 359–60.

8 THE CLIMAX OF BRITISH DECOLONIZATION IN AFRICA

1. In addition to the works cited in chapter 5, note 3, students interested in the Gold Coast/Ghana may also refer to David E. Apter, *Ghana in Transition* (Princeton, 2nd rev. ed., 1972).

2. Robert Blake, *A History of Rhodesia* (London, 1977) pp. 296–306.

3. Ibid., pp. 300–1.

4. The course and consequences of these disturbances are narrated in Clyde Sanger, *Central African Emergency* (London, 1960).

5. Harold Macmillan, *Pointing The Way, 1959–61* (London, 1972) pp. 116–77.

6. Ian Macleod, 'Trouble in Africa', *Spectator*, 31 January 1964.

7. This important episode has recently been treated at length in Otto Geyser, *Watershed for South Africa: London, 1961* (Cape Town, 1983).

8. A political outline of Northern Rhodesia's decolonization can be found in David C. Mulford, *Zambia: The Politics of Independence, 1957–64* (Oxford, 1967).

9. For two different, if not always conflicting, versions of the Central African Federation's demise see Sir Roy Welensky, *4000 Days: The Life and Death of the Federation of Rhodesia and Nyasaland* (London, 1964) and Lord Alport, *The Sudden Assignment: Central Africa 1961–63* (London, 1963).

10. Blake, *History of Rhodesia*, pp. 348–51.

11. Kenneth Young, *Rhodesia and Independence* (London, 1969) pp. 171–5.

12. For a more detailed coverage see Blake, *History of Rhodesia*, pp. 374–84.

13. Andrew Porter, 'Iain Macleod, Decolonization in Kenya and Tradition in British Colonial Policy', *Journal for Contemporary History*, 2 (1975/6) 37–59.

14. Charles Douglas-Home, *Evelyn Baring: The Last Proconsul* (London, 1978) p. 242.

15. J. M. Kariuki, *'Mau Mau' Detainee* (Oxford, 1963) pp. 126–43.

16. Lord Chandos, *Memoirs* (London, 1962) pp. 393–407.

17. For an excellent biography see David Goldsworthy, *Tom Mboya: the man Kenya wanted to forget* (London, 1982).

18. See above, pp. 205–9.

19. Sir Michael Blundell, *So Rough A Wind* (London, 1964) pp. 247–58.

20. Gary B. Wasserman, *The Politics of Decolonization: Kenya Europeans and the land issue 1960–65* (Cambridge, 1976) pp. 157–62.

21. George Bennett, *Kenya. A Political History: The Colonial Period* (London, 1963).

9 BRITISH DECOLONIZATION IN THE MEDITERRANEAN

1. Stanley Mayes, *Makarios: A Biography* (London, 1981) p. x.
2. Sir Anthony Eden, *Full Circle* (London, 1960) pp. 219–23.
3. David Goldsworthy, *Colonial Issues in British Politics 1945–61: From 'Colonial Development' to 'Wind of Change'* (Oxford, 1971) p. 310.
4. For Grivas' version of Cypriot events see Charles Foley (ed.), *The Memoirs of General Grivas* (London, 1964).
5. G. M. Kahin, *The Asian–African Conference, Bandung* (New York, 1956).
6. Goldsworthy, *Colonial Issues in British Politics 1945–61*, p. 312.
7. Sir Hugh Foot, *A Start in Freedom* (London, 1964) pp. 143–88.
8. The most suggestive introduction to Maltese society, and the place of the Catholic Church in island life, is Jeremy Boissevain, *Saints and Fireworks: Religion and Politics in Rural Malta* (London, 1965).
9. The linkage between language and nationalism in Malta is discussed in Henry Frendo, *Party Politics in a Fortress Colony: The Maltese Experience* (Valletta, 1965).
10 The two standard texts on the various stages towards Malta's self-government in the 1950s and 1960s are Dennis Austin, *Malta and the End of Empire* (London, 1971) and E. Dobie, *Malta's Road to Independence* (Oklahoma, 1967).
11. Dobie, *Malta's Road to Independence*, p. 163.

10 THE ASSERTION OF A POST-COLONIAL AGE

1. J. B. Kelly, *Arabia, the Gulf and the West* (London, 1981).
2. See, for example, Suzanne Cronje, *Lonhro: Portrait of a Multinational* (London, 1976).
3. Peter Lyon, 'Transfer and Transformation: An Introduction' in Peter Lyon and James Manor (eds), *Transfer and Transformation: Political Institutions in the New Commonwealth. Essays in Honour of W. H. Morris-Jones* (Leicester, 1983) pp. 1–2.
4. The events leading up to Britain's final entry into the EEC are described in U. Kitzinger, *Diplomacy and Persuasion: How Britain Joined the Common Market* (London, 1973).
5. For EEC–Third World relations see I. William Zartman, *The Politics of Trade Negotiations between Africa and the EEC: The Weak Confront The Strong* (Princeton, 1971) and Chris Stevens (ed.), *The EEC and the Third World: a survey* (London, 1981).
6. See Phillip Darby, *Britain's Defence Policy East of Suez 1947–1968* (London, 1973).
7. For a wide-ranging survey of south Arabian problems during the 1960s see Fred Halliday, *Arabia Without Sultans* (London, 1974). A military appreciation of the debacle in Aden can be found in Julian Paget, *Last Post: Aden 1964–67* (London, 1969).
8. Harold Wilson's version of events in Aden appears in his memoir, *The Labour Government, 1964–70: A Personal Record* (London, 1971) pp. 138, 213, 231, 235, 376, 381, 396, 405, 444–5.
9. Darby, *Britain's Defence Policy East of Suez 1947–68*, pp. 134–65.
10. Humphrey Trevelyan, *The Middle East in Revolution* (London, 1970) pp. 254–66.
11. For further reading see Miles Hudson, *Triumph or Tragedy?: Rhodesia to Zimbabwe* (London, 1982); Elaine Windrich, *Britain and the Politics of Rhodesian Independence* (London, 1978); David Martin and Phyllis Johnson, *The Struggle for Zimbabwe: The Chimurenga War* (London, 1981).
12. For a biography see H. Kay, *Salazar and Modern Portugal* (London, 1970).
13. See Neil Bruce, *Portugal's African Wars* (London, 1973).
14. There is, as yet, no major study of Portugal's African decolonizations. Malyn Newett, *Portugal in Africa: The Last Hundred Years* (London, 1981) affords a general

coverage. Two short but informative accounts are Neil Bruce, *Portugal: The Last Empire* (London, 1975) and Kenneth Maxwell, 'Portugal and Africa: The Last Empire' in Prosser Gifford ad Wm Roger Louis (eds), *The Transfer of Power in Africa: Decolonization 1940–60* (Yale, 1982) pp. 305–37. Gervase Clarence-Smith, *The Third Portuguese Empire, 1825–1975: A Study in Economic Imperialism* is to be published by Manchester University Press during 1984.

Select Bibliography

Rudolf von Albertini, *Decolonization: the administration and future of the colonies, 1919–60* (New York, 1971).
Lord Alport, *The Sudden Assignment: Central Africa 1961–63* (London, 1963).
Dennis Austin, *Malta and the End of Empire* (London, 1971).
J. Ayodele, *Pan-Africanism and Nationalism in West Africa, 1900–45* (Oxford, 1973).
A. Banani, *The Modernization of Iran, 1921–41* (Stanford, 1961).
George Bennett, *Kenya. A Political History: The Colonial Period* (London, 1963).
Robert Blake, *A History of Rhodesia* (London, 1977).
Sir Michael Blundell, *So Rough a Wind* (London, 1964).
Russell Braddon, *Suez: The Splitting of a Nation* (London, 1973).
Judith Brown, *Gandhi's Rise to Power: Indian Politics, 1915–22* (Cambridge, 1972).
——, *Gandhi and Civil Disobedience: the Mahatma in Indian Politics, 1928–36* (London, 1977).
Neil Bruce, *Portugal: The Last Empire* (London, 1975).
Alan Bullock, *Ernest Bevin: Foreign Secretary, 1945–51* (London, 1983).
John F. Cady, *A History of Burma* (Ithaca, 1958).
Alan Campbell-Johnson, *Mission with Mountbatten* (New York, 1953).
Miriam Camps, *Britain and the European Community, 1955–63* (London, 1964).
David Carlton, *Anthony Eden: A Biography* (London, 1981).
Lord Chandos, *Memoirs* (London, 1962).
Michael J. Cohen, *Palestine. Retreat from the Mandate: The Making of British Policy 1936–45* (London, 1978).
J. S. Coleman, *Nigeria: Background to Nationalism* (Berkeley, 1960).
A. R. Conan, *The Sterling Area* (London, 1952).
Michael Crowder, *West Africa Under Colonial Rule* (London, 1968).
Phillip Darby, *Britain's Defence Policy East of Suez 1947–68* (London, 1973).
John Darwin, *Britain, Egypt and the Middle East: Imperial Policy in the Aftermath of War, 1918–22* (London, 1981).
T. R. H. Davenport, *South Africa: A Modern History* (London, 1977).
Eric Davis, *Challenging Colonialism: Bank Misr and Egyptian Industrialization 1920–41* (Princeton, 1983).
A. C. L. Day, *The Future of Sterling* (Oxford, 1954).
Phillippe Devillers and Jean Lacouture, *End of a War: Indo-China 1954* (London, 1969).
Peter Duignan and L. H. Gann (eds), *Colonialism in Africa, 1870–1960. Volume Four: The Economics of Colonialism* (Cambridge, 1975).
Sir Antony Eden, *Full Circle* (London, 1960).
Leon D. Epstein, *British Politics and the Suez Crisis* (London, 1964).
Bernard B. Fell, *Street Without Joy: Insurgency in Indo-China, 1946–63* (Harrisburg, 1963).
D. K. Fieldhouse, *Unilever Overseas: The Anatomy of a Multinational* (London, 1978).
J. Gallagher, A. Seal and G. Johnson, *Locality, Province and Nation: Essays on Indian Politics, 1870–1940* (Cambridge, 1973).

J. Gallagher, *The Decline, Revival and Fall of the British Empire* (Cambridge, 1982).
R. Gardner, *Sterling–Dollar Diplomacy: Anglo-American Collaboration in the Reconstruction of Multilateral Trade* (Oxford, 1956).
Prosser Gifford and Wm Roger Louis (eds), *The Transfer of Power in Africa: Decolonization 1940–60* (Yale, 1982).
David Goldsworthy, *Colonial Issues in British Politics, 1945–61: From 'Colonial Development' to 'Wind of Change'* (Oxford, 1971).
——, *Tom Mboya: the man Kenya wanted to forget* (London, 1982).
Henri Grimal, *Decolonization: the British, French, Dutch and Belgian empires* (London, 1978).
Fred Halliday, *Arabia without Sultans* (London, 1974).
Ellen Hammer, *The Struggle for Indo-China* (Stanford, 1954).
Keith Hancock, *Smuts: The Fields of Force* (Cambridge, 1968).
David Harkness, *The Restless Dominion: the Irish Free State and the British Commonwealth of Nations, 1921–31* (London, 1969).
Kenneth Harris, *Attlee* (London, 1982).
Houghton D. Hobart, *The South African Economy* (Cape Town, 1964).
H. V. Hodson, *The Great Divide: Britain–India–Pakistan* (London, 1969).
R. F. Holland, *Britain and the Commonwealth Alliance, 1918–39* (London, 1981).
A. G. Hopkins, *An Economic History of West Africa* (London, 1973).
Alistair Horne, *A Savage War of Peace: Algeria, 1954–62* (New York, 1978).
R. Hyam and Ged Martin, *Reappraisals in British Imperial History* (London, 1975).
John Iliffe, *A Modern History of Tanganyika* (Cambridge, 1979).
G. M. Kahin, *Nationalism and Revolution in Indonesia* (New York, 1952).
George M. Kelly, *Lost Soldiers: The French Army and Empire in Crisis* (Cambridge, Mass., 1963).
J. B. Kelly, *Arabia, the Gulf and the West* (London, 1981).
Charles P. Kindleberger, *The World in Depression, 1929–39* (London, 1978).
Gavin Kitching, *Class and Economic Change in Kenya: The Making of an African Petit Bourgeosie* (Yale, 1980).
A. J. Latham, *The Depression and the Developing World, 1914–39* (London, 1981).
J. M. Lee and M. Petter, *The Colonial Office, War and Development Policy: Organization and the Planning of a Metropolitan Initiative, 1939–45* (London, 1982).
J. D. Legge, *Sukarno* (London, 1972).
Rene Lemarchand, *Political Awakening in the Congo* (Berkeley, 1964).
S. H. Longrigg, *Iraq, 1900 to 1950: A Political and Economic History* (Oxford, 1953).
Wm Roger Louis, *Imperialism at Bay: The United States and the Decolonization of the British Empire, 1941–45* (Oxford, 1977).
Harold Macmillan, *Pointing the Way, 1959–61* (London, 1972).
Andrew G. Maguire, *Towards 'Uhuru' in Tanzania: The Politics of Participation* (Cambridge, 1969).
Nicholas Mansergh, *The Commonwealth Experience. Volume Two: From British to Multiracial Commonwealth* (London, 2nd ed., 1982).
John Marlowe, *The Seat of Pilate: An Account of the Palestine Mandate* (London, 1959).
Stanley Mayes, *Makarios: A Biography* (London, 1981).
John T. McAlister, *Viet Nam: The Origins of Revolution* (Princeton, 1969).
Elizabeth Monroe, *Britain's Moment in the Middle East* (London, 1963).
J. H. van Mook, *The Stakes of Democracy in South-East Asia* (London, 1950).
Penderell Moon, *Divide and Quit* (London, 1961).
R. J. Moore, *Churchill, Cripps and India, 1939–45* (Oxford, 1979).
——, *Escape from India: The Attlee Government and the Indian Problem* (Oxford, 1983).
D. J. Morgan, *The Official History of Colonial Development*, 5 vols (London, 1980).

W. H. Morris-Jones and Georges Fischer, *Decolonization and After: The British and French Experience* (London, 1980).

Edward Mortimer, *France and the Africans, 1944–60: A Political History* (London, 1969).

David C. Mulford, *Zambia: The Politics of Independence, 1957–64* (Oxford, 1969).

Jeremy Murray-Brown, *Kenyatta* (London, 1972).

Malyn Newytt, *Portugal in Africa: The Last Hundred Years* (London, 1981).

Conor Cruise O'Brien, *To Katanga and Back* (New York, 1962).

Leslie Palmier, *Indonesia and the Dutch* (Oxford, 1962).

R. D. Pearce, *The Turning Point in Africa: British Colonial Policy 1938–48* (London, 1982).

Margery Perham, *The Colonial Reckoning* (London, 1961).

Jan Pluvier, *South-East Asia from Colonialism to Independence* (Kuala Lumpur, 1974).

Lucien W. Pye, *Guerrilla Communism in Malaya: Its Social and Political Meaning* (Princeton, 1956).

Rajat K. Ray, *Industrialization in India: Growth and Conflict in the Private Corporate Sector, 1914–47* (Delhi, 1979).

P. J. Robb, *The Government of India and Reform, 1916–21* (Oxford, 1976).

Charles Robequain, *The Economic Development of French Indo-China* (Oxford, 1944).

A. Arthur Schiller, *The Formation of Federal Indonesia, 1945–9* (The Hague, 1955).

Andrew Shonfield, *British Economic Policy Since the War* (London, 1958).

Anthony Short, *The Communist Insurrection in Malaya, 1948–60* (London, 1975).

A. J. Stockwell, *British Policy and Malay Politics during the Malayan Union Experiment, 1942–48* (Kuala Lumpur, 1979).

Richard Storry, *Japan and the Decline of the West, 1894–1943* (London, 1979).

Susan Strange, *Sterling and British Policy: A Political Study of an International Currency in Decline* (Oxford, 1971).

John Talbot, *The War Without a Name: France in Algeria, 1954–62* (London, 1981).

Christopher Thorne, *Allies of a Kind: The United States, Britain and the War against Japan, 1941–45* (Oxford, 1978).

Hugh Tinker, *Race, Conflict and the International Order: From Empire to United Nations* (London, 1977).

B. R. Tomlinson, *The Indian National Congress and the Raj, 1929–42: The Penultimate Phase* (London, 1976).

——, *The Political Economy of the Raj, 1914–47: The Economics of Decolonization* (London, 1979).

Humphrey Trevelyan, *The Middle East in Revolution* (London, 1970).

Gary B. Wasserman, *The Politics of Decolonization: Kenya Europeans and the land issue, 1960–65* (Cambridge, 1976).

Sir Roy Welensky, *4000 Days: The Life and Death of the Federation of the Rhodesias and Nyasaland* (London, 1964).

C. M. Woodhouse, *The Struggle for Greece, 1941–9* (London, 1976).

Crawford Young, *Politics in the Congo: Decolonization and Independence* (Princeton, 1965).

Kenneth Young, *Rhodesia and Independence* (London, 1969).

Index

Abadan, 126
Abyssinia, 63
Accra, 131
Aden, 274–9
Adoula, Cyrille, 189
Algeria, 163–75
Allenby, Field Marshal Viscount, 18
Amritsar Massacre, 18
Angola, 292–7
Annam, 4, 46
Arden-Clarke, Sir Charles, 133, 213–14, 217
Armitage, Sir Robert, 94
Aswan Dam, 195–6
Atlantic Charter, 53
Australia, 15, 26, 204

Baghdad Pact, 252
Bamako Congress, 156
Banda, Hastings, 141, 223–4, 227
Bandung Conference, 254
Bao Dai, Emperor, 98–102
Baring, Sir Evelyn, 148, 237
Basutoland, 271
Bechuanaland, 271
Beel, Louis van, 90
Belgium, 175–90
Bengal, 60, 77, 79, 85
Bevin, Ernest, 115–16, 118
Bihar, 79
Birla, G. D., 7
Blue Streak, 204
Blundell, Sir Michael, 242
Bourne, Sir Frederick, 217
Boyd Commission, 289–90
Brazzaville, 155, 179
British Guiana, 271
Buisseret, Auguste, 178
Burns, Sir Alan, 131

Cabral, Amilcar, 293

Cairo Conference, 52
Cambodia, 100
Canada, 15, 25–6
Cao Bang, 100
Carrington, Lord, 289
Catroux, Georges, 167
Central African Federation: events leading to formation, 139–44; early political problems of Federation, 221–3; origins and course of the 1959 'emergency', 224–5; change in British approach to regional affairs, 225–31; formation of Rhodesia Front ministry in Southern Rhodesia, 231–2; dissolution of Federation, 232–3
Chiang Kai-shek, 52
Chilembwe, John, 8
China, 74, 99–100, 102, 107
Churchill, Sir Winston, 53, 58, 193
Cochin, 3–4, 46, 94, 96
Cohen, Sir Andrew, 66, 142–3
Corsica, 171
Cranborne, Lord, 67
Creech-Jones, Arthur, 140–1
Cyprus: growth of Enosis movement, 250–2; outbreak of EOKA violence, 253–4; course of rebellion, 254–7; agreement on independence constitution, 258–9; the costs of revolt, 259–60

Dahomey, 155
Dalat Conference, 96
d'Argenlieu, Admiral Thierry, 94
Deferre, Gaston, 160
Defiance Campaign, 138
de Gaulle, General Charles, 160–3, 170–3, 191, 206
Devlin Commission, 225
Dien Bien Phu, 94, 100, 167
Djokjakarta, 94, 100, 167

Douglas-Home, Sir Alec, 233–5, 278, 284–5
Dulles, John Foster, 197, 202
Dutch East Indies: character of pre-1939 nationalism, 8; Islam in national life, 10–11; impact of the 1930s depression, 14; incorporated into Japanese empire, 40; situation during Japanese occupation, 42–4; post-war events leading to consolidation of Indonesian Republic, 86–92; dispute over West Irian, 92–3; post-colonial relationship of Netherlands and Indonesia, 93

Eden, Sir Anthony, 192–200, 262
Egypt: termination of British Protectorate status, 17–18; political crisis during 1942, 51–2; situation in aftermath of the Second World War, 123–5; events leading to the Suez War in 1956, 191–9
Eisenhower, General Dwight, 195, 197
Elisabethville, 184, 186, 228
Erskine, General, 237
European Economic Community, 162–3, 173, 201, 206, 209–10, 271, 273
Evian Agreement, 174

Fagan Commission, 96
Falklands War, 291–2
Fawzi, Mahmud, 197
Fianna Fail, 25
Field, Winston, 234–5
Foot, Sir Hugh, 256–7
France: achievement in Indo-China before 1939, 4–5; modus vivendi with Japan in Indo-China after 1941, 44; struggle for mastery in Indo-China after 1945, 93–103; decolonization in West Africa, 154–62; the European Economic Community in national foreign policy, 162–3; the rebellion in Algeria and the collapse of the Fourth Republic, 163–75; involvement in the Suez War, 197–8
Fraser, Malcolm, 290
FRELIMO, 286–7
Front de Libération Nationale, 166, 168–9, 174–5
Front for the Liberation of South Yemen, 286–7

Gaitskell, Hugh, 226
Gandhi, Mohandas K., 6, 19–20, 22, 57, 59, 75, 77
Gibraltar, 249, 283
Glubb, General, 120, 195
Gold Coast: economic change in British West Africa, 13; indirect rule, 31–2; political and constitutional change in the 1940s, 130–5; course of decolonization after 1951, 212–19
Gonzi, Archbishop, 262
Gracey, General, 93
Great Britain: character of 'imperial unity' goals before 1939, 26; shifts in public opinion during the Second World War, 40–1; nature of strategic position, 47–8; loss of export markets after 1939, 48; new emphasis on colonial development, 54; friction with the United States over post-war planning, 55–6; dilemmas of post-war foreign policy, 119; importance of colonies to British interests, 200–2; changing world role after Suez War, 202–7; domestic party politics and decolonization, 208–9; transformation in economic attitudes to non-advanced world, 273
Greece, 119, 252, 254, 258
Grivas, George, 253–4, 258
Guiné, 292, 295–6
Gurney, Sir Henry, 110

Hailey, Lord, 65
Haiphong, 97
Hammarskjöld, Dag, 188
Harding, Sir John, 255–6
Healey, Dennis, 276
Heath, Edward, 278, 284–5
Hertzog, J. B. M., 23, 25
Hiroshima, 40
Ho Chi Minh, 44, 46, 88, 96–8, 102
Hofmeyr, Jan, 136
Huggins, Sir Godfrey, 139, 141–4, 221–2

Imperial Conference (1926), 24
India: population growth after 1900, 2; bourgeois elements in nationalist politics, 6–8; growth of nationalism and constitutional developments after 1918, 18–23; events during the Second World War, 56–63; approach

to partition after 1945, 74–84;
becomes a republic within the British
Commonwealth, 84–86
Indian National Congress, 7–8, 57,
59–63, 74–9
Indo-China: economic conditions before
1939, 2–5; events during the Second
World War, 41–7; Franco-Viet Minh
struggle after 1945, 93–103
Indonesia, *see* Dutch East Indies
Iran, 278–9
Iraq, 120, 122–3
Irish Free State, 24–5, 85, 200
Irwin, Lord, 23
Israel, 197–9, 272, 277
Istanbul, 254
Ivory Coast, 162

Japan: significance of military victory
over Russia (1905), 9;
industrialization during 1930s, 38;
war aims in December 1941, 39–40;
character of rule in South-East Asia,
42–3
Java, 10, 87
Johnson, Louis, 58
Jordan, *see* Transjordan

Kadalie, Clement, 30
Kalenjin, 244
Kamba, 236
Karamanlis, Constantine, 253
Kasavubu, Joseph, 181, 185, 187
Kashmir, 84
Katanga, 64, 185–7, 228–9
Kaunda, 224, 231, 284–5, 287
Kennedy, John F., 203–4
Kenya: trusteeship formula in inter-war
years, 32–3; Closer Union movement
in British East Africa, 35; increase in
food production during Second
World War, 67; destabilization in
post-war period, 144–9; the Mau
Mau Emergency, 237–9; political and
constitutional transition to
independence, 240–8
Kenyatta, Jomo, 145, 244–8
Khilafat Movement, 18–19
Kikuyu, 145, 236–8, 245

Lacoste, Robert, 168–9
Lampson, Sir Miles, 51

Lancaster House (Conferences), 242–3,
247, 257–8
Laos, 100
Lebanon, 120, 193, 203
Lennox-Boyd, Alan, 219, 241
Leopoldville, 178, 180, 184, 186
Linggadjati Treaty, 87
Linlithgow, Lord, 22, 57–8, 61–2
Lomé Convention, 273
Luanda, 297
Lugard, Lord, 31
Lumumba, Patrice, 185, 187–8
Lyttelton, Oliver, 111, 143, 240

Macgillivray, Sir Donald, 111
Machel, Samora, 290, 296
Macleod, Iain, 227, 231, 241–3
Macmillan, Harold, 202–4, 206–7, 231,
234, 242–3, 257, 274
Macpherson, Sir John, 135
Makarios, Archbishop, 250–5, 258–9
Malan, Daniel, 137–8
Malaya: character of pre-war
nationalism, 8; impact of depression
during the 1930s, 14; situation during
the Japanese occupation, 41–2; post-
war events leading to Communist
insurgency, 103–8; the Emergency,
108–11; the approach to
independence, 111–12
Malta: linguistic and religious roots of
island conflict, 260–2; issue of
integration with Britain, 262–3;
suspension of constitution in 1958,
263; independence attained, 264
Manchuria, 38
Marshall Plan, 201
Masai, 236, 244
Massu, General Jacques, 169
Mboya, Tom, 240, 245
Mendès-France, Pierre, 103, 112, 163–4,
166
Meru, 236
Milner, Viscount, 18
Mitchell, Sir Philip, 144–5, 147
Mitterand, François, 157
Mintoff, Dominic, 261, 263–4
Misr Bank, 6
Mollet, Guy, 167–8, 199
Monckton Commission, 226–7, 229
Mook, Hubertus van, 88–9
Morocco, 164
Mossadeq, Mohammed, 125–6

Mountbatten, Lord Louis, 42, 75, 82–4
Mozambique, 30, 292–6
Mugabe, Robert, 286, 290–2
Muslim League, 59–63, 75–9
Muzorewa, Bishop Abel, 286, 290–2

Nairobi, 147, 238
Nassau Agreement, 204
Nasser, Gamal Abdul, 51, 191–9, 275
Nehru, Jawarharlal, 22, 75–6, 83, 85, 92
Netherlands, 86–93
New Zealand, 15–17
Nicosia, 249, 253, 255
Nigeria: economic change in British
  West Africa, 13; increase in
  commodity production during the
  Second World War, 48; 'Richards'
  constitution (1946), 131; growth of
  Ibo-Yoruba rivalries, 135;
  independence attained (1960), 162
Nixon, Richard, 288
Nkomo, Joshua, 144, 227, 230, 232, 288
Nkrumah, Kwame, 130–1, 134, 212–19,
  301
Northern Rhodesia, 30, 64, 135, 138–44,
  221, 224, 230–1
North Yemen, 275
Nyasaland, 30, 135, 140, 221, 223–4,
  227
Nyerere, Julius, 284–5, 301

Odinga, Oginga, 241, 245
Olivier, Borg, 262–3
OPEC, 272, 278
Organisation armée Secrète, 173–4

Pakistan, 84
Palestine: Balfour Declaration on Jewish
  homeland in territory (1917), 113–14;
  developments in inter-war period,
  114–15; situation during the Second
  World War, 115; post-war crisis,
  115–20; formation of Israel and war
  with the Arab nations, 120–1
Pan-Africanism, 129–30
Pearl Harbour, 38, 53
Peel, Lord, 115
Pflimlin, Pierre, 171
Polaris, 205
Portugal, 292–8
Punjab, 60–1, 77–8

Radcliffe, Lord, 255

Rassemblement Démocratique Africaine, 156
Renison, Sir Patrick, 246–7
Renville Agreement, 89
Richards, Sir Arthur, 131
Roosevelt, F. D., 52–3, 55, 57–8
Rubber, 14, 48

Saigon, 47, 94
Saintény, Jean, 96
Salazar, Antonio, 292–4
Saudi Arabia, 52, 113, 178–9
Senghor, Leopold, 256
Sétif Massacre, 165
Sharpeville Massacre, 228
Sjahir, Sutan, 91
Sikhs, 83–4
Simla Conference (1945), 63
Sind, 20–1
Singapore, 41, 107
Smith, Ian, 233–5, 280–92
Smuts, Jan, 23, 29, 68, 136–7
Soustelle, Jacques, 166
South Africa: political change in the
  1920s, 23; development of
  segregationist practices before 1939,
  27–30; British apprehension of South
  African power, 30–1; expansion of
  influence during Second World War,
  68–9; emergence of apartheid state,
  136–8; Macmillan addresses Union
  Parliament (1960), 226; exit from
  British Commonwealth, 228; external
  policies after 1970, 288–90, 297–8
Southern Rhodesia: 1922 referendum
  on political future, 31; growing
  sentiment for amalgamation with
  Northern Rhodesia after 1945, 139;
  negotiations leading to new
  Federation, 140–4; for 1953–63
  period see Central African Federation;
  events leading to Unilateral
  Declaration of Independence (1965),
  233–5; course and final demise of
  UDI regime, 279–92
Soviet Union, 193, 202–4, 273, 277
Spinola, Antonio de, 296–7
Stanleyville, 188–9
Sterling, 119, 130, 205, 271–2
Sudan, 103
Suez Canal, 192, 196–9, 252, 256
Sukarno, Achmed, 43, 67
Sumatra, 86
Syria, 120

Tata, J. N., 6–7
Thatcher, Margaret, 290–2
Thuku, Harry, 240
Todd, Garfield, 222
Tonkin, 3–4, 46, 95–6
Torch Commando, 138
Transjordan, 120, 122–3, 192–5
Trevaskis, Sir Kennedy, 275
Truman, Harry S., 91, 117–20, 201, 203
Tshombe, Moise, 185–7
Tunisia, 164, 170
Turkey, 114, 252, 254–5, 257

United Nations, 120, 188, 197, 277
United States: isolationist culture after
    First World War, 26; attitudes to
    European colonialism during Second
    World War, 52–5; move towards
    economic 'internationalism', 55–6;
    dilemma of post-war relationship
    with Great Britain, 119, 199–201;
    supports Jewish state in Palestine,
    117–18; role in Angolan
    decolonization, 297–8

U Ottama, 9–10

Valetta, 263
Versailles Treaty (1919), 1
Verwoerd, J. W., 138
Volta, 155
Vorster, John, 287–8

Waruhiu, Chief, 148
Watchtower Movement, 8
Wavell, General Sir Archibald, 62–3, 81
Welensky, Sir Roy, 139, 221–8, 278–9
West Indies, 12, 54, 207, 271
Westminster (Statute of), 24–5
Whitehead, Sir Edgar, 222, 224–8,
    231–2
Wilson, Harold, 234–5, 271–2, 275–6,
    280–4
World Bank, 195, 247

Zimbabwe African National Union,
    286–92
Zimbabwe African Peoples Union, 286,
    289